Human–Computer Interaction Series

Editors-in-chief
Desney Tan, Microsoft Research, USA
Jean Vanderdonckt, Université catholique de Louvain, Belgium

HCI is a multidisciplinary field focused on human aspects of the development of computer technology. As computer-based technology becomes increasingly pervasive – not just in developed countries, but worldwide – the need to take a human-centered approach in the design and development of this technology becomes ever more important. For roughly 30 years now, researchers and practitioners in computational and behavioral sciences have worked to identify theory and practice that influences the direction of these technologies, and this diverse work makes up the field of human-computer interaction. Broadly speaking it includes the study of what technology might be able to do for people and how people might interact with the technology. The HCI series publishes books that advance the science and technology of developing systems which are both effective and satisfying for people in a wide variety of contexts. Titles focus on theoretical perspectives (such as formal approaches drawn from a variety of behavioral sciences), practical approaches (such as the techniques for effectively integrating user needs in system development), and social issues (such as the determinants of utility, usability and acceptability).

Titles published within the Human–Computer Interaction Series are included in Thomson Reuters' Book Citation Index, The DBLP Computer Science Bibliography and The HCI Bibliography.

More information about this series at http://www.springer.com/series/6033

Nicholas S. Dalton • Holger Schnädelbach
Mikael Wiberg • Tasos Varoudis

Editors

Architecture and Interaction

Human Computer Interaction in Space
and Place

Editors
Nicholas S. Dalton
Department of Computer Science
  and Digital Technologies
University of Northumbria
Newcastle upon Tyne, UK

Mikael Wiberg
Department of Informatics
Umeå University
Umeå, Sweden

Holger Schnädelbach
Mixed Reality Laboratory
Department of Computer Science
University of Nottingham
Nottingham, UK

Tasos Varoudis
The Bartlett School of Architecture
University College London
London, UK

ISSN 1571-5035
Human–Computer Interaction Series
ISBN 978-3-319-30026-9   ISBN 978-3-319-30028-3   (eBook)
DOI 10.1007/978-3-319-30028-3

Library of Congress Control Number: 2016943077

Printed on acid-free paper

This Springer imprint is published by Springer Nature
The registered company is Springer International Publishing AG Switzerland

Preface

This book emerged from a chance collision of the editors, and others, at an ACM SIGCHI conference in 2011 in Vancouver. We were a disparate collection of academics and researchers who came together, all of us surprised that there were others who held an interest in, or connection to, architecture and the built environment at a conference on human-computer interaction (HCI). While we talked about it, it became clear that we were not the only ones who had this singularly quixotic preoccupation. In the process of creating a workshop for the subsequent ACM SGICHI conference, we were able to begin to articulate the nascent synthesis of the hitherto seemingly divergent areas of human computer interaction and architecture. Through the process of creating and running the workshop, we have begun to feel that these areas are both complementary and likely to share a future together.

As the chapters in this book will attest, architecture is exploring the use of digital technology and, at the same time, many digital technologies are exploring their integration into buildings, contexts and places. Given other prior and ongoing research and events in this area, our meeting and subsequent workshop appears less the consequence of chance and more the inevitable process of building/computer convergence.

This book and this field are still highly formative, much of the work we did in editing the book was identify themes, issues and concerns. As two disciplines collide, it is inevitable that new terms and new languages have to be shared and mutually comprehended. This is not an inconsequential task and in overcoming these early communication problems we hope we are creating the foundations for later research to build upon. The objective of this book is to initiate discussions, initiate collaborations and reveal a shift in perspectives.

Historically, when human computer interaction moved from command line interfaces to early graphic user interfaces, it was realized that the domain of graphic design was not a trivial area of expertise which could be easily discounted or subsumed into the interaction process. Visual design became a domain of knowledge which added to the richness of the interaction process and interaction research.

Similarly, as we move into the realm of interaction in the built environment, human computer interaction researchers might then see those with knowledge of space, inhabitation and architecture as bringing new knowledge and expertise into the realm of interaction design. Fundamentally Weiser's vision of ubiquitous computing was that of 'technology beyond the desktop', embedded in the fabric of the world around us. While interaction specialists see the potential benefits, both in the utility and simplification of interaction that this 'embeddedness' brings, they are less likely to be aware of the wealth of design expertise which has developed over many millennia in the design of built form. The objective of this book is to introduce those design professionals and interaction researchers to each other, so that the possibility of solutions to their current problems already existing might be discovered.

At the same time, we hope that some of the wealth of projects in this book show that architecture is not a passive partner or a consultancy in waiting to HCI. We hope to show that architects are highly passionate about the integration of digital components into the design of the build environment. From an interaction point of view, there is a great deal about the process of designing for interaction, which the architectural world is equally unaware of.

The central task, therefore, of this book is one of introduction. If this book could encourage those on either side of the divide to cross over, as our workshop participants did, then its purpose will be fulfilled and the efforts of the authors, editors and organizers will be well rewarded.

Finally, we would like to use this space to acknowledge the organizers of the original workshops: Prof. Keith Green, Professor of Architecture and Electrical and Computer Engineering at Clemson University; Prof. Christoph Hölscher, Chair of Cognitive Science at ETH Zurich; Prof. Ruth Dalton, Department of Architecture, Northumbria University; Dr Paul Marshall, UCL Interaction Centre, University College London; and Dr Anijo Mathew from the IIT Institute of Design. They, along with the editors, committed a great deal of time, energy and effort to both the workshop and the formulation of the book. Without their energy and commitment, this project might not have happened. We would like to thank them for their time, energy and effort.

Newcastle upon Tyne, UK   Nicholas S. Dalton
Nottingham, UK   Holger Schnädelbach
Umeå, Sweden   Mikael Wiberg
London, UK   Tasos Varoudis
February 2016

Contents

Contributors

Ben Bedwell Horizon Digital Economy Research Institute, The University of Nottingham, Nottingham, UK

H.H. Bier Department of Architectural Engineering & Technology (AE&T), Faculty of Architecture/AE&T/Hyperbody, TU Delft/BK, Delft, The Netherlands

Cameline Bolbroe Adaptive Environments, IT University of Copenhagen, Copenhagen, Denmark

Nicholas S. Dalton Department of Computer Science and Digital Technologies, University of Northumbria, Newcastle upon Tyne, UK

Ruth Conroy Dalton Department of Architecture and the Built Environment, University of Northumbria, Newcastle upon Tyne, UK

Parag Deshpande HiQ Stockholm AB, Stockholm, Sweden

Jonathan Hale Department of Architecture and Built Environment, University of Nottingham, Nottingham, UK

Christoph Hölscher Department of Humanities, Social and Political Sciences, ETH Zurich, Zurich, Switzerland

Andy Hudson-Smith Centre for Advanced Spatial Analysis (CASA), The Bartlett School of Architecture, University College London, London, UK

Nils Jäger Mixed Reality Laboratory, Department of Computer Science, University of Nottingham, Nottingham, UK

Petros Koutsolampros Space Syntax Laboratory, The Bartlett School of Architecture, University College London, London, UK

Bess Krietemeyer School of Architecture, Syracuse University, Syracuse, NY, USA

Jakub Krukar Institute for Geoinformatics, University of Münster, Münster, Germany

Rachael Luck   The Design Group, Department of Engineering and Innovation, The Open University, Milton Keynes, UK

Anna Luusua   University of Oulu, Oulu, Finland

Nemanja Memarovic   University of Zurich, Zürich, Switzerland

Fatemeh Moradi   Department of Informatics, Umeå University, Umeå, Sweden

S. Mostafavi   Department of Architectural Engineering & Technology (AE&T), Faculty of Architecture/AE&T/Hyperbody, TU Delft/BK, Delft, The Netherlands

Nadia Pantidi   School of Applied Psychology, University College Cork, Cork, Republic of Ireland

Henrika Pihlajaniemi   University of Oulu, Oulu, Finland

Kerstin Sailer   Space Syntax Laboratory, The Bartlett School of Architecture, University College London, London, UK

Holger Schnädelbach   Mixed Reality Laboratory, Department of Computer Science, University of Nottingham, Nottingham, UK

Peter Scupelli   School of Design, Carnegie Mellon University, Pittsburgh, PA, USA

Tasos Varoudis   The Bartlett School of Architecture, University College London, London, UK

Mikael Wiberg   Department of Informatics, Umeå University, Umeå, Sweden

Johanna Ylipulli   University of Oulu, Oulu, Finland

Martin Zaltz Austwick   Centre for Advanced Spatial Analysis (CASA), The Bartlett School of Architecture, University College London, London, UK

Chapter 1
Introduction

Nicholas S. Dalton, Holger Schnädelbach, Mikael Wiberg, and Tasos Varoudis

Abstract Ubiquitous computing has a vision of information embedded in the world around us. Yet the built environment, while familiar is also the subject of design. Recently, architects have also seen digital elements incorporated into the fabric of buildings as a way of creating advanced spaces and environments to meet the dynamic challenges of future habitation. Historically, both sides have progressed based on their own practice in largely mutual non awareness.

This book, based on a series of workshops held at the prestigious international ACM CHI conference seeks to bring these research communities together. This chapter introduces the ideas, themes and issues approached in the book.

To the average reader it might feel rather incongruous as to the necessity for a book on Architecture and Human Computer Interaction (HCI). However, the editors feel that these subjects are not discordant. While there are clearly differences, Architecture, as a design profession is hundreds of years old, while human computer interaction is relatively new, but they offer many similarities. The editors would argue that in terms of complexity, Architecture and Urban planning are one of the few technologies which exhibit the same kinds of scales, heterogeneous hardware, distributed ownership and complexities that large software and digital technologies

N.S. Dalton (✉)
Department of Computer Science and Digital Technologies, University of Northumbria, Newcastle upon Tyne, UK
e-mail: Nick.dalton@northumbria.ac.uk

H. Schnädelbach
Mixed Reality Laboratory, Department of Computer Science, University of Nottingham, Jubilee Campus, Wollaton Road, Nottingham, UK
e-mail: Holger.Schnadelbach@nottingham.ac.uk

M. Wiberg
Department of Informatics, Umeå University, Umeå, Sweden
e-mail: mwiberg@informatik.umu.se

T. Varoudis
The Bartlett School of Architecture, University College London, Gower Street, WC1E 6BT, London, UK
e-mail: t.varoudis@ucl.ac.uk

© Springer International Publishing Switzerland 2016
N.S. Dalton et al. (eds.), *Architecture and Interaction*,
Human–Computer Interaction Series, DOI 10.1007/978-3-319-30028-3_1

do. It seems natural that we explore the existing commonalities between these two fields as a source of more than inspiration; in this book we hope to show how the destinies of the two fields strongly intersect.

From the days when computing abandoned the command line interface, Human Computer Interaction has dealt, rather implicitly, with space. From the earliest two-dimensional graphical user interface to three-dimensional representations, gaming and virtual reality, emerging into mobile computing, context aware computing, urban computing, public displays, ambient computing, tangible computing and ubiquitous computing, our awareness of space and its role in the interaction process is becoming more distinct. As computing becomes embedded in our homes, our streets and our buildings, the demands to understand the role of space and architecture are becoming critical to HCI.

At the same time, architecture is becoming far more engaged with the digital experience. Architects are already introducing digital components into buildings. For example, architects at ART+COM have designed a museum for BMW using complex projections and ambient displays (ART+COM 2008). Hyposurface by Mark Goulthorpe et al. (2001), Blur Building by Diller et al. (2002), and Bubbles by Michael Fox et al. (2006). Kas Oosterhuis and Ilona Lénárd (1998) and Oosterhuis et al. (2002) have used digital projectors to create complex adaptive spaces. Yet these practitioners have had little access to the techniques and methodologies of human computer interaction, potentially compromising the user's or occupant's experience.

With the rise of the graphical user interface and later with the web-based Internet, HCI evolved by extending it's collaboration to those from a graphic design background (Mackay et al. 1997). Historical precedence suggests that computing will, by necessity, begin to engage with architecture much in the way that it did with the graphics community. Yet this can only happen well if both sides are aware of their own expert knowledge, have some understanding of the expertise of others, and, finally, have some awareness of their own ignorance regarding the other discipline.

This book emerged from a series of workshops at a succession of ACM/CHI conferences (Dalton et al. 2012, 2014), which attempted to bring these diverse communities together to explore what mutual cooperation might bring to each field. The organizers included computer scientists, architects, architectural robot designers, cognitive psychologists, human computer interaction researchers, and architectural researchers, just to give an idea of the scale of the community brought together. What we discovered was not only a number of overlapping concerns, but also divergences over methodology, terminology, and practice. This book is an attempt to record some of these perspectives and begin to create an overarching framework to understand how these two communities could begin to interact and collaborate. Our hope for this book is to begin to form a roadmap for future collaboration and research. To do this we must begin by understanding that both communities have different research arcs which seem to be drawing towards the same point: that there will be a merging of digital information flows embedded in the built environment which we will occupy.

The purpose of this book, much like the workshops, is to initiate and facilitate this partnership rather than ossify the positions. Our aim is to create awareness, define terms, and map out research. To facilitate this, the book is aimed at both human computer researchers and practitioners, and those engaged in the architectural profession. The editors and authors believe that a number of forces have set both disciplines on a collision course resulting in circumstances where incomprehension can no longer be tolerated. These collision vectors come from two directions, which we will now describe in turn.

Space in the Direction of Human Computer Interaction Research

If we scratch the surface of Human Computer Interaction (HCI) we see architecture as a metaphor buried beneath (Chen and Rada 1996) it. HCI is awash with spatial and architectural metaphors. We have the home button, we navigate to a page, we surf the web or the information super highway, we click the back button, we mine information, the website is under-construction, we get lost in cyberspace, we follow 'trails of bread crumbs' to navigate 'up' to the top level and software is built by software architects who perform 'cognitive walkthroughs'. Even Donald Norman's seminal work (1988) is littered with architectural details such as door push plates, and shower systems as examples of affordance and cognitive models. It is of little surprise then that cognitively computing, like architecture, is one of those systems which cannot be wholly appreciated from one perspective. Like a building, to operate complex software it needs to be explored and learned, forming a cognitive model. For complex software and websites new software users behave like new residents to a building or neighborhood, they move beyond initial fixed memorized paths and memorized routes to combine different paths through software flexibly. Eventually routes and commands become like words in a sentence, almost infinitely interchangeable in pursuit of a goal. Like a pedestrian or a driver, an expert user can navigate through a digital habitat with very little consideration or apparent mental effort. Even in the realms of previously two-dimensional interaction space does not escape from the potential influence that research into space might bring. There is some evidence to suggest that users who have difficulty navigating space have difficulty navigating websites (Kim 2001; Jones et al. 2007; Chen and Rada 1996). This introduces questions into the field of Human Computer Interaction. When we talk about being 'lost on a website' or interface, are we talking metaphorically or literally in a cognitive sense? If the answer is literal, what can one of the most established professions, dealing with navigation design, tell us about the construction of software for navigability? Given that architecture isn't free to perform empirical experiments, can the insights of interaction design help us to redesign more navigable landscapes? Navigation is an on-going concern in Human Computer Interaction, as it is indeed in architecture, and environmental psychology. As such it is likely that these two fields will begin to overlap to ever-stronger degrees.

Ubiquitous Computing

Moving beyond the graphical user interface, Marc Weiser's (1993) original vision of ubiquitous computing, saw computing receding into the background, and by background he meant the fabric of the world around us including clothes but specifically the built environment. In his 1991 Scientific American article, terms from architecture fill most of the world, very different to the writing in Doug Engelbart's 'mother of all demos'. Weiser's Sam character distinctly moves between rooms to create new contexts. Sam has an urban context of a neighborhood, a home, she navigates traffic to go to work, she shops, buys coffee. She looks through windows, uses offices, signs, meeting rooms and leaves items near doors. In short the very thing which computers were receding into, was the architectural structure around us. Direct descendants of Weiser's vision, smart homes like Georgia Tech's aware home (Kidd et al. 1999) were built around the turn of the millennium. In a review of smart homes, Chan et al. (2008) reported on 54 papers discussing smart home installations mostly with a Tele-care bias. Significant by it's absence in this work, is any information about the homes as buildings. There seems to be an implicit assumption of neutrality to the level of naturalness. The built environment that computing was meant to recede into did not come around accidentally; it is also the product of much investigation and reflection, the extent of which is currently unclear in Computer Science.

Spatial Approaches in Interaction Research

There are also research perspectives that view space as an active participant in the interaction system. Proxemics (Ballendat et al. 2010), for example, shows how an understanding of space, occupant, and device may lead to new interactional dynamics. Ishi and Ulmer (1997) and Wisneski et al. (1998) describe ambient computing as fusing architectural surfaces with active interfaces, but, by doing so includes the role of space, spatiality, and architecture in interaction as mentioned in (Wiberg 2011). From a theoretical perspective, Rodden and Benford (2003) point to new directions in HCI observing that ubiquitous interaction had so far focused on 'stuff' and had failed to explore space. Kostakos et al. (2006) also argues that, *"We have no fundamental theory, knowledge base, principled methods, or tools for designing and building pervasive systems as integral elements of the urban landscape."* He further contends that space is a fundamental part of this urban picture. Numerous authors have also written to challenge our notions of context. Brignull and Rogers (2003), for example, are a strong proponent of leaving the lab and engaging with ecologically valid contexts, part of which is the role of the building and space. Hornecker and Nicol (2012) observed that re-contextualizing museum interfaces from the living laboratory to the museum environment changed many factors of the interaction model. Fischer and Hornecker (2012) discuss the complex arrangement of seven types of space in an interactive media façade, yet this highly specific framework for media facades seems to be the most complex description of space yet available.

While space in interaction is as old as Fitt's Law (MacKenzie et al. 1992) and while there have been some very notable exceptions, architecture and space have always been approached on an ad hoc and extemporaneous basis. The field of HCI has very little well-organized literature on the role of space in interaction. This is echoed by Harrison and Dourish (1996) who reviewed the simplistic models of space in CSCW and suggested that place, rather than space, should configure interaction.

The lack of well-organized literature should not suggest that the HCI community is ignorant of architecture and space. On the contrary, there is a growing interest in HCI in the overlap of architecture and interaction design. This growing interest surfaces right now in many ways, stretching from a new ACM interactions forum on architecture and interaction (Wiberg 2015) to the coining of new terms such as "architectural informatics" (Wiberg 2011). Further on, Wiltse and Stolterman (2010) suggest that in many ways interaction has already been informed by and drawn on architecture design principally through the use of virtual reality as an interface metaphor. They go on to suggest that through the mediation of permeability and co-presence computing is moving slowly to overlap a realm previously exclusive to architecture. They argue that the growth of digital technologies mediating the awareness of the world, computing is becoming more like architecture. They suggest that with the arrival of third wave HCI (Bødker et al. 2006) computing could benefit from an architectural perspective and critique of interaction. One significant example they identify is the holistic approach of architecture, which they compare to the focus on specific goals and specific tasks common in interaction design. They argue we should see interactive spaces not as just functions and workflows, that we should think about experiencing experiential wholes in for the functional parts, and that we should link specific design decisions to potential social dynamics. In this context, research by Schnädelbach (2012) and Varoudis et al. (2011) have moved into the liminality between Architecture, digital communications and Virtual Reality by using digital techniques to merge physically remote spaces to redefine both CSCW and architecture. This area known as 'hybrid' architecture (Harrison et al. 1996) is hard to fully place within the realm of human computer interaction research, being so critical to the knowledge of and rethinking of architecture.

In his article *Learning from Architecture* (Ingram 2009) Ingram highlights that HCI can also learn from the deep historical precedence that architecture brings to the table. He also suggests that interaction design is very similar to the profession of architecture in the manner in which it melds art and engineering along with its deep impact on the cultural landscape. This immediately leads to questions about how we, as interaction experts, can both expand our understanding, approaches, and methodologies using architectural insights. Bratton (2008) goes one stage further and suggests that interaction design and architecture are set on a convergent course. As computing effects the way that we live, work, and communicate, Bratton foresees the evolution of 'universal interface design' which is a fusing of both subjects. In her paper Thomsen (2008) reinforces this use of contemporary architectural concepts of space and inhabitation as a way of allowing for a new framing of interactive experiences.

Mikael Wiberg in his book *Interactive Textures for Architecture and Landscaping* (Wiberg 2010) has also promoted the many complex ways in which spatiality has existed within interaction design. While computers have frequently promoted the concept of 'the death of distance' (Cairncross 1997; Wiberg 2014) he points out that computers are always used in some kind of spatial context. Wiberg promotes the spatialising of interaction via *Architecting Interactables*, the use of space and flows as a way of dealing with interactional complexity. This suggests that the design process would overlap with that of architecture to deal with the notion of flow.

Smart Cities

Up to this point we have discussed the role of architecture and space in HCI's core role of creating, extending and simplifying the user interaction process. Any discussion of HCI and Architecture would not be complete without briefly identifying some of the related areas where Architecture isn't an agent in the interaction process but the interaction process is an agent for architecture. One principle research area is that of 'Smart Cities'. The considerable interest in the field of smart cities combined with expenditure by research funding organizations suggests that urban interaction (Fischer et al. 2012) will be a considerable field in the near future. The growth of computing research into smart cities where digital technology is drawn together with urban intellectual and social capital can extend and rejuvenate many of the traditional physical infrastructures (mobility, places of living and work, social and electronic networks, energy). Smart cities demand that we cannot exclude, an understanding of the complex social and cultural dynamics that defined the streets we live in. As Rogério de paula says "*A city is not just a static backdrop against which our everyday lives as city dwellers unfold. Rather, it plays a critical role in shaping how its inhabitants experience their everyday lives*" (De Paula 2013). This suggests that Urban HCI is moving towards a position in which the city no longer plays a passive role. For Smart Cities to be more than a vague marketing term it seems that computer scientists and interaction designers should be as aware of what cities can do for computing as well as what computing can do for the city. It seems natural then that HCI will begin to explore the regularities between these two fields as a source of more than inspiration.

Finally, if the Weiser vision (Weiser 1993), where computing is at least partially embedded in the physical environment, is to become a practical reality, it seems reasonable to assume HCI will have to engage with architecture and architectural design to the same extent it did with graphic design with the introduction of the graphic 2-D interface and later the web. Human computer interaction, like architecture, is a diverse and consciously evolving community. While the delivery of data by means of the environment is not the only possible direction for computing, it is currently a significant research direction. Given the developments in ubiquitous and pervasive computing already taking place, it seems natural that computing is becoming more spatial and that the context of digital technology in the build environment will become a significant factor in the Human Computer Interaction process.

Directions of Architectural Research

Architects have long been interested in the architectural opportunities of digitally enhanced spaces (McCullough 2005; Mitchell 1995). As far back as 1966, architects like Iannis Xenakis were incorporating electronic elements into their work as a fundamental aspect of the building's experience (Xenakis and Kanach 1976). In 1992, architect Prof. Michael L. Benedikt published his book *Cyberspace*: *First Steps* (Benedikt 1992), a collection of articles dedicated to the impact of virtual worlds on the world of architecture. Architectural and computing pioneer John Frazer preempted many developments in tangible interaction and digital inhabitation back in the early 1990s (Frazer 1995), yet his developments are unknown to many in the field of ubiquitous computing research. Many of the architectural ramifications of early digital technologies on the physical environment were explored by authors such as William J. Mitchell. In *City of Bits*: *Space*, *Place*, *and the Infobahn* (Mitchell 1995), for example, MIT Professor of Architecture Mitchell, discussing the future impact on the city of digital connectivity, augured the laying of ever shorter fibre-optic cables for algorithmic trading.

Architecture has always seen itself as engaging with modern social and technological innovations, so it comes as no surprise that it has engaged with digital computing on a dizzying number of fronts. To further facilitate the comprehension of these fronts, we categorized the principle ones under the twin streams of process of design and product of design.

Process of Design

Thinking and imagining in three dimensions is a complex cognitive activity, so it is natural that architects might use digital means to augment their design processes to explore new creative designs. Thus, even buildings with no digital components can be highly influenced by digital technology. Computer aided architectural design (CAAD) is certainly the most visible adaptation architecture has made to computing. In his book *Hybrid Space*: *Generative Form and Digital Architecture* (Zellner 1999) Peter Zellner identifies that, by engaging with computer aided design, architects have been able to define forms that would previously have been unachievable. Frank Gehry's Guggenheim Museum in Bilbao (Fox and Kemp 2009), for example, would be impossible without software and Gehry's practice had to engage in a software development process to build something that possessed the right degree of expressiveness. The roof of the Great Court at the British Museum, designed by architects Norman Foster and Partners, is also a good example, where every triangular component of the curved roof was of a slightly different specification. Without the use of specifically designed software to compute every triangle, and machine it, this approach wouldn't have been attempted (Harrison et al. 1996).

While HCI works with digital technology as a 'product', the above examples demonstrate how the field can also lay claim to having changed what is achievable in the architectural design and manufacturing process. There is much to learn about the practice of augmenting the design process with software, which Patrik Schumacher, a partner at Zaha Hadid Architects, approaches through parametric design as a creative process. This blurs the boundary between the designer and the machine, giving some control over the design process to the digital partner. This process stretches as far as Marcus Novak in the 1990s who employed algorithmic techniques to define form, creating something which has yet to be achieved in the world of interaction design. With popular software, such as Grasshopper 3-D showing that augmentation of the architect with digital software in the design process is not an idiosyncratic digital retreat of the few. Here the architect is using code as a reflective sketchbook.

Product of Design

While the use of digital technology in the design process is not the subject of this book, it does highlight that architects are seriously and reflectively engaging with digital materials as part of their design process. It can be of little surprise then that architects would begin to incorporate digital elements in the products of the design process. As part of the process for engaging with social and cultural issues, architects from the modernist school, such as Frank Lloyd Wright and Le Corbusier, believed that new technology rendered all traditional styles of building obsolete. The work of architects like Ludwig Mies van der Rohe's Seagram Building in New York (1956–1958) (Carter 1974) was an attempt to honestly reflect the new materials being used in construction at the time (steel and glass). It seems natural that, when new digital media became available, architects would begin to try to create new types of architecture based on these new materials. Parallel to the way that artists, like Thomson and Craighead (Sánchez et al. 2009), began to engage with digital multimedia as a cultural response to the social rise of pervasive computing, it would seem natural that architects will also try to engage with digital elements as part of the lived hermetic of building occupation. In his book, *The Digital Turn in Architecture 1992–2010*, Mario Carpo (Picon 2010) gives a comprehensive anthology of digital architecture using papers by many well-known authors in the field to give a historical context to the many future trends. In a similar way, architect Neil Spiller, who reports on the numerous digital architects in his book, *Digital Architecture Now: A Global Survey of Emerging Talent*, (Spiller et al. 2008) shows architects and discusses how architects are engaging with digital experience as well as digital processes. These and many more architects fall under the general rubric of

'Interactive Architecture'. In their book, Michael Fox and Miles Kemp (2009) see architecture with digital technology becoming more process orientated, dynamic and, in many ways, humanistic. Like their contemporaries in the Netherlands, Prof Kas Oosterhuis and Xin Xia (Oosterhuis et al. 2010), they use practice as a means of further reflecting on their materials and process. The sheer momentum behind all these projects suggests that architects will more fluidly engage with digital technologies than computer scientists might first suspect.

Historically, Nicholas Negroponte, architect and founder of the media lab, had a vision of a more robotic environment where the building would conform around the needs of the user, he foresaw "a man-made environment that responds to and is 'meaningful' for him or her" (Negroponte 1975). The notion of the robotic building has a long history going back to the psychotropic house in J.G. Ballard's *The Thousand Dreams of Stellavista* and is currently a subject of study as 'architectural robotics'. Sitting comfortably between robotics and architecture, 'architectural robotics' (Gross and Green 2012; Weller et al. 2007) creates a whole number of design affordances which could be used to change both buildings and future cities. This work sits firmly in the practice of architectural research, as Gross and Green say, "*Perhaps the greatest challenge for architectural robotics is defining its community*" (Gross and Green 2012). That is, technical architectural research like this lacks a clearly defined path from research to industrial uptake, something the HCI community seems more familiar with.

From an academic perspective it seems clear that both sides of this divide are becoming slowly mutually aware. In his 2011 book, Dade-Robertson (2011) begins to discuss the impact of ubiquitous computing from an architectural and architectonic perspective. The importance here is the growing awareness that architects will not only be the users of computers and digital technologies, but will play a part in the configuration and presentation of those technologies to users/occupants. Malcolm McCullough's book *Digital Ground* (McCullough 2005) is probably the most well- known book dealing with architecture and pervasive computing. Here McCullough introduces pervasive computing to the world of architecture from an architectural perspective. Using architectural theory and criticism, McCullough challenges the notion that computing is an a-spatial technology, and argues that it is the spatiality which can reconfigure the interface. From the perspective of architecture, he argues that pervasive computing is another in a historic line of cybernetic technologies that architecture has previously responded to. Comparing pervasive computing to virtual reality technologies, he says, "*Whereas previous paradigms of cyberspace threatened to dematerialize architecture, pervasive computing invites a defence of architecture.*"

McCullough argues that pervasive computing probes fundamental aspects of architecture and, to a similar degree, that pervasive computing challenges fundamental aspects of interaction design. Above all, *Digital Ground* poses the fundamental necessity for the two disciplines to work more closely together. "*The need to connect architecture and interaction design comes from overlapping subject matters and escalating social consequences.*" What McCullough does for the building, Mark Shepard's book, *Sentient City*, demonstrates for the city. He suggests that urban design is also becoming aware of the growth of ubiquitous computing. This is still an active and on-going area of investigation from the architectural and urban design perspective, as witnessed by the 2013 Urban Interaction (UrbanIDX) (Smyth et al. 2013) Symposium.

The Collision

Given the literature described, it seems inevitable that, despite different practices and histories, both architecture and interaction will eventually stand over almost literally the same ground. Both are concerned with an artefact (the building of technology) and how that artefact informs and changes the experience of the inhabitant/user.

The purpose of this book is to begin to create a framework in which this collaboration can take place. For this purpose, the two conceptual lenses of space and interaction are useful tools to frame the work included in this book. We present these two lenses very briefly here.

Space

For many in the field of HCI, location and space become synonymous, yet in architecture numerous diverse spatial representations allow architects to more fully understand the role of space within the social organization of a building. One important translation, which needs to be established, is the notion of space in architecture versus computing. Helen Couclelis (1999) gives a good introduction to the use of space in geography, stating that there are five uses of the term for that field alone. The first term is that most common in mathematics, a series of orthogonal attributes' specific values which form a 'point' in space. This kind of space derives from the geometric notions and is most familiar in the notion of 'Cartesian' space— coordinates which are infinite, measureable, infinitely scalable and inseparable.

For architectural historian Adrian Forty (2000), the concept of space was absent from architectural vocabulary until the 1890s. For him, the previous term was that of 'volumes' and 'voids' with space used as a synonym or in the context of 'void spaces'. Frank Lloyd Wright is quoted as saying, "*Space is the breath of art*" or "*The space within becomes the reality of the building*" or "*All architecture is shelter, all great architecture is the design of space that contains, cuddles, exalts, or stimulates the persons in that space,*" or Le Corbusier, "*'Architecture is the learned game, correct and magnificent, construction of space assembled in the light*." These quotes appear to be based on the belief that architects make space, which, from a scientific concept, seems incomprehensible. From a practical point of view, buildings are typically sold on the amount of space they contain, developers don't sell a certain number of meters of wall but square meters of floor space. So architectural use of space is closer to that of 'place' but leaving it in the realm of the designable. Architectural space is the kind of space you experience when you enter a large room in a house and remark on how 'spacious' it is. It is best to leave this translation with the observation that architecture typically specifies and records only the item, which defines the boundary of the thing which it actually designs—space.

Interaction

Interaction is as familiar a term to Human Computer Interaction specialists as space is to architects. For HCI designers, the core desire is to create a smooth dialog between user and machine. While you could speak about the interaction between a user and a can while drinking a beverage, this diminishes the level of sophistication digital interaction can achieve. While wanting to avoid delving into the deeper aspects of 'present-at-hand vs. ready-to-hand (Heidegger 1962), a more familiar experience of what HCI means by interaction might be understood from computer gaming. The gaming community talks about the diaphanous 'playability' (Sánchez et al. 2009) of a game. This is separate from the plot, graphics or music of a game, it is the measure of the intangible pleasure the responsiveness of the game has to the user. A game might be difficult to control, yet this might contribute to the experience and lead to high 'playability'. This 'playability' is at the aesthetic extreme of interaction but does highlight the general interpretation of interaction to HCI. More recently, emphasis has started to move away from the interaction with a single software artefact, such as a game, production application or distributed system. 'User experience' captures our interaction with software in situ and covers many of the concerns architecture has with space. The organisational and spatial context of software use is critically important, as Suchman has highlighted (Suchman 1987). With the rapid expansion of computing into all aspects of our lives, the scope of this context is expanding at an equally rapid pace, with, for example, UrbanIXD specifically looking at the integration of user experience across the city.

Using these two lenses we hope that you can begin to view the chapters in this book not as two distinct areas of research but the boarders of one continuous area of enquiry which need to be knitted together. We see this book as the beginning of this process and hope that you, like us, are as excited by the research potential as much as the outcome for both future architecture and future interaction.

References

ART+COM Kinetic Sculpture. 2008 http://www.artcom.de/en/projects/project/detail/kinetic-sculpture/

Ballendat T, Marquardt N, Greenberg S (2010) Proxemic interaction: designing for a proximity and orientation-aware environment. ACM conference on interactive tabletops and surfaces. ACM, New York, pp 121–130

Benedikt M (1992) Cyberspace: first steps. MIT Press, Cambridge

Bødker S (2006) When second wave HCI meets third wave challenges. In: Proceedings of the 4th Nordic conference on human-computer interaction: changing roles. ACM, New York, pp 1–8

Bratton B (2008) The convergence of architecture and interface design. Interactions 15(3):20–27

Brignull H, Rogers Y (2003) Enticing people to interact with large public displays in public spaces. In: Proceedings of INTERACT. ACM, New York, pp 17–24

Cairncross F (1997) The death of distance: how the communications revolution is changing our lives. Harvard Business Press, Boston

Carter P (1974) Mies van der Rohe at work. Pall Mall Press, London

Chan M, Estève D, Escriba C, Campo E (2008) A review of smart homes—present state and future challenges. Comput Methods Prog Biomed 91(1):55–81

Chen C, Rada R (1996) Interacting with hypertext: a meta-analysis of experimental studies. Hum Comput Interact 11(2):125–156

Couclelis H (1999) Space, time, geography. In: Geographical information systems: principles and technical issues 1, pp 29–38

Dade-Robertson M (2011) The architecture of information: architecture, interaction design and the patterning of digital information. Routledge, New York

Dade-Robertson M (2013) Architectural user interfaces: themes trends and directions in the evolution of architectural design and human computer interaction. Int J Archit Comput 11(1): 1–20

Dalton N, Green KE, Dalton R et al (2014) Interaction and architectural space. CHI'14 extended abstracts on human factors in computing systems. ACM, Toronto, pp 29–32

Dalton N, Green K, Marshall P et al (2012) Ar-CHI-Tecture: architecture and interaction. CHI'12 extended abstracts on human factors in computing systems. ACM, pp 2743–2746

De Paula R (2013) City spaces and spaces for design. Interactions 20(4):12–15

Diller E, Scofidio R, Murphi D (2002) Blur: the making of nothing. Harry N Abrams, New York

Fischer PT, Hornecker E (2012) Urban HCI: spatial aspects in the design of shared encounters for media facades. In: Proceedings of the 2012 ACM annual conference on human factors in computing systems. ACM Press, New York, pp 307–316

Forty A (2000) Words and buildings: a vocabulary of modern architecture. Thames and Hudson, London

Fox M, Franklin S, Kilian A, Miao M, Lin J (2006) Bubbles. http://foxlin.com/category/process/bubbles/

Fox M, Kemp M (2009) Interactive architecture. Princeton Architectural Press, New York

Frazer J (1995) An evolutionary architecture. Architectural Association Publications, London

Goulthorpe M, Burry M, Dunlop G (2001) Aegis hyposurface: the bordering of university and practice. In: Proceedings of the ACADIA, New York, pp 344–349

Gross MD, Green KE (2012) Architectural robotics, inevitably. Interactions 19(1):28–33

Harrison S, Dourish P (1996) Re-place-ing space: the roles of place and space in collaborative systems. In: Proceedings of the 1996 ACM conference on computer supported cooperative work. ACM, New York, pp 67–76

Heidegger M (1962) Being and time (trans: Macquarrie J, Robinson E). Harper & Row, New York

Hornecker E, Nicol E (2012) What do lab-based user studies tell us about in-the-wild behavior?: insights from a study of museum interactives. In: Proceedings of the designing interactive systems conference. ACM Press, New York, pp 358–367

Ingram B (2009) FEATURE learning from architecture. Interactions 16(6):64–67

Ishii H, Ullmer B (1997) Tangible bits: towards seamless interfaces between people, bits and atoms. In: Proceedings of the SIGCHI conference on human factors in computing systems. ACM, New York, pp 234–241

Jones SJ, Burnett GE (2007) Spatial skills and navigation of source code. In: Proceedings of the 12th annual SIGCSE conference on innovation and technology in computer science education. ACM, New York, pp 231–235

Kidd C, Orr R, Abowd G et al (1999) The aware home: a living laboratory for ubiquitous computing research. In: Cooperative buildings. Integrating information, organizations and architecture. Springer, Berlin/Heidelberg, pp 191–198

Kim KS (2001) Implications of user characteristics in information seeking on the World Wide Web. Int J Hum Comput Interact 13(3):323–340

Kostakos V, O'Neill E, Penn A (2006) Designing urban pervasive systems. Computer 39(9):52–59

Mackay WE, Fayard AL (1997) HCI, natural science and design: a framework for triangulation across disciplines. In: Proceedings of the 2nd conference on designing interactive systems: processes, practices, methods, and techniques. ACM Press, New York, pp 223–234

MacKenzie IS, Buxton W (1992) Extending Fitts' law to two-dimensional tasks. Proceedings of the SIGCHI conference on human factors in computing systems. ACM Press, New York, p 226

McCullough M (2005) Digital ground: architecture, pervasive computing, and environmental knowing. The MIT Press, Cambridge, MA

Mitchell WJ (1995) City of bits: space, place and the Infobahn. MIT Press, Cambridge

Negroponte N (1975) Soft architecture machines. MIT Press, Cambridge, MA

Norman D (1988) The design of everyday things. Doubleday, New York

Oosterhuis K, Bouman O, Lénárd I (2002) Kas Oosterhuis: programmable architecture. L'Arcaedizioni, Milano

Oosterhuis K, Lénárd I (1998) vrmlSITE. http://v2.nl/archive/works/vrmlsite

Xia X, Sam EJ (2010) Interactive architecture. episode publishers, Rotterdam

Picon A (2010) Digital culture in architecture. Birkhauser, Basel

Rodden T, Benford S (2003) The evolution of buildings and implications for the design of ubiquitous domestic environments. In: Proceedings of the SIGCHI conference on human factors in computing systems. ACM Press, New York, pp 9–16

Sánchez JLG, Zea NP, Gutiérrez FL (2009) From usability to playability: Introduction to player-centred video game development process. In: Human centered design. Springer, Berlin/Heidelberg, pp 65–74

Schnädelbach H (2012) Hybrid spatial topologies. J Space Syntax 3(2):204–222

Smyth M, Helgason I, Brynskov M, Mitrovic I, Zaffiro G (2013) UrbanixD: designing human interactions in the networked city. CHI'13 extended abstracts on human factors in computing systems. ACM New York, pp 2533–2536

Spiller N et al (2008) Digital architecture now: a global survey of emerging talent. Thames & Hudson, London

Suchman LA (1987) Plans and situated actions: the problem of human-machine communication. Cambridge University Press, Cambridge

Thomsen MR (2008) Sites of flux: imagining space in the dance-architectures of the changing room and sea unsea. Personal Ubiquitous Comput 12(5):383–390

Varoudis T, Dalton S, Alexiou K, Zamenopoulos T (2011) Subtle interventions: how ambient displays influence route choice in buildings. RESPECTING FRAGILE PLACES-29th eCAADe conference Proceedings, eCAADe, pp 933–941

Weiser M (1993) Some computer science issues in ubiquitous computing. Commun ACM 36(7):75–84

Weller MP, Do EY-L (2007) Architectural robotics: a new paradigm for the built environment. EuropIA 11:19–21

Wiberg M (2010) Interactive textures for architecture and landscaping: digital elements and technologies. IGI Global, Hershey

Wiberg M (2011) Making the Case for "Architectural Informatics": a new research horizon for ambient computing? Int J Ambient Comput Intell (IJACI) 3(3):1–7

Wiberg M (2014) Interaction design research and the future. Interactions 21(2):22–23

Wiberg M (2015) Interaction design meets architectural thinking. Interactions 22(2):60–63

Wiltse H, Stolterman E (2010) Architectures of interaction: an architectural perspective on digital experience. In: Proceedings of the 6th Nordic conference on human-computer interaction: extending boundaries. ACM Press, New York, pp 821–824

Wisneski C, Ishii H, Dahley A et al (1998) Ambient displays: turning architectural space into an interface between people and digital information. In: Cooperative buildings: Integrating information, organization, and architecture. Springer, Berlin/Heidelberg, pp 22–32

Xenakis I, Kanach S (2008) Musique, architecture. Pendragon, Marseille

Zellner P (1999) Hybrid space: generative form and digital architecture. Rizzoli International Publications, Inc., New York

Part I
Interdisciplinary Dialogue

In the introduction we highlighted the rise of pervasive computing over the last three decades. Technological and architectural developments have been rapid, while they have sometimes occurred in relative isolation, 'protected' by disciplinary boundaries. Such separation can lead to multiple false starts, when things are tried and tested even though someone else has already discovered that there is an issue. This separation will also lead to missed opportunities when potential synergies between sets of expertise are not realized. We have argued that separate research arcs are coming to the same nexus and the two chapters in this section react to this.

Krukar begins with a view that seems to be at odds with many of the preconceptions someone from human-computer interaction might bring to this book. Rather than looking at computing as the young discipline with much to learn from the older design professions of architecture, Krukar's work declares that buildings are also artefacts and talks about looking to human-computer interaction to bring user-centred design to architectural design. Citing the rise of the evidence-based design movement, Krukar discusses the use of HCI familiar personas in architectural design. In many ways, this opening chapter underlines the reciprocal nature of design enquiry exchange to both HCI and architecture. Beneath the headline messages, there are some themes that will be reflected repeatedly in later chapters.

Luck's work begins by stating some of the obvious changes that have occurred to office buildings partly or wholly engendered by digital technologies. Once upon a time, computers occupied buildings and now, to some extent, she suggests we are approaching the world where buildings occupy computers. Commercial office architecture has had to respond to the demands that computational furniture has placed upon it. This may be the datacentre with the massive air conditioning requirements or the floor and ceiling increases along with ventilation problems caused with the rise of the extensive use of desktop computing. Even today the electromagnetic properties of the building can limit the use of wireless network connections. This chapter examines the changing interactions between people, buildings and computation, using the re-design of the office as a building type to illustrate. **Luck** suggests that 'the design of the physical locations for work (the built form) has more in common with the design of technology for work than these largely separate, fields acknowledged.'

Like the other writers in this chapter, Luck suggests that analytic ethnography under the rubric of 'work place studies' is a way to study activities in their natural habitats. Further Luck suggests that 'The setting, location or place of work is integral to its analysis and thus are concerned with far more than jobs and tasks; rather, the focus has always been on entire 'workscapes''.

These workscapes are not strange new objects of inquiry but, in fact, admission of elements that have always been present. As Luck states '*at Xerox, we understand that we cannot separate the operation of a photocopier by people from its setting-situated contexts of use provide import insights for design important. What these studies all point up is that the places where we work, in various ways, become part of the work that gets done there.*' All this must be done with a clear realization that the practice of work has become mutable. At work we use the technology resources for play (fun would be a better choice) but with the rise of mobile technologies the workplace can extend to our homes and third places like coffee shops. As Luck points out the rise of drop-down spaces, the introduction of cafes into the workplace, all speak to a blurring distinction between the workplace and other environments. This is a chapter about digital technology, and the reconceptualization of the workplace, from an embodied phenomenological perspective, as such it seems to be the Keystone on the bridge between computing and architecture.

Chapter 2
Applying HCI Methods and Concepts to Architectural Design (Or Why Architects Could Use HCI Even If They Don't Know It)

Jakub Krukar, Ruth Conroy Dalton, and Christoph Hölscher

Abstract The act of designing a building is indirectly, but conceptually very closely, linked to the user experience of its final outcome. It is this experience which often constitutes a major criterion for assessing the quality of the architect's work. And yet, it would be a gross overstatement to suggest that architectural design is a user-centered process.

On a more generic level, designing any physical object acting as a catalyst for the final experience can be viewed as an act of designing a human-artifact interaction where the 'artifact' (be it a building or a computer device) serves as an interface for the ultimate behavior or emotional reaction. This chapter argues, that the field of Human-Computer Interaction (HCI) can be viewed as a source of inspiration for architects wishing to incorporate, or enhance, user-centric planning routines in their creative workflows.

Drawing from the methodological toolbox of HCI, we demonstrate how user-centric planning can be placed in a structured framework, with tested and easy-to-apply methods serving as the vehicle for holistic user-centered planning processes.

The chapter proposes a formal model for understanding usability and user experience in the architectural context, demonstrates a number of methods suitable for its application, and concludes with a case study of an attempted use of one of such methods in an award-winning (yet, not necessarily user-friendly) public library project.

J. Krukar (✉)
Institute for Geoinformatics, University of Münster, Münster, Germany
e-mail: krukar@uni-muenster.de

R.C. Dalton
Department of Architecture and the Built Environment, University of Northumbria,
Newcastle upon Tyne, UK

C. Hölscher
Department of Humanities, Social and Political Sciences, ETH Zurich, Zurich, Switzerland

© Springer International Publishing Switzerland 2016
N.S. Dalton et al. (eds.), *Architecture and Interaction*,
Human–Computer Interaction Series, DOI 10.1007/978-3-319-30028-3_2

Introduction

It should be self-evident that architects design buildings for the people who will ultimately come to inhabit them and therefore it could be assumed that the architectural design process might exemplify a user-centred design approach. The reality unfortunately falls short of this ideal. Frequently, the needs of a building's end-user/s fade into the background due to the fact of being subsumed by numerous other, and often conflicting, design constraints: these include the needs of the client (where the client and end users are not one and the same) or functional, programmatic, structural, material and legal requirements. Conversely, the needs of the user may receive less consideration, as experienced architects may believe that they can intuitively (and hence implicitly) design for building's inhabitants without any need to make this an explicit part of the design consideration. Sometimes this is true; sometimes it is not. It is the position of this chapter that by explicitly placing the needs of users at the centre of the architectural design process, the overall quality of public architecture and cities can be increased. If so, how might this be achieved? One suggestion is to look to another field where the needs of the users are integral to their methodologies, namely human-computer interaction (HCI; see e.g. Dix et al. 1997; Preece et al. 2011).

Ultimately, human-computer interaction is a type of human-artifact interaction, and HCI research is characterized by analyzing human behavior, cognitive processes and task structures faced by the user. Buildings can also be understood as artifacts, and humans interact with these artifacts in numerous ways. In the behavioral sciences, this has been investigated under the label *environmental psychology* since the 1970s and, more recently, also within the *spatial cognition* domain. While a large number of studies in these two fields have tried to identify how people react to environmental settings (e.g. Kopec 2006) and how they mentally represent spatial relations (e.g. McNamara 1986), such research has had little impact on architectural design practice in comparison to the established role of HCI professionals and their methodology in contemporary software and IT systems design.

In the last 10 years there has been an important revitalization of the interaction between cognition and architecture. One example is the *evidence-based design* movement in architecture, which calls for better understanding of human behavior inside buildings. The main thrust is to obtain performance measures of implemented designs (existing buildings) and/or derive predictions of such measures for design options under consideration. The *evidence-based architectural design* movement has emphasized the need for adopting a human-centered, empirically grounded perspective and for developing scientifically appropriate evaluation methods (Hamilton and Watkins 2009). This approach is most prominent in health care and office architecture (e.g. Suttell 2007; Ulrich et al. 2004; Sailer et al. 2008). Evidence-based design has been significantly inspired by the success of evidence-based medicine with its core demand for decision-making based on unbiased, reliable data-sets that often question expert intuitions and long-held preferences (Sackett et al. 1996). Besides issues such as energy-efficiency, human factors are now seen as a component of building performance, involving perception, emotion and aesthetic appraisal, psychological well being, as well as behavioral and cognitive factors of movement in a building or through cities.

In HCI, the usability of a digital system typically can be described by a triangle of user characteristics, task properties and system features (including the user interface and underlying functionality). In architectural design we find a similar triangle, here of the building user, building-specific tasks, and the features of the building. Consequently, methods for capturing the usability of buildings must be able to take these factors into account. In order to do this, we must first, however, unpick what exactly is meant by the term *usability* when applied to architecture rather than to a digital system. And since in HCI the importance of usability is most often seen through the wider lens of the holistic *user experience* we must define the relation between these two concepts in the architectural context; this will be addressed in the first section of this chapter.

Building Usability and User Experience

Reviewing the Existing Usability Models in HCI

Understanding what is a *usable building* varies significantly between publications (Hölscher et al. 2006; Leaman and Bordass 2000; Norman 2002) and a universal acceptance of quantifiable measures defining it is still a distant goal. Such an understanding is necessary on an interdisciplinary level, since many design-related fields could benefit from such knowledge transfer (Ingram 2009) – particularly with respect to architecture, where emerging, reliable means of measuring usability require a clear framework of reference. One of the aims of this chapter, therefore, is to contribute to the debate on building usability by appropriating existing knowledge from the field of human-computer interaction.

In software engineering usability has been investigated thoroughly and has been clearly defined in ISO standards; defining the concept from different perspectives. Abran et al. (2003) provide a review of some existing definitions, identifying the two most widely accepted ones:

1. [Usability is] "the capability of the software product to be understood, learned and liked by the user, when used under specific conditions" (ISO/IEC 9126-1, 2000).
2. "Software is usable when it allows the user to execute his task effectively, efficiently and with satisfaction in the specified context of use" (ISO 9241, 1992/2001).

It should already be noted that both of these definitions encompass similar ideas, describing the ability to be "*understood, learned and liked*" by the user in the former example and used "*effectively, efficiently and with satisfaction*" in the latter one.

Fig. 2.1 Enhanced usability
model (After Abran et al.
2003)

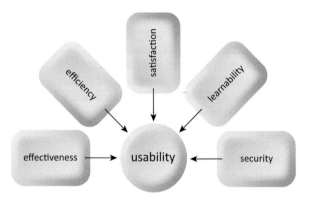

All of these concepts relate to how well a user is able to perform a given task whilst
using a given interface (or whilst 'using' a given building in the new context to
follow), as well as what resources or features he or she must make use of in order
to perform their undertakings (whatever they may be) successfully. The reference to
"*specific conditions*" and "*specified context of use*" are also important parts of both
definitions, emphasizing the need to take into account various meanings of usability
if and when a different context of use is being considered. Using these ISO standards
as a starting point, Abran et al. (ibid.) combined a number of existing definitions
with their own interpretations and presented an *enhanced usability model*. This is
shown in Fig. 2.1.

This model can be explained as follows:

- *Effectiveness* relates to how many mistakes people make while performing a task;
- *Efficiency* is described by how much time and resources it costs to perform a task;
- *Satisfaction* could be measured as the ratio of favorable to unfavorable opinions
  about or comments on the process as elicited from the users;
- *Learnability* describes the time required to learn how to perform a task;
- *Security* is important in terms of access controllability.

In architecture, each of these factors has been considered for decades, if not
centuries, but almost only in isolation from each other. *Effectiveness* has been
studied, for example, by counting the number of wayfinding errors at decision points
(Golledge 1992; Williamson and Barrow 1994). *Efficiency* might be indicated by
the time needed to find a specific room in a wayfinding task. *Satisfaction*, from
the building experience perspective, has been measured as part of standard Post-
Occupancy Evaluation research (Leaman and Bordass 2001). *Learnability* in the
building context indicates how long it may take a user to become familiar with a
building (Peponis et al. 1990). *Security* in an architectural context relates to the
way in which buildings have to accommodate the needs of different user groups
with differing levels of control, access, and hierarchy (medical staff vs. patients
vs. visitors in a hospital or the myriad complex levels of non-intersecting access,
occupation and egress required by the different groups such as judge, lawyers, jury,
prisoners, police and the public in a courtroom; Pati et al. 2007).

Abran's model, combining numerous, existing definitions of usability in the field of human-computer interaction indicates that usability is a quality of a product (or of a building, in this case) that makes it safe, easy, pleasant and stress-free to operate. At a very fundamental level, usability is about nothing more than avoiding frustrating the user. While, currently, this is certainly implemented in any major software development project, in contrast, this *bottom-line goal* has rarely been explicitly formulated (and planned for) in architectural practice. The result of this omission is that our built environment, despite being composed of numerous multi-million pound/dollar/euro projects, does not lack frustrating, annoying, confusing, stressful, or mentally tiring spaces. Is it any surprise, therefore, that the concept of usability remains somewhat under defined, and certainly underused, in an architectural context? The following section will aim to reinterpret what has already been written about usability, and convert it into a format that has the potential to be beneficial to architectural researchers and practitioners.

Introducing a Usability Model for Architecture

We have just suggested that usability is fundamentally about avoiding frustrating your user and there is clearly no reason why such an aim should be any different for an architect than for a software engineer: it is about intentionally placing your future users at the very center of the design process. In reality, however, things are never quite this simple and, of course, all design processes include limitations: financial, spatial and procedural, to name but a few. But such constraints are no different, whether the designer is a software engineer or an architect; the essence of their task remains the same, namely, to satisfy the final user with the delivered product. To demonstrate the similarity of the concepts and of the design processes, we can start by replacing the software-related words in the ISO usability definitions presented above with alternative terms relating to architectural design. This action produces the following initial re-interpretations:

1. [Usability is] the capability of the **BUILDING** to be understood, learned and liked by the user, when used under specific conditions.
2. A **BUILDING** is usable when it allows the user to execute his/her tasks effectively, efficiently and with satisfaction in the specified context of use.

Buildings essentially exist for the structuring or organization of different functional spaces: this is the purpose of their existence (Hillier et al. 1984). They can be considered a physical *interface* (an environment) that facilitates the undertaking of a range of everyday actions – from a guard supervising inmates in a prison to a child reading a book in a library. Likewise, computer software offers an *interface* (an environment) through which to conduct many everyday actions – from computing mathematical equations to communicating with a distant relative. Both artifacts (buildings and software) stand between us, the action-performers, and the action's outcome. This is irrespective of whether the action is mental or physical and notwithstanding of the scale of the action. Both, buildings and software, therefore serve as an *interface* and this principal fact requires them to be usable. These artifacts-as-interfaces determine how well we, the end user, can perform our actions. This aspect of building usability is both captured and emphasized by the re-definitions provided above: buildings should be "*understood, learned and liked*" by their users, so they are able to do what they want, or need, to do "*effectively, efficiently and with satisfaction*".

In terms of satisfaction, it is worth mentioning that how users 'like' a product or are 'satisfied' with it frequently relates more to a *lack of negative feelings* about the interaction than to an abundance of positive ones. This is a widely accepted understanding of usability in HCI (Hassenzahl 2010) since users, in general, do not expect to have positive experiences of their everyday equipment. For example, an alarm clock would rarely be a source of positive feelings, but users will get frustrated if their interaction with it is not flawless (i.e. if they could not reprogram easily the time of the alarm). This is not equivalent to saying that designers should limit themselves to providing only 'tried and tested' solutions. Even alarm clocks can remain a source of innovation.[1] But each such innovative departure is treated with the highest caution and consequently is preceded by extensive user testing. The same is not true in an architectural context, even though the financial and social consequences are usually much larger (e.g. a potential user might not be able to choose to ignore and avoid a confusing train station building).

In terms of the kinds of tasks that building users might wish to perform, there is a striking departure from the analogy with digital systems as described above. This is because an architectural setting demands a sub-categorization of the types of tasks that can be performed. These can be broadly held as: (a) the task of moving from one place to another in the building and (b) conducting a subsequent action once that place or context has been reached. Therefore, another distinction can be made, between 'dynamic' and 'static' activities, i.e. those involving wayfinding through the, often complex, spatial structure of a building and those actions which take place within a single space. This distinction is important, since a change of spatial location in a building often produces a change of context (e.g. moving from a cafeteria in a hospital to the emergency room) and also because wayfinding can be an extremely challenging task in its own right, demanding careful user-centric planning (e.g. Wiener et al. 2009). As a result, the model of building usability illustrated above can be further modified (Fig. 2.2).

This model of building usability now permits us to present both wayfinding and the full range of other actions facilitated by a building within a single framework allowing for considerations of successful and comfortable task performance. As mentioned previously, both of these aspects of building use are extensively studied, although the second category (the static actions) is dispersed across a range of research and literature. Many examples can be found, for instance, in the

---

[1] Consider, for instance, the case of integrating alarm clocks into touch-screen-based devices, e.g. by means of a 'wheel' metaphor as used in an iPhone.

Fig. 2.2 Enhanced usability model after Abran et al. (2003), applied to architecture

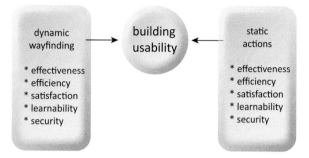

post-occupancy evaluation studies (e.g. Leaman 2000; Leaman and Bordass 2000, 2001). For instance, Leaman and Bordass (2000) name perceived control, speed of building's response, lighting, noise and health-comfort-productivity interaction as the crucial aspects influencing human comfort, and hence productivity, in places of work.

From Usability to User Experience

However, to subordinate everything to mere usability would imply total and rigid coherence to functionality within the building. To give an example from HCI, Hassenzahl (2010) cites a Microsoft Games employee who once said that *"if a usability engineer designs a game, it would be most likely a single button announcing >To win press here<"* (Hassenzahl 2010, p. 43). Considering building usability, it must be remembered that building design cannot pursue an ever-increasing spatial simplification with the aim to efficiently support users' needs/actions (The building's equivalent of *"To win press here"*). What excites and stimulates us, what we love about architecture is its diversity. To promote usability above all other criteria in the design process would be to destroy the very identity and uniqueness of our buildings.

For this reason, usability's *"lack of frustration"* is merely a starting point for creating a pleasant and satisfying experience of being in a place. It is a prerequisite, if such a satisfying experience is to emerge, but it is not the only factor required for it. Therefore, in human-computer interaction, another distinction is proposed which takes user-centered design a step further through the concept of User Experience (often abbreviated as UX). Hassenzahl (ibid) describes Experience Design as a process of designing for users' goals, where all of these goals are equally taken into account.[2]

---

[2]We will base further discussion on this particular work, although the reader should bear in mind that there are many approaches to UX design in HCI, some of which are less formalised than the one here cited.

Discovering what these goals are is the aim of user-centered design. But the users' explicit goal is rarely, *not to experience frustration*. Rather they expect, and even seek, positive and memorable experiences while interacting with designed products (Hassenzahl 2010). The same seems to be true within an architectural context, since the buildings that win architectural awards and those that gain public recognition often stand out, either visually or conceptually, from the everyday and commonplace buildings. This appears to be true even when some of these acclaimed buildings are, at the same time, relatively 'unusable' (Carlson et al. 2010).

As Hassenzahl (2010) writes, *"Even the best usability may never be able to put a smile on users' faces, because it only makes the difference between bad and acceptable."* (Hassenzahl 2010, p. 28). In contrast, Experience Design addresses the issue of achieving a positive experience, rather than merely an acceptable one. He therefore reformulates existing psychological theories (see Hassenzahl 2010 for details) and introduces a three-level hierarchy of goals:

- *Motor goals* answer to the question of '*how*' something is achieved, e.g. how does one get from A to B (in a building) or find a particular menu item (in software);
- *Do goals* answer the '*what*' question and relate to the action itself, i.e. what is it that a user is trying to do (e.g. read a book in a library or send an email from a given software);
- *Be goals*, however, answer the most important '*why*' question and reveal the motivation behind every action.

A book can be read in many different places other than a library and paintings can be viewed from the computer screen at home instead of on a museum wall. Answering *why* people do things they do (i.e. go to libraries or museums) is the most crucial element of a user-centric design. Making a library usable by allowing its users to find books easily is a fundamental necessity but it is not, and should never be, the only aim of the buildings' design. Figure 2.3 presents so-defined relations between the introduced hierarchy of goals and the Usability-UX distinction. Yet, since every user is different, and therefore every single experience of any space must vary from individual to individual (Thompson 1990), how can this final user experience be planned and designed?

Fig. 2.3 Three-level hierarchy of goals based on Hassenzahl (2010)

If we accept that all mindful user-activities are goal-driven,[3] the key of successful user-centric design lies in revealing these goals and correctly evaluating their importance. Turning this theory into design practice requires the use of methods that have to be reliable, reproducible and easy to apply in a fast-paced design studio environment often run by a team of people responsible for different parts or aspects of the same end product. Understanding the users' motivations is one aspect of this process, but effective communication within the team and applying this understanding to all stages of the design process might prove to be a more difficult challenge. As this is an issue equally present in HCI, one of the intentions of this paper is to present an example method, usage of which might be beneficial to architects just as it is to software and product designers. First we will take some time to briefly outline some of the range of methods taken from HCI, which we believe could be usefully appropriated by architects, in order to later take a closer look at one particular method.

A Brief Overview of Human-Computer Interaction Methods Available

HCI Methods in HCI Practice

We believe that the methodological toolbox of HCI researchers and practitioners can be valuable for understanding the challenges of designing buildings that meet user needs. It is important to note that the number of theoretical approaches, methods and specific tools used within HCI is diverse and our focus here lies on those that emphasise the cognitive, goal-oriented perspective (as opposed to e.g. the ethnographic perspective).

One family of methods broadly used within Human-Computer Interaction is *task analysis*. It aims at understanding the nature of potential interactions with a system being designed by decomposing the cognitive processes and behavioural actions required from the user in order to accomplish the desired task. *Behavioural scenarios* (Sutcliffe 2003) as well as *cognitive and computational models such as GOMS* (Olson and Olson 1995) *and ACT-R* (Anderson et al. 2004) were, among other methods, used to describe, structure, and analyse such tasks. *Personas* (which we will review in more detail below) are yet another tool often used for this purpose. In principal, *task analysis* is applied at the earliest stages of the design process, but remains relevant until its end (Diaper and Stanton 2003).

Collection of empirical user data in HCI occurs at all stages of the design process. Early ideas are tested through *interviews* and *focus group* meetings with potential users (see e.g. Lazar et al. 2010). These are often facilitated by simple *prototypes*

---

[3]Even if the goals are implicit.

such as paper prototypes (Snyder 2003), or prototypes believed to be functional while in reality they are operated by a human (so-called *Wizard of Oz studies*; Dahlbäck et al. 1993). Their goal is to make the discussion more focused, and to identify potentially critical areas of the user-system interaction. Under the lack of prototypes, other tools are available to extract the user's understanding of the structure of the potential task. *Card sorting* (e.g. Hudson 2005), for instance, is often used for guiding the design of menu items in a more complex software/websites, as it makes it easy for the participant to communicate which items in his or her mind 'belong' to similar categories.

More advanced versions of the device or software under development are often tested with a battery of usability studies, where participants are asked to perform specific tasks within the system. Behaviour of the user is then monitored, so that potential errors (but also emotions demonstrated during these errors) can be analysed. Some examples include *video recording* the interactions and *monitoring physiological processes* (Park 2009) or *eye-movement* (Poole and Ball 2005; Holmqvist et al. 2011). Additionally, HCI studies often involve *Think-Aloud-Protocols*, where the participant is asked to say what he or she thinks while performing the task (van Someren et al. 1994). Such behavioural studies take place both inside psychological laboratories and in-the field (Wynekoop and Conger 1992).

After public release of the new system, evaluation can continue as the usage data is gathered from the users of the system and new improvements can be studied with the so-called *A/B tests* (e.g. when a subset of users of an exisiting mobile application is presented with an alternative version of the main screen layout on their phone; see e.g. Nielsen 2005).

HCI-Like Methods in Architecture

A reader well familiar with the methods described in the previous section might be surprised that there are design-related fields which *do not* follow a similar work plan. A reader familiar with the architectural studies, on the other hand, might find many linkages to some of the methods used in the (still, almost exclusively academic) world of architectural usability studies. Those assumptions are only partially correct.

Early stages of the architectural design are very often proceeded by interviews with the client (note: who is not always the final user). Some versions of *task analysis* are employed throughout the analysis of functional spaces required for the particular structure (note: although they tend to be very generic and space-, instead of user-oriented). Prototypes (both virtual and physical) are constructed in order to explore multiple design alternatives (note: and not to test them with the potential users). Finally, Post-Occupancy Evaluation studies are employed to test the actual building performance (note: which is done extremely rarely; Cooper 2001; Roberts 2001).

In the academic sphere, multiple other methods were employed for testing building usability: *Virtual Reality A/B tests* (Kuliga et al. 2015), *physical mock-up A/B tests* (Krukar 2015), *Think-Aloud-Protocols* (Hölscher et al. 2006), or *Eye-Tracking* (Krukar 2015) to name but a few. What differs the academic world from the architectural practice, however, is that academics typically do not conduct their studies as a means to designing a specific product, but rather to generate generalisable insight or evaluate the current state-of-the-art solutions (namely: completed buildings). Perhaps for this reason, there is a number of methods available to test an existing (or a virtual) building (the slow adoption of which by practitioners is an issue deserving its own book chapter), but relatively little tools for facilitating the user-centric thinking at the earliest stages of the design process.

In the next section we are going to take one of the above methods, namely that of *personas* (a subset of task analysis) and demonstrate how they may be directly used in the architectural design field to address this gap. We will give one example of where something akin to a persona has already been used to great effect in architectural design, but where the architect was possibly unaware of its precedent usage.

Personas

If we summarize the chapter so far, and we concur that a usable building is one that can *"be understood, learned and liked by the user"* and that to move beyond mere usability is to be able to design an enriching and enjoyable *"user experience"* of a building, one needs to understand something about the goals and motivations of the user (Hassenzahl 2010). How might an architect or team of architects go about doing that? And more importantly what kinds of processes might be involved? The vast majority of architectural practices are small and 'micro' firms of two to ten staff with, in the UK for example, only 3–4 % of chartered architectural practices having more than 50 staff (RIBA 2012). For the most part, the majority of their work is of a domestic scale and their clients will also be their end-users and therefore the challenge of understanding the end user is simply one of getting to know, and developing a good relationship with, the client. This is, in fact, the familiar *modus operandi* for most architects and the way in which the majority of architects are trained in schools of architecture. However, what happens in larger practices, when architects are commissioned to build large-scale, public buildings (such as airports, hospitals or libraries)? The client may then be an amorphous institution and the end-users a separate group distinct from the client. In this situation the client's needs frequently do not map onto the end-users' needs. It is not a coincidence that these are frequently the building types that are beset with usability issues such as wayfinding difficulties.

If you cannot design for the client (since the client is not the end user any more) and you cannot design for every single user (since they are too many) the option that is left is to design for a sub-set of the future user-group. After all, designing for some of the users might still be better than designing for none of them. For that reason, even the simplest, evidence-based representations of a potential, future building user can help guide the design process and result in the building being significantly more usable. HCI designers faced the very same problem and noticed that every product (or, correspondingly – a building) belongs to a different 'product category' and serves many different people trying to perform different actions (described in the form of behavior scenarios). As a result, an HCI tool called *personas* (Cooper 2004; Cooper and Reimann 2003) has been developed and successfully used to provide customer/market research for websites or handheld interface designs. A persona, as Cooper writes, is a characterization of a user or groups/types of users that exhibits the most prominent attributes of the whole group: in other words, it is an archetype presented in the guise of a fictional character (Cooper 2004). In the architectural context, there is no reason why such behavior scenarios and the inspired personas could not be evidence-based, as architectural user studies are increasing and, at the same time, automated methods of behavioral data generation are more readily available.

There can be as many descriptions of archetypal users, or personas, as it makes sense (to the designer) to differentiate, but in general they should remain concrete and distinct from each other. They are a point of reference for a designer to help him or her keep the project consistent and suitable throughout the design process. At the same time, if confronting the goals of different possible users, through the use of different personas, the designer can ensure that the building will be flexible enough to be used by many dissimilar people once it has been completed. The most powerful personas are frequently based on focus groups and user interviews and, as such, they can also protect the researcher from forming false assumptions. So methodologically being very simple, they remain a tool, or, better to say, a way of thinking about interaction design, which can help architects just as much as they helped HCI designers.

The following bullet points identify some of the key features of using personas:

- A persona is a portrayal of an archetypical user intended for use in the design process;
- A persona's character may be constructed from surveys/interviews and obser- vations of real would-be users: this data is then analyzed and distilled into the characteristics of the persona;
- In situations where it is impossible or impractical to consult with real end-users the persona/s serve as ersatz versions for the designer's guidance;
- The use of personas may provide inspiration without the need to engage directly with end-users;
- Personas may also be termed 'user archetypes', 'target customer characteriza- tions', and 'user profiles'.

The use of personas is not without controversy or criticism. These include the criticisms of the method as being non-scientific (not based on real data but meta-data), as being insufficiently rigorous, methodologically under-developed and un-verifiable (Chapman and Milham 2006). Additional criticism points out that their use results in less, rather than more, user-centered design by lulling the designer into a sense of false security that they are being user-focused when in reality they are not, since the persona is only ever a substitute user (Portigal 2008; see also: Matthews et al. 2012). However, despite these reasonable criticisms, the authors of this chapter argue that the architectural profession could benefit from their use, particularly when designing large-scale public buildings with a varied user-group. Friess (2012) argues that it is the sole involvement in the process of creating personas that facilitates more user-centric thinking by individual members of the design team. Thus, even though their value might not be obvious throughout the process, it 'forces' the planners to consider the potential user within a relatively structured framework. Due to the growing number of technologies and sensors for monitoring human behavior in the built environment, the process of constructing personas can easily become much more evidence-based. This evidence can potentially be available, inputted and modified in real-time, as users interact with increasingly 'smart' buildings and cities. Simultaneously, the newly established design workflows and the benefits of truly user-centric thinking will remain unchanged. In the following section we will present a single case study illustrating the tentative steps into using persona-like methods in architectural design. This case study is given not as a best-practice example, since, as it will be demonstrated, its outcome can be considered far from ideal for any usability engineer. It is rather here in order to emphasise the key aspects of persona-building process (namely, its grounding in real data) which has been already mentioned above and remains equally relevant in the architectural design context.

Case Study: Seattle Public Library

The Seattle Public Library in Seattle was designed in 2004 by the Office for Metropolitan Architecture (Rem Koolhaas and Joshua Ramus) in partnership with LMN Architects. It is an enigmatic building having both won a significant number of awards whilst simultaneously dividing the opinion of its users, some of whom find it practically dysfunctional (Conroy Dalton et al. 2013). In our quest to unearth the source of its dysfunctionality we examined OMA's design process and discovered a strong focus on the user: in particular, a series of diagrams or 'scenarios' that OMA produced in order to develop the design (Ferré et al. 2004).

Each diagram represents a different type of 'user' of the library, indicated by a black question mark (?) and their questions or queries are expressed as speech bubbles. Each archetypal user has a need that can only be met by successfully navigating through the library and a dotted red line indicates their resultant trajectory or path. In one of such diagrams (Ferré et al. 2004), the user is characterized as a research student in conversation with a roving librarian. They ask the question, *"My professor claims that OMA is a postmodern practice, and I'd like to prove her wrong."* Further up the library (and further into their search indicated by a dotted line traversing across the simplified layout of the library) they encounter a second librarian, of whom they ask, *"Maybe I should refer to Mies van der Rohe ... do you have any publication of his works?"* This is an example of the type of user that OMA characterizes as a 'knowledge acquirer' (those seeking a holistic understanding – a deeper and wider body of knowledge) in contrast to an 'information gatherer' (who requires ease of access, efficiency and speed; Kubo and Prat 2005). This alternative 'user type' – the 'information gatherer' is shown in a different diagram, with the accompanying speech bubble query, *"Which way to the latest Tom Wolfe Book?"*. Other Reference Strategy Scenarios show yet another a user wanting to buy tickets to a concert in the auditorium and another, asking in Spanish, *"¿Dónde están los libros de ingles como segundo idioma?"* (Where are the books of English as a Second Language?). Although these are not fully developed personas in the way that is typically used in software and product design, this does represent an innovation in terms of architectural practice.

Through firsthand accounts of OMA's design practices (Yaneva 2009), we are relatively confident that OMA architects were not consciously employing personas in order to create these Reference Strategy Scenarios. Rather, we suspect, it was the architects own intuitive response to how to 'get inside the head' of what otherwise would have been an amorphous and intractable multiple-user group. The personas represented above can be characterized as the 'Research Student', the 'New Fiction Reader', the 'Concert Lover' and the 'English-Language Learner'. In these scenarios, depicted visually rather than in text or data, each persona has a specific task, which necessitates them travelling to a different part, and hence to a different floor, of the library. The resultant journey through the building is calculated and visualized (and hence part of the *'usability'* of the building would be dependent upon them being able to effectively navigate from one part of the library to their destination, without getting lost, confused or disorientated). However, despite the superficial similarities between OMA's Reference Strategy Scenarios to HCI personas, these attempts fall short of the real thing. First, they are probably not based upon survey data about library user or derived from interviews or focus groups. If, for example, they had survey data from the library indicating the 14 % of library user were enrolled in college and were using the library for college work, then the 'Research Student' persona could have been based upon this statistic. As mentioned above, the most effective personas emerge from a rich dataset that is then analyzed and distilled into the characteristics of the persona. Second, if they were true personas, they may well have been presented in the guise of a fictional character. The 'Research Student' would have been called Sally, aged 24, who would have been a grad student enrolled on the Master of Architecture Program in the Department of Architecture at University of Washington. She lives only a few blocks from the library, has a liking for espresso coffee, yoga and a phobia of enclosed spaces. Of course, all of this is fiction, but that is the joy of personas: when real users are not available to you, personas act as substitutes, willing and able to be as 'fleshed out' as necessary to whatever level of detail the architect needs for design inspiration. In this way the 'Research Student', the 'New Fiction Reader', the 'Concert Lover' and the 'English-Language Learner' (or Sally Meacham, Mrs A. Johnson, Chuck B. Headley and Rodrigo Lopez as they might have become under their new persona transformations) could have, collectively, represented the much larger community of would-be library users.

The benefit of using personas lies not only in structuring the individual architects' thinking about the complexity of the designed building in user-centric terms. Most importantly, it forms a 'common ground' for understanding this complexity by multiple members of larger design teams. Personas provide an inspiration for discussing critical user-centric design issues and focus individual efforts of many team members in the direction of well-defined design challenges.

The example presented above has been included in order to demonstrate what we believe to be the receptiveness for this approach by the architectural profession, despite the fact that their use of personas is rare. It is our conviction, that could the methodology be further adapted for architectural design, there would be considerable interest and uptake within the profession. Furthermore, we suggest that the use of personas may be a highly efficient method of designing with a building user in mind. It is our theory that by focusing on the user, architects can design better buildings and that any technique that helps this shift in focus is beneficial. From the example above, it should be noted that personas can be used both in the design-phase and in the post-occupancy evaluation stage in order to understand the building once it is in use. The use of both together, may form a 'virtuous circle' in which knowledge of previous schemes helps in the design of subsequent ones.

Additionally, we suggest that the use of personas could serve as a valuable tool in architectural education, where the students are frequently disadvantaged through lack of access to a real client; there is evidence that the use of personas in education produces higher quality student work (Long 2009). Finally, in terms of the criticisms of the use of personas, we do not disagree with them, rather suggest that this is a greater incentive to research this area and provide evidence for the methodology.

Conclusion

The use of personas is but one of the many sets of methods developed in HCI that might be adapted for use in architectural design. We chose just one of these methods, in order to illustrate how easy it is to transfer the methods from one arena to the other and to suggest the potential receptiveness for this approach. The field of human-computer interaction has the potential to provide a methodological framework for investigating how people understand buildings and cities and how the cognitive processes of their orientation and navigation behaviors are structured. Analytic methods such as cognitive task analysis and cognitive walkthroughs have already been adapted to the task performance of building users (e.g. Hölscher et al. 2006). Similarly, observational techniques such as video analysis (e.g. Tomé et al. 2015), movement tracking (e.g. Tröndle et al. 2014; Dalton et al. 2012) and virtual reality simulations (Conroy Dalton 2001) have been employed, increasingly relying on usability metrics (e.g. error classification).

Currently, however, the majority of architectural research (such as the previously mentioned Post-Occupancy Evaluation), happens *after* the building is in use with the assumption that the insights generalised from such studies might potentially be disseminated and applied as a guideline for future cases. The field of HCI demonstrated that shifting the user-centric efforts into early stages of the design process can result in an overally higher quality of an average end-product. It is important to note, that the methods which make this possible in architectural design are already in place, and need not be expensive or sophisticated. Personas, as presented earlier in this chapter, only facilitate a particular way of thinking, rather than enhance it with any novel, previously unavailable data. This early focus on the user is also visible in other methods used within *usability* and *user experience* design, such as preparing (and testing) prototypes (e.g. paper prototypes) even of very early versions of the device or software. Similar 'prototypes' are available to architects both in the form of 3D virtual models, as well as physical, miniaturised maquettes. What perhaps differs these two fields is therefore not the technological, financial, or procedural availability of such prototypes, but the aim they serve. In HCI, those methods revolve around the user's needs and goals. The aim of a simple paper prototype is to make the vague assumptions about the particular behavioural scenarios (and the mediating interactions between the artifact and the user) more concrete. This leads to earlier detection of potentially critical elements of the design. In architecture, it seems, prototypes make the vision about the shape and structure of a designed building more concrete, but the concept of the user is present there barely as a meaningless placeholder in images, maquettes and visualisations. Those, primarily aim to encapsulate the atmosphere of the designed spatial experience (as it is envisioned by the planner) or to explore multiple design alternatives but rarely, if ever, serve as a platform where any data-driven (or at least data-inspired) representation of a user would play the central role. As a result, the focus of the work heavily lands on what is visible, while neglects the more subtle characteristics of a building – those, which have been shown to influence its usability. These include the configurational functionality of its sub-spaces (e.g. Peponis et al. 1990), the visibility of key building elements (such as staircases) from the viewpoint of a potential user (e.g. Hölscher et al. 2006), or the building's suitability for diverse preferences and limitations (both mental and physical) of its potential occupants (e.g. Heitor et al. 2013). The commonly accepted assumption that architects prioritise the visible, outer shell of a building over its functionality might in this case not be true at all as the priorities are rarely explicitly set as such; they simply happen to influence the final outcome more, given the currently existing design workflows.

Taking HCI methods to architecture therefore requires a rigorous framework for capturing environmental properties not clearly conveyed with traditional maquettes or 3D models, which refer to the aspects other than the visible outer shell of a building, like saliency of landmarks or complexity of layout geometry. Space Syntax techniques, for example, are just one tool with the potential to make building features accessible to quantification and capture features relevant for understanding cognitive deficits of buildings (Franz and Wiener 2008; Conroy Dalton et al. 2005).

In addition to this, 'big data' increasingly captured via sensor-enabled buildings and cities, contribute to the corpus of user data allowing the researchers and practitioners to verify their theoretical assumptions, often in real-time. With this chapter, we are not only calling for more user studies in architecture (although that would naturally be welcome) but rather for a uniformed approach to measuring building usability and integrating it into the design process. Important questions to be addressed for the future include how to establish a user-centered perspective in the architectural design process, and how to refine analytic techniques suitable for use in design practice. Here, the field of HCI can serve as a model of best practice for evidence-based approaches in architectural design.

References

Abran A, Khelifi A, Suryn W, Seffah A (2003) Usability meanings and interpretations in ISO standards. Softw Qual J 11(4):325–338

Anderson JR, Bothell D, Byrne MD, Douglass S, Lebiere C, Qin Y (2004) An integrated theory of the mind. Psychol Rev 111(4):1036

Carlson L, Holscher C, Shipley TF, Conroy Dalton R (2010) Getting lost in buildings. Curr Dir Psychol Sci 19(5):284–289, http://doi.org/10.1177/0963721410383243

Chapman CN, Milham RP (2006) The personas' new clothes: methodological and practical arguments against a popular method. In: Proceedings of the human factors and ergonomics society annual meeting, vol 50, San Francisco, pp 634–636, http://www.hfes.org/publications/ProductDetail.aspx?ProductId=79

Conroy Dalton R (2001) Spatial navigation in immersive virtual environments. Unpublished Doctoral Dissertation, University College London, London

Conroy Dalton R, Hölscher C, Turner A (2005) Space syntax and spatial cognition. World Archit 185(41–47):107–111

Conroy Dalton R, Kuliga SF, Hölscher C (2013) POE 2.0: exploring the potential of social media for capturing unsolicited post-occupancy evaluations. Intell Build Int 5(3):162–180

Cooper I (2001) Post-occupancy evaluation – where are you? Build Res Inf 29(2):158–163

Cooper A (2004) The inmates are running the asylum: why high-tech products drive us crazy and how to restore the sanity. Sams Publishing, Indianapolis

Cooper A, Reimann R (2003) About face 2.0: the essentials of interaction design. Wiley, New York

Dahlbäck N, Jönsson A, Ahrenberg L (1993) Wizard of Oz studies: why and how. In: Proceedings of the 1st international conference on intelligent user interfaces, Orlando, pp 193–200, http://dl.acm.org/citation.cfm?id=169892

Dalton NS, Conroy Dalton R, Hölscher C, Kuhnmünch G (2012) An iPad app for recording movement paths and associated spatial behaviors. In: Spatial cognition VIII. Springer, Berlin, pp 431–450

Diaper D, Stanton N (2003) The handbook of task analysis for human-computer interaction. CRC Press, New York

Dix A, Finlay J, Abowd G, Beale R (1997) Human-computer interaction. Prentice-Hall, Upper Saddle River

Ferré A, Hwang I, Kubo M, Prat R, Sakamoto T, Salazar J, ... Tetas A (2004) Verb Architecture Boogazine: connection: the changing status of the city, of architecture, of Urbanism. The generation of activity, physically linking programs, people, and uses. Actar, Barcelona

Franz G, Wiener JM (2008) From space syntax to space semantics: a behaviorally and perceptually oriented methodology for the efficient description of the geometry and topology of environments. Environ PlanB: Plan Des 35(4):574–592

Friess E (2012) Personas and decision making in the design process: an ethnographic case study. In: Proceedings of the SIGCHI conference on Human Factors in Computing Systems, ACM, New York, pp 1209–1218

Golledge RG (1992) Place recognition and wayfinding: making sense of space. Geoforum 23(2):199–214

Hamilton DK, Watkins DH (2009) Evidence-based design for multiple building types. Wiley, Hoboken

Hassenzahl M (2010) Experience design: technology for all the right reasons. Synth Lect Hum-Centered Inf 3(1):1–95

Heitor T, Nascimento R, Tomé A, Medeiros V (2013) (IN)ACCESSIBLE CAMPUS: space syntax for universal design. In: Proceedings of ninth international space syntax symposium, vol. 2013, pp 084:–17

Hillier B, Hanson J, Peponis J (1984) What do we mean by building function? In: Designing for building utilisation, E & F.N. Spon Ltd: London, UK, pp 61–72, http://discovery.ucl.ac.uk/15007/

Holmqvist K, Nyström M, Andersson R, Dewhurst R, Jarodzka H, Van de Weijer J (2011) Eye tracking: a comprehensive guide to methods and measures. Oxford University Press, Oxford

Hölscher C, Meilinger T, Vrachliotis G, Brösamle M, Knauff M (2006) Up the down staircase: wayfinding strategies in multi-level buildings. J Environ Psychol 26(4):284–299

Hudson W (2005) Playing your cards right: getting the most from card sorting for navigation design. Interactions 12(5):56–58

Ingram B (2009) Learning from architecture. Interactions 16(6):64–67

Kopec D (2006) Environmental psychology for design. Fairchild/Troika Distributor, New York/London

Krukar J (2015) The influence of an art gallery's spatial layout on human attention to and memory of art exhibits. University of Northumbria, Newcastle

Kubo M, Prat R (2005) Seattle public library, OMA/LMN. Actar, Barcelona

Kuliga SF, Thrash T, Dalton R, Hölscher C (2015) Virtual reality as an empirical research tool – exploring user experience in a real building and a corresponding virtual model. Comp Environ Urban Syst 54:363–375. ISSN 0198-9715

Lazar J, Feng JH, Hochheiser H (2010) Research methods in human-computer interaction. Wiley, Hoboken

Leaman A (2000) Usability in buildings: the Cinderella subject. Build Res Inf 28(4):296–300

Leaman A, Bordass B (2000) Keeping occupants "Satisficed". Energy Environ Manag 2nd Q 2:23–27

Leaman A, Bordass B (2001) Assessing building performance in use 4: the Probe occupant surveys and their implications. Build Res Inf 29(2):129–143

Long F (2009) Real or imaginary: The effectiveness of using personas in product design. In: Irish ergonomics review, proceedings of the IES conference, Dublin

Matthews T, Judge T, Whittaker S (2012) How do designers and user experience professionals actually perceive and use personas? In: Proceedings of the SIGCHI conference on human factors in computing systems, Austin, pp 1219–1228

McNamara TP (1986) Mental representations of spatial relations. Cogn Psychol 18(1):87–121

Nielsen J (2005) Putting A/B testing in its place. Retrieved August 14, 2015, from http://www.nngroup.com/articles/putting-ab-testing-in-its-place/

Norman DA (2002) The psychopathology of everyday things. In: Levitin DJ (ed) Foundations of cognitive psychology: core readings. MIT Press, Cambridge, MA, pp 417–443

Olson JR, Olson GM (1995) The growth of cognitive modeling in human-computer interaction since GOMS. In: Baecker RM, Grudin J, Buxton WA, Greenberg S (eds) Human-computer interaction. Morgan Kaufmann Publishers, San Francisco, pp 603–625

Park B (2009) Psychophysiology as a tool for HCI research: promises and pitfalls. In: Jacko JA (ed) Human-computer interaction. New trends. Springer, Berlin, pp 141–148

Pati D, Bose M, Zimring C (2007) Rethinking openness: courthouses in the United States. J Archit Plann Res 24:308–324

Peponis J, Zimring C, Choi YK (1990) Finding the building in wayfinding. Environ Behav 22(5):555–590

Poole A, Ball LJ (2005) Eye tracking in human-computer interaction and usability research: current status and future. In: Ghaoui C (ed) Encyclopedia of human-computer interaction. Idea Group, Pennsylvania, pp 211–219

Portigal S (2008) Persona non grata. Interactions 15(1):72

Preece J, Sharp H, & Rogers Y (2011) Interaction design-beyond human-computer interaction. Wiley, New York

RIBA (2012) The RIBA and the architect in practice. Retrieved August 13, 2015, from https://www.architecture.com/Files/RIBAProfessionalServices/Regions/NorthWest/Education/Part3/StudyPacks2012/ChesterMarch/TheRIBAandthearchitectinpractice-AdrianDobson.pdf

Roberts P (2001) Who is post-occupancy evaluation for? Build Res Inf 29(6):463–465

Sackett DL, Rosenberg WM, Gray JA, Haynes RB, Richardson WS (1996) Evidence based medicine: what it is and what it isn't. BMJ: Br Med J 312(7023):71

Sailer K, Budgen A, Lonsdale N, Turner A, Penn A (2008) Evidence-based design: theoretical and practical reflections of an emerging approach in office architecture. In Undisciplined! Proceedings of the design research society conference 2008, Sheffield Hallam University, Sheffield, pp 119/1–19

Snyder C (2003) Paper prototyping: the fast and easy way to design and refine user interfaces. Morgan Kaufmann, San Diego, https://books.google.de/books?id=YgBojJsVLGMC&printsec=frontcover&source=gbs_ge_summary_r&cad=0#v=onepage&q&f=false

Sutcliffe A (2003) Scenario-based requirements engineering. In: Requirements engineering conference, 2003. Proceedings of the 11th IEEE international, pp 320–329

Suttell R (2007) Evidence-based design shapes healthcare facilities. Buildings, January. Retrieved from http://www.buildings.com/article-details/articleid/3535/title/evidence-based-design-shapes-healthcare-facilities.aspx

Thompson D (1990) An architectural view of the visitor-museum experience. In: Bitgood S, Benefield A, Patterson D (eds) Visitor studies: theory, research, and practice. Center for Social Design, Jacksonville, pp 72–85

Tomé A, Kuipers M, Pinheiro T, Nunes M, Heitor T (2015) Space–use analysis through computer vision. Autom Constr 57:80–97

Tröndle M, Greenwood S, Bitterli K, van den Berg K (2014) The effects of curatorial arrangements. Mus Manag Curatorship 29(2):140–173

Ulrich R, Quan X, Zimring C, Joseph A, Choudhary R (2004) The role of the physical environment in the hospital of the 21st century: a once-in-a-lifetime opportunity. The Center for Health Design, Concord

Van Someren MW, Barnard YF, Sandberg JAC et al (1994) The think aloud method: a practical guide to modelling cognitive processes, vol 2. Academic, London

Wiener JM, Büchner SJ, Hölscher C (2009) Taxonomy of human wayfinding tasks: a knowledge-based approach. Spat Cogn Comput 9(2):152–165

Williamson J, Barrow C (1994) Errors in everyday routefinding: a classification of types and possible causes. Appl Cogn Psychol 8(5):513–524

Wynekoop JL, Conger SA (1992) A review of computer aided software engineering research methods. Department of Statistics and Computer Information Systems, School of Business and Public Administration, Bernard M. Baruch College of the City University of New York, New York

Yaneva A (2009) Made by the office for metropolitan architecture: an ethnography of design. 010 Publishers, Rotterdam

Chapter 3
What Is It About Space That Is Important in Interaction? . . . Let's Take the World from a Situated Point of View

Rachael Luck

Abstract The spatial relationships between architectural form and computation are changing. They have been changing ever since the computer left a dedicated room in an office building leading to evolution, not only in the design of the office as a building type but also new forms of interaction with computing technology that are changing our ways of working and living within the built environment. In this chapter we study how this relationship has changed both the nature of 'work' and its locations. Building on this insight and understanding from the field of workplace studies we suggest a particular approach, analytic ethnography, to inform the design of environments for the new ways that computation, architecture and interaction intersect.

Introduction

The spatial relationship between architectural form and computing is changing. It has been changing ever since the mainframe computer left a dedicated room in an office building and migrated onto our desktops. Since computation has moved off the desktop there has been increased concern where it might have gone (Dourish and Bell 2007). In Negroponte's digital quest to 'move bits not atoms' he offers an answer, '*Computing is not about computers any more. It is about living.* The giant central computer, the so-called mainframe, has almost been universally replaced by the personal computer. We have seen giant computers move out of air-conditioned rooms into closets then onto desktops and now into our laptops and pockets' (Negroponte 1995 p. 6 [emphasis added]). This re-location of computing was most famously foreseen in Mark Weiser's vision of a world where computing is ubiquitous and 'the most profound technologies are those that disappear. They weave themselves into the fabric of everyday life until they are indistinguishable

R. Luck (✉)
The Design Group, Department of Engineering and Innovation, The Open University,
Milton Keynes, UK
e-mail: Rachael.Luck@open.ac.uk

© Springer International Publishing Switzerland 2016
N.S. Dalton et al. (eds.), *Architecture and Interaction*,
Human–Computer Interaction Series, DOI 10.1007/978-3-319-30028-3_3

from it' (Weiser 1999). We are now living within (designed) environments (think workplaces, spaces, rooms, buildings and the interstitial spaces between buildings in cities that are all part of our experience of built environment) that have been aptly described by Negroponte (1995) as places 'where people and bits meet'.

At this point in time, although we know the location of computing is changing we don't yet know the spatial implications of this. Like Dourish and Bell (2007) we 'want to know something of the spaces into which computation moves' and also, how to design the spaces where computing has re-located. These themes chime with the emergent field of architecture and interaction and are central in this argument.

In this chapter we examine the changing interactions between people and buildings and computation, using the re-design of the office as a building type to illustrate. These concerns intersect with how we design the built form (spaces, locations and places both within and between buildings), the design of technology for its new locations and the design of bodily interactions with technology (computation and architectural form, people and tech/buildings). The intellectual and practical questions that are raised through this inquiry are, just what is it about space that is important in interaction? and how, methodologically, can we study this?

In response this argument interleaves current thinking from architecture, workplace studies, systems and interaction design, and sociologists that study interaction, as well as corporate real estate analysts and space planners within organisations. Each of these fields has an interest in understanding human interaction in space. It is suggested that an analytic route to study new forms of interaction within complex technologically augmented environments already exists. Although the name 'workplace studies' seemingly limits its application, analytic ethnography is offered as a way to study activities in their natural habitats. What we show is that the design of the physical locations for work (the built form) has more in common with the design of technology for work than these, largely separate, fields acknowledge. We also suggest that key thinkers from different disciplines share a common critique of the over-simplification of an 'anytime, anywhere' view of the future. Instead, more nuanced understandings of places that work, it is suggested, are underscored by the detailed study of *particular* places. In sum, by taking the world from a situated view.

The argument is structured in three parts. First, tracing the path taken in the re-location of computing, examining its spatial relationship with architectural form. Next the field of workplace studies is introduced to show how different applications of this analytic orientation have informed the design of systems in the workplace and 'work' interactions in other places. To conclude we reflect on what these insights can tell us about the design of technologically augmented places, for the new ways that computation, architecture and interaction intersect.

Locating Computing (in Buildings) in History

First we examine the changing locations of computing and its relationship with work, taking the mainframe computer as a starting point.

Fig. 3.1 Computing, a room?

White Heat of Technology

When computers were housed in a computer room their spatial relationship with the built, physical form was easier to describe. Computer rooms were designed spaces within buildings. There was a designated, serviced (air-conditioned) location for the instrumentation, which occupied most of a room. At this time a computer was almost indistinguishable from the configuration of the room. Ideally a room was designed to house a computer (Fig. 3.1).

Unusual though it may seem, in the advance of digital technologies we have taken a convoluted route to arrive at a similar position, where space is once again important in HCI. Now however, instead of computers being housed within a building the numerous processors in our lives are part of the fabric that surrounds us, embedded within the walls of buildings, in the external facades of real estate and that we carry with us, as we move within and between different environments. "Digital networks are no longer separate from architecture ... pervasive computing has to be inscribed into the social and environmental complexity of the exiting physical environment" (McCullough 2004 p. xiii). This story of computation at work starts by tracing its movement around office buildings.

Crawling Out of the Computer Room

In Duffy's (2007) re-evaluation of the office as a building type he noticed that when computers were liberated from the computer room they crawled along the corridors of office buildings and settled on our desks. The design of office buildings prior to that point centered on Taylorist models of production and the ability to see people sitting at their desks was a way to monitor the workforce. The organisation of the spatial layout became a means of surveillance. Locating employees in rows, at repetitious workstations standardised the workplace and enabled the comparison of the performance and efficiency of one person relative to another.

Workstation, Worksetting, Workscape

When the desktop computer landed in the workplace it was personal and more near proximal layout space was needed, to accommodate a computer and the published materials that were still migrating around an office. Additional pieces of equipment, printers and photocopiers also needed housing. At this point in time Xerox, the document management company, focused on the design of photocopiers. Research at Xerox Parc become renown for questioning what technological systems are and how people relate to them (Turkle 2007; Suchman 1995; Orr 1996). People's interactions with machines were understood as social and technical but the technician's work to establish whether there was a malfunction or failure of a machine component was also fragile, variable and improvised, in shaping the user's perceptions and understanding (Orr 1996 p. 3). At this time there was already an appreciation that human machine interaction is more than an interface problem.

  The configuration of the office workplace took on several characteristic forms. Open plan offices were a standard workplace configuration. Space planning escalated as a service, as did the design of office furniture systems to create reconfigurable landscapes of screened workspaces within an office. Overtime the proportions for the size of an office floorplate were standardized, calculating the depth of plan and the distance from each desktop to the external facade or natural lighting. Artificial lighting systems were designed to provide an even lumen reading at each desk. Channels for trunking were housed within the floor and suspended ceiling voids were the design solutions universally adopted to distribute services, including cabled IT networks, to workers in deep plan offices now further away from perimeter walls. Fewer services were fixed to the external fabric of a building, which increased the potential glazed area. Although there are early examples of iconic office buildings that led to innovation in cladding technology and progressive workforce management (for example Foster's Willis Faber and Dumas, Niels Torp SAS HQ Norway) there was rapid standardization in workplace features and ways to optimize productivity were openly discussed. Over time North American norms were adopted (Duffy 1992 p. 237) and in UK the BCO (British Council of Offices) specification for the design of office buildings became a standard.

In this spatial configuration although you can see when people are at work (reinforcing the understanding of work as a location defined activity), working in an open plan office it was less easy to see what people are actually doing. The work primarily takes place on a computer screen. Through a network, remotely an organisation can know what their employees are doing at any moment in time. Indeed working collaboratively on shared files (for example, architects and engineers sharing BIM models) letting other people know when new information is available is an important part in the coordination of this work. In the workplace we can see people working on collaborative tasks at several locations in an office, showing that design work is evidently not just bound to a workstation (Luck 2015).

In 1980s it was unclear what the spatial organisation of collaborative work using groupware over a network would look like, would people still need to meet? In the later twentieth century workplaces were increasingly designed with a typology of settings in mind, acknowledging that different kinds of work require different levels of collaboration. Not all shared tasks are the same. Different kinds of work require varying degrees of individual concentration to complete it, and places to meet to discuss the coordination of their collaborative work.

In an attempt to build contingency into the lifespan of buildings (Brand 1994) there was less attention on defining the activity for each room. Instead it was flexibility in the use of workplaces (Gibson and Luck 2004; Duffy 1992 p. 216) designing a range of workscapes that to a greater and lesser extent encourage social interaction, all underpinned by the constant connectivity that characterised workplaces. Hubs, coffee areas, touch-down spaces are later twentieth century framings for the kinds of spaces organisations are considered to need. Organisations were freed by and yet utterly dependent on information technology. "The office building is now part of the computer. Office space has become the infrastructure of servicing upon which commercial success more or less depends. If the computer fails, or if buildings obstruct the computer's operations, then the consequences for everyone can quickly become expensive" (Duffy 1992 p. 185). Computers were understood to be mission-critical to accomplish work and the office building was viewed as just another layer of its casing.

Changing the workplace is one way of organising and explaining variation in physical terms (Duffy 1992 p. 88). Time is another organising mechanism. Hot-desking is a serviced-solution where people no longer have a dedicated workspace and instead will locate at an available desk when working in the office. Similarly 'hoteling' (where workspace is hired for a period of time) is guided by the rationale that if employees are away from their desks, at meetings, visiting other organisations, on leave, why provide premium deskspace if it is under-occupied. From a space planning and property portfolio management perspective hoteling is more efficient use of resource. Again it is advance in computation that has transformed the ways that 'work' gets done. The laptop and access to the internet, on wi-fi on trains in public buildings, open up new, prospective locations for work. The introduction of a new category of worker, the nomadic worker, also reinforces the notion of working 'anytime and anywhere'. This view is not uncritically received

(Wiberg 2005; Perry et al. 2001) and, as an alternative to this ubiquity, one design challenge for pervasive computing is to uphold the value of place (McCullough 2002).

There is a blurring of work and life that accompanies mobile computation, although some locations do block cell-phone reception and bar some work activities (Dourish and Bell 2007). Indeed, if we progress the flexible and teleworking argument further, justifying a dedicated place for work becomes increasingly difficult. The mobile nature of electronic communications is in danger of rendering the permanent office as we know it extinct (Bullivant 2005) and the viability of the office as a building type is being questioned (Duffy 2007). These observations pose profound challenges when planning corporate real estate and the future shape of our cities.

Walls of Buildings, Eyes of the Skin

The walls within office buildings that once housed corporate art increasingly provide locations for hanging computation. Teleconferencing screens are permanent fixtures on the walls in some meeting rooms, enabling interactions with global audiences to take place in local locations. Smart boards often replace white boards and can capture the diagrams and ideas generated in workshops. Plasma screens increasingly replace notice boards in reception locations. The term 'spatial computing' was introduced when walls became interactive, to describe the augmented reality afforded in a digitally enhanced workspace (Krogh and Grønbaek 2001). The walls of exhibition spaces are also increasingly interactive (Ciolfi 2004) and in more nuanced ways, both our interactions with art work and our understanding of how we interact with exhibition spaces are re-configured (Luff and Heath 2013).

The external facades of buildings are not exempt from this technological advance. In some (un)subtle ways the capabilities that we associate with computers, which might include cameras and sensor technologies for surveillance, can be subsumed into a building's envelope, in the walls that envelop our everyday lives (Moran et al. 2012). The very fabric of the built form acts as a host for these technologies. Architecture is now injected with the plasticity of digital bits, 'we are living within a world built of "habitable bits" … living within "synthetic" space' (Takeuchi 2014). As Weiser and Seeley-Brown described "electricity … surges invisibly through the walls of every home, office, and car. Writing and electricity become so commonplace, so unremarkable, that we forget their huge impact on everyday life. So it will be with UC" (Weiser and Brown 1996). The facades of buildings are now hosts for visual displays (sculptural works in light, such as the Tower of Wind by Toyo Ito), sensors monitoring air-quality and cameras for the surveillance of the urban streetscape. Computation has a new expression in material and aesthetic form through architecture (Vallgarda 2014). Paradoxically, these technologies do have physical manifestation but also a loss of visibility. A building's façade may house 'intelligence' but this intelligence merges into the background, sending and receiving data about the local environment (McCullough 2004 p. 127). Although, it is questioned, if buildings are intelligent (Cole 2009) who has access to this information? "Pervasive technologies promise to transform the ways we experience and live in the world. But did anyone ask for our permission?" (McCullough 2004). It is contested precisely where the big data collected in smart cities resides. There has been a transition from buildings that house computers to buildings that are (infused with) computers, now that the skins of buildings are sensing devices.

In the City, Interstitial Spaces Between Buildings

At the city scale the spaces between buildings construct a cityscape and provide the ever-changing backdrop to everyday life. There is also an expectation, in a world that is increasingly networked and composed of cosmopolitan cities that computing is ubiquitous, available anytime, anywhere. It is against this backdrop that Duffy sees the future for our (working) lives.

In a similar manner Dourish and Bell (2004) sees that 'cities exhibit a physical layering of complex topologies ... that operate in more than three dimensions, with physical settings that reflect their historical evolution and many forms of cultural experience. It is this experience that is disrupted and transformed when new technological opportunities enter those spaces'. Paay also describes the city as a digital layer cake (Paay et al. 2007) composed of hybrid spaces for serendipitous interactions. It is the city locations that foster the exchange of ideas that are important, and have been since the eighteenth century- in places such as a coffee houses and members clubs (Duffy 2007). Noticeably Duffy does not describe an homogenous view of what our digitally augmented cities will become. Instead he paints two present day scenarios. At Canary Warf an atmosphere of surveillance prevails. This is in contrast with the buzzing streetlife and serendipitous exchange of ideas in the media industry in Soho. Two tales of the same city, London.

Space and place, evidently, are different. There is a 'distinction between place, a situated location with cultural patterns and norms, and space as an abstract construct' (Harrison and Dourish 1996). To design technologically enhanced places that matter we need to be able to articulate the life that makes one place more alive than another. We need a vehicle (a method) to provide praxiological accounts of places in use. This is the task that Duffy sets, "If you had to explain to a creature from outer space what place was about, what arguments would you assemble in order to justify it?"

In the next section we provide a response. We offer *workplace studies* as an analytic method that is able to connect interaction with the characteristics of a *particular* place: to be able to show, just what is it about space that is important in interaction.

Workplace Studies

Workplace studies "are concerned with the social and interactional organisation of technology in the workplace. … They are concerned … with *the work to make technologies work*; with the tacit and 'seen but unnoticed' resources through which organisational activities are accomplished in and through tools and technologies" (Luff et al. 2000 p. xii–xiii emphasis added). These studies provide important contributions to our understanding of work, technology and interaction.

More substantively, "Workplace studies are returning technology to action, and beginning to show how the use of particular systems is dependent upon the social and organisational competencies upon which participants rely to produce accountable actions and interaction with *particular* settings" (Heath and Luff 2000 p. 224 emphasis added). Workplace studies are always situated.

These forms of analyses provide insights to inform the design of workspaces and work environments. "The more significant contribution will be in reshaping the ways in which we conceive of everyday social actions and interactions in the workplace" (Luff et al. 2000 p. 3). Indeed, unpicking how collaborative activities are actually accomplished in workplace settings can suggest new ways of reconceptualising key concepts in the analysis of technology-oriented activities and the design of computer systems (Luff et al. 2000 p. 11).

Workplace studies involve more than the study of activities in workplace settings. There is a specific theoretic and analytic ground to analytic ethnography, informed by ethnomethodology. It is this analytic ground that we examine next.

Theory and Method

The field of workplace studies was developed by Harold Garfinkel and provides inspiration for how we now understand 'work' and also the analytic route of ethnomethodology to study this (Rawls 2008). Workplace studies have a particular analytic rigour. 'These empirical case studies have … concentrated on revealing the complexities of everyday social interaction and emphasise the relevance of particular analytic orientations for the examination of empirical materials and drawing out the implications these analyses have for critical conceptions underpinning the study of work activities' (Luff et al. 2000 p. 12).

This distinct analytic approach is without deviation from the members' 'ethnomethods'. In other words, their actions and accounts reflexively document 'what is going on' as it is being accomplished in their situated actions (Garfinkel 1967 [1984]). These practical actions are 'witnessable' by others as accomplishing things, and this 'noticing' includes the observers of actions who have an analytic interest in noticing them (Garfinkel 1967 [1984]). This way of documenting action has been described as, "the strong sense of the observeability of real world activities" (Baccus 1986 p. 3). What an ethnomethodological (EM) orientation offers is a rationale to inform which aspects of 'context' to bring into an account.

'Ethnomethodology's original purchase was a critical one, drawing attention to the failings of psychological models on which design was predicated, and the need for design to be responsive to the social circumstances of work within which IT systems are embedded in their use' (Crabtree 2004). Dreyfus is similarly critical of the mapping of information processing onto everyday practices in the physical world (Dreyfus 1992 p. 166). In studies for systems design there is criticism that 'cognitivism' obscures the 'actualities of work' and that the principles that underpin some forms of cognitive science cannot fully account for human behaviour. "Ethnomethodology, for good or ill, is concerned with critiquing a model of the relationship between the mind and the world, not with denying that people plan and think" (Randall et al. 2007). In analytic ethnography it is not 'thinking' as a mental process that is witnessable in a sequence of actions, but what it is that a sequence of actions accomplishes (without assuming insight into thought processes, or interpretation of the motive behind an action).

The challenge has become one of understanding the collaborative character of work and the ethnomethodology response has been to move from 'design critique to design practice and the invention of the future' (Button and Dourish 1996). We need to be able to analyse and articulate how things work in the places we inhabit, to inform the design of new settings.

Studying Our Interactions with the Built Form

In this section we introduce three central characteristics of analytic ethnography, to give a flavour of the kinds of insights that workplace studies recover.

Setting, Place, Context ... More Than a Container

The setting, location or place of work is integral to its analyses. "These studies have been from the start committed to a *holistic* understanding of work, and thus are concerned with far more than jobs and tasks; rather, the focus has always been on entire 'workscapes' – configurations not only of people and their communal practices (the methodological means that they use to organise and accomplish their work) but also the environments where the work gets done and the artefacts and devices that populate these sites are thus intimately involved in the work's achievement" (Szymanski and Whalen 2011 p. 6).

This approach builds on an understanding in the field of workplace studies, where the setting in which activities happen is viewed as more than a container (Garfinkel 1967; Heath et al. 2000). Human interaction and communication involves space in multiple ways. It is understood that the environment shapes activities. For example, how the bodily movement of the participants within the confined space of a police interrogation room, in their appropriation of the material surroundings constituted a spatial order that made possible certain arguments that steered a suspect towards the confession of a crime (LeBaron and Streeck 1997).

The location in which activities take place is interwoven in our sense-making, to understand how the things that take place in a situation are viewed and received. The setting, however, is not only an attribute of space or location but the people present, their patterns of interaction are interwoven in our ability to understand actions in particular ways. For example, in a setting where the plan drawings pinned to a wall were some distance away from where the residents were sitting, it became an artful, interactional accomplishment to show that there was a problem in the design of a housing scheme, the nature of the problem and to know that the architects and residents were discussing the same design feature (Luck 2012). The configuration of the room and ways the residents adjusted their orientation to the drawings and to each other, bringing them into conversation at specific moments in time, were mundane but also remarkable actions to progress the design work. We begin to get a sense that although the setting (a place, location) is regarded as part of the context, at other times other materials feature as context in the analysis. It is this ability to show *when* and *how* their attention was attracted that was remarkable, not just that they were able to do this.

The setting is more than a container for embodied spatial interactions, social interaction and the embodied ways people interaction with technology is always determined by the physical space in which it takes place (van Dijk and Mitchell 2014). Returning to the foundational work at Xerox, we understand that we cannot separate the operation of a photocopier by people from its setting- situated contexts of use provide import insights for design improvement (Turkle 2007; Heath et al. 2000; Suchman 1987). Indeed Xerox has shifted its market from the design of photocopiers to designing a document management service and more recently, the design of organisational workscapes (Szymanski and Whalen 2011).

What these studies all point up is that the places where we work, in various ways, become part of the work that gets done there.

Work ... Doing Things

There has been a re-alignment in the relationship between work and workplace and a shift in understanding from work as a 'location' to work as an 'activity'. A further development has been to examine the nature of work. Button argues for a more complete appreciation of what constitutes 'work' in ethnomethodological studies of work?' (Button 2012). It is evident that design's interest in social networking and gaming in non-work settings such as the home are equally suitable for ethnomethodological studies of work (Button 2012). What is increasingly acknowledged is that an ethnomethodological understanding of work involves effort in purposeful activity and not just activities connected with gainful employment (Suchman 1995). This opens up a broad range of activities and locations for 'workplace studies' examining different 'activities' in different'places' (locations, settings, built environments). For example, the socio-material organisation of space and interaction in a coffee shop becomes the workplace setting for a knowledge worker (Laurier et al. 2001). The home continues to be a place where computation re-locates. The setting-up of a network in the home (Crabtree 2003) is both an art in placing ubicomp in an environment to enable both 'work' and 'play' to take place at home (Rodden et al. 2004) and to be able to interface with virtual city environments outside the home (Crabtree 2004). Not only has the location of work migrated from office locations but the nature of work has also expanded. 'Work' has now become 'doing things', the detailed study of the ways that we actually 'get stuff done'.

Praxiological Accounting Practices . . . Lived, Occasioned, Sequential Actions

There are characteristics that mark workplace analyses as distinct from other accounts of practice: in their attention to ordered, situated sequential actions. Ethnomethodologically-informed approaches explore the distinctiveness or 'just-thisness' of particular situations. "Being able to account for the work in terms of its endogenous organization provides the basis for writing 'praxiologically valid' accounts (Garfinkel 1996). Unlike constructive analytic accounts, praxiological accounts do not attempt to make workpractice available through a generic inferential apparatus but instead, through description of the 'lived work' of a particular, distinctive, real world setting of human jobs (Garfinkel et al. 1981)". The art in preparing a praxiological account is in 'recovering the machinery of interaction,' to show how practical actions are occasioned (Crabtree et al. 2013). A concrete example of the 'work' that is involved in the act of visiting a place reveals that when and where to go and what to do is more involved than a generic sociological characterisation of visiting rural places (Crabtree et al. 2013). While there is insufficient space here to show what the preparation of a praxiological account entails, many of the references cited in this argument present detailed accounts. It is by showing how practical actions are occasioned (through detailed analysis) that we are able to see what matters, to see what makes something work at that particular moment in time.

Implications for Design

Whatever we interact with, be that touching a wall, a screen or picking up materials and technological devices in a setting, all play a momentary part in how we experience that environment. Providing an analytic account of situated interactions will shed light on the order of things in that setting, on how things are occasioned (accomplished, get done) and these insights can then inform the careful design, tailored to the specific contexts of future (computational) places.

Designing Environments with the Place Implications for Computation in Mind

In numerous ways computation has changed the way we work and has also impacted on the design of office buildings, the configuration of workplaces and the newly nomadic places of work. We now 'work' ubiquitously, anytime, anywhere and constantly. We work within buildings that are infused with computation, in the equipment we use, in constant connectivity and communication with the environment around us. The fabric of the architectural form is also imbued with computation, to sense the environment, to send and receive information. We are the donors, content creators and recipients of this data. Computers regulate the controls of the systems within a building and the skin of a building is another sensing device. The distinction between a building and its services is now less clear. When we design buildings are we designing yet another (computer) interface?

Yes and No. It is a matter of framing, whether buildings are viewed as wholes, systems or as parts, as objects (after Alan Kay) or as a collection of object components and systems of built environment services (Brand 1994 p. 13). One response it that "Interface design has become interaction design, and interaction design has come into alliance with architecture" (McCullough 2004 p. xiv). In McCullough's use of the concept 'digital ground', he expresses an alternative to the anytime-anyplace sameness in computing. He acknowledges that *context* not only shapes usability but ideally becomes the subject matter of interaction design, and is a characteristic that technology may serve and not erode (McCullough 2004). This call for design attention to the situated details of place echoes and, in many respects, reinforces Duffy's (2007) argument. By questioning the need to justify (work)space Duffy highlights that office buildings are a legacy location for work, now there are more opportune locations for serendipitous interactions in the city.

Place, evidently, still matters, even though many actions and activities in the conduct of work are virtual and given the new locations for computation. It is this agreement, arriving at a shared understanding of the importance of place, from different disciplinary perspectives that is insightful. It champions a shared critique of the over-simplification of an 'anytime, anywhere' view of the future.

Instead we see that more nuanced understandings of places that work are needed. It is the ability to describe occasions, situations and locations that work well that are increasingly important. Situated insights are equally important for the design of technology as well as the re-configured places where people work. It is this attention to design detail that supports a more general turn to the study of interaction.

The Turn to Interaction

There has been re-newed inspection of embodied interaction and the bodily encounters between people and technology since the move of computation off the desktop (Dourish and Bell 2007). Our interactions with computation are moving beyond button pushing and flat-screen display, towards tangible and embodied interaction, and raise important questions about how we might study them (Buur et al. 2014). It also has implications for how we might design for interaction in this technologically-entangled hybrid space (Lootsma 1999; Dourish 2006). There is a growing body of research that questions, at a basic level, how we interact with the things around us (Boer et al. 2015), experimenting, for example, in the embodied simulation of a large revolving door (Mitchell and Raudaskoski 2013) and the interplay between computation and the materiality of the world around us (Vallgarda 2014; Wiberg 2014). This line of inquiry, questioning how proximity to things in an environment actually brings about a change, is being developed in the field of adaptive architecture, where a range of methodological perspectives are applied (see for example Schädelbach et al. 2015). We are at a point in time when exploring what is revealed from different methodological vantage points will strengthen the advance of the field of architecture and interaction studies.

Conclusion

This argument has developed an appreciation of how the fields of architecture and (human computer) interaction strongly connect by examining how computation has changed the way we work, where we work and how work is understood. In this argument we suggest that now workplaces and buildings are not only run by computers but are computers, sending and receiving data, they have added additional digital layers in the relationship between people and their experience of the built form. Boundaries between the design of the built form and the technology it houses become artificial. Therefore, as we continue to question relationships between space and interaction at different architectural scales, we need to be able to articulate the life that makes one place more alive than another. Workplace studies are suggested as an analytic route in this direction. These analyses are able to migrate across different scales, to recover just how computation is important to get 'work' things done. Through fine-grained attention to the occasioned, situated practices in locations of 'work' the ubiquity and relativism of working 'anytime, anywhere' is tempered by an appreciation that the nature of why some places work better than others can only be shown in the details of situated practice.

Acknowledgments The National Museum of Computing at Bletchley has kindly given permission for the photograph of the Harwell Dekatron, the world's oldest working computer, to be re-produced in this publication. This paper revisits several themes and develops the argument from a paper at CHI 2014, One of a CHInd conference in Montreal.

References

Baccus MD (1986) Sociological indication and the visibility criterion of real world social theortiz-
   ing. In: Garfinkel H (ed) Ethnomethodological studies of work. Prentice-Hall, New Jersey
Boer L, Mitchell R, Caglio A, Lucero A (2015) Embodied technology: unraveling bodily action
   with normative types. CHi 2015
Brand S (1994) How buildings learn: what happens after they are built. Viking Penguin, London
Bullivant L (2005) Intelligent workspaces: crossing the thresholds. AD 4Dspace Interact Archit
   75:38–46
Button G (2012) What does 'work' mean in 'ethnomethodological studies of work?' Its ubiquitous
   relevance for systems design to support action and interaction. Des Stud 33(6):673–684
Button P, Dourish P (1996) Technomethodology: paradoxes and possibilities. In: CHI '96
   Proceedings of the SIGCHI Conference on human factors in computing systems. ACM, New
   York, pp 19–26
Buur J, Caglio A, Jensen L (2014) Human actions made tangible: analysing the temporal
   organization of activities. Paper presented at the DIS 14 Designing Interactive Systems
Ciolfi L (2004) Understanding spaces as places: extending interaction design paradigms. Cogn
   Technol Work 6:37–40
Cole R (2009) Gaining intelligence through feedback. Intell Build Int 1:235–238
Crabtree, A. (2003). Designing collaborative systems: A practical guide to ethnography. Springer,
   London
Crabtree A (2004) Taking technomethodology seriously: hybrid change in the ethnomethodology-
   design relationship. Eur J Inf Syst 13:195–209
Crabtree A, Tolmie P, Rouncefield M (2013) "How many bloody examples do you want?"
   Fieldwork and generalisation. In: Bertelsen O, Ciolfi L, Grasso MA, Papadopoulos G (eds)
   ECSCW 13th European conference on computer supported cooperative network. Springer
   Verlag, Berlin
Dourish P (2006) Implications for design. CHI 2006. ACM, Montreal, 22–27 April 2006
Dourish P, Bell G (2004) Getting out of the city: meaning and structure in everyday encounters
   with space. Ubicomp, Nottingham
Dourish P, Bell G (2007) The infrastructure of experience and the experience of infrastructure:
   meaning and structure in everyday encounters with space. Environ Plann B Plann Des 34(3):
   414–430
Dreyfus HL (1992) What computers still can't do: a critique of artificial reason. The MIT Press,
   Cambridge, MA
Duffy F (1992) The changing workplace. Phaidon Press Limited, London
Duffy F (2007) Justifying place in a virtual world. Design + planning [online]. Available:
   http://www.aecom.com/deployedfiles/Internet/Capabilities/Designand Planning/Strategy Plus/
   FDuffy_Connected Real Estate.pdf. Accessed 28th Jan 2014
Garfinkel, H. (1967[1984]). Studies in ethnomethodology. Prentice-Hall, Englewood Cliffs
Garfinkel H (1996) Ethnomethodology's program. Social Psychol Q 59(1):5–21
Garfinkel H, Lynch M, Livingston E (1981) The Work of a Discovering Science Construed with
   Materials from the Optically Discovered Pulsar. Philosophy of the Social Sciences 11(2):131–
   158
Gibson V, Luck R (2004) Flexible working in central government: leveraging the benefits. Office
   of Government Commerce OGC, London
Harrision S, Dourish P (1996) Re-place-ing space: the roles of place and space in collaborative sys-
   tems. In: CSCW '96 proceedings of the ACM conference on computer supported cooperative
   work. ACM, New York
Heath C, Luff P (2000) Technology in action. University Press, Cambridge
Heath C, Knoblauch H, Luff P (2000) Technology and social interaction: the emergence of
   'workplace studies'. Br J Sociol 51:299–320

Krogh P, Grønbaek K (2001) Roomware and intelligent buildings: buildings and objects become computer interfaces! Architectural research and information technology. Nordic Association for Architectural Research. Århus School of Architecture

Laurier E, Whyte A, Buckner K (2001) An ethnography of a neighbourhood cafe: informality, table arrangements and background noise. J Mundane Behav 2:195–232

Lebaron C, Streeck J (1997) Built space and the interactional framing of experience during a murder interrogation. Hum Stud 20:1–25

Lootsma B (1999) Hybrid space: emergent dimensions, information technologies and evolutionary architectures. In: Zellner P (ed) Hybrid space: new forms in digital architecture. Thames & Hudson, London

Luck R (2012) Kinds of seeing and spatial reasoning: examining user participation at an architectural design event. Des Stud 33:557–588

Luck R (2015) Organising design in the wild: locating multidisciplinarity as a way of working. Archit Eng Des Manag 11:149–162

Luff DVL, Heath C (2013) Isolating the private from the public: reconsidering engagement in museums and galleries. CHI 13. ACM, Paris

Luff P, Hindmarsh J, Heath C (eds) (2000) Workplace studies: recovering work practice and informing systems design. Cambridge University Press, Cambridge

Mccullough M (2002) Digital ground: fixity, flow and engagement with context. Doors of perception 7: flow. MIT Press, Cambridge, MA

McCullough M (2004) Digital ground: architecture, pervasive computing and environmental knowing. MIT Press, Cambridge, MA

Mitchell R, Raudaskoski P (2013) Whose line is it anyway? Ccollaborative turn-making. In: Participatory innovation conference 2013. LUT Scientific and Expertise Publications Tutkimus-raportit, Lahti Finland

Moran S, De Vallejo IL, Nakata K, Conroy-Dalton R, Luck R, Mclennan P, Hailes S (2012) Studying the impact of ubiquitous monitoring technology on office worker behaviours: the value of sharing research data. In: 2012 IEEE international conference on pervasive computing and communications workshops, PERCOM workshops. IEEE

Negroponte N (1995) Being digital. Vintage Books, New York

Orr J (1996) Talking about machines: an ethnography of a modern job. Cornell University, New York

Paay J, Bharat D, Howard S (2007) Understanding and representing the social prospects of hybrid urban spaces. Environ Plann B Plann Des 34:446–465

Perry M, O'hara K, Sellen A, Harper R, Brown B (2001) Dealing with mobility: understanding access anytime, anywhere. In: Transactions on computer-human interaction ToCHI. ACM

Randall D, Harper R et al (2007) Fieldwork for design: theory and practice. Springer, London

Rawls A (2008) Harold Garfinkel, ethnomethodology and workplace studies. Organ Stud 29:701–732

Rodden T, Crabtree A, Hemmings T, Koleva B, Humble J, Åkesson KP, Hansson P (2004) Between the dazzle of a new home and its eventual corpose: assembling the ubiquitous home. DIS, ACM Press, Cambridge, MA

Schädelbach H, Slovak P, Fitzpatrick G, Jager N (2015) The immersive effect of adaptive architecture. Pervasive and mobile computing

Suchman L (1987) Plans and situated actions. Cambridge University Press, Cambridge

Suchman L (1995) Making work visible. Commun ACM 38:56–64

Szymanski M, Whalen J (eds) (2011) Making work visible: ethnographically ground case studies of work practice. Cambridge University Press, Cambridge

Takeuchi Y (2014) Towards habitable bits: digitizing the built environment. ITS 2014 Touch, pressure and reality, 2014 Dreseden. pp 209–218

Turkle S (2007) Evocative objects: things we think with. MIT Press, Cambridge, MA

Vallgarda A (2014) Giving form to computational things: developing a practice of interaction design. Pers Ubiquit Comput 18:577–592

Van Dijk J, Mitchell R (2014) Co-embodied technology: a design space for human being. In: TEI 14 Tangible Embodied Interaction. Munich

Weiser M (1999) The computer for 21st century. ACM SIGMOBILE Mob Comput Commun Rev 3:3–11

Weiser M, Brown JS (1996) The coming age of calm technology [online]. Xerox PARC, Stanford. [Accessed 12 April 2011]

Wiberg M (2005) "Anytime, anywhere" in the context of mobile work. Encyclopedia of information science and technology I–V. Idea Group, Calgary

Wiberg M (2014) Methodology for materiality: interaction design through a material lens. Pers Ubiquit Comput 18:625–636

Part II
Approaching Interaction in Space

Within the emerging field that combines architecture and computing, whether one might call this adaptive, interactive or reactive architecture, a multitude of approaches have been developed to address interaction. Interaction here refers to that between people, with artefacts and with the environment. The field has developed tools and methods that use computation to evaluate interaction through measurement and to support design. This section presents work by researchers who have drawn on standard observational techniques to observe interaction in workplaces, learning spaces and the urban environment, with a view to supporting design. The section also presents work that has considered existing design frameworks and developed new frameworks to discuss interaction in space.

Pantidi brings the focus of this discussion away from the confusing general and abstract and is reassuringly concrete about the specific learning spaces which are approached. Whereas **Luusua's** work (below) occurs in the external space that can be used in many diverse ways, Pantidi studies a single function learning space providing three cases to compare and contrast. This work finds that the technology and the space influence three principal elements. The *legibility* of infrastructure and social systems, the *legitimacy* and sense of *ownership* and the customization and appropriation of the technology. This work reinforces and clarifies some of the concepts introduced by **Luusua**. This work while also founded in *phenomenology* and the use of *ethnographic* and embodied approaches is interesting in that while it seems to reinforce much of Luusua's architectural work it is a text grounded firmly in human-computer interaction research yet each smoothly work alongside the other. When we stripped away the languages used we seem not to have an interdisciplinary dialogue but the dialogue of two halves of the same whole.

Scupelli's work is in many ways a mirror of that of Pantidi. They both study the design of learning spaces. Whereas Pantidi is strongly ethnographically bound and was drawn initially as the study of interaction technology in learning situation that discovered the value of space Scupelli's comes from a makers perspective; Scupelli is a practitioner, educator, and designer. Thinking to extend pedagogic thinking by using the built form along with augmentation by numerous digital technologies to support the postgraduate curriculum. This work largely based on well known human computer interaction methodologies also absorbs methods such as *time lapse photography* and *space syntax* analysis (an architectural research method mentioned by *Krukar*). Scupelli's future learning design studio overlaps in many ways with that of *Luck's* description of contemporary workplace design. Participants fluidly cycle through multiple activities such as socializing, eating, individual work and group work. Scupelli highlights that privacy seems to be an important factor when deciding impromptu workplace location. This result from the education sector potentially gives insight into a wider range of work choice locations and has a number of technology implications.

"*In our contemporary digital life, culture is dynamic rather than stationary – it is more about routes than roots.*" begins **Moradi**. The paper reminds strongly of Weisner's vision of ubiquitous computing. This would be a partial distraction from the papers content. Moradi sees mobility as an extension of place. Yet Moradi argues that while the mobility of sociality has changed radically, computing has also introduced a very sedentary way of life. Moradi's work also uses the notion of *embodied* perception but this time in office space. This work reinforces some of Deshpande's findings of the role of technology creating the potential for social interaction in *space* and the creation of *place*. When reading this text, it is difficult to decide if it is written from an architectural or computer science perspective. This paper strongly overlaps with that of Deshpande (see below). While the objectives are to investigate the ways in which natural movement in a building can be used to resist the natural sedimentary tendencies that computing leans towards, the paper emphasizes the role that technology has in the creation of place through the manipulation of movement and encounter. The paper's championing of the use of Labanotation as a means of recording the detail of bodily spatial interaction definitely seems like a pointer to methodologies of the future.

Sailer's contribution is a study over a large number of different work environments. The interplay here between architecture and technology is interesting, beginning with ideas of digital technology making the office obsolesce. Sailer begins by identifying that many flagship offices are being created by the very technology companies that seem to benefit by disrupting traditional office design. Most significant of all is the idea that Yahoo has banned home working in an effort to return to the benefits of co-location. This work founded in the architectural technique known as *space syntax* reinforces that of *Moradi*. This paper is an important one for interaction designers to study carefully. It seems to contradict many of the natural assumptions about office interaction that a technology designer may bring to the design process. In many ways communication technologies exist to facilitate interaction. Office architecture from this perspective is a pre-existing technology to create interaction. Sailer points out that **Open Plan workspaces** and cellular spaces account for tiny fractions of interaction events. While the programmed activities of meeting spaces account for most interactions, it's significant that alternative and informal areas count for the next largest fraction. This suggests that it is the informal and *serendipitous* interaction that buildings most facilitate. Sailor comes from an architectural tradition that maintains that space is never simply in the *background it* *is not neutral.* In many ways, it goes beyond its architectural theology and suggests that *space* and *time* become important factors in the crafting of *interaction.* This perspective was based on observations of human to human interaction and while not simple it appears to have many implications for the design of human to machine interaction. This work also has tantalizing implications and synergies with that of *Luusua* when considering the role of technology in the creation of place.

Chapter 4
Supporting Fluid Transitions in Innovative Learning Spaces: Architectural, Social and Technological Factors

Nadia Pantidi

Abstract Innovative learning spaces (ILS) are a response to the ubiquity of technologies in our everyday lives and a shift towards a student-centered pedagogical approach in higher education. As an inhabited, technologically enriched architectural space, ILS embody multi-purpose agendas that are intended to support a variety of activities, often simultaneously. Yet, we know very little about the everyday lived experiences of those who use and inhabit them, and whether they are used as anticipated by their creators. This chapter reports on three ethnographic investigations into ILS. Our analytic themes provide an account of the everyday interactions in these spaces focusing on how diverse activities coexisted, how people collaborated and socialized and identify factors that were found to mediate user interactions, and support – or obstruct – fluid transitions in these spaces. The three factors are: (i) Legibility (infrastructural and social) (ii) Legitimacy and sense of ownership (iii) Customisation and appropriation.

Introduction

As digital technologies become increasingly ubiquitous in our everyday lives the field of education is taking up on this trend by incorporating technologies into learning in all its manifestations. Examples include online learning environments and courses, using tablets and mobile phones as part of the school curriculum, and introducing interactive surfaces such as whiteboards and tabletops to support collaboration in classrooms. The last 10 years has seen universities and colleges around the world investing in a new type of learning environment, in which digital technologies feature prominently in spaces built to facilitate formal education and informal learning. These new environments, coined as twenty first century learning spaces (JISC 2009), blended learning spaces (Milne 2006) or more broadly, *innovative learning spaces* (ILS) (Groff 2013; Oblinger 2006), harness a combination

N. Pantidi (✉)
School of Applied Psychology, University College Cork, North Mall, Cork, Republic of Ireland
e-mail: konstantia.pantidi@ucc.ie

© Springer International Publishing Switzerland 2016
N.S. Dalton et al. (eds.), *Architecture and Interaction*,
Human–Computer Interaction Series, DOI 10.1007/978-3-319-30028-3_4

of digital technology and flexible architectural design to enact a major shift in how education is delivered. They are designed to accommodate a student-centered, peer-learning pedagogical approach as well as a variety of formal and informal learning activities where collaboration and socializing are key. Depending on the overall institutional agenda, the specifics of the ILS pedagogical agenda may vary. For example, the Saltire Center's agenda, UK's first ILS, is described as *"the hub of the learning activities in the university, providing a range of functions related to learning; from social areas and student services to wireless-enabled group learning spaces and library facilities"*.[1] As this example illustrates, the agendas for ILS are multi-purpose, which can vary from supporting formal teaching activities (lectures, labs) to informal peer learning and socializing all within the same space.

In this chapter, we take a closer look into three examples of ILS to gain a better understanding on how their multipurpose agenda is supported (or not) on a day-to-day basis. We consider their anticipated use based on their pedagogical agenda and juxtapose it with the observed actual use. More specifically, we look at how formal and informal learning activities and, most important, people co-exist within the same physical space, how people collaborate and socialize within ILS, how they interact with the technologies, the space and each other within context. By addressing those questions, the present work contributes to an empirically-grounded understanding of how ILS are being used and appropriated compared to the envisioned usage. The analysis reveals tensions between actual and anticipated use, the situated nature of flexible design, as well as the complex and contested processes through which interactions in innovative learning spaces are accomplished, adapted or superseded. The findings suggest a set of critical factors that account for the tensions between desired and actual use of such spaces. Issues of legibility, legitimacy and sense of ownership and appropriation supersede the existing views and guidelines of adaptable design as presented in the current literature and can be used to inform the design and evaluation of ILS.

Related Work

Innovative Learning Spaces

Innovative learning spaces (ILS) are higher education spaces that have been designed to support a variety of learning activities, by means of technological infrastructure and flexible architectural design. The creation of ILS has been motivated by a shift away from traditional approaches of learning – where learning is seen as knowledge that can be delivered only by the tutor in the auditorium – and towards student-centred approaches that emphasise on learning taking place

---

[1] https://jiscinfonetcasestudies.pbworks.com/w/page/45407218/Glasgow%20Caledonian%20 University%20-%20Saltire%20Centre.

anywhere and anytime, students being active participants in their learning through socializing and collaboration with peers. As Oblinger (2006) describes: "*The key, therefore, is to provide a physical space that supports multidisciplinary, team-taught, highly interactive learning unbound by traditional time constraints within a social setting that engages students and faculty and enables rich learning experiences*". There are many examples of such spaces across the world including the Stanford D. School (Doorley and Witthoft 2012) and the HCId Graduate Design Studio at University of Indiana School of Informatics (Callison 2011) in the US, the Learning Lab at the University of Melbourne's School of Chemistry (Tregloan 2009) and the Teaching Grid in the University of Warwick in the UK.[2]

The creation of such spaces has been talked about as long overdue and necessary in keeping up with the technological advances and as an investment for future education. For example, in an article in the Times Higher Education, Davidson (2011) commented on how US Higher Education is still driven by the industrialisation model and stressed the need for renewal: "*My students live an extracurricular digital life that is as rich, varied and ever-changing as is the world of work that lies ahead of them. Sadly, in between their digital personal lives and the digital work life ahead stands the institution of education as stern and unyielding as Taylor with his stopwatch (...)*".

Having a *flexible, comfortable architectural design* (e.g. movable walls. variety of furniture including armchairs and couches, chairs and tables on wheels) and up-to-date *technological infrastructure* (wifi, interactive whiteboards, laptops, desktops) are seen as key in supporting the new pedagogical agenda and this is where the innovation lies. Below, we outline how architectural layout and technological infrastructure are discussed in the ILS literature.

Architectural Layout and Furniture

In terms of the architectural layout, a main concern voiced in the literature is moving beyond the traditional architectural design that has been prevailing since the nineteenth century (McGregor 2004; Schratzenstaller 2010; Long and Holeton 2009; Van Note Chism 2006). Traditional design being (i) the uniformity of design where all spaces on a campus look the same and (ii) the tutor/teacher-based design where the whole learning experience is oriented towards passively attending to whoever is lecturing (auditoriums and lecture theatres). Such traditional educational architectures translate to a particular social context of pedagogies where the teacher has all the power and control over the students – in sharp contrast with the student-centered approach upheld by ILS.

Two approaches have been prominent in informing the design of ILS: the notion of flexibility and use of metaphors. A flexible architecture can support a variety

[2]http://www2.warwick.ac.uk/services/library/staff/teaching/teachinggrid/what_is_the_teaching_grid/

of learning activities (Oblinger 2006; Fischer 2005) and consists of a variety of comfortable, often portable furnishings (wheeled chairs and tables) in combination with an architectural layout that can be transformed such as movable walls, combinations of open and enclosed areas within the same space. Spatial arrangements fit for purpose, such as using round tables to better support collaboration or having partitions to separate private work areas from social areas, has been suggested (Oblinger 2006; Dudek 2000; JELS 2009; Doorley and Witthoft 2012). Yet as many authors – in particular architects – contest (Jamieson 2008; Boys 2011; Radcliffe 2009), architectural flexibility in the context of ILS is presented in a rather simplistic or vague manner: as if it would work for any space and all users. As Jamieson puts it (2008: 58): *"What is meant by flexibility? Does it refer to the capacity to move and re-arrange furniture at the discretion of the user, allowing the use to change according to need? Does it refer to the range of activity that can be supported in a single space simultaneously?"*

Metaphors (such as streets, hubs, learning cafes) are also used in the design of ILS to describe or imply architectural features with relation to learning activities. As Boys (2011) pointed out, it is unclear whether these metaphors are understood and shared across the different stakeholders. To better understand these and most importantly the complex interrelationships between features of architectural design and use (and then learning), Boys (2011) and Temple (2007) note that more qualitative approaches to understanding ILS is needed.

Technological Infrastructure

With respect to technological infrastructure, the main demand is that the technology in ILS should support diverse user activities and mechanisms of learning that take place anywhere and anytime. The technological infrastructure in ILS at the time of our studies comprised commercial, off-the-shelf technologies (e.g. laptops, desktops, tablets, interactive whiteboards) that aimed to support formal and informal learning, collaborative and individual work. However, a number of technologies are being developed that aspire to assist the vision and practice of ILS even more. For example, Kaplan et al. (2009) propose using technology to enhance active and collaborative learning, through providing students with various kinds of *interpersonal computers*, that is technologies that several people can interact with at the same time, in the same place. Examples of such technologies include the DOCKLAMP, a portable smart lamp that augments people's interactions on tables by projecting images and documents (Kaplan and Dillenbourg 2010) and the REFLECT table where individual contributions to the discussion are represented by LEDs on the table's surface (Bachour et al. 2010). Another example is having an ecology of networked interactive multi-touch surfaces e.g. tabletops could support collaboration and vertical displays awareness and reflection for the whole classroom (AlAgha et al. 2010), very similar to what Fox et al. (2000) designed as part of the Interactive Workspaces project. However, until now these technologies have only been tested in lab settings and not in real settings, so their benefits remain uncertain.

It is unclear whether ILS will be fitted with more customized technologies in the near future, but looking into what people do with the current technology in these spaces can prove a useful starting point.

Assessing Innovative Learning Spaces: Understanding Lived Use and Experience

Whether the technological infrastructure and the flexible architectural design result in innovating teaching and learning and whether the effort, time and costs involved in building ILS has had the desired impacts is still being debated especially as the costs only are usually quite high – for example, the cost of the Saltire Center mentioned previously was approximately £24 M. Recently, in the UK Guardian newspaper, Baker (2011) argued that the benefit of ILS is that they attract prospective students, enhance their experiences and prepare them for their future jobs. In contrast, Day (Shepherd 2007) questions whether having such spaces can be beneficial for the students: "*I am not convinced that students will learn any more about what is expected of them academically in such an environment*". Similarly, the Secretary of Education in the UK enforced a policy of "*simplified architectural design*" for educational buildings – as opposed to "*a decade of wasteful extravagance*" (Booth 2012).

While many examples of such spaces exist around the world, there is still no consensus about their impact or what should drive their technological and overall design (Davidson 2011; Shepherd 2007; Temple 2007; Radcliffe 2009). Several assessments have been carried out, guidelines provided and frameworks have been developed (JISC 2009; Jamieson 2008; Temple 2007; Siddall 2006; Radcliffe 2009). Yet, these studies have done little to diffuse the debate around the benefits and impact of ILS, as they have not been able to clearly articulate success metrics and evaluation criteria, or agree on which concepts to prioritise in the design. A report from the Scottish Funding Council (2006) recognized that very few empirical studies of ILS link to the actual environment where learning takes place. In the same report, it was argued that the relationship between the environment and learning is not a straightforward one and hence a more complex form of assessment is needed. How do these innovative features of technological infrastructure and architectural design materialize as part of the day-to-day learning context?

The challenges involved in the design of ILS, both in terms of the pedagogical agenda and their architectural and technological layout, are well recognised. However, less consideration has been given to understanding their lived use and experience. The work of Christopher Alexander on patterns of architecture (Alexander 1979) shows how occupancy can shape architectural design. Alexander stressed the connection between spatial/structural patterns and events – as in people's interactions and lived experiences. A sensible architectural pattern is not necessarily a successful pattern in terms of how the space is used; as Alexander puts it: "*A pattern only works, fully, when it deals with all the forces that are actually present in the situation*" and in practice before a structure is complete "*we have no reliable way of knowing exactly what the forces in a situation are*" (p. 285). In other words, when a design is put in place, it is uncertain, as to how the social context surrounding any designed artefacts will materialize; it is unclear in what ways people will adapt to what they are being offered and how learning may take place. Studies that consider ILS in the context of their everyday use and lived experience can provide useful insights regarding design.

An example of a post-occupancy study of two secondary schools, was carried out by Sutherland and Sutherland (2010). They studied the effect of various architectural features on the interactions that took place in them. They found that in school A in contrast to school B, there were a number of physical transient spaces where "*semi-informal*" learning was taking place, such as corridors. In that school, the corridors were wide, lit with natural light and as a result "*street-like and casual conversations were possible and visible*"; whereas in school B, the corridors functioned as fire escape routes which meant students couldn't decorate them, they had only artificial light, were leading off the atrium and were very narrow. There are a number of important implications from studies such as Sutherland and Sutherland that inform the work presented in this chapter. The first is how design priorities can be informed by occupancy and points to the importance of re-visiting architectural and design choices after they have been deployed.

Second, it shows the effects that architectural and interior design decisions in a space can have, in this case, either constraining or facilitating spontaneous conversations and gatherings. Technological infrastructure is only considered briefly by Sutherland and Sutherland in that it "*should be taken into account and blend in with the overall architectural design.*" Dourish and Bell (2011) advise that studies of technological infrastructures should be sensitive to the social meanings, norms and traditions in which they are embedded, as only then will it be possible to develop and adopt technologies that are relevant and appropriate for existing practices. In this work, we take a closer look into three examples of ILS to gain a better understanding on their everyday use and lived experience and consider this with respect to their design and anticipated use.

Research Methodology

The focus of this work is to capture the role of the technological infrastructure and the architectural design in ILS as a *lived experience* by those who use and inhabit them; and to establish whether they are used as anticipated. This work takes up on this challenge and investigates three ILS through an ethnographic approach that, following the analytic orientation of Suchman's situated action, considers and juxtaposes anticipated versus actual use.

Analytic Orientation

The analytic orientation of this ethnographic work is located in the theory of situated action and the work of Lucy Suchman (2007). Suchman critiqued the mismatch between how creators of technology assumed people would use their technology and how this was actually accomplished in the real world. In her observations of how people used a photocopy machine, she found that people did not follow a specific procedure, even for the 'simple' task of photocopying. Rather, their plans and actions adapted depending on the specifics of the situation: *"the resources and constraints afforded by material and social circumstances"*. Context provides a point of reference: a frame where associations can be generated and a means that allows distinctions to be made. But context also indicates what distinctions are useful to be made. It is possible that some distinctions are only useful in some settings. In line with Suchman, our analysis is an examination of the relationship between action and the particular circumstances in which it occurs. Our work views the interactions taking place in ILS as co-constructions of complex interdependencies between people and artefacts situated in context. Since situated action is neither pre-determined, nor random, we are able to build generalisations (such as design guidelines) grounded in empirical evidence from qualitative, in depth investigations, while maintaining the locality of the situation.

Study Methods

This work investigates the everyday interactions between people, space and technology in ILS. The methodological approach taken was an ethnographic one, as the nature of the investigation focuses on issues that need to be understood in context. Ethnography is combinative, immersive, detailed and contextual (Hammersley and Atkinson 2007). It considers how people's practices and interactions become immersed in their everyday routine to the extent that they are often not recognised consciously by the actors themselves. The ethnographic approach provides the benefit of combining data collected from in-situ observations and semi-structured interviews to understand practices and interactions.

The use of ethnography in this work focused on producing detailed accounts of the situated interactions that took place in three ILS (Dspace, Qspace, Cspace). The activities observed were considered and treated as 'strange'. No preliminary hypotheses were formed beforehand and no particular feature of use or interaction was given a priori significance. Each of the settings studied was different – in terms of their spatial layout, but also in terms of their running and managing circumstances. That meant that the way data was collected also differed, as it had to be decided and negotiated with respect to its individual circumstances.

The duration of the fieldwork for each setting varied from periods of continuous observation and recurring short-term visits depending on the specifics of the setting's operation and use and what was considered a sufficient time for gaining an understanding of the setting. The study in Dspace was carried out 2–3 days a week over a period of 2 months (Feb-April). Dspace was open during library working hours. The whole spectrum of daily activity was covered, by dividing each day into three sessions: morning (9 AM–12 PM), noon and early afternoon (12 PM–3 PM) and late afternoon (3 PM–7 PM). The majority of the data was gathered from the noon-early afternoon sessions, since the researcher found that there was little occupancy or activity in the other two sessions. Qspace was only open when an event took place. Two events were studied taking place in Qspace, an academic workshop and an exhibition event. The researcher visited the space before each event and also observed the planning meetings prior to the academic workshop between the workshop organisers and the managers of the Qspace.

Cspace was open every day from 9 am to 9 pm with the exception of national and university holidays. Data collection in Cspace was completed in three phases, which provided the opportunity to observe a broad diversity of its everyday practices. The first observational phase took place in May for a 3-day period. This coincided with the beginning of the Easter term exam period; as a result examination sessions, individual and group study sessions for exam purposes were taking place. The second phase took place the following October for the duration of a week. The second phase took place at the beginning of the academic year so that newcomers' interaction could be observed. The interest in newcomers arose out of findings from the Dspace study, where newcomers' assumptions and use of the space were found to be influenced by the activities already taking place in the space. The third phase of the study was conducted in February for a period of 2 days. During this period, issues that emerged from the analysis of the previous two phases were followed up.

Data were collected through a variety of techniques: participant observation (primarily), semi-structured interviews and questionnaires (See Table 4.1). The data collected consisted of fieldnotes, photos, audio and video recordings, printed and digital documents. Participant observation allowed the researcher to observe but also experience first hand the use of each space. Semi-structured interviews were conducted with one manager from each space, as well as users of the space who were

Table 4.1 Data collection methods used and materials collected in each studied setting

	Dspace	Qspace	Cspace
Participant observation	✓	✓	✓
Semi structured interviews	[1 Manager, 1 returning user, 6 first time users]	[1 Manager, 3 returning users, 7 first time users]	[1 Manager, 3 returning users, 2 first time users]
Questionnaires	✗	✗	✓
Video	✗	✓	✓
Documents	✓	✓	✓

categorized as first-time users or returning users. The interviews aimed to establish an understanding of the space's vision, design and anticipated use as well as how its current use was viewed by its managers. The interviews with the managers aimed to inform the researcher's understanding of the design and anticipated use of each space while the ones with the users aimed to provide information about the specifics of the everyday use. Questionnaires with open-ended questions were disseminated to the users of Cspace to query the specifics of their experience using the space. This method was chosen for the particular space due to its large number of users (40+).

The rapport that the researcher built up with the managers/designers of the spaces as gatekeepers provided with a unique opportunity to gain insight into the managers'/designers' ideas, feelings, aspirations and concerns about the space, the technology and its use. Analysis of the data compared situated actual use with use as envisioned by the managers/designers of those spaces. Our findings comprise themes that emerged as central to how people co-existed, socialised and collaborated as part of the everyday interactions in ILS.

The Three Settings: Dspace, Qspace, Cspace

Dspace was situated on the ground floor of a university's library building. Its door was the first in a line of office doors and required a university staff/student key card in order to gain access. At the time of the study, Dspace had been in use for approximately 15 months. Dspace was designed to support various learning activities – mostly informal – taking place simultaneously, such as brainstorming, research collaborations and experimentation with digital technologies. Dspace users were postgraduate students and members of academic staff. The managers of the space explained how it was envisioned that Dspace would be a drop-in space where all visitors of the library could have access; that would allow for brainstorming and collaborating by means of low and high tech artefacts. Dspace was a non-bookable, non-facilitated, public space and a number of low tech props could be found scattered around the space such as Lego, plasticine and bendy sticks. Further, the designers and managers wished to provide users of Dspace with the opportunity to trial emerging commercial technologies and inspire potential applications of those in educational materials. For this purpose, in Dspace one could find a large collection of current video games and their consoles (Nintendo Wii, Xbox360, Sony PS3, PSP, Nintendo Ds), a selection of smartphones, PDAs and iPods. Other technological equipment chosen to support or enhance the learning and gaming experiences included a projector, an LCD screen, an interactive whiteboard and a home theatre speaker system. Apart from being a space where users could familiarise themselves with new technologies, it was also hoped that Dspace's comfortable layout and informal atmosphere would bring together academics with common interests and ignite future work opportunities and collaborations. Comfortable and flexible furniture was chosen for Dspace to help visitors relax and allow for a variety of seating arrangements; comprising a big U-shaped couch with movable parts,

Fig. 4.1 Overview of Dspace

beanbags, desk chairs, armchairs and tables with wheels (see Fig. 4.1). A coffee machine that served free coffee and other hot beverages was also available in Dspace to accommodate for a relaxed atmosphere. The library was chosen as common ground between all the departments and disciplines. As the manager pointed out, they had put a lot of thought and effort to make Dspace approachable to everyone on campus: "(. . .) *Library was neutral that is why it was chosen. If Dspace happened in a department people would feel strange, like invading in others' offices*".

Qspace was a Centre of Excellence in Teaching and Learning (CETL) that was created as part of the Higher Education Funding Council for England (HEFCE) joint initiative. Qspace was a bookable intentionally unconventional space – all-white and minimalist – meant to be spatially reconfigured through movable walls, depending on the needs of the activities taking place. Its furniture was versatile and portable: it included chairs, stools, bean bags and tables stored in a separate area, to be added to the space depending on the needs of a particular event. White curtains hung from the ceiling to enable creating smaller spaces, or to be used as projection surfaces for creating immersive environments. Immovable PLASMA screens were mounted on the walls and the space featured an integrated audio-visual (AV) system. Several projectors, and individually adjustable multi-coloured LED lighting were mounted on the ceiling (see Fig. 4.2).

Qspace's pedagogical agenda as described by its managers was to bridge formal teaching with informal learning, as well as use technology to creatively augment – and even revolutionise – teaching; where students would be offered "*exciting opportunities to work in an environment that fosters collaborative, self-directed and experiential learning*". For most events taking place in Qspace, chairs were replaced with beanbags as they were thought to provide a relaxing demeanor that would encourage creative ideas. Providing the users with maximum flexibility was considered a priority; both the physical layout and the technology in Qspace had been designed so that users would be encouraged to configure and explore them. However, due to health and safety regulations, specialised training was required to reconfigure the layout of Qspace. This meant that only a specific number of trained people were allowed to do so. Further, the AV system embedded in the space was not a commercial system – it was developed specifically for Qspace – and its control

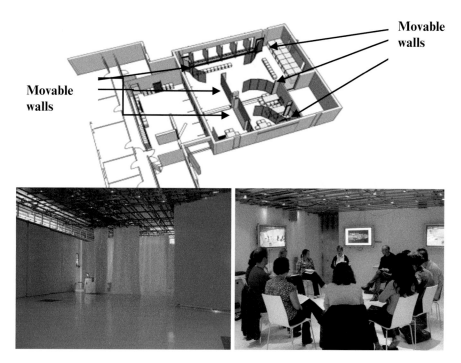

Fig. 4.2 On the *top*, a 3D floorplan of Qspace showing its reconfigurable parts, on the *bottom left* a view of Qspace empty with an array of LEDs and on the *right*, an arrangement of Qspace during the academic workshop

interface was password protected ensuring only a small number of people who knew the password were allowed access. Qspace was open only when an event was taking place in it. For our studies, we observed Qspace being used during two different events: an academic workshop and an exhibition event. In this chapter, we will focus on observations from the academic workshop. The workshop was a 2-day event with approximately 50 international academic attendees (students, researchers and staff).

Cspace was a CETL in Computer Science, situated on the third floor of the Engineering Department building in a UK university campus. Access to the space was controlled via the use of a swipe card – similarly to Dspace – which was available to Computer Science and Engineering students and staff. Cspace consisted of ten booths – five on each side of the room separated by a large corridor of high tables with laptops on them – that could accommodate from six to eight students each (see Fig. 4.3). Each booth contained an interactive SmartBoard, one or two tablet PCs and laptops. Lighting in the booths (top and back lit to avoid glare on screens) could be controlled independently by dimmer switches. The booths had some soundproofing qualities; ensuring groups working in adjoining booths did not disturb each other. Benches and a vending machine that sold snacks and drinks were placed near the entrance to the space.

Fig. 4.3 A typical american diner (*left*) contrasted with the design of Cspace (*right*) with high tables and stools and booths with tables and facing couch seating to allow for prolonged use

Table 4.2 Main features of each observed setting

	Dspace	Qspace	Cspace
Bookable	No	Yes	No
Plug and play tech	No	No	Yes
Movable furnishings	Yes	Yes	No
Facilitators	No	Yes	No
Users	University staff and students	Academic/non academic, event organisers and participants	University students and staff - mostly CompSci
Opening hours	Library hours	Organised event hours	University opening hours

According to its creators, Cspace's main purpose was to support collaborative work among computer science students. In addition, it aimed to support a variety of other activities:

- Teaching; labs and formal tutor-led sessions took place in it
- Thinking; as "*a quiet study area for individuals*"
- Coding and testing
- Communication; as an area where informal *group discussion is facilitated (…) where students can email, use mobile phones, have coffee and lunch without disrupting others.*

To accomplish these aims the manager and director of Cspace chose the booth design for the space so that it resembles a diner. The inspiration for the design came from the director's vivid memories of spending hours in a Pizza Express, with diner style booths, while working on group assignments as an undergraduate student. Table 4.2 provides a brief overview of the main features of each setting.

Findings

In this section we provide an account of the everyday interactions taking place in three ILS – Dspace, Cspace and Qspace focusing on how diverse activities and people coexisted, how people collaborated and socialised.

Supporting Diverse Activities Within the Same Space

As presented earlier, supporting formal and informal learning activities simultaneously within the same space was a key point in the ILS pedagogical agenda. In this section we describe our observations of how users of the three ILS managed their activities while in the presence of others. In each space we observed its users attempting to maintain a semblance of privacy through regulating noise levels and visibility.

Dspace aspired to bring together academics from all levels and departments to discuss and collaborate in an informal atmosphere. However, users of the space were found to avoid co-existing with other people, whenever possible. There were several occasions when people entered the space with the intention to use it and then left immediately because someone else was already there. Even when people co-existed in Dspace their demeanour revealed it was not preferred and that they were displeased by the presence of others. Facial expressions, annoyed looks, stares and body language were indicators that users often were disturbed by the presence of others. When having to co-exist, people were seen to whisper and *create corners*. Creating corners (see Fig. 4.4) was a strategy where each group tried to physically isolate itself from others by retreating into a corner of the room; and also, when this was not possible, groups created corners where they did not exist (e.g., the couch) with their posture or the movable furniture. Apart from not wanting to use Dspace when someone else was there, it was found that some people – mostly newcomers – simply did not know it was possible to use the space while others were there, as they

Fig. 4.4 Creating corners in Dspace (*left*) and Qspace (*right*)

assumed it was a booking-only space. All of the newcomers interviewed identified Dspace as a private space and referred to the key-card locked door: "*a room that requires key-card access is not public, even if it is in the library*"; "*(. . .) it feels like a room that you have to book*". Several also pointed out how if they entered Dspace and someone else was already there, they would feel they are interrupting and leave and conversely, they would feel interrupted in a similar occasion. The manager of Dspace in her interview acknowledged how often people didn't realize Dspace was a public and non-bookable space and they were trying to advertise this more prominently. She also mentioned how often they got requests from people that wished to book the room and she had to explain how it is a non-bookable space: "*I always go back to them and explain that we do have a non-booking policy, (. . .) and they are usually fine with that and they will either come back and say we understand and still come and use the room or they will find a meeting space that they can book*".

Qspace was all about being flexibly reconfigurable so that students, staff and general public could engage in various formal and informal activities, from the movable walls to the lack of permanent furniture and the white curtains running through the space as potential dividers. However, due to the unconventional design of Qspace and the reality of health and safety regulations only Qspace's management staff was allowed to move the walls and for people to use the space, management staff had to be present at all times. As a result of this, Qspace had to be pre-booked and was not a walk-in and use space. Only one event was booked at any time, so whether diverse activities co-existed depended on whether the type of event called for it. The academic workshop we observed, provided this opportunity in the form of a breakout session where groups of participants had to discuss and design various artefacts, while others took a break and socialized. However, this co-existence was not supported very successfully mainly due to sound disturbance. While the movable walls provided the breakout groups with some privacy with respect to visibility, there was no privacy with respect to noise. Qspace had no soundproofing mechanisms and the lack of furniture or any other objects/materials meant that sounds were not absorbed, which made it very difficult for the breakout groups to converse and work unobtrusively. Similar to Dspace people were also seen to whisper and create corners when they were engaging in conversation so that they could hear each other above the noise, but also to maintain some degree of privacy (see Fig. 4.4).

In Cspace formal and informal activities occurred in parallel at the different booths, be it during software engineering sessions, exams or other events. In contrast to the cornering and whispering behaviours observed when people co-existed in previous settings, users of Cspace were not disturbed by others' activities, and engaged in diverse activities simultaneously. For example, a common occurrence in Cspace during lunchtime involved a group of students having lunch in one booth and in the adjacent booth another group discussing or working on an assignment. The noise generated by the group having their lunch break did not seem to bother the focused readers and similarly the quietness of those working did not seem to discourage those having lunch from being loud. The body language and the

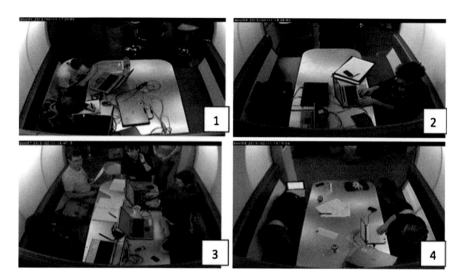

Fig. 4.5 Diverse activities co-existing in Cspace: (**1**) Working in pairs on a group assignment, (**2**) Individual study, (**3**) Practical software engineering sessions with the tutors present, and (**4**) relaxing

overall demeanour of the students on both sides indicated they were comfortable co-existing; no whispering, no angry staring and no creating corners were observed. Figure 4.5 shows four screenshots of the interactions that took place at the same time in four booths. In (1), two students are working on a joint assignment; in (2) one student is studying individually; in (3), one of the student teams is reporting to the tutors on their progress; and in (4), two students are relaxing after having spent a few hours working in the booth. The most extreme example of how formal and informal activities took place unobtrusively in Cspace was during an exam event where two booths were occupied by students chatting and having lunch while in the remaining booths students were examined on their final year project presentations.

This coexistence of diverse activities not only was unproblematic but also went unnoticed by the inhabitants (students and tutors). The unproblematic coexistence of the different activities seemed to come from – at least to some extent – the efficacy of the cocoon-like design of the booths. As mentioned earlier, the booths were soundproofed to some extent. Apart from the booths' soundproofing quality, they restricted visibility to outsiders. By blocking the view to/from others, the booth design might have allowed students and tutors to occasionally forget the presence of others and work as if it was only them in the room.

In summary, of the three settings observed, Cspace was the only setting that was found to accommodate a diversity of activities from socialising to formal learning at the same time and unobtrusively. On the contrary in Qspace and Dspace, there were few instances where learning activities co-existed but this co-existence was problematic.

Supporting Collaboration

Another important feature for ILS and specifically for the three settings observed was that the design of the spaces (layout and technological infrastructure) had to support collaboration among its users. In this section, we describe our observations of how two or more users performed joint work in the space.

In Dspace, specific features had been chosen by the designers of the space to enable groups of people to view and discuss their work such as the projector screen and the big LCD screen. In terms of the furniture, the wheeled chairs with individual tables were chosen to allow for users to move them around and work in groups. However, observations of the everyday use of the space revealed that people very rarely used the chosen technology and furniture to collaborate. This is attributable to the observation that people very rarely used Dspace for group activities. The most common use of Dspace involved individuals having lunch, browsing the web, and pairs of people chatting. On the few occasions where groups of people collaborated, they used their own laptops to share content with others or they used the desktops in the space – mainly the technology not intended for purposes of collaboration by the creators of Dspace. Several people unsuccessfully tried to use the projector or the LCD, as they either had trouble locating the control interface that turned the devices on or could not configure the system so that they could plug in their personal laptops. A few people attempted to override the main control interface and plug their device directly to the LCD screen but found that this was not possible, as the cabling was locked inside a cupboard, purposefully done so by the managers as there had been incidents in the past where people interfered with the setup and this was considered a health and safety hazard.

In Qspace, we observed how collaboration was obstructed, rather than supported, by the unconventional design of the space. Collaboration did take place although the workshop participants found it rather difficult. The minimalist furniture in the space meant that groups had no tables to work on. Workshop participants were seen to balance holding their laptops, notepads and refreshments in their laps. Many of them noted the lack of tables as "*unusual and inappropriate for a workshop*" and several expressed scepticism about Qspace's value as a collaborative workspace. One of the participants – who happened to be the manager of another CETL space – was particularly annoyed with the lack of tables: "*I don't understand how this is a collaborative workspace . . . it doesn't even have tables! How are we supposed to work?*". We observed how participants worked around this problem by appropriating chairs, stools, cardboard boxes and other features of the physical space to 'create' tables. Any surface they could find to put their materials on, they did. These make-shift tables served a number of functions: tall cardboard boxes and stools were used by participants to place laptops, print-outs and other material; the tall cardboard boxes were also used as work surfaces for some groups during the breakout sessions to build paper and other low-tech prototypes on (see Fig. 4.6). The stools further were appropriated as tables for individual use; participants used them to write, draw or place their coffee cups, notepads, pens and pencils on (see Fig. 4.6).

Fig. 4.6 Use of various surfaces to create make-shift tables in Qspace: from *top left*, tall cardboard boxes and chairs used to place equipment; group using the surface of a cardboard box; *bottom*, stools were appropriated as individual tables for placing personal objects or working on them

A second issue with the unconventional design of Qspace had to do with the use of the digital infrastructure. As described earlier, power outlets and cabling were hidden under tiles or behind the moving walls and therefore were only accessible to the managers of the space. Using the projectors or the LCD screens was hard-wired and controlled via a passworded control interface and a desktop computer located at the managers' office. This meant – similarly to Dspace earlier – that users could not spontaneously plug in their personal devices or use the projectors and LCD screens to share content with others while collaborating and several of the workshop participants were astonished and disappointed that they could not do so. Some participants asked the managers if they could use the projectors during the breakout sessions but the response was that this required significant set up time due to the system's software specifications.

In Cspace collaborative work was observed to be a common occurrence. Students collaborated over assignments and exam preparations in a variety of ways, both within the booth and across booths; most importantly these collaborative configurations were seen to happen intuitively and effortlessly. Students using Cspace were found to bring in their own personal devices (e.g. laptops, netbooks and smart phones) and seamlessly integrate them with the existing technology. For example, during the practical sessions, students brought their laptops into Cspace and connected them to the SmartBoards in the booths in order to share their work with the group and the tutors. Students plugged their personal devices into the existing infrastructure without asking for help and without being instructed on how to do so. Plugging was performed in such a familiar and automated way that it was barely noticeable to the observer. Moreover, students felt comfortable unplugging other students' devices from the shared display without asking specifically for permission. Users could connect and disconnect their devices from the shared SmartBoard display with a single tap of the keyboard, which allowed them to easily switch between making their screen visible to the group, or keeping it private so they could perform more private online activities such as checking emails or social media.

In most cases students were observed collaborating in pairs. The booth layout promoted such pairings to occur; both through the configuration of the seating and by restricting space, which enforced physical proximity between users. We observed how the booth design and the technological infrastructure available in the booths allowed for various seating arrangements and for the use of different technologies during collaborative work (see Fig. 4.7). For example in a group of four students sharing one booth, two students on one side of the booth could share one laptop and a notepad or alternate between using one another's laptops (see top left). Students working in pairs and seated across from one another, vertically or diagonally could use either the SmartBoard to acquire a shared view of the task or document at hand (see bottom right) or turned their screens for the other person to see/contribute to the task (see bottom left). When a group of more than two people was working together (and not in pairs as described previously), they would use the SmartBoard to share content with the rest of the group (see top right). While the booth design enabled within-booth collaborations, it restricted across-booths collaborations. If students needed to interact with their peers in other booths, they had to physically move from one booth to the other, and they often did so. These visits were motivated by the need to request some information or clarification about a work related subject but equally allowed students to socialize.

Relaxing and Unwinding

Another important feature of the multipurpose agenda of ILS was that its users would be able to take a break from 'work', relax, unwind and socialize. In this section, we describe our observations of the various ways in which users achieved this in the three settings.

As presented earlier, Dspace had a wide range of gaming consoles and other playful artefacts (e.g. Lego bricks, robot) so that users could try them out, consider them as potential tools in the context of learning but also simply use them to unwind and socialize with one another. While many of Dspace's users were excited with the possibility of coming to Dspace to play, they were not observed to engage in any playful activities. Our interviews revealed two reasons for this observation. First is that users felt playing in a library was not appropriate. Further, they felt that

Fig. 4.7 Patterns of collaboration in Cspace: *Top left*, students working in pairs side by side sharing one screen or alternating between monitors and notes; *top right* whole group collaboration while sharing information on the SmartBoard and; *bottom*, students working in pairs across the booth and either using the SmartBoard or turning their monitors

they did not want to engage in play while someone else was using the space for serious work, for fear of disturbing them. Participants reported that playing video games was problematic due to the difficulty in using the interface that controlled the projector. Despite not observing users playing video games, we did observe users of Dspace unwinding and relaxing in other ways. Whether it was on their lunch break, a tea/coffee break or while waiting for the bus back home, participants explained in the interviews how they enjoyed being in Dspace alone or with colleagues and friends sitting on the comfortable couch and beanbags and relaxing. The free coffee encouraged further such behaviours. Compared to the rest of the library, Dspace was seen to be more informal, playfully decorated and thus was appropriated by its users as an informal meeting and relaxing space.

In Qspace, the beanbags and the ambient lighting also allowed for a relaxing atmosphere and users to unwind. For example, during the breaks and after the end of the workshop, participants sat on the beanbags in a laid back manner while chatting with others. Some even laid completely flat on the large-sized beanbags and closed their eyes. During our observations, participants also were talking about the unconventional design of the space. This talk functioned an ice-breaker among people who did not know each other, allowed people to overcome any initial social embarrassment and have relaxed conversations with one another.

In Cspace, as described earlier, relaxing, socializing and work related activities co-existed harmoniously. Users were also switching between work and break activities. In one booth, students could be observed working on an assignment, while in the next booth another group of students could be observed having lunch, socialising and relaxing. Similar variations were equally observed within the same booth. The booth seating design allowed for students to even lie and have a short nap as pictured in Fig. 4.5. Eating, drinking browsing social media or watching online videos were regular relaxing and unwinding behaviours observed in Cspace. In addition to what was observed, the students' responses in the questionnaires asking for "*A waiter, a menu*" illustrate how they thought of Cspace very much to be like a diner where they could relax.

Discussion

In this work we have studied three settings that share a multi-purpose agenda and examined how the technology and the architectural design of these settings enabled or obstructed the realisation of the multi-purpose agenda. Our analysis of the everyday use of these spaces highlight how challenging the realisation of a multi-purpose agenda may be despite the careful planning carried out by its creators at the design stage. At the heart of this challenge lies a dynamic feature of everyday use of a space identified in our studies – fluid transitions. Below, we discuss what we mean with fluid transitions and then we present the factors supporting fluid transitions grounded in our empirical evidence.

The Challenge of the Multi-purpose Agenda: Fluid Transitions

In our studies of ILS we observed how their creators integrated the technological and architectural infrastructure to support users in coexisting harmoniously, working collaboratively and socializing. We have identified how users of Dspace and Qspace found co-existence within the one space difficult, as they navigated issues around the physical layout and the social etiquette. They had to overcome noise issues and lack of privacy, and did so by 'creating corners' and whispering. This finding resonates with the work of R. Sommer (1969) on personal space and people as shapers of their environment. But, it also goes beyond that as in Cspace, despite the restricted physical layout of the space (booth design), privacy could be found when needed, and diverse activities took place unobtrusively.

With respect to supporting collaboration, in all three spaces there was architectural and technological infrastructure in place that was intended to support collaborative work. Yet in Dspace and Qspace, we observed that people had difficulty using the resources provided as they were faced with issues of access and control. In most cases, the difficulty arose when people wanted to plug their personal devices to the existing infrastructure, e.g. plugging their laptops to a projector, and then were not able to do so. In contrast, this 'plug and play' feature was visibly laid out and socially encouraged in Cspace and therefore allowed for collaboration among its users to take place.

With respect to relaxing and unwinding, people were found to do so in all three settings. The main difference was that in the case of Cspace, relaxing and socialising was weaved in with the pace of the learning work and not a separate state.

The evidence presented in this chapter has shown that realising a multi-purpose agenda might be a big and difficult task, yet not an impossible one. A multi-purpose agenda is not problematic per se; if the mechanisms that support this multiplicity and consequently bridge actual and anticipated use are better understood. Accounting for these differences between anticipated and actual use requires an analysis that goes beyond the arrangement of the flexible furniture and technologies. Instead, it requires an understanding of how *fluid transitions* are supported; that is how users of these space can be supported in seamlessly switching back and forth between individual and group work, between different types of activity (e.g. from working to socializing), between digital and non-digital, between various devices, between private to public spheres.

The analysis of Cspace showed that it is possible for one space to support a wide range of activities in the same space and at the same time. However, this was not achieved due to – or at least not only due to – its technological infrastructure and physical layout. Cspace's success was shown to be relating to how a number of transitions (e.g. from one activity to another, from work to socialising, from formal to informal, from private to public, from familiar to unfamiliar) took place fluidly. In Cspace, various activities from snoozing to being examined took place unobtrusively at the same time, students switched from socialising to working, from working privately to working in groups. On the other hand, in the other two settings tensions often arose when transitioning from one to another. For example, in Dspace conflicts arose when people wanted to use the space for playful, informal activities, while other users were using it for more formal activities (interview, work demo, etc.). Even for less conflicting activities (concurrent informal meetings), people were seen to leave the space instead of co-existing and returning later when it was free. In Qspace, the minimal and unconventional design of the space, made it difficult for people to engage with the technology in the desired way as familiar devices were arranged and/or controlled in very unfamiliar ways. So the question is how can we better support fluid transitions in spaces with multi-purpose agendas?

Supporting Fluid Transitions in Innovative Learning Spaces

We propose three factors, empirically grounded in our ethnographic studies, that mediate the way people interact and further support – or obstruct – fluid transitions in ILS. These three factors, informed by our ethnographic work, present a coherent vocabulary that has a role to play in the design decisions relating to these spaces and can be valuable to various stakeholders (policy makers, architects, designers, managers). By considering each of these aspects both before and after an innovative space has been designed, anticipated and actual use can be closely aligned.

These factors are:

  (i) Legibility (infrastructural and social)
 (ii) Legitimacy and sense of ownership
(iii) Customisation and appropriation

These factors are interdependent and need to be considered as such.

Legibility

Legibility refers to whether people understand how they can use the space and its infrastructure (technological and physical), what kinds of activities can or are expected to take place in it. It is useful to think of legibility in two ways: infrastructural and social. These are interrelated.

Infrastructural legibility refers to whether technological devices or the furniture or the physical layout is arranged or positioned in such a way that it helps people understand what it is for, i.e. its purpose and affordances. The spatial architectural setup and the technological artefacts in ILS should be sufficiently visible and legible for users – and in particular newcomers – to approach and interact with, while at the same time provide ways this infrastructure can be extended to those that have more advanced needs (see later customisation).

As shown in the findings, the arrangement of devices and furniture in the three settings made it easier or more difficult for users to understand how or even whether, they could be used. In Cspace the power sockets, the cabling and all the controls for using the laptops and the SmartBoard screens were visibly laid out on the tables of the booths. In Qspace, the same infrastructure was hidden from view. In both Qspace and Dspace one interface to control multiple functionalities went hand in hand with poor legibility. Physical structures can encourage or hint on specific interactions. Hornecker and Buur (2006) describe this as "embodied constraints" in their framework for Tangible Facilitation. Embodied constraints refer to the "set up or configuration of space and objects" and they can: "ease some types of activity", "limit what people do" or "provide implicit suggestions to act in a certain way". This does not suggest that physical space determines behaviour; it simply says that there is an interplay between physical and social, which brings us to the notion of social legibility.

Social legibility refers to how the social context or social cues can help people understand how to use and interact with the space and others. Social context, social cues and/or perceived social etiquette can support – or hinder – fluid transitions, hint towards or discourage specific activities and interactions. For example, Dspace being in the library building and a library's social etiquette potentially conflicted with its playful, experimental agenda. Social cues can be embedded in or implied by the architectural layout and the technological infrastructure. An example of this is Cspace's design based on a diner setting. Its booth-like design had strong associations with what it feels/means to be in a diner; a casual eating and drinking coffee place where people come together in a relaxed setting. As such it encouraged a wide range of interactions to take place without any conflicts.

Legibility is the basis for appropriation and customisation and further contributes to notions of legitimacy.

Legitimacy and Sense of Ownership

Legitimacy refers to how the normative status regarding interactions in ILS is conferred and established; and sense of ownership refers to whether and how people perceive they are allowed to interact and use the physical and technological artifacts. For people's interactional transitions to take place fluidly in ILS, it was shown it is important that users have a sense of ownership or at least co-ownership on the space.

Notions of ownership and legitimacy regarding use of technology vary among places, private and public ones. Sanusi and Palin's ethnographic work (2008) showed how there were varying ways of granting access to the use of Wifi in coffee shops and people relied on social conventions to make sense of these. Humphreys' ethnography (2005) similarly showed how the use of mobile phones in public spaces was mediated by social norms. When legitimacy is unclear and individuals are unsure as to whether they are allowed to use a space or the technology in it, they will often conform to social norms or the closest appropriate etiquette. In this respect social and infrastructural legibility are central. In Dspace, people were observed to be confused as to whether they were allowed to use the space when others were already using it or play games, which clashed with the commonly accepted social etiquette of a library.

Poor legibility and the fact that for each event there was a new set of users made it very difficult for Qspace users to experience a sense of ownership over the space with clear implications on the appropriation, customization and use of the space (see next section). Health and safety issues regarding the moving of the walls and the cabling infrastructure of Qspace intensified the managers' role and limited further the sense of ownership of the users. A mixed message was also delivered: the space was designed and advertised to be fully configurable by the users and for the users and yet all these had to take place within very strict constraints that were set by the managers. On the contrary, in Cspace, legitimacy was not problematic and people were seen to use the space and interact with each other with ease. The users were co-deciders and co-constructors of what was allowed to take place and as such they exhibited a strong sense of ownership over the space. The lack of legibility issues as well as the fact that the community of users was a coherent and well bounded group further contributed to Cspace being used as well as appropriated.

Customisation and Appropriation

Customisation refers to providing the option for an artefact – or a space – to be adapted, appropriated by its users. Appropriation refers to how the users took the space and used it as their own. The studies showed that it is important for ILS to provide customisable tools or infrastructure along with mechanisms that will allow for users to appropriate. However, there is a delicate balance to be handled when users are appropriating for their own rather than intended use. Appropriation can be a plus but can equally create more tensions between actual and anticipated use.

Customisation and appropriation further depend on the previous concepts of legibility and legitimacy. Our analysis has shown that the less clear it is to users what resources are available and how and when and where those resources are, the less likely the users are to appropriate them. For example, in Qspace, despite having the most flexible/reconfigurable design, the poor legibility of the tailored control interface and the unconventional physical layout made it very hard for people to appropriate the technology in the space. Further, issues of legitimacy made it problematic for people to use their own devices in the space. It is not that appropriation was impossible in Qspace but it certainly required significant effort. In both Dspace and Qspace, users appropriated for their own use and needs rather than the intended ones. In Qspace, they appropriated various surfaces to make tables, which, apart from their functional use, provided a *"social shield"* (Goffman 1963) through shared and private space. In Dspace, people had coffee and lunch and informal meetings, but very rarely played with the games in the space or interacted with people already in the space. Also, issues with the legibility and the legitimacy of the space (mentioned earlier) impeded more creative or playful appropriations.

In Cspace, users appropriated the space both in the intended ways and also in ways that were not expected when it was designed. These unexpected uses (such as having a nap) were not relevant to the anticipated use of the space but at the same time they were not conflicting. The technology in Cspace was also appropriated by its users. They both used the existing set up of devices in the space and further added a number of other devices (personal ones) customising the existing infrastructure to their needs.

Conclusion and Future Work

Innovative learning spaces lie at the interface of learning activities, flexible architecture and technological infrastructure. Looking into how various off-the shelf technological devices are being integrated in one single space with the purpose of supporting a range of learning activities, collaboration and socialising and into how users appropriate them, is an essential activity to justify the costs – in terms of money, effort and time – of developing such spaces.

Three ILS were investigated through an ethnographic approach that considered the situated interactions and juxtaposed anticipated versus actual use. The findings contribute to an empirically-grounded understanding of how ILS are being used and appropriated on an everyday basis, which has implications for the (re)design of current and future ILS. In accounting for the differences between anticipated and actual use the integral role of *fluid transitions* emerged from the analysis. We elaborated three factors that were found to mediate user interactions, and support – or obstruct – fluid transitions in ILS. The three factors are: (i) Legibility (infrastructural and social) (ii) Legitimacy and sense of ownership (iii) Customisation and appropriation. These factors can be applied in two ways: (i) as a coherent vocabulary for supporting stakeholders in discussing and reasoning about the design of ILS, and (ii) as a set of guiding concepts against which an existing space can be evaluated and anticipated and actual use be better aligned. A natural continuation of this work would be to apply these three factors in the inception phase of an ILS before it is built and to expand the locus of the investigation to larger size settings – perhaps entire buildings.

References

AlAgha I, Hatch A, Ma L, Burd L (2010) Towards a teacher-centric approach for multi-touch surfaces in classrooms. In: Proceedings of the ACM international conference on interactive tabletops and surfaces 2010 (ITS 2010), Saarbrücken, 7–10 November

Alexander C (1979) The timeless way of building. Oxford University Press, New York

Bachour K, Kaplan F, Dillenbourg P (2010) An interactive table for supporting participation balance in face-to-face collaborative learning. IEEE Trans Learn Technol 3(3):203–213

Baker D (2011) Why UK higher education institutions should invest in technology. Retrieved May 2011, from The Guardian: http://www.guardian.co.uk/higher-education-network/blog/2011/apr/18/higher-education-investing-in-technology?INTCMP=SRCH

Booth R (2012, December 31) Michael Gove faces rebellion over no-curves school plans. Retrieved January 2013, from The Guardian: http://www.guardian.co.uk/education/2012/dec/31/michael-gove-rebellion-no-curves-schools

Boys J (2011) Towards creative learning spaces. Routledge, New York

Callison M (2011) A design case featuring the Graduate Design Studio at Indiana University Bloomington's Human Computer Interaction Design Program. Int J Designs Learn 2(1) https://scholarworks.iu.edu/journals/index.php/ijdl/issue/view/98

Davidson C (2011, April 28). So last century. Retrieved June 10, 2011, from Times Higher Education: http://www.timeshighereducation.co.uk/story.asp?sectioncode=26&storycode=415941

Doorley S, Witthoft S (2012) Make space: how to set the stage for creative collaboration. Wiley, Hoboken

Dourish P, Bell G (2011) The infrastructure of experience and the experience of infrastructure: meaning and structure in everyday encounters with space. Environ Plan B 34(3):414–430

Dudek M (2000) Architecture of schools. Architectural Press, New York

Fisher K (2005) Research into identifying effective learning environments. http://www.oecd.org/dataoecd/26/7/37905387.pdf

Fox A, Johanson B, Hanrahan P, Winograd T (2000) Integrating information appliances into an
    interactive workspace. IEEE Comput Graph Appl 20(3):54–65
Goffman E (1963) Behaviour in public places: notes on the social order of gatherings. Free Press
    of Glencoe, New York
Groff J (2013) Technology-rich innovative learning environments. (OECD paper). Retrieved from
    http://www.oecd.org/edu/ceri/Technology-Rich Innovative Learning Environments by Jennifer
    Groff.pdf
Hammersley M, Atkinson P (2007) Ethnography: principles in practice, 3rd edn. Routledge,
    London
Hornecker E, Buur J (2006) Getting a grip on tangible interaction: a framework on physical
    space and social interaction. In: Proceedings of the SIGCHI conference on human factors in
    computing systems, ACM, New York, pp 437–446
Humphreys L (2005) Cellphones in public: social interactions in a wireless era. N Media Soc
    7(6):810–833
Jamieson F (2008) Creating new generation learning environments on the university campus.
    Woods Bagot Research Press, Southbank
Joint Information System Committee (JISC) (2009) JELS project final report at www.jisc.ac.uk/
    870 media/documents/projects/jelsfinalreport30.06.09.doc. Retrieved on 13 Jan 2013
Kaplan F, Dillenbourg P (2010) Scriptable classrooms. In: Mäkitalo-Siegl K, Zottmann J, Kaplan
    F, Fischer F (eds) Classroom of the future: orchestrating collaborative spaces. Sense Publishers,
    Rotterdam, pp 245–257
Kaplan F, Do-Lenh S, Bachour K, Kao GY, Gault C, Dillenbourg P (2009) Interpersonal computers
    for higher education. In: Dillenbourg P, Huang J, Cherubini M (eds) Interactive artifacts and
    furniture supporting collaborative work and learning. Springer, Lausanne, pp 129–145
Long P, Holeton R (2009) Signposts of the revolution? What we talk about when we talk about
    learning spaces. EDUCAUSE Rev 44(2):36–49
McGregor J (2004) Space power and the classroom. FORUM 46(1):13–18
Milne A (2006) Designing blended learning space to the student experience. In: Oblinger D (ed)
    Learning spaces. Educause, Boulder
Oblinger D (ed) (2006) Learning spaces. Educause, Boulder
Radcliffe D (2009) A pedagogy-space-technology (PST) framework for designing and evaluating
    learning places. In: Radcliffe D, Wilson H, Powell D, Tibbetts B (eds) Learning spaces in higher
    education: positive outcomes by design. The University of Queensland and the Australian
    Learning and Teaching Council, Brisbane
Sanusi A, Palen L (2008) Of coffee shops and parking lots: considering matters of space and place
    in the use of public Wi-Fi. Comput Supported Coop Work 17:257–273
Schratzenstaller A (2010) The classroom of the past. In: Mäkitalo-Siegl K, Zottmann J, Kaplan F,
    Fischer F (eds) Classroom of the future: orchestrating collaborative spaces. Sense Publishers,
    Rotterdam
Scottish Funding Council (2006) Spaces for learning: a review of learning spaces in further and
    higher education. SFC, Edinburgh. http://www.jiscinfonet.ac.uk/Resources/externalresources/
    sfc-spaces-for-learning
Shepherd J (2007, July 10) Comfort zone. Retrieved March 2013, from The Guardian: http://www.
    guardian.co.uk/education/2007/jul/10/highereducation.students?INTCMP=SRCH
Siddall SE (2006) The Denison learning space project, mission and guiding. http://www.denison.
    edu/academics/learningspaces/checkl.pdf
Sommer R (1969) Personal space: the behavioural basis of design. Prentice-Hall, Inglewood Cliffs
Suchman L (2007) Human-machine reconfigurations: plans and situated actions, 2nd edn. Cam-
    bridge University Press, Cambridge, UK
Sutherland, Sutherland (2010) In: Mäkitalo-Siegl K, Zottmann J, Kaplan F, Fischer F (eds)
    Classroom of the future: orchestrating collaborative spaces. Sense Publishers, Rotterdam,
    pp 41–63

Temple P (2007) Learning spaces for the 21st century. Higher Education Academy, London

Tregloan P (2009) Learning lab: transforming a learning experience. In: Radcliffe D, Wilson H, Powell D, Tibbetts B (eds) Learning spaces in higher education: positive outcomes by design. The University of Queensland and the Australian Learning and Teaching Council, Brisbane

Van Note Chism N (2006) Challenging traditional assumptions and rethinking learning spaces. In: Oblinger D (ed) Learning spaces. Educause, Boulder

Chapter 5
Creative Workplace Alchemies: Individual Workspaces and Collaboration Hotspots

Peter Scupelli

Abstract Much like creative knowledge work environments, studio-based design education environments are changing rapidly to include: multidisciplinary teams, information technology, geographically distributed teams, and flexible workspaces. Factors such as, architectural space design, furniture choices, technical infrastructure features, acoustics, socio-cultural norms, and privacy and visibility of wall-sized displays support or hinder workers in creative environments. In this chapter, I describe a case study of a graduate design studio at the School of Design at Carnegie Mellon University. The studio has four connected spaces: individual workspaces, collaborative spaces, a kitchen and social café area, and a distance-learning classroom. In earlier work, researchers evaluated student satisfaction through fieldwork, pre-post occupancy surveys, and interviews. In this chapter, I analyze a design studio environment through time-lapse photography, Space Syntax analysis, and semi-structured interviews. This research identifies locations where people and teams work and the factors that support collaboration, such as space configuration, wall-sized display affordances, furniture configurations, and support infrastructures. Teams worked more often in locations that were less visible from other locations, provided greater laptop screen and display privacy, had whiteboards, and electrical outlets. Students did individual work throughout the studio-suite regardless of the function assigned to the spaces.

Introduction

Knowledge workers in creative workplaces often engage in individual and collaborative work. Workspaces optimized for collaborative tasks may facilitate the often-noisy teamwork but may disrupt collocated co-workers engaged in quiet focused work. Likewise, optimizing the workplace for quiet focused work may hinder collaboration between co-workers. Team members can be collocated in the same workplace or working remotely. A design challenge for the creative workplace

P. Scupelli (✉)
School of Design, Carnegie Mellon University, Pittsburgh, PA, USA
e-mail: scupelli@cmu.edu

© Springer International Publishing Switzerland 2016   85
N.S. Dalton et al. (eds.), *Architecture and Interaction*,
Human–Computer Interaction Series, DOI 10.1007/978-3-319-30028-3_5

is to shape a flexible work environment to support workers' dynamically changing needs without hindering co-workers. For example, some aspects of collaborative teamwork require face-to-face discussion, which can interfere with co-workers quiet focused work. Likewise, one worker's phone and conference calls can interfere acoustically with other work. Another challenge for creative workplace design includes providing a range of options that support different types of tasks and fluid transitions between tasks.

Even collaborative team tasks require different types of spaces based on task. Radically collocated teams may benefit from working together uninterrupted (Olson et al. 2002). Other types of intellectual work may benefit from serendipitous interaction with co-workers (Kraut et al. 1990). The arrangement of a physical space, such as the hallways, offices, and common areas in a building, can influence the frequency of informal interaction among inhabitants of that space (e.g., Allen 1977; Festinger et al. 1950; Hatch 1987; Kraut et al. 1990). Even when the same distance separates people, visual barriers such as walls and stairways reduce opportunities to make eye contact with one another (Festinger et al. 1950) and initiate interaction (Kraut et al. 1990).

Seen from an ecological psychology perspective, both structural and dynamic attributes influence behavior in a setting (Barker 1968). On the structural side, *behavior settings* consist of standing patterns of behavior that can be defined as a bounded pattern in human behavior with unique spatial-temporal coordinates (e.g., classroom lecture, coffee break). On the dynamic side, the *behavior setting* has a dynamic relationship with the *behavior-milieu*. The *milieu* surrounds the behavior in question often is an intricate complex of times, places, and things. The *milieu* is similar in structure as the behavior in a *behavior setting*. For example, the boundary of a class lecture is both class time and the classroom boundaries.

Barker's ecological psychology research illustrates, places, time, and things come together to shape human behavior in the built environment. The geometry and features of the environment in turn influence where people choose to interact. Furthermore, people's position in an environment affects where other people choose to position themselves. For example, the "line of talk" between people interacting limits where others situate themselves (Goffman 1963).

The location of people and artifacts in space influence behavior. For example, the location of information displays is linked to whether people engage with large displays (Huang 2007; Huang et al. 2008). In surgical suites, heavy foot traffic in a hallway hindered the use of a large schedule-board to coordinate surgery schedule changes on the day of surgery (Scupelli et al. 2010). Preferred seating locations for group tasks at tables were associated with the type task one is doing (Sommer 1969 p. 62). In the library setting, students preferred to sit with their back to the wall at smaller tables facing away from the entrance to reduce distractions and facing the entrance to defend their table from unwanted invasion (Sommer 1969 p. 49).

Visibility and privacy likely play a critical role in psychological comfort. Appleton's prospect-refuge theory, posits that environments that allow one to see (prospect) without being seen (refuge) helps one feel psychologically more secure (Appleton 1975).

Privacy and visibility of information displays is associated with interaction as well. With respect to display visibility and display privacy, where should wall-sized displays be located in relation to furniture, hallways, and individual and team workspaces?

Other factors affect where people choose to work and collaborate. For example, in cafes or airports, laptop screen privacy, glare from windows, and access to electric outlets are often associated with where people prefer to sit. How might the type of work environments available change where people choose to collaborate or work individually? How does the mobility of people in the environment affect work activities? What features such as windows, whiteboards, electric outlets, and large displays support individual and group work? Questions remain about spaces workers prefer when given autonomy to choose between multiple work settings for individual and team tasks.

Architecture Environments and Interaction

Extensive research on the influence of architecture in organizations has shown that the built environment shapes how much interaction people have (e.g., Allen 1977; Hatch 1987; Kraut et al. 1990; Sommer 1969). Physical proximity increases the quantity of communication among co-workers in office buildings (Allen 1977).

In a research organization, smaller distances between researchers' offices predicted a greater likelihood that researchers would co-author (Kraut et al. 1990). Yet, in open plan offices, it is possible to be too close. In one study of an open office plan, office walls and doors encouraged interaction because they created a private territory that allowed for confidential communication and reduced interruptions (Hatch 1987). Other research suggests that open office plan decreases opportunities for focused work (Kaarlela-Tuomaala et al. 2009).

The arrangement of a physical space and the objects in the space affects interaction. The shape and design of the places where people interact inevitably shape their dynamics: for good and for bad. The arrangement of spaces and displays mediates not just interaction but also people's access to information and objects. Retail stores size passageways to allow both circulation space and activity zones for customers standing or seated around counters and displays. In retail environments, narrow aisles increase the likelihood that customers circulating interrupt other customers viewing products. Such interruptions were associated with decreased sales (Underhill 1999).

Furniture shape and location limit the positions in which people can place themselves. In dyadic interactions there are essentially four positions people can place themselves in relative to one another: face-to-face, at right angles, side-by-side, and back-to-back. Sommer (1969) showed that choice of seating location depended largely upon the type of task. Two people who are co-acting rather than interacting (e.g., sitting at the same table working on different things) choose seats that are not face-to-face. When collaborating or having an informal conversation, people prefer to sit at right angles, whereas for competitive tasks, they tend to sit opposite one another. Thus, the physical arrangement of benches, chairs, and tables can determine whether people are able to interact comfortably.

Architectural Space and Large Displays

The architecture of a building affects people's access to information sources. The creative workplace contains both information technology and people engaged in cooperative work, using technology. Schmidt and Bannon (1992) introduced the concept of common information spaces to describe the activities and cooperative work that may emerge around shared computer-based information resources. People create common information spaces by discussing and negotiating the meaning of shared objects and information.

The configuration of architectural space may affect the creation and maintenance of common information spaces. When information artifacts and people are in different physical locations, people must travel or use technology to create a common information space. The arrangement of displays depicted on computer screens, the placement of large displays, notes, and charts, and information spoken aloud may support or inhibit the creation and maintenance of a common information space (e.g., Suchman 1997; Goodwin and Goodwin 1996). Challenges in the creative workplace regard time-sharing places for unrelated projects, unlike high reliability organization (HRO) control rooms that have defined purposes (e.g., air traffic control, underground rail system).

Whittaker and Schwarz (1999) compared the effects on task scheduling of physical whiteboards vs. calendaring software in software development teams. The public nature of a centrally located wall-sized display promoted group interaction and collaborative planning around the board. In the creative workplace, less central, visible, and private large displays may better support team workspaces for focused team tasks, whereas, more central, visible, and less private locations can support tasks that benefit from interactions with others.

The location and visibility of displays are associated with people's interaction with the display. Hawkey et al. (2005) found that being close to a display makes direct input interaction easier, but compromises effectiveness of collaboration in using the board. Being close to a display also reduces opportunities to establish eye contact and initiate interactions with others, creating a tradeoff. Researchers found that mounting public large displays high on the wall discouraged viewers' engagement with the displays (Huang 2007; Huang et al. 2008). Huang et al. (2008) suggest that system designers consider the position and context of the large display in the design phase rather than after deployment.

There are multiple ways to engage with large displays. People position themselves at different distances from the display and from one other. Rogers and Rodden (2003) describe the area around large displays as composed of three activity areas: the direct interaction activity area nearest the display; the focal awareness activity area a medium distance from the display; and the peripheral awareness activity area furthest away. People move from peripheral activities to focal awareness activities, overcoming commitment thresholds before interacting with the system. The space among people engaged in an interaction defines an area not available for others to stand in or walk through (Goffman 1963). Crowding limits people's choice of position and thus access to things and other people.

Physical space and social context (i.e., place) affect engagement with public interactive displays. In the creative workplace, the visibility and degree of privacy of visual displays' make public displays more or less desirable depending on task.

In the creative workplace, the human factors of large displays are likely to affect usage. For example, Wigdor et al. (2006)) found that people prefer a display location and input device arrangements that give them personal comfort more than they want an uncomfortable arrangement with better performance. Su and Bailey (2005) determined that large displays should be separated on a horizontal plane up to 45°, should not be placed behind people, and if that position is needed, the displays should be offset relative to their users.

Likewise form factor of interactive displays impact how users notice displays, are motivated to interact, and socially interact with the public display. Flat configurations trigger the strongest honey pot effect. Hexagonal screen configurations are associated with low social learning. Concave display configurations trigger the smallest amount of simultaneously interacting users (Koppel et al. 2012). Systems such as, Screenfinity, allow to rotate, translate, and zoom content in order to enable reading while passing by very large displays (Schmidt et al. 2013). Ambient displays can augment the principal static elements of architecture, such as walls, transforming space into a dynamic and ever-changing environment used to refine navigation paths (Varoudis et al. 2011). The challenges to design, implement and embed large-scale distributed ambient display systems in buildings raise many issues and require a range of approaches including non-user centered such as bricolage and consultation (Hazlewood et al. 2010).

Space Syntax to Predict Human Behavior in the Built Environment

Human movement through built environment is predictable. As mentioned previously, visibility and geometry of the physical environment play roles in shaping where people choose to move and pause.

The term space syntax describes a group of theories and methods for the analysis of spatial configurations. Researchers studied many buildings typologies ranging from: museums (Choi 1999), airports, hospitals (Peponis and Zimring 1996), and other places. Pre-post occupancy studies linked visibility and accessibility, increased face-to-face interaction, and improved perceived privacy in new office in an open plan office (Rashid et al. 2009). Space syntax methods are able to predict correlation between spatial layouts and social effects such as crime, movement, and sales per unit area (Hillier et al. 1993; Scoppa and Peponis 2015).

One of the main ideas in Space Syntax is that people make choices as they move through space. Analysis of sub-components that make up whole spaces describe components and analyzed as networks of choices people make as they move through space. Space Syntax is based on three ways of thinking of space: isovist, convex space, and axial space.

An isovist is the set of all points visible in all directions from a given vantage point in space (Benedikt 1979). Isovist analysis allows one to see how visible one point is from all other points. By calculating isovists from each point in the floor plan one can see what are the most and least visible portions of the floor plan in general (Batty 2001; Turner et al. 2001). It is also possible to calculate isovists for particular points to see how visibility compares between several positions.

Isovist analysis allows designers to create visibility maps for floor plans of proposed alternatives. Visibility measures can be used to position public displays for maximum salience. There is a complex pattern of interactions between the size and shape of spaces where displays are situated and memory of different types of representations depicted (Dalton et al. 2013). Different representations were more memorable when positioned in different shapes of spaces, but the memorability of text and images differed with the size and jaggedness of the space where they are displayed (Dalton et al. 2013). Patterns of interaction around shared schedule boards in surgical suites were associated with quantity of isovist overlap. Researchers used isovist analysis of a shared display in surgical suites to determine display placements that would enhance coordination between groups (Scupelli et al. 2007).

Convex space is a space that someone can occupy; if imagined as a diagram, no line between two points goes outside the perimeter. All points in a convex space are visible from all other points (Peponis et al. 1997). Integration measures how many turns are necessary to reach all other segments in a network. Integration measures of convex spaces in a floor plan describe how connected convex spaces are to each other. Connectivity measures the number of links to each node. The relationship between visibility and connectivity of regions of space allows predicting where people are most likely to be in a space (Batty 2001; Turner et al. 2001). Connectivity describes how connected portions of a space are to other spaces. More connected spaces are more likely to have more foot traffic (Hillier 1996).

Axial space is a straight sight line and a possible path through space (Hillier and Hanson 1984). An axial map is made of the least amount of axial lines that to cover all connections between convex spaces. Axial lines are the longest views across spaces. An axial map represents the sense of connections a persons has while moving through a building. Initially, axial lines were difficult to calculate by hand, Turner developed a computer program to calculate axial lines (Turner 2001). Integration is a measure of how connected an axial line or to all other axial lines in a building. Spaces that are more integrated require fewer connections between axial lines to connect all convex spaces in a building. More integrated spaces are closer other spaces; less integrated spaces are more separate (Haq 2003).

While Space Syntax helps to explain how people move through space, there is more to guiding human behavior in the built environment than visibility, connectivity, and geometry of spaces. For example, in the workplace setting, the type of work engaged affects workers' movements through space. There is a distinction between "strong" and "weak" program buildings (Hillier et al. 1984).

In a "strong" program building, the layout "strongly" controls the movement of people through space. For example, the design of a courthouse separates prisoners, employees, and visitors. Instead, in a "weak" program building, the elements of the building shape how users move more than the program of the building. One of the limitations for Space Syntax research is that the visibility and geometry of a space certainly play a role in how people use a space but other factors matter as well.

The program of a building along with the processes pursued in the space together influence where people choose to move and pause. In office environments, where people move, work, and talk is a critical factor (Hillier and Penn 1991). For example, in organizations where communication occurs in very connected areas, information tends to spread across the organization widely. Conversely, in organizations where communication occurs far away from connected spaces, individual groups reinforce the differences between cultures.

Robotic Architecture Environments and Beyond

Technological advances in work and living environments are likely to change visions for flexible and reconfigurable workplaces. Notable examples span building automation, Internet of Things (IoT), responsive environments, and robotic furniture. Building automation covers a broad range from: heating and cooling systems, alarm systems, and automated lighting systems. Commercially available IoT systems can empower non-programmers to sense user activity and control smart things (e.g., lights, thermostats, doors). Examples include, SmartThings, a home automation sensor and actuator kits (http://www.smartthings.com/), Nest thermostat (https://nest.com/), and Phillips Hue personal lighting systems (http://www.meethue.com). Such systems can further empower office workers to shape their work environment to better support their preferences.

Reconfigurable hybrid physical-digital work environment prototypes allude to futures with increased flexibility in workplace environments. In the Animated Work Environment (AWE) robotic work environment, end-users can program six-panels to dynamically shape and support individual creative workplaces (Green et al. 2009). An example of robotic furniture includes, modular robots reconfigured into adaptive furniture (Sproewitz et al. 2009). An interesting vision of a domestic robotic environment reduces the total amount of space necessary to live by allowing rooms, partitions, and furniture to shift based on user needs (Georgoulas et al. 2014). Such promising areas of research are early signals of the future of flexible creative workplace environments.

Given the challenges of fluid transitions between different work tasks such as individual work vs. teamwork, and the possible opportunities afforded by research into robotic architecture, and robotic furniture, workplace designers may need to explore environments that respond dynamically to user needs. However, such advances in the merging of robotics and architecture pose interesting challenges for how to evaluate and optimize spatial configurations based on user needs and evaluation criteria. Fleming et al. (1992) developed 2D-layout design systems of constraint satisfaction techniques that used an orthogonal 2D grid and used algorithmic optimization. Bier et al. (2008) created a prototype called FunctionLayouter (FL) to automatically generate 2D layouts of functional objects in 3D-space. Even though algorithmic optimization and robotic architecture is not the focus of this chapter, reviewing these areas links this case study to other relevant research areas. In the next section, I describe a case study of a graduate design studio at a North American first-tier research university.

Case Study: A Design Studio Environment

Much like creative workplaces, design studio education is rapidly changing to keep abreast with global trends. Design and architecture schools have been shifting away from solely individual projects to team projects (Koch et al. 2002). Design studio environments therefore need to support individual work and teamwork. Public display of work during a critique supports meaningful discussion grounding the conversation around design artifacts. Likewise, desk critiques for individual projects and table critiques for team projects and informal discussion in the studio require shared visual displays to ground conversations.

Increasingly, design and design thinking are receiving much attention (Brown and Kātz 2009). "Design thinking" is an innovation design method that relies on field research, prototyping, iteration, and refinement. Typically, people learn "design thinking" through design studio courses in a studio setting. Universities are rethinking their design studios. For example, the d.school at Stanford University chronicles their design space transformations in the book, Make Space (Doorley and Witthoft 2012). The School of Design at Carnegie Mellon University remodeled the Graduate Interaction Design Studios in fall 2012 (Scupelli and Hanington 2014; see Fig. 5.1).

Figure 5.1 shows a floor plan with the design studio furniture. The studio suite is 400 m^2 and includes four interconnected spaces to support multiple work preferences: (a) an area with individual workspaces for 40 students (Desks A, Desks B); (b) collaborative spaces and an enclosed team room; (c) social spaces with a kitchen and social cafe area; and (d) a distance-learning capable classroom. A glass garage door separates the collaborative space and distance-learning classroom. During classes and lectures, the garage door acoustically separates the two spaces. Students are free to use the classroom for individual or collaborative work when the garage door is open and class is not in session. Additional features included wall-to-wall

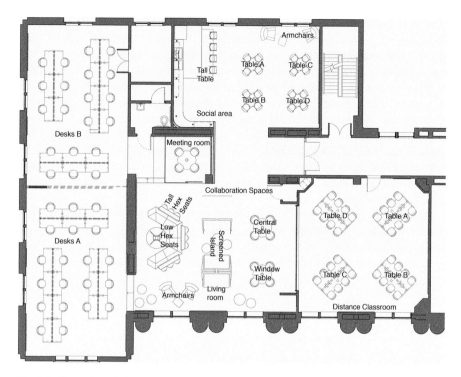

Fig. 5.1 Floor plan of the remodeled graduate design studio in the school of design at Carnegie Mellon University to support individual work areas (*A*, *B*), social interaction spaces, team-based collaborative work in flexible spaces, and a distance-learning classroom

whiteboards, six 50-in. video monitors, dynamic screen-sharing technologies, and teleconference abilities. The large video monitors are situated as follows: (a) the classroom has four large video displays mounted in the corners, one for each rectangular table; (b) one mobile large video monitors allows students to move it where needed in the studio; and (c) the small-enclosed team room has a large video display mounted on the wall. Furnishings were specified in collaboration with Steelcase Learning Environments. See prior research for more details about the graduate design studio and pre-post occupancy evaluation (Scupelli and Hanington 2014).

Methods: Time-Lapse Data, Space Syntax, and Field Interviews

In this study, three main data sources were used: time lapse data, space syntax analysis, and field interviews. Time-lapse data was collected with five Brinno TLC 200 Pro HDR time-lapse cameras for 1 week at a time. Pictures were taken every minute to capture where people stop to work in the graduate design studio. The cameras were placed in five locations: two in the individual workstation areas, two in the collaborative work areas, and one in the social space area. Each image in the time-lapse movies had a timestamp. We used an annotated floor plan to code where people were working in the graduate design studio in a spreadsheet for each minute of footage. The five cameras bore the same timestamps to provide a snapshot of where people worked in the graduate studio at any given minute.

Two types of space syntax analyses were conducted on a floor plan of the graduate design studio, isovist and connectivity analysis with DepthmapX software 0.30 MacOSX version. Given the focus of the study is an interior space, we conducted both analyses on empty rooms, and with main furniture not easily moved (e.g., tables, couches).

Interviews were semi-structured in nature. Participants were asked to clarify the type of work observed in the time-lapse data collected. Participants were asked general questions while reviewing a time-lapse video clip such as: Can you please comment on what is happening here? What are the pros and cons of this location?

Results

The results for time-lapse analysis, Space Syntax analysis, and interviews are discussed in two sections: first, an analysis of the design studio as a whole and second a detailed analysis of the four areas: collaborative spaces, social spaces, individual workspaces, and the classroom.

Overall Studio Time-Lapse Data Overview

A time-lapse video of the graduate design studio was filmed for 2 weeks (February 25–March 5 2014 and April 1–8, 2014). A total of 361.5 h (15 days) were recorded with five studio time-lapse cameras. One camera was in the kitchen/social space, two in the collaborative spaces, and two in the individual desk areas. Pictures were taken every minute to capture were people worked.

The time-lapse videos were coded to count the number of people working at each location each minute (e.g., table, desk, chair). Occupancy was calculated by taking the average number of occupants and dividing it by the number of students enrolled in the graduate design programs in the academic year 2013–2014 ($n = 37$).

In the 2 weeks of time-lapse observations, on average the design studio was occupied by at least one person 67 % of the time (53 % occupied on weekdays, and 13.5 % on weekends) and empty 33 % of the time. The overall average weekday occupancy was approximately four students (SD 4.78) 10 % of students, median two students. Overall, peak occupancy was 23 students (62 % occupancy).

Table 5.1 Student occupancy in design studio on weekdays and weekend based on 37 graduate students in a 2-week time-lapse study, pictures taken every minute, (February 25–March 5, 2014 and April 1–8, 2014)

	Morning	Lunch	Afternoon	Evening	Late night
Weekday	13.56 %	33.36 %	36.60 %	17.34 %	2.99 %
Weekend	2.12 %	12.50 %	16.34 %	8.03 %	1.14 %

Table 5.2 Weekday student occupancy in the individual workspaces, collaborative spaces, and social spaces in the design studio based on 37 enrolled graduate students based during a 2-week time-lapse study (February 25–March 5, 2014 and April 1–8, 2014). The time-lapse pictures were taken at 1-min intervals to capture where students stopped to work

	Morning	Lunch	Afternoon	Evening	Late night
Individual desk area	4.81 %	16.17 %	13.95 %	9.16 %	1.94 %
Collaboration spaces	3.12 %	7.34 %	8.96 %	3.50 %	0.32 %
Social spaces	3.48 %	7.07 %	7.10 %	3.31 %	0.47 %
Classroom	2.15 %	2.78 %	6.58 %	1.38 %	0.27 %

Weekday morning occupancy (7–11:29 am) ranged from 0 to 21 students with an average of five students (SD 3.75), approximately 14 % occupancy (median five students). Weekday lunchtime occupancy (11:30 am–1:29 pm) ranged from 2 to 23 students with an average of 12 students (SD 4.78) approximately 33 % occupancy, median 11 students. Weekday afternoon occupancy (1:30–4:29 pm) ranged from 3 to 23 students with an average of 12 students, approximately 37 % occupancy, median 12 students. Weekday evening occupancy (4:30–6:29 pm) ranged from 1 to 17 students with an average of six students, (SD 3.31) approximately 17 % occupancy, (median five students). Weekday late-night occupancy (6:30 pm–6:59 am) ranged from 0 to 11 students with an average of two students (SD 1.75) approximately 3 % occupancy (median one student).

Table 5.1 shows the average student occupancy calculated for weekdays and weekends according to the different times of day. Unsurprisingly, on the weekend compared to weekdays, the regular morning time was six times less popular, lunchtime and afternoon were two and half times less popular, and the late night times were half as popular.

Where the 37 graduate students choose to work in the studio varied according to the time of day. The individual workspaces were by far the most popular place to work compared to the collaboration spaces, social spaces, and the classroom. In Table 5.2, occupancy in the individual spaces was calculated by dividing the total number of people counted in each location during the particular time periods divided by the total number of graduate students enrolled in the 2013–2014 academic year (n = 37).

Table 5.3 illustrates where people worked in studio during weekdays. For the main studio areas—individual workspaces, collaboration spaces, social spaces, and

Table 5.3 Total counts of people on weekdays by studio area and percent of the total observed in each space for 2 weeks based on a 2-week time-lapse study (February 25–March 5, 2014 and April 1–8, 2014). The time-lapse pictures were taken at 1-min intervals to document where people work

	Individual desks	Collaboration spaces	Social spaces	Classroom
People counted	34,260	18,459	14,458	9753
Percent of total	44.53 %	23.99 %	18.79 %	12.68 %

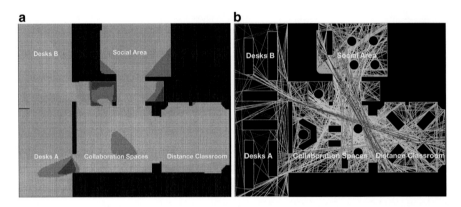

Fig. 5.2 (**a**, *left*) isovist visibility graph of the graduate design studio. *Red* indicates the most visible locations and blue indicates the least visible locations. Shades in-between have intermediate visibility. (**b**, *right*) The most connected lines are *red*, the least connected lines are *blue*, and the shades in-between represent intermediate connectivity

classroom. The total number of people counted working in the main four studio areas and the percentages of the total people counted by area.

Students worked in the classroom outside of scheduled class times or during in-class work-sessions. Usually during class lectures the garage door was closed to avoid bothering other people working in the studio spaces. The people working in the classroom were counted only when the garage door between the collaboration spaces and the classroom was open. Where people worked in the classroom was visible in the time-lapse footage only with the garage door open.

Space Syntax Isovist Analysis and Connectivity Analysis of Whole Studio

In this section, the Space Syntax analysis of the overall studio is described from the perspective of visibility of spaces and connectivity between spaces.

Figure 5.2a is an isovist visibility graph that shows how visible each in a space is to all other points in that space. An isovist for a point shows all the points are visible from that point. In the visibility graph, red indicates the most visible locations and blue indicates the least visible locations. Shades in-between have intermediate visibility. In areas that are more visible, one can see more of the surrounding areas but also is more exposed to the surrounding areas. In the individual desk areas, the more visible spaces coincide with the bottom left portion of Fig. 5.2a and the center portion of the collaboration space. Less visible areas coincide with the private conference room and the lower right section of the social space. Notice two of the large displays on the left side of the classroom are less visible than the other two displays on the right side of the classroom.

Connectivity is the second measure of interest in the graduate studio. It allows one to infer where are people more likely to be in a space. Connectivity measures the links possible from one location in a space to other locations in a space. More connected locations are more likely to have more foot traffic compared to other less connected locations. Chance encounters are more likely in more connected locations compared to less connected locations. In a studio setting, more connected areas are more desirable to meet people but less desirable for teams or individuals focused on completing a task uninterrupted.

In Fig. 5.2b, the most connected lines are red, the least connected lines are blue, and the shades in-between denote intermediate connectivity. The most connected paths form a pathway from the kitchen headed to the classroom and a path across the collaborative space to the classroom.

In the sections that follow, the time-lapse data and excerpts from interviews are used to describe where participants choose to work in the various spaces to uncover usage patterns. The names of participants in the field notes were changed preserve privacy. Observed behavior is explained with Space Syntax analysis and features of the furniture and environment. There are four parts to this section: first, the social space; second, the collaborative spaces; third, the distance learning classroom, and fourth, the individual workspace areas. For each section I describe: (a) an overview of the area; (b) time-lapse counts for subareas, (c) space syntax visibility analysis and connectivity analysis, and (d) anecdotes from the semi-structured interviews.

Social Space

In the social space there are four round tables, a standing height table near to the fridge and sink, and two tall-back armchairs (Fig. 5.1). Figure 5.3a, b are photographs from the time-lapse footage of the social space. The main entrance to the studio connects to the social space and the collaboration space.

Table 5.4, shows the number of people counted in at each location in the social area. The tall table is by far the most popular destination in the social space. It is on wheels and located close to the fridge, sink, microwave, and counter, it accommodates eight people standing comfortably and has four tall stools. It is a clear destination for socializing and informal interaction. People eat, work, and interact socially there. The standing height makes it easy for people to stop by without having to sit down and commit to occupying a chair. There are four round

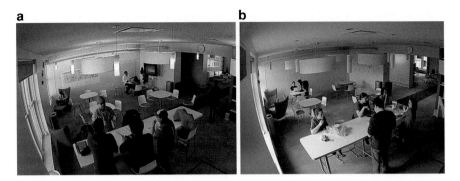

Fig. 5.3 Still images from the social space. (**a** *left*) In the far left student does individual work, at the Tall Table students socialize and work, and in Table D faculty member and student discuss. (**b** *right*) Work and social at Table C and students eating at the Tall Table

Table 5.4 Social space time-lapse data as number of people counted at each location for in the social space during a 2-week time-lapse study (February 25–March 5, 2014 and April 1–8, 2014). A summary of the Space Syntax analysis (i.e., isovist, connectivity) is provided with of the main values present in Fig. 5.2a, b

Time-lapse	Tall table	Table A	Table B	Arm chair	Table C	WB1	Table D	WB2
Morning	1123	260	244	54	613	0	1101	126
Lunch	964	470	644	102	453	58	610	11
Afternoon	933	735	737	322	1624	94	939	122
Evening	468	174	112	286	244	12	351	24
Late-night	478	25	54	2	140	0	196	332
Weekday total	3966	1664	1791	766	3074	164	3197	615
Space Syntax								
Isovist	4	4	4	3	3	3	2	2
Connectivity	8	5	7	3	3	3	3	3
Features								
Window	Nearby	Nearby	Far	Nearby	Nearby	Nearby	Far	Far
Whiteboard	None	None	None	Yes	Yes	–	Yes	–
Seat Height	Standing	Chair	Chair	Low	Chair	–	Chair	–
Number of seats	8 (4 stools)	4 chairs	4 chairs	1–2	4 chairs	–	4 chairs	–
Power outlets	None	None	None	Yes	Yes	–	Yes	–
Screen privacy	None	None	None	Yes	Some	–	Some	–

tables. Closest to the tall table is table A next to the window; table B is closest to the entryway. Closest to the wall sized whiteboards are table C next to the window and table D in the corner. Table C and table D are close to electrical outlets whereas Table A and Table B are not. Teams using the whiteboard tend to work in table D. Table C usually is occupied when the armchair is empty, and the whiteboard near the table is used less than the whiteboard near Table D.

Evident in the time-lapse videos are the transitions from one space to the other. For example, two students may be hanging out at the tall table waiting for team members to show up for a meeting. The field interview notes below illustrate how students transition through multiple activities ranging from individual work, socializing, and teamwork. I posit that the popularity of the tall table might be explained other known effects such as the "water cooler" effect and the "kitchen" effect (e.g., Allen and Henn 2007). People are drawn to the access to food and drink there. Furthermore, the standing height table makes it easy for people to have a pit stop with a brief social encounter, and then head elsewhere to work.

The high visibility and high connectivity reinforce the Tall Table as a destination for congregating and also a central departure point.

> You can socialize with people arriving in studio getting water. You can ask people about whether they've started a homework!

The excerpt below illustrates how people transition from individual work, socializing, and teamwork.

> Around 5:30 p.m., Francine is sitting at table (D). Different people come up to her and join her for a few minutes at a time. At some point, it turns into a group project meeting. At 6:15 p.m., Francine and her three partners turn toward the whiteboard and James stands there to write things. Around 6:30 p.m., Janct and someone else are having dinner together at the tall table. They leave around 6:45 p.m. Francine's group is still meeting.

Below the field notes describe how people transition through multiple activities in the social area:

> At 11:30 a.m., class ends and a few people come out to the tall table to hang out and eat. They hang out for about 15 minutes, then it's down to just James and Randal. They're gone by 12 noon.
>
> James and Randal like to talk about pop culture and video games and how they relate to design. "If there's a critical mass of people at the tall table, more than 5 or 6, then I don't want to hang more than a minute or two because I'm introverted." Randal went on to say "Whenever I work with James on a group, we always work in the kitchen, by the whiteboard near the window in the kitchen (e.g., Table C)."

The armchair has a tall back that affords some screen privacy. One armchair is often next to the window by a warm radiator. This location is a prime location for individual work. Some students chose to work there for long stretches of time. When the armchair is available, teams may use it together with Table C.

As is clear from the field notes above, that not all locations receive the same amount of patronage from students. For example, the Tall Table receives lots of action during weekdays. Visibility, Connectivity, and proximity to windows do not seem to explain the differences between the Tall Table, Table A, and Table B.

The key distinctions are based on distance to the kitchen, and height of table. The Tall Table is closer to the filtered water dispenser, refrigerator, sink, microwave, and so forth. The height of the table seems more conducive to brief uncommitted social interactions compared to a sit down meal.

The round tables A and B receive similar action, but half of the use of tables C and D. Tables A and B are quite visible and quite connected compared to the less visible and connected Tables C and D. Other key differences between the more used and less used tables are: the lack of electric outlets, lack of whiteboards, and inability to use the large screen on wheels at tables A and B compared to Tables C and D. The Tall Table, Table A, and Table B afford little laptop screen privacy.

In summary, proximity to the windows, visibility, and screen privacy alone do not explain where people position themselves. The whiteboard nearest to Table D is used more than the whiteboard near Table C. At Table C at least one person can sit with his back to the whiteboard. At Table D two can achieve greater privacy of their laptop screens by sitting in the corner with their backs to the wall. Greater laptop screen privacy, access to electric outlets, and access to whiteboard seem to invite teams to collaborate at Table C and Table D. The proximity of Table A and Table B to the more trafficked areas of the room make it a good location to share a meal or have a seated conversation. The Tall Table is the best location for mostly standing fast interactions around food and drink.

Collaborative Spaces

The collaborative space hosts a range of areas: a private meeting room, two round tables for team work, a hexagonal shaped low seating area near a large whiteboard, a private couch area surrounded by screens, and lounge chairs and couches near the windows (Fig. 5.1). All areas have power outlets. The collaborative spaces are used for both individual and group work (Fig. 5.4).

Table 5.5 shows the counts of locations where people were during weekdays by time. The low height half-hexagonal shape low seating area and the living room

Fig. 5.4 Time-lapse video footage of the collaborative workspaces. (*left*) View from garage door towards meeting room. (*right*) View onto the hex seating area, individual work along the windows, and a view into the classroom with garage door open

Table 5.5 Collaborative space time-lapse data for number of people counted at each location based on a 2-week time-lapse study (February 25–March 5, 2014 and April 1–8, 2014). A summary of the Space syntax analysis for isovist and connectivity is presented, along with key features for each area

Time-lapse	Meeting room[a]	Low Hex seats	Tall Hex seats	Window chairs	Screened island	Living room	Central table	Window table
Morning	313	674	155	712	195	1440	84	86
Lunch	380	864	5	1032	342	694	355	279
Afternoon	480	2557	595	713	350	1417	596	589
Evening	246	479	92	13	120	614	122	220
Late night	673	226	43	4	0	446	4	250
Weekday total	2092	4800	890	2474	1007	4611	1161	1424
Space Syntax								
Isovist	1	4	5	5	7	5	5	5
Connectivity	5	3	4	5	5	7	8	7
Features								
Window	No	No	No	Yes	No	Yes	No	Yes
Whiteboard	Yes	Yes	Yes	No	No	Yes	No	No
Seat height	Chair	Low	Stool	Low	Low	Low	Chair	Chair
Number of seats	4	8	9	2	4	4	4	4
Power outlets	Yes	Yes	Yes	Yes	Yes	Yes	Yes	Yes
Visual privacy	Yes	Some	None	Some	Yes	Some	None	Some

[a]Due to frosted glass on the meeting room walls, we counted when the conference room was in use, not how many were in it. There were four chairs in the conference room

"couch area" were by far the most popular. The meeting room was used quite a bit as well. It has a large screen display and a large whiteboard. Due to the frosted glass on the walls, we were unable to count how many people occupied it. The meeting room was used both for individual work and teamwork.

From a space syntax perspective, two of the most connected pathways, based on the geometry of the space, run through and intersect in the collaborative space (Fig. 5.2b). The first path connects the social space kitchen with the classroom. The second path connects Desk Area B to the classroom. These two paths intersect in proximity of a centrally located round table.

Visibility between spaces varies along with space connectivity. The collaboration space is a central hub because it is connected to every other space ranging from the entryway, social space, classroom, meeting room, individual workspaces, and the bathroom.

Interestingly, the collaborative areas are being used for individual work, collaboration, and social activity. The half-hexagonal low seating area is being used for teamwork. The central regions are being used for collaborative work (i.e., hex shaped seating, round tables, meeting room). Counter intuitively, in the middle of the collaboration spaces, on a blue couch surrounded by grey screens some nap, work, and others talk.

The hexagon shaped seating area near the whiteboard is another focus area for teamwork and individual work. The lower seating areas are used for longer meetings and the tall stools seem to be used for shorter meetings. Students collaborate on fun activities as well.

> 8:10 p.m. Several students stand behind the hexagonal couch to watch something on the TV on wheels. They're playing video games, starting around 9 pm. They were too tired to work. Wanda was helping Jenna write an essay; James and Randall are being loud with the video games so Wanda and Jenna join in. They play for almost two hours.

As with the social area described previously, students transition fluidly between individual tasks, socializing, and teamwork. The field notes below describe transitions around the central and window round tables.

> 10 a.m.: several people sitting at round tables during class, until 11:30 a.m.
>
> 11:50 a.m.: Louise, Christine, Kendall, and Lannie sit at round table. Dan walks up. They are chatting during lunch. People come and go as Christine and Lannie stay there. Kendall sits down around 12:25 p.m. By 12:40, only Christine is. By 1 p.m., others return and wait for design studio class to begin at 1:30 pm.
>
> Dan's is back, just to hang out. King says they like to have lunch between the two classes, "transition design seminar" and "graduate design studio." If they want to meet as a group before the "graduate design studio" class, they like to do it at the round tables. Otherwise they just have lunch and socialize during that time. (11:30 am to 1:30 pm)
>
> Noon: Zane, Jenna, and two others sit at a round table for a meeting. Zane writes on the whiteboard on wheels. They disperse after about 2 hours. Zane stays behind for a bit and works on stuff by himself.

Individual work is done in spaces near the windows: the tall back armchairs, the low blue couches, and the round table near the window. At times the blue couches and the round table are used for group work. The work areas closest the windows are popular for individual work. The high back chairs, and the grey screens behind the blue couch allow some privacy to laptop displays. Facing outside allows people doing individual work to have a view onto trees, lawns, and campus bustle and give their back to the nearby distractions in the studio. Individuals working at the round table near the window tend to face inside the studio thus placing themselves with their back to the wall. There are two plausible explanations: first, laptop screen privacy is more important than a view out the window; and second, facing into the studio is a defensive strategy to avoid unwanted intrusion to the round table (Sommer 1969 p. 62). From the observations four factors seem important for individual work: laptop screen privacy, having ones back covered, avoiding unwanted distraction, and defending a territory from intrusion.

In summary, quite surprising is the range of uses that the students used the collaborative spaces for ranging from sleep, to individual work, teamwork, socializing, and play. Individual work occurs predominantly in near the windows with seating arrangements that maximize laptop screen privacy. As with the social spaces, the conditions around the collaborative spaces along with the features help to determine the uses.

Classroom

The classroom is used for classes and is a place for students to work. Sometimes teams work in the classroom during class and other times they work in the classroom outside of scheduled class times (Figs. 5.5 and 5.6). As described previously, glass garage door separates the classroom from the rest of the studio (Fig. 5.1).

Food and drinks are not allowed in the classroom because the tables have built in video conferencing technology. Some professors lecture with the "glass garage door" open that separates the classroom and the collaboration spaces to allow

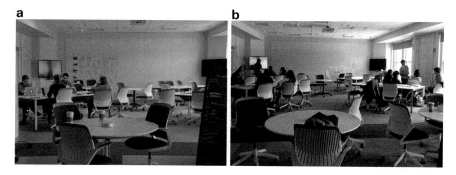

Fig. 5.5 Classroom seen from the collaboration spaces with the garage door open. (**a** *left*) One student group working at Table D. Notice the drinks in the foreground on the collaborative space round tables outside of the classroom. Food and drinks are not allowed in the classroom because the tables have built in video conferencing technology. (**b** *right*) Student teams work during design studio class at Tables A, C, and D

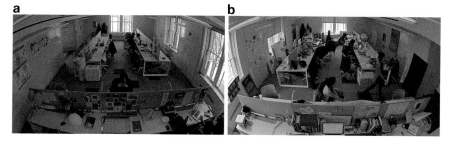

Fig. 5.6 (**a** *left*) The individual workspaces in desk Area A on the left with an opening next to the collaborative spaces were occupied less frequently than desks in Area B on the right side next to the bathroom and printers (**b** *right*)

Table 5.6 Classroom
time-lapse data for number of
people counted at each
location based on a 2-week
time-lapse study (February
25–March 5, 2014 and April
1–8, 2014). A summary of the
Space syntax analysis for
isovist and connectivity is
presented, along with key
features for each area

Time-lapse	Table A	Table B	Table C	Table D
Morning	969	205	383	677
Lunch	384	299	363	315
Afternoon	1597	602	1347	1127
Evening	156	123	332	64
Late-night	98	0	394	318
Weekdays total	3204	1229	2819	2501
Average people	0.24	0.09	0.21	0.18
Space Syntax				
Isovist	4	4	4	4
Connectivity	3	3	5	5
Features				
Window	No	Yes	Yes	No
Whiteboard	3.5	2.5	1	2
Seat height	Chair	Chair	Chair	Chair
Number of seats	8	8	8	8
Power outlets	8	8	8	8
Visual privacy	No	No	No	No
Large display	Visible	Visible	Private	Private

students to eat and drink during class. The glass garage door provides acoustic separation between the classroom and the rest of the studio environment. Other times professors open the "glass garage door" after a lecture to transition from lecture to group work. Students often go on to work elsewhere in the studio. When the classroom is available, teams and students work in there.

Table 5.6 shows where students worked during weekdays. Unsurprisingly, Table A, with the large whiteboard was most used has 3.5 whiteboard panels (on average 0.24 people on weekdays). Table C, with the smallest whiteboard close to a window was the second most used table had 1 whiteboard panel (on average 0.21 people on weekdays). Table D was the third most used table had two whiteboard panels (on average 0.18 people on weekdays). Table B has the second largest whiteboard next to a window but is the least used table (on average 0.09 people on weekdays).

While the average number of people at a table explains what table was most popular for groups, the average occupancy by at least one person tells the story of what tables were most occupied. Table C, next to the window, with was most occupied (0.12), Table A and Table D were occupied about the same (0.09), and Table B was occupied the least (0.07). The patterns of occupancy differ less than the average number of people per table described in the previous paragraph.

Average number of occupants and average times the table is occupied by at least one person tells a different story. Table B had almost less than half the number of people compared to Table D, but was occupied only 22 % less. The discrepancy in average number of people and occupancy may suggest that Table B was used by individual occupants wanting to be close to the window whereas Tables A and

D were more popular for team work. The second highest average number of people and the highest occupancy for Table C can be interpreted to mean that it was popular for both teamwork and individual work.

When counting the whiteboard panels available, one would expect Table B, with the second largest quantity of whiteboard panels, to be the second most popular table instead of the least used table. One possible explanation is that Table A and Table B share a whiteboard. Students likely first pick Table A because it has whiteboards on two sides of the table, but in so doing Table B becomes less attractive because it has a shared whiteboard with Table A (see Fig. 5.5 above).

Less effort to reach the tables from the studio might explain why tables C and D are so popular. Table C and Table D are closest to the rest of the studio whereas Table A and Table B are furthest away from the rest of the studio. From a connectivity perspective, Table A and Table B are less connected to the rest of the studio compared to Table C and Table D.

Distance between tables is another variable to consider. The largest distance between tables is on the diagonals of the room. Table A is furthest from Table C and Table B is furthest from Table D. Conversely Table A is closest to table B, and Table C is closest to Table D. Hence, when tables are already occupied, trying to maximize distance from that table may partially influence where choose to people. The heuristic of maximizing distance between occupants to reduce acoustic interference and interruptions is a relative heuristic depending on what spaces are occupied, and what spaces are available. Such a heuristic is possible only with low occupancy.

Being close to a window can provide a pleasant view if one is facing outside, but can be a source of glare on a laptop screen. However the tables close to the window, Table B is least popular and Table C is second most popular. Based on the observations in the classroom, for teamwork it does not seem as if being close to a window seems to add great value. Clearly other variables are at play to explain the use of the tables.

Each of the four tables has a large display. While there are no significant differences in visibility for participants in the four tables, two tables have more private large displays. As is clear in Fig. 5.2a, the large displays have different levels of visual privacy. The large displays at Table D and Table C have the most visual privacy and were the second and third most used tables. It would seem that privacy of the large displays is a valuable feature for teamwork.

Table A is the most used, lacks large display privacy, the most whiteboard space, and is the furthest away from the studio. Table C has: large display visual privacy, the smallest whiteboard, adjacent to the window, and close to the studio. Table D has large display privacy, the second largest whiteboard, and is close to the studio. In short, Table A has the largest whiteboard and that seems to be more important than large display privacy (Tables D, C). However, having to pick between two tables with equal large display privacy (Tables D, C), students tend to pick Table C. It has the smallest whiteboard, a window and is the furthest one from the most occupied place (Table A).

In summary, where people choose to work in the classroom is quite complex. Students likely consider multiple factors to decide what the spaces best might support their work. The table by the window that is appealing for individual work differs from the best table for team whiteboarding sessions, and two tables have more private large displays. Another factor to consider, is that occupants may use heuristics such has preferring tables that maximize distance from other occupied tables to reduce sound interference.

Individual Workspaces

The individual workspace areas A and B were conceived as individual quiet work areas (Fig. 5.1). Some students worked frequently at their individual desk, and others mostly used their desk to store belongings in the locked desk drawers.

Table 5.7 illustrates weekday raw counts by time of occupancy. As described previously (Table 5.3), the individual desk areas account for approximately 45 % of the counts of students in the whole studio on weekdays. Students preferred individual desk area A less (17 % of total weekday data) than individual Desk Area B (28 % of weekday data). Both areas have similar features: surface areas, number of windows, whiteboards, and similar connectivity to the rest of the studio.

Overall, in average there were 1.71 (SD 2.38) students in the individual workspace areas (15 max; 0 min). On average, fewer people occupied the individual workspaces A (0.62 people; SD 1.21; max 10, min 0) compared to the individual

Table 5.7 Individual workspace time-lapse data for number of people counted at each location based on a 2-week time-lapse study (February 25–March 5, 2014 and April 1–8, 2014). Space syntax analysis for isovist and connectivity along with key features for each area are provided

Time-lapse	Desks A	Desks B
Morning	2743	2518
Lunch	3672	4250
Afternoon	3928	6754
Evening	1403	3067
Late-night	1076	4849
Weekdays	12,822	21,438
Space Syntax		
Isovist	5–7	3–4
Connectivity	1–2	1–2
Features		
Window	3	3
Whiteboard	4	3
Seat height	Chair	Chair
Number of seats	20	20
Power outlets	20	20
Visual privacy	4	7

workspaces B (1.09 people, SD 1.49; max 9, min 0). The Desk Area A were occupied by at least one person 54 % of the time, compared to individual workspace B desk area occupied 52 % of the time.

One key difference between individual desk areas A and B regards visibility and prospect refuge exposure. From the Isovist Map perspective, Individual Desk Area A is more visible compared Individual Desk Area B (Fig. 5.2). Furthermore, fewer desks in Desk Area A allow students to work with their backs to the wall (4 of 20 desks) compared to Desk Area B (7 of 20 desks). Individual Desk Area A is further away from the bathroom and printers compared to Individual Desk Area B.

Other factors to consider include class schedule differences in first and second year students. First year students usually spend more time in classes and hence have fewer hours to work at individual desks in the afternoon hours. However, schedule alone does not seem to fully explain the differences at times when classes are not being held.

In summary, as with the other areas of the studio, in the individual workspace areas, it is possible to see how multiple factors are at play, and users parse many variables to decide where to work. The individual workspace area occupancy differences highlight how individual and group choices mutually influence each other. For example, the second year students picked the better desks from a visibility and privacy perspective, and such group behavior influenced what seats were available for the first year students. The first year students perhaps then sought out the best available places to do their individual work elsewhere in the studio (e.g., social spaces, collaboration spaces, classroom).

Summary and Future Work

Given the recent changes in design studio education and the increasing interest in design thinking in other disciplines, it is important to identify and describe the individual work and collaboration hotspots in design studios accurately. In this chapter, I described a graduate design studio in first tier research university with three methods: time-lapse movies, Space Syntax analysis of visibility and connectivity, and semi-structured interviews. The design studio described includes four interconnected spaces to support multiple work preferences: an area with individual workspaces for 40 students, collaborative space with an enclosed team room, a kitchen and social cafe area and a distance-learning capable classroom. Even though this case study is in an academic setting, the insights likely apply more broadly to creative workplaces.

In the social space, participants fluidly cycled through multiple activities such as: socializing, snacking, individual work, and groupwork. The location of the Tall Table next to the kitchen, its connectedness to other spaces, and the tall table height converged to create a dynamic location for quick informal interactions around work, food, and drink. The two less used round tables for teamwork were used for informal meetings and socializing had the following features: lacked electric outlets and whiteboards, and were near connected spaces with foot traffic. The two more used round tables were in less connected and visible portions of the room, were next to wall-sized whiteboards, and had electrical outlets. Occupancy of the armchair next to the window in the corner seemed to co-occur with teams working at the furthest available table with a whiteboard. Teams tended to prefer the tables with most privacy, whiteboard surface available, and less connected.

In the collaboration spaces, surprisingly there was a broad range of activities ranging from group work, individual work, collective play, sleeping, meals, and waiting for classes to begin. Individual work mostly occurred close to the windows in armchairs, couches, and a round table. Collaborative work mostly occurred in the half-hexagon low seating facing the whiteboard, in the closed meeting room, at the round tables, and in the couch areas. The two round tables were used to wait for a class to begin, or during class when the garage door to the classroom was open. Surprisingly, only three of the collaborative areas had a whiteboard surfaces, the half-hex seating, meeting room, and couch area near the window.

The classroom tables were used for both individual and groupwork. The four classroom tables, each with a large display and eight chairs, were used very differently outside of scheduled classes. Features such as proximity to whiteboards, windows, privacy of shared display, and distance from other tables seemed to most influence occupancy patterns. The table with the most whiteboard surface was preferred over tables that had more private large displays.

In the two individual desk areas, occupancy differed to a large extent. Features such as visibility, acoustics, and prospect-refuge seemed to best explain the occupancy differences. One limitation to this work is that unlike professional design studios where going to work is required, in a university design studio, outside of scheduled class times, students are free to work anywhere they choose. The freedom to work anywhere' may in part explain the low occupancy percentages observed in this study. However, the low occupancy allowed students to discriminate between available spaces and pick the best available. The least used spaces were then examined in detail to explain why that might be so.

Further research is necessary to explore alternative explanations to phenomena described in this chapter. For example, in the social spaces, might table occupancy patterns for the central tables significantly change with the introduction of electric outlets and mobile whiteboards? Or would replacing the Tall Table with a regular height table and chairs deeply change the social dynamics?

In the collaboration spaces, might replacing the quiet "private island" screened couch used for sleeping and conversations with a standing height table for collaboration, large display, and whiteboards on wheels, create a dynamic team space?

In the classroom, would the addition of whiteboards on wheels allow teams to increase the visual privacy of large displays shift the usage patterns?

In the Individual Desk Area A, might adding a frosted glass door reduce visibility and acoustic interference from the collaborative spaces thus increasing occupancy of the desks?

This on-going research illustrates how nuanced users are of work environments, and how important even minor features are to usage patterns. As HCI engages with interior spaces including Space Syntax analysis of visibility and connectivity and a detailed analysis of features such as sitting height of furniture, access to large displays, and so forth will play critical roles in the success of the new generation of technologically enhanced work environments.

Acknowledgements I would like to thank the Berkman Faculty Development Fund at Carnegie Mellon University for partially supporting this research; Andrea Fineman, Xiaowei Jiang, Yin Wang for their assistance with field observations, data collection, and time-lapse coding; Chang Liu for her assistance with the Space Syntax analyses; Professor Bruce Hanington, the Director of Graduate Studies, for his support of this research effort; and three anonymous reviewers for their insightful suggestions.

References

Allen TJ (1977) Managing the flow of technology. MIT Press, Cambridge, MA
Allen TJ, Henn G (2007) The organization and architecture of innovation: managing the flow of technology. Elsevier, Amsterdam
Appleton J (1975) The experience of landscape. Wiley, London
Barker RG (1968) Ecological psychology. Stanford University Press, Stanford
Batty M (2001) Exploring isovist fields: space and shape in architectural and urban morphology. Environ Plan B 28(1):123–150
Benedikt ML (1979) To take hold of space: isovists and isovists fields. Environ Plan B 6:47–65
Bier H, De Jong A, Van Der Hoorn G, Brouwers N, Heule M, Van Maaren H (2008, Jan) Prototypes for automated architectural 3D-layout. In: Proceedings of the 13th international conference on virtual systems and multimedia, Springer, Berlin, pp 203–214
Brown T, Kātz B (2009) Change by design: how design thinking transforms organizations and inspires innovation. Harper Business, New York
Choi YK (1999) The morphology of exploration and encounter in museum layouts. Environ Plan B: Plan Des 26(2):241–250
Dalton N, Marshall P, Dalton R (2013) Extending architectural theories of space syntax to understand the effect of environment on the salience of situated displays. In: Proceedings of the 2nd ACM international symposium on pervasive displays, ACM, Mountain View, pp 73–78
Doorley S, Witthoft S (2012) Make space: how to set the stage for creative collaboration. Wiley, Hoboken
Festinger L, Schacter S, Back K (1950) Social pressures in informal groups: a study of human factors in housing. Stanford University Press, Palo Alto
Flemming U, Baykan CA, Coyne RF, Fox MS (1992) Hierarchical generate-and-test vs constraint-directed search. Springer, Dordrecht, pp 817–838
Georgoulas C, Linner T, Bock T (2014) Towards a vision controlled robotic home environment. Autom Constr 39:106–116
Goodwin C, Goodwin MH (1996) Seeing as a situated activity: formulating planes. In: Engeström Y, Middleton D (eds) Cognition and communication at work. Cambridge University Press, Cambridge, pp 61–95
Goffman E (1963) Behavior in public places; notes on the social organization of gatherings. Free Press of Glencoe, New York

Green KE, Walker ID, Gugerty LJ, Witte JC, Houayek H, Kwoka M, Johnson J, Teja K Kuntzi N
    (2009) AWE: a robotic wall and reconfigurable desk supporting working life in a digital society.
    In: IEEE/RSJ International Conference on Intelligent Robots and Systems, 2009 (IROS 2009),
    pp 406–407
Haq S (2003) Investigating the syntax line: configurational properties and cognitive correlates.
    Environ Plan B: Plan Des 30(6):841–863
Hatch MJ (1987) Physical barriers, task characteristics, and interaction activity in research and
    develop-ment firms. Adm Sci Q 32:387–399
Hawkey K, Kellar M, Reilly D, Whalen T, Inkpen KM (2005) The proximity factor: impact of
    distance on co-located collaboration. In: Proceedings of GROUP '05. ACM Press, New York,
    pp 31–40
Hazlewood WR, Dalton N, Marshall P, Rogers Y, Hertrich S (2010) Bricolage and consultation:
    addressing new design challenges when building large-scale installations. In: Proceedings of
    8th ACM conference on designing interactive systems, Aarhus, Denmark, pp 380–389
Hillier B (1996) Space is the machine: a configurational theory of architecture. Cambridge
    University Press, Cambridge
Hillier B, Hanson J (1984) The social logic of space. Cambridge University Press, Cambridge
Hillier B, Penn A (1991) Visible colleges: structure and randomness in the place of discovery. Sci
    Context 4(01):23–50
Hillier B, Hanson J, Peponis J (1984) What do we mean by building function? In: Powell JA,
    Cooper I, Lera S (eds) Designing for building utilisation. E & F.N. Spon Ltd, London, pp 61–72
Hillier B, Penn A, Hanson J, Grajewski T, Xu J (1993) Natural movement: or, configuration and
    attraction in urban pedestrian movement. Environ Plan B: Plan Des 20(1):29–66
Huang EM (2007) When does the public look at public displays? In Companion proceedings of
    the conference on Ubiquitous Computing, UbiComp 2007, Innsbruck, Austria
Huang EM, Koster A, Borcher J (2008) Overcoming assumptions and uncovering practices: when
    does the public really look at public displays?. In: Lecture notes in computer science, vol 5013,
    Pervasive 2008, Springer Link, Sydney, pp 228–243
Kaarlela-Tuomaala A, Helenius R, Keskinen E, Hongisto V (2009) Effects of acoustic environment
    on work in private office rooms and open-plan offices – longitudinal study during relocation.
    Ergonomics 52(11):1423–1444
Koppel MT, Bailly G, Müller J, Walter R (2012) Chained displays: configurations of public
    displays can be used to influence actor-, audience-, and passer-by behavior. In: Proceedings
    of CHI 2012. ACM, Austin, pp 317–326
Koch A, Schewennsen K, Dutton T, Smith D (2002) Redesign of studio culture: a report of the
    AIAS studio culture taskforce. American Institute of Architecture Students, INC, Washington,
    DC. Demystified. Architectural Press, Oxford
Kraut RE, Fish R, Root R, Chalfonte B (1990) Informal communication in organizations: form,
    function, and technology. In: Oskamp S, Spacapan S (eds) Human reactions to technology:
    Claremont symposium on applied social psychology. Sage, Beverly Hills, pp 145–199
Olson JS, Teasley S, Covi L, Olson G (2002) The (currently) unique advantages of collocated
    work. Distributed work, 113–135
Peponis J, Zimring C (1996) Designing friendly hospital layouts. The contributions of space-
    syntax. J Healthc Des 8:109–116
Peponis J, Ross C, Rashid M (1997) The structure of urban space, movement and co-presence: the
    case of Atlanta. Geoforum 28(3):341–358
Rashid M, Wineman J, Zimring C (2009) Space, behavior, and environmental perception in open-
    plan offices: a prospective study. Environ Plan B: Plan and Des 36(3):432–449
Rogers Y, Rodden T (2003) Configuring spaces and surfaces to support collaborative interactions.
    In: O'Hara K, Perry M, Churchill E, Russell D (eds) Public and situated displays. Kluwer
    Publishers, Dordrecht, pp 45–79
Schmidt K, Bannon L (1992) Taking CSCW seriously: supporting articulation work. J Comput
    Supported Coop Work 1(1):7–40

Schmidt C, Muller J, Bailly G (2013) Screenfinity: extending the perception area of content on very large public displays. In: Proceedings of CHI2013. ACM, Paris, pp 1719–1728

Scoppa MD, Peponis J (2015) Distributed attraction: the effects of street network connectivity upon the distribution of retail frontage in the City of Buenos Aires. Environ Plan B: Plan Des 42(2):354–37

Scupelli P, Hanington B (2014) An evidence-based design approach for function, usability, emotion, and pleasure in studio redesign. In: Lim Y-K, Niedderer K, Redström J, Stolterman E, Valtonen A (eds) Proceedings of DRS 2014: design's big debates. Umeå Institute of Design, Umeå University, Umeå

Scupelli P, Kiesler S, Fussell SR (2007) Using isovist views to study placement of large displays in natural settings. In: CHI'07, ACM, San Jose, pp 2645–2650

Scupelli P, Xiao Y, Fussell SR, Kiesler S, Gross MD (2010, April) Supporting coordination in surgical suites: physical aspects of common information spaces. In: Proceedings of the SIGCHI conference on human factors in computing systems, ACM, pp 1777–1786

Sommer R (1969) Personal space: the behavioral basis of design. Prentice-Hall, Englewood Cliffs

Sproewitz A, Billard A, Dillenbourg P, Ijspeert AJ (2009) Roombots-mechanical design of self-reconfiguring modular robots for adaptive furniture. In: IEEE International Conference on Robotics and Automation, 2009 (ICRA'09), 4259–4264

Su R, Bailey B (2005) Towards guidelines for positioning large displays in interactive workspaces. In: Proceedings of INTERACT 2005, LNCS 3585, 337–349

Suchman L (1997) Centers of coordination: a case and some themes. In: Resnick L, Saljo R, Pontecorvo C (eds) Discourse, tools, and reasoning: essays on situated cognition. Springer, Berlin

Turner A (2001) Depthmap: a program to perform visibility graph analysis. In: Proceedings of the 3rd international space syntax symposium, Atlanta

Turner A, Doxa M, O'sullivan D, Penn A (2001) From isovists to visibility graphs: a methodology for the analysis of architectural space. Environ Plan B 28(1):103–121

Underhill P (1999) Why we buy: the science of shopping. Simon & Schuster, New York

Varoudis T, Dalton S, Alexiou K, Zamenopoulos T (2011) Ambient displays: influencing move-ment pat-terns. In: CHI'11. ACM, Vancouver, pp 1225–1230

Wigdor D, Shen C, Forlines C, Balakrishnan R (2006) Effects of display position and control space orientation on user preference and performance. In: Proceedings of CHI2006, ACM Press, New York

Whittaker S, Schwarz H (1999) Meetings of the board: the impact of scheduling medium on long term group coordination in software development. Comput Supported Coop Work (CSCW) 8(3):175–205

Chapter 6
Getting It Going: Explorations at the Intersection of Moving Bodies, Information Technology and Architecture

Fatemeh Moradi and Mikael Wiberg

> *"Space is a hidden feature of movement and movement is a visible aspect of space."*
>
> Rudolf von Laban

Abstract Our bodily experience of space and time is primarily con by the architecture around us. Through architecture we fuse our image of self with our experience in the world. It articulates our experience of being-in-the-world and shapes our bodily movement. Moreover in this new age of technological development we inhabit architectural spaces with both material and digital fabrications. The concept of space is both socially and materially constructed through our daily lives. One space in which we spend much of our adulthood is the office or workplace. Throughout history, designers and technocrats have planned workspaces and thereby (in)directly influenced our bodily movements during work hours. Their designs have tended to make our bodies stationary and passive in these social and architectural spaces. This chapter examines the intersection of moving bodies, Information Technology, and architectural spaces, asking how contemporary workspace design affects bodily movements in working hours. During our studies we have conceptualized "Moving Bodies" as an interactive element in office spaces, and we conclude the chapter by introducing a sensory ambient display designed for "Moving Bodies" in offices and exploring its impact on their social and architectural space.

Introduction

As the world becomes more computational, our awareness of space and its influence on interaction design is increasing. This awareness includes a recognition of opportunities to introduce new modalities of human-computer interaction including approaches based on touch, gesture and body movement (Benyon et al. 2010).

F. Moradi (✉) • M. Wiberg
Department of Informatics, Umeå University, Umeå, Sweden
e-mail: fatemeh.moradi@umu.se; mwiberg@informatik.umu.se

© Springer International Publishing Switzerland 2016
N.S. Dalton et al. (eds.), *Architecture and Interaction*,
Human–Computer Interaction Series, DOI 10.1007/978-3-319-30028-3_6

Our interactive and autonomous behaviors are embedded in material objects and architectural spaces whose design blends the digital and the physical (Loke and Reinhardt 2012; Camurri et al. 2000). Users of an interactive system make physical, perceptual, and conceptual contact with its interface, all of which must be accounted for during the system's design (Benyon et al. 2005). Therefore, designers must consider the effect of their system designs on bodily movements in social and architectural spaces.

As adults we spend the majority of our daily time in workspaces. According to the United States' Department of Labor, adults aged 25–54 spend more than 8 h a day in offices or doing work-related activities (see e.g. http://www.bls.gov/tus/charts/). Therefore, we are particularly interested in investigating bodily movements in workspaces, which are perhaps the most common arenas in which social space is defined by the interaction of Information Technology and architectural space. Over the last 80 years, workspace designs have been influenced by the modernist view of scientific management (Moradi and Wiberg 2013). Based on Taylor's time and motion studies (Barnes 1968), most office spaces have been designed with the explicit aim of eliminating physical movement in order to increase productivity. As a consequence we find our bodies being mostly passive when interacting with information technologies and we have become accustomed to prolonged sitting in the context of office work (McAlpine et al. 2007). The project outlined in this chapter seeks to identify novel ways of understanding movement and mobility in office-based spaces. "Moving Bodies" is a concept that was generated on the basis of a historic review of workplace design and a series of ethnographic studies. This concept guided our effort to develop a new approach to designing for interaction in social and architectural spaces such as offices, which is centered on body movements.

The transdisciplinary InPhAct (Increasing Physical Activity) research project was initiated in the fall of 2012 and involves researchers from the departments of Informatics and Medicine as well as the School of Architecture and the Design Institute of Umeå University. As part of the project, more than 5 months of intensive ethnographic observation were conducted in two workspaces in order to investigate "Moving Bodies" within the social and architectural space. This chapter begins with a brief overview of workspace design in the past few decades and its effect on bodily movements in workplaces. We introduce "Moving Bodies" as a concept for designing prototypes in which the body functions as an interactive element within the social and architectural space. The second section of the chapter describes the methods we used to gather ethnographic data in office spaces. Based on observations from our first ethnographic study and the "Moving Bodies" concept, we designed our first sensory ambient display prototype, which is described in the chapter's third section. In the fourth section, we describe how this prototype was evaluated in our second ethnographic study and the notable outcomes of this investigation. Finally, the chapter concludes with a discussion on the use of ambient light and its relationship with "Moving Bodies" in the social and architectural space. Creating an interaction between "Moving Bodies" and architecture by means of ambient displays is a way of inhabiting the space; as Grosz and Eisenman (2001) asked, "Can architecture inhabit us as much as we see ourselves inhabiting it?" Our prototype forms a union between "Moving Bodies" and architectural space through the use of sensors, and can thus be seen as a novel example of an intersection between interaction design and architecture.

First Step: Conceptualizing Moving Bodies

Our efforts to develop "Moving Bodies" as a guiding concept for interaction design in architectural spaces have been informed by theories concerning bodily movements. These theories bear on the relationship between mobility and modernity, and its effects on "Moving Bodies" as a concept, describing the body in terms of movement and as a temporal material of existence in social and architectural spaces.

Mobility and Modernity

In our contemporary digital life, culture is dynamic rather than stationary – it is more about routes than roots (Haggett 1965). Bodily movements on different scales are associated with different meanings. In addition to simply being a displacement between locations, movement can be seen as a dynamic equivalent of place (Cresswell 2006). Mobility as a socially produced motion, is practiced, experienced and embodied. In general, mobility is a way of being in the world; as David Delaney (1999) has observed, "human mobility implicates both physical bodies moving though material landscapes and categorical figures moving through representational spaces." Moreover, mobility is part of the process of social production of time. The entrance of technology into our lives and the way it has shaped modern societies has made mobility a defining characteristic of city life.

As mobility became a major characteristic of modern life in western society, researchers studied it in various sociological contexts (Cresswell 2006; Delaney 1999; Haggett 1965). According to Lowe and Moryadas (1975), "movement occurs to the extent that people have the ability to satisfy their desire with respect to goods, services, information, or experience at some location rather than their present one, and the extent that these other locations are capable of satisfying such desires." Before mobility became a key characteristic of modern life, moral values were imagined to be closely associated with a sense of place and rootedness. It was thought that culture could only be preserved through the maintenance of class hierarchy and a strong attachment to places and regions. Culture and home were so closely linked that movement could even be seen as a threat to cultural distinctiveness (Cresswell 2006). Despite these concerns, access to mobility increased and became a dominant characteristic of modern life. In this process, mobility changed our way of knowing the world (Cresswell 2010).

The Mechanistic World View

In parallel with the molding of our worldview by modernity, scientific management arose as the manifestation of a phenomenon and a way of thinking that originated in the natural and physical sciences during the nineteenth century (Reeves et al. 2001). Reeves and his colleagues (2001) claim that, "this approach represented an important change in knowledge development paradigm and involved breaking down complex phenomenon into component parts and putting them back together in an effort to better understand the whole, appreciate interrelationships, and eventually improve efficiency". In other words, the motion and time studies that underpinned scientific management were a consequence of new ways of understanding reality and productivity.

This deterministic belief in the existence of cause and effect, uncertainty reduction, quantification and measurement, and continuity in design resulted in a mechanistic, clockwork-like view of reality (Shephard 1974). The same culture and thought process influenced society on a larger scale by changing the way work was managed. The new understanding of process relationships, which included only those elements that are absolutely necessary for the performance of the task at hand, increased the efficiency of movement within workplaces (Moradi and Wiberg 2013). The ultimate goal of scientific management according to this worldview was to understand how motions related to one another and how they could be optimally connected so as to increase the efficiency of work (Reeves et al. 2001).

The analysis of body movements in the context of scientific management was predated by studies on movement within the performing arts (e.g. theater and dance), which were pioneered by Delsarte, Dalcroze, and von Laban (Rothe 2012). These studies inspired long-running efforts in modernity to eradicate superfluous motion. The nature of movement in dance seems different to that during work: work movements appear to be obligatory and constrained whereas dance is regarded as a realm of freedom, pleasure and play. But the history of dance, like that of work, relays on arrays of disciplinary practices and deep-rooted ideologies of mobility (Cresswell 2006). There have long been scholars such as Desmond who are keen to see bodily movements primarily as social phenomena through which we enact our place in society. At the turn of twentieth century, dance, bodywork and labor were connected by the concept of rhythm (Rothe 2012).

Moving Bodies at the Individual Level

As noted above, mobility became a key characteristic of modern life on multiple levels and scales (Cresswell 2010). However, at the level of individuals and their bodies, the transition to modernity was accompanied by a gradual reduction in mobility. Even though movement of the body is the most fundamental form of mobility, and it is through the body that mobility is experienced, we are very sedentary in our daily lives (Moradi and Wiberg 2013). This may be because our current ways of knowing are insufficiently mobile at the individual level of moving bodies, leaving us stuck with sedentarist metaphysics (Cresswell 2006).

Shortly after the beginning of the modern period, researchers developed ways of capturing mobility with snapshots (Barnes 1968). Historical records show that these snapshots were used to construct charts depicting the tension between the threat of embodied motion and the potential benefits of increasing mobility. These charts in turn were used to rationalize and abstract mobility (Corlett 1983). The aim of philosophers, planners, technocrats, and others was to make mobility functional, ordered, and ultimately, knowledge-bearing (Das and Grady 1983; Grandjean et al. 1983).

Moving Bodies in Workspaces

Throughout history, there has been a tendency to design artifacts with the aim of promoting a sedentary state. Moreover, the growing tendency to view the world in mechanistic terms gradually affected our ways of designing work and workspaces (Barnes 1968; Kvålseth 1983; Shephard 1974). With the dawn of the age of industrialization, new methods and theories of work were developed in order to maximize economic efficiency and labor productivity (Giordano 1992). These ideas and approaches, which included Taylorism, time studies, and motion studies, prompted a trend in workplace design that aimed to minimize movement during the working day.

Time studies were pioneered by Taylor and involve conducting repeated measurements of the time required to complete a given work task, while the motion studies developed by the Gilbreths focused on characterizing workers' bodily movements as they work and finding ways to increase their efficiency (Cresswell 2006). In the 1930s, both of these techniques were used to identify better and simpler methods of getting specific jobs done. They were subsequently recognized to be complementary and combined in so-called time and motion studies.

The measurement of human movement was not limited to planners and technocrats such as Taylor and Gilbreths. Laban (Laban and Ullmann 1971) was a famous choreographer and movement analyst who invented a language for describing the shapes of different movements and the effort involved in performing them. His analysis provides a clear picture of the relationship between movement, space and time. The aim of his work was to formalize and describe the characteristics of human movement, something which is useful when studying both dance and everyday working practices (Davies 2007; Maletic 1987). Laban's work has consequently been used in a range of contexts outside dance, especially in the development of gestures and interaction models (Chi et al. 2000; Fagerberg et al. 2003). As someone who played a major part in shaping the modern Central European dance movement (Hodgson 2001), Laban believed that dance grows naturally out of the rhythms experienced by all individuals in their everyday lives. He therefore paid attention to the developing relationship between the human body and mechanization, and used his studies as the basis for the creation of contemporary folk dances that drew inspiration from the modern industrial environment. To Laban, dance was the supreme expression of the human condition. Perhaps because of this, he considered the most interesting and beautiful aspects of operating a machine to be the effort and shaping of the body required to perform common tasks. This is linked to his best-known invention and legacy – Labanotation (Maletic 1987), which he developed to record and analyze human movement.

Although Labanotation was originally developed for recording dance and for use in dance therapy, it also enabled a deeper and more scientific approach to analyzing human movement at work. Notably, it was used to characterize the movements of workers performing specific tasks in agriculture and industry in order to identify the most efficient ways of performing those tasks. This required an ability to describe the movements that were made and a way to assess their quality in terms of space, time and pressure. Laban's findings indicated that no two people perform a given task in quite the same way. In other words, we all have our own individual movement patterns. As Davies (2007) states in his book Beyond Dance, "Analysis of our movement pattern reveals not only how we will perform in work situations, but also a great deal about our personality and our capacity for personal relationships." Laban subsequently applied his principles to redesign assembly lines, notably one in a factory producing Mars Bars.

Second Step: Experiencing the Real

To obtain a deeper understanding of office work and its associated bodily movements, we spent more than 5 months in total conducting ethnographic studies in order to gather qualitative data on movement in workplaces. Two separate studies were performed. The first was undertaken in the fall of 2013 and examined the patterns of daily movement in an office setting over a period of 80 days. This investigation helped us to refine and optimize our methods for conducting ethnographic studies in offices and prompted the development of the concept of "Moving Bodies" as interactive elements in workspaces. Data were gathered by mapping the walking paths taken by workers, making drawings, taking notes and photographs, and conducting informal interviews (see Fig. 6.1). Eventually the data gathered in this study along with the guiding concept of "Moving Bodies" led to the design of our first prototype.

Based on the results of this first ethnographic observation and an analysis using the concept of "Moving Bodies", we attempted to design artefacts that would promote movement in the workspace. Our first attempt at such a design was a sensor-based movement artifact that has been named the "NEAT Lamp". The second study, which was conducted in the fall of 2014, was an exercise in ethnographic observation whose aim was to evaluate and prototype the "NEAT Lamp" in an office space. Like the first study, it involved recording patterns of daily movement

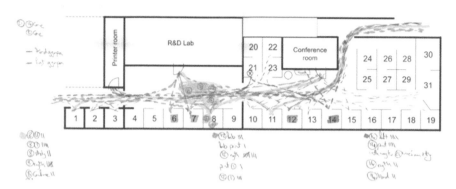

Fig. 6.1 An example of the data collected during our ethnographic studies. In this data set that was gathered during the second ethnogarphy, the six participants volunteered for testing the "NEAT Lamp" have been color coded to be distinguished from other office workers. Also the gymnastic breaks or 'pausgympa' has shown along with the other movement patterns in the office space

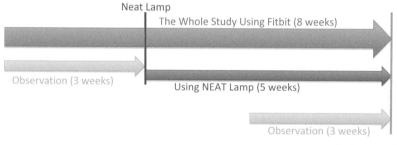

Fig. 6.2 Study plan of our second ethnographic study, evaluating "NEAT Lamp". As illustrated in the plan the six participants were equipped with Fitbits during the whole study

by making drawings, taking notes and photos, and conducting semi-structured interviews. The original aim in this work was to complement the qualitative data sources with quantitative information obtained by issuing the workers in the studied environments with Fitbits that counted their steps. As shown in Fig. 6.2, our initial plan was to conduct 6 weeks of ethnographic observation over a total period of 8 weeks. During these 8 weeks, six volunteer participants in the office were equipped with Fitbits during their working hours. After the first 3 weeks of ethnographic observation, our six volunteers were introduced to our prototype lamp. This section briefly outlines the methods used in our workspace studies, with reference to similar investigations reported by other authors. We then describe how we defined moving bodies in workspaces and present the key results and experiences gained from our first ethnographic study in the office environment.

Approach -Design Ethnography

Design is an activity that concerns both thought and planning. It is practiced in various forms including industrial design, architectural design, service design, and human-computer interaction design, and is widely regarded as a major source of cultural production and change (Gunn et al. 2013). In contrast, anthropology is the comparative study of societies and cultures based on detailed empirical research in concrete social contexts (Hammersley and Atkinson 2007). Although as a discipline it originally focused on the study of non-western social settings, its methods gradually came to be applied in a much wider range of contexts, ranging from high-tech companies to rural villages in underdeveloped countries (Atkinson and Hammersley 1994). During the twentieth century, participant observation became the dominant method of conducting field studies in anthropology and a core component of ethnography, which aims to describe the culture, practices, and norms of everyday behavior within the studied group through immersion in the social setting in order to facilitate comprehensive data gathering (Clarke 2010). This is achieved by having the researchers spend a considerable amount of time in the social setting of interest, interacting with the people who live or work within it. Major areas of interest in ethnographic research include processes of social and cultural change, human creativity and innovation. As Clarke (2010) states the current relationship between design and anthropology blossomed during the 1970s, when designers became aware of the value of ethnographic data and methodologies, in particular for understanding the needs and experiences of product users and the contexts in which products and computer systems were used. This awareness led to the development of a genuine affinity between design and ethnography as processes of inquiry and discovery. Ethnographic methods quickly became popular in very different fields of design including architecture, urban design, city planning, interaction design, and Human-Computer Interaction.

Ethnographic approaches are also widely used by researchers to study behavior in workspaces (Blomberg and Karasti 2013). While many such investigations have been conducted by technocrats and researchers who adhere to the positivist tradition of designing workspaces on the basis of time and motion studies (Barnes 1968; Shephard 1974), observational studies in offices have also been undertaken by researchers with different aims and perspectives. For example, one of the most dominant figures in the field of Human-Computer Interaction (HCI), Lucy Suchman, conducted anthropological studies at Xerox PARC (Suchman 1995). In addition, Computer Support Collaborative Work (CSCW) researchers often perform ethnographic studies to investigate various aspects of workplaces. In the beginning, these studies mainly aimed to understand cooperation and collaboration during working practices. Later on, while investigating office work and the role of computerization in such social spaces during the early days of informatics research (Bellotti and Bly 1996; Luff and Heath 1998), researchers became interested in mobility within workplaces. In these investigations, mobility was generally regarded as a factor that increased collaboration among office workers.

While more HCI researchers are adopting ethnographic methods in their studies and designs, there is a degree of confusion about how ethnography should be practiced in this field. In addition, it is not wholly clear what criteria should be used to evaluate the results of ethnographic studies in the context of HCI research. As argued by Dourish (2006), the value of ethnographic investigations in workplaces is not in their implications for design per se but in their ability to provide insights into the organization of the social setting. As such, a key goal of ethnographic research in the context of design for workplaces is to provide models for thinking about those settings and the work that is conducted there. Ethnography is regarded as a process of creating and representing knowledge based on the experiences of the researcher (Pink 2013). Therefore, the aim in our ethnographic investigations was to gain a holistic understanding of movement and mobility in the studied workspaces rather than to specify a set of requirements for system development or to obtain guidelines for design.

Office Workers as "Moving Bodies" in Architectural Spaces

Before discussing the data collection protocols and design processes used in this project, we should explain how we define the office as an architectural space and office workers as "Moving Bodies" within this space. An office environment can be regarded as a social establishment with social barriers in which a particular kind of activity regularly takes place (Goffman 2012). This social establishment can be viewed from technical, political, structural and cultural perspectives. In an office there are performers and actors who act on the *front stage,* and interact with one-another *back stage.* In addition there are *audience* members, i.e. people visiting the office to receive a service, who interact with the actors on the front stage. The office environment and the architectural designs of the front and back stages are different and all affect the ways in which actors move around in the space.

People experience the world and the office environment in particular via embodied perception (i.e. perception through the body) and their interactions within the architectural space (Loke and Reinhardt 2012). These interactions influence both our movements and the space around us (Martin 2004). The architectural space affects the spatial practices that we perform (Brown 2010) and our spatial behaviors disturb the way the space is traditionally seen and experienced. As it was stated earlier, space is considered as a precondition of movement and "movement as a visible aspect of space" (Doolittle and Flynn 2000). In other words, it is the interaction between our bodies and the environment that makes spaces speak.

Implementation and Data Collection

The first step taken in our project was to reshape the methods of design ethnography to fit our objectives of (i) understanding bodily movements and mobility in current contemporary office spaces, and (ii) using this understanding to design an interactive prototype artefact that would encourage movement. When seeking to design interactive artifacts that blend into an existing culture, it is not sufficient to simply study people and the space they work in; it is necessary to immerse oneself in that space to acquire a deeper understanding of its context, forms, materials and cultural values. Prolonged immersion is necessary in studies of this sort because it is impossible to know in advance what sort of information is important to gather or what you will observe in the workspace (Clarke 2010). Therefore, while gathering data is important, it is also essential to discuss and re-evaluate one's observations with other researchers in order to determine how the qualities of individual objects in their context within the studied setting could be reflected in a new design. The gathering of data in this way supports the focused examination of relevant contexts as well as the thorough characterization of elements and details that may provoke intrigue or movement within workspaces. To this end, we chose to focus on elements such as objects, social interactions, and architectural spaces that oblige office workers to engage in whole body movement, creating "Moving Bodies" that function as interactive elements in the office's social and architectural space. The core practices adopted in this project were gathering various sources of data such as visual documentation, reviewing and revisiting the gathered records, and finally discussing and storytelling with team members.

Awareness and attention to detail are essential during all stages of ethnographic observation and data collection. A fundamental point in any ethnographic investigation is to seek inspiration everywhere in the studied environment and to always be sensitive towards objects and their contexts because the relationships between the two can provide valuable inspiration for design and have profoundly influenced approaches to design in social and architectural spaces. Such sensitivity towards objects and their contexts in the setting of interest facilitates the development of new interactive models that may harmonize more effectively with the space than those in current use. This awareness makes it possible to create new interactive designs that evoke new experiences and promote body movements during interaction within the workspace. However, when attempting to create such designs, it is also impossible to reflect on how "Moving Bodies" will perceive these qualities and their justification in the architectural space.

During our first ethnographic study, we developed a strong awareness of the roles played by different objects in the workspace. These non-human agents include office equipment such as printer, shared resources and even personal belongings. Every object involved in an interaction between office workers or which an office worker interacted with in a way that required movement was recorded. Some of these objects were only involved in small-scale interactions – for example, the list included rubber finger pads used to facilitate counting and scrolling. Conversely, others offered the possibility of full-body interaction. Some of the interactions associated with these objects were work-oriented (e.g. using the printer to print documents) while others were less so (e.g. watering the office plants). Figure 6.3 shows some of the objects that served as sources of interaction in the office's social

Fig. 6.3 Objects involved in different physical interactions in the office

and architectural spaces. The objects shown in this figure include a circular white standing table, a printer, a notice board, and the adjacent TV.

These objects trigger and shape the architectural space but also create social spaces. For example, the small noticeboard shown in the bottom right of Fig. 6.3

was used by the office workers to reserve company vehicles. As such, the board created a point of interaction for "Moving Bodies" in the architectural space but also encouraged short informal meetings between the office workers with the aim of identifying optimal ways of allocating vehicles to meet everyone's needs. The social spaces created within this specific architectural section of the workspace were clearly distinct from those created elsewhere in the office. We do not believe that a comparable social space would have been created if vehicles were reserved using online/digital tools. Such social spaces created within the architecture as a result of interacting with non-human agents occur daily in workplaces. Other informal social spaces were created by interactions with different objects, such as when two office workers went to fetch the watering cans shown in Fig. 6.3 at the same time. Since these watering cans were usually kept on either a standing table or the library shelves, these meetings were necessarily brief, with both individuals standing up. Several such meetings were recorded during the observational study. The role of these non-human agencies within the social and architectural space on "Moving Bodies" in offices was so clearly evident that it became our main source of inspiration. Consequently, it was decided that our first prototype, the "NEAT Lamp", would be a non-human agent that would interact with "Moving Bodies" in the workplace. The following section introduces the "NEAT Lamp" and explains how it was designed to interact with and promote "Moving Bodies".

Third Step: Designing for Moving Bodies

Designing interactive elements for "Moving Bodies" similar to any other novel design that aims for creating new spaces of interaction, requires a detailed knowledge and understanding of movements associated with specific interactions (Benyon et al. 2010). Based on the experience gained during our ethnographic studies in workspaces (see above), we became interested in the agency created by objects that foster movement in social and architectural spaces. As a way of promoting movement through interaction in office spaces, we designed a prototype sensor-based movement artifact known as the NEAT lamp. This section begins with a discussion of the practical considerations relating to the design of the "NEAT lamp" as an interactive artifact. This is followed by a detail description of our second study in which this prototype was evaluated in the office setting.

Concept and Design

Our first ethnographic study clearly demonstrated the importance of objects and artifacts as triggers for bodily interaction in the architectural and social spaces of offices. To further explore the intersection between moving bodies and architectural space, we designed a novel interactive sensory-based movement artifact. We chose to make our artifact a lamp because they are found in all kinds of offices. The

Fig. 6.4 The "NEAT Lamp"

"NEAT Lamp" (see Fig. 6.4) provides a sensory reminder approximately every 25 min to workers who are sitting in front of it. It is a USB-connected interactive lamp consisting of a LED and a sensor that recognizes movement. The lamp utilizes proximity sensors that is sensitive to lighting and shadow depending how far you are away of it. As it was mentioned previously the study was prolonged due to technical difficulties. One of the main challenges ahead of the study was related to the sensor utilized in the design of the prototype. Due to the differences of the lighting in the office space, the "NEAT Lamps" required manual calibrations in their sensitivity parameters.

The acronym NEAT stands for Non-Exercise Activity Thermogenesis (Levine 2004; Levine et al. 1999), a concept that has been investigated extensively in Public Health studies. Put simply, NEAT is any physical activity other than volitional exercise. It has considerable effects on the physiology of weight change and reduces the risk of chronic disease associated with prolonged sitting (McAlpine et al. 2007). By installing this interactive artifact in the workspace and tunings its settings, we hoped to 'hack' the sedentary habits of office workers and foster NEAT-type bodily movements within the architectural space. By sedentary behaviour we refer to all activities whose energetic cost is less than 1.5 metabolic equivalents, including sitting and lying down while working, eating, or commuting and transporting.

Although the "NEAT Lamp" is designed to modify office workers' sedentary behaviors, it should also avoid disrupting the progress of work when installed in a workspace. To this end, the lamp is static and silent, with no intrusive notifiers; it simply turns green to indicate that the worker has been sedentary in front of it for more than the specified length of time. The green color along with the plant-like pattern of the LED was chosen deliberately to resemble the plants in offices. An important goal was to avoid causing any disturbance or stress to the workers when they interacted with the lamp. Therefore, its design went through three cycles and it was tested in a pilot study before being evaluated in the second ethnographic study.

The "NEAT Lamp" is a concept-driven design (Stolterman and Wiberg 2010) that is intended to highlight a lack of "Moving Bodies" in a social and architectural space, and encourage workers to address this lack by moving. The prototype was designed to alert workers to their own sedentariness in the workspace by varying the ambient light. Because it is essential for vision, light plays a central role in shaping our perceptions, and vision is arguably our dominant sense. However, lived experiences are mostly shaped by peripheral unfocused vision, and this must be taken into account when designing for offices in their capacity as everyday social and architectural spaces. As described by Pallasmaa (2012), there is an exchange that occurs during our experiences of our daily lives: we tend to lend our emotions and associations to the space around us, and the space in turn lends us its aura, which shapes our perceptions and thoughts. The reality of an architectural space is fundamentally dependent on peripheral vision, not least because information gleaned via the peripheral vision is highly prioritized by the human perceptual system. Appropriate ambient displays experienced through the peripheral vision can thus integrate people into a social and architectural space as "Moving Bodies" whereas focused vision disconnects us from such spaces.

Public health workers have promoted "booster break" programs for office workers to address concerns about the amount of time that such workers spend in front of computers (Taylor et al. 2013). Although some of these programs have proven to be effective at breaking the habit of sitting for prolonged periods, we did not seek to emulate their design. Our basic idea was to design an artifact tailored for "Moving Bodies" in the social and architectural space, so a simple reminder on the computer or a phone screen would not have had the desired effect. Instead, the vision underpinning the prototype was to exert agency through an object that would foster mobility among office workers, encouraging them to become "Moving Bodies" in the workspace rather than disembodying the workers and disconnecting them from their spatial surroundings. This prompted us to explore the use of ambient light displays, perceived via the peripheral vision. The idea of using ambient displays to "hack" the habit of prolonged sitting and encourage users to be more active has previously resulted in several studies (Fan et al. 2012; Forlizzi et al. 2007; Hazlewood et al. 2011; Jafarinaimi et al. 2005). However, none of these designs have been subjected to intensive user evaluation in everyday settings. Moreover, our goal was not just to study the interaction between the user and the prototype but to comprehensively explore the way in which the "NEAT Lamp" functions as an interactive agent that alters the social and architectural space, influencing not only its user but also other "Moving Bodies" in the office.

The Study Plan and Objectives

As mentioned above, an intensive ethnographic study was conducted to evaluate the "NEAT Lamp" in an office-based company. The original plan was to conduct a 3 week ethnographic study in the office to gather reference data before introducing

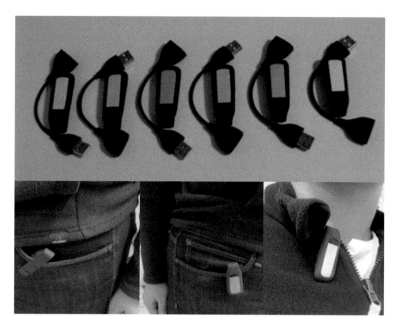

Fig. 6.5 (*Top*) The Fitbits used in this study each color coded for a specific participant. (*Bottom*) The way each of the participant carried their Fitbits

the prototypes into the setting (see Fig. 6.2). To complement the qualitative data that we planned to collect, we decided to issue our six participants in the office with Fitbits that would provide quantitative data on movement in the workspace. Six of the office staff were willing to evaluate the "NEAT Lamps", each of whom was given a Fitbit and a charger for it at the start of the study. To ensure that the participants' behavior was not influenced by the Fitbits and their step-counting capabilities, the units' displays were covered (see Fig. 6.5). In addition, the participants were not given USB connectors for the Fitbits to prevent them from looking up their step counts on the product's website. The Fitbits were collected for data retrieval on a weekly basis. As can be seen in Fig. 6.5, each participant (and their Fitbit) was assigned a unique color, which was also used when making qualitative observations of each participant's movements (see Fig. 6.1). The participants were asked to only wear the Fitbits when they were in the office.

As shown in Fig. 6.2, six "NEAT" lamps were introduced to the same six participants after the initial 3-week ethnographic study had been completed. Before conducting the second round of observation, the lamps were left in place for 2 weeks so that our six participants could familiarize themselves with the prototypes. By adopting this approach we were able to gain a comprehensive overview of the lamps' influence on bodily movement in the office setting that was based on both qualitative (observation notes) and quantitative (Fitbit measurements) data gathered before and after the installation of the "NEAT Lamps". At the end of the second observation period, we conducted semi-structured interviews with each of our six participants. The data gathered in this way revealed several interesting changes induced by the prototype in terms of the participants' behavior as "Moving Bodies" as well as the social settings of the office and its architectural space.

It is important to note that difficulties can be expected in any study, and this was no exception. A major challenge we encountered related to the calibration of the "NEAT Lamp" because some of its sensors did not respond well to the existing lighting in the office. This malfunction obliged us to extend the study for a week. Moreover, as anticipated, some of the participants forgot to only use the step counters during working hours; consequently, reliable quantitative data could only be obtained for three of the six individuals issued with Fitbits. In this chapter only one of the data sets will be presented thoroughly. Since the other two data sets will no add any new contribution to the chapter, we will avoid discussing them for now.

Fourth Step: Comprehending the Experience

As mentioned above, the main objective of the ethnographic study was to determine how the "NEAT Lamp" altered the social and architectural space of the office, and what this alteration meant in terms of interactive "Moving Bodies". The process of meaning making and knowledge production in our study began during the first few days of the data gathering phase, in the form of the observations and asides that are inevitably included with field notes. Although the written word is commonly regarded as the best tool for recording ethnographic information, we also used visual methods to record data. According to Pink (2013), "visual images, objects, descriptions should be incorporated when it is appropriate, opportune or enlightening to do so". Our field notes, interview transcripts and other sensory material that we have gathered along with the quantified data gathered by the Fitbits, created meaningful insights for us. This section reviews the key findings of our study.

Setting the Field

As in any field study, there was a time span required for us to become familiar with the overall setting of the office space. By becoming familiar with the setting we specifically mean recognizing the nature of the office workers' jobs, hierarchical positions in the company, and the personal characteristics of the participants and other office workers in the setting. The office consisted of two sizable rooms with one open cubicle for each worker, as shown in Fig. 6.1. The rooms were separated by a door. This door was almost always open during our study, so we treated the two rooms as a single space; indeed, we only became aware of the door's existence towards the end of the study, when it was briefly closed by accident. The workers in the left hand room participated in gymnastic breaks ("pausegympa") two times a day. Most of the workers in the office were engineers and designers whose jobs involve designing and testing electronic artifacts. Therefore, their daily routines included collaborative meetings and testing sessions in the laboratory located in one of the rooms (see Fig. 6.1).

From the first day of the study, the participants were equipped with Fitbits to use while they were in the office. One interesting observation was that the participants carried their Fitbit in different ways (see Fig. 6.5): three tried to hide the devices in their pockets while two carried them more overtly and one left it hanging from his shirt pocket! While these devices were gathering quantitative data on the workers' movements, we collected qualitative data in the form of our observations. During the first 3 weeks of our ethnographic study, we quickly realized that the office workers were active as "Moving Bodies" in the architectural space. Previous studies have shown that collaboration is a key source of mobility in workspaces (Bellotti and Bly 1996; Luff and Heath 1998), and this appeared to be the case here as well. The articulation of work is one of the main reasons for office workers' micro-movements and mobility. "Moving Bodies" create dynamic patterns of movement and mobility in the social and architectural space which are shaped by different workflow factors including temporal factors, challenges, obstacles and responsibilities. By labeling these patterns dynamic we aim to clarify their interdependencies and the fact that they are subject to change. Some of the workers' movements were repeated daily and acted as the basic elements of their roles as "Moving Bodies" in the studied space whereas other movement patterns occurred more rarely, typically when the office was busy. The aim of designing for "Moving Bodies" as interactive elements in space is not to focus on days when activity is already high; instead, the aim is to increase micro-mobility on days when workers are more detached from the social and architectural space, immersed in their work, and mainly focused on the computer screen. We consider ambient displays to be very well suited to this purpose because they are unobtrusive and easily ignored during busier periods.

Placing the Lamp

As noted in the preceding section, the "NEAT Lamps" were installed in the office space for 6 weeks. During this time the office workers continued using their Fitbits, and ethnographic observations were conducted for approximately 4 weeks. Because difficulties with the lamps' calibration were encountered, the ethnographic observations were continued for a week longer than had originally been planned. After the end of the observation period, semi-structured interviews were conducted with all six participants. This section presents some highlights from the field notes gathered during the observation period and then presents key findings based on our interviews and quantitative data.

Ethnographic Notes

By placing the prototypes in the offices of our participants, we introduced to them a new artifact. As is the case for any design, we as the designers were unable to anticipate the exact use cases of our designs in their dynamic context. One unexpected use case was observed shortly after the lamps were introduced into the setting: one of the participants placed a mug in front of its sensor, causing the lamp to permanently remain in the green 'notification' state. He subsequently claimed to have done this because he liked the green light.

There were a number of other similar instances in which the participants tuned the prototype to suit their needs and preferences. By tuning the space and artifacts around us, we can align them with our preferred state; this can be regarded as a process of hacking the parameters of the space (Coyne 2010). These small and subtle shifts can have large effects in the environment. Other such hacks used by participants included moving the lamps to new locations based on their preferences or 'tricking' the sensor by placing it in front of a wall in order to get a notification in 25 min' time.

During our observation we realized that participants reacted differently when their lamp was on. Some increased their movements within the workspace and some went further, inducing their colleagues to move around as well, for example by taking a gymnastic break (pausegympa) earlier than the would have otherwise and inviting other employees to join them. However, some ignored the lamp's green light, turned it so its sensor faced in some other direction, moved away from the sensor, or conducted some light stretches while sitting. This diversity of responses to the artifact was taken as a positive sign, indicating that the "NEAT Lamp" had met the goal of increasing bodily movements without imposing a burden on office workers. We were particularly interested in promoting deliberate movement among the workers, who thereby become "Moving Bodies" in the social and architectural space. Gradual changes occurred over the period of 4 weeks when we were present in the office – specifically, we observed that the number of participants and other workers taking time to stretch or increasing their micro-mobility rose gradually over the observation period. This increase was identified by comparing notes made during the second observation period (after the lamps' installation) to those made during the first 3 weeks of the study, when the lamps had not yet been introduced. In addition to these effects, the subtle design of the prototype appeared to provoke a degree of frustration and impatience with the artifact among some of the participants.

The social effect of "NEAT Lamps" became more and more visible as we spent time in the setting. Initially we assumed that the lamp itself would provide an impetus for individual workers to change their movement patterns. However, as we observed and prototyped the lamp in the setting, we became aware of a secondary impetus whereby a single lamp could influence the movement patterns of several workers (or Moving Bodies). When a lamp was activated by sedentary behavior on the part of a worker in a cubicle housing a lamp, the lamp's light illuminated the ceiling above the cubicle. Because the office consisted of a set of cubicles in an open

Fig. 6.6 The reflection of the "NEAT Lamp" on the ceiling represents an intersection between interaction design and architecture

space, this light on the ceiling was visible to everyone in the space (see Fig. 6.6). Therefore the interaction of one individual (e.g. a study participant) with the lamp affected the tendency of other office workers to act as "Moving Bodies" in the social and architectural space. This display of the participants' movement habits (or lack thereof) by the lamps provoked others to reflect on their own movement habits in the workspace and those of their colleagues. Often these reflections and considerations provoked verbal dialogue between individual "Moving Bodies" as they passed one-another in corridors or during informal meetings. The illumination of the ceiling thus helped to fulfil the shared human desire to feel and become part of our buildings. In this way, it also helped to reveal the scarcity of "Moving Bodies" in the architectural space. As Wodiczko (1999) states, "We feel a drive to complete the building and we desire to be completed by it."

Interviews and Quantified Data

The interviews were conducted in a semi-structured format and were begun by showing the participants the data gathered by their Fitbits. Some general background questions were then asked, followed by specific inquiries about the participants' experiences during the study and with the "NEAT Lamp". As soon as the quantitative data were presented, most of the participants said that it had been challenging to use the Fitbits in the way they had been asked to (see Fig. 6.7). Therefore, we only present Fitbit data for the two participants who made sure to only use their step counters during working hours.

The majority of the participants had experienced muscle pains as a result of prolonged sitting. In addition all of them had participated in a step count competition 2 years prior to our study. They described their work as mostly being done while sitting and involving extensive collaboration with other workers in the office.

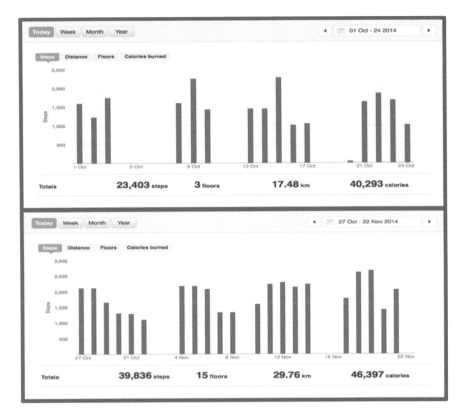

Fig. 6.7 The results of the Fitbits from one of the participants as a sample of our quantified data. The data belongs to the purple participant and are marked by Phase One and Phase Two, each refereeing to a separate part of the study

Interestingly all of them mentioned that their current perceptions of the prototype differed from those they had when it was first introduced to them. They had expected to be an artifact that would provoke dramatic change and encourage them individually to be more active rather than a subtle design intended to modify the office's social and architectural space. Many of the participants regarded the demands of their work as the main motivation for their bodily movement and mobility in space. As one put it: "*I move because I have to do other things.*" Most of the participants reported the lamp to be a more practical tool for office environments than the step counters they had previously tested; one participant neatly expressed the group's feelings about wearing the step counters by saying "*It can be a fun thing to do but to have all the year is not fun at all.*"

During the interviews, all of the participants reported that the "NEAT Lamp" had positive effects by reminding them of their sedentary behavior while working at their computers. One of the participating workers described its effect as being like a "*tap on the shoulder*". In the Fig. 6.7 the quantified data from one of the participants that have used the Fitbits according to the instruction is presented as an example. As stated earlier, the other two sets of data are spared in order to avoid redundancy in the text. The data is presented represents step counts of the purple participant. The first data set relates to the days that the prototype has not yet been presented to the office workers and it is tagged as Phase One. Similarly the dataset beneath represent the Phase Two where that the "NEAT Lamps" were presented in the office space. As it was stated before, the first 2 days of the study partially because of our presence in the office conducting ethnography and also due to some challenges in the company the level of movement in all of the participants was irregular in comparison to other days. Therefore the data gathered from these 2 days are excluded in the Fig. 6.7. When we asked the participants regarding their level of movement in these 2 days, they mentioned a break in one of their systems. In addition they added that our presence was their source of increasing their micro mobility. The blue participant stated, *"In the beginning to know that someone is measuring how much you are walk[ing] made me try to walk more."* Majority of the participants have an increase in the level of their steps in the first days except from one of the participants. During the interview he mentioned that he avoided coming out of his cubical the first days of the study since he was being observed.

However soon they became used to our presence in the office space and so in our analysis we do not consider the first 2 days of the quantified data. Based on the Fitbit data (see Fig. 6.7), the purple participant increased his daily number of steps by 337 in average per day as a result of interacting with the lamp. The results indicate that the maximum number of steps taken in a day during Phase One of the study is 2289 and the maximum steps per day in the second phase are 2679. In average the participant took 1560 steps/day in the first phase and after the lamp was introduced in the setting the average increased to 1897 steeps/day, which reveals 21.6 % increase in the number of steps per day. When asked about the lamp's effect on their work routine, the purple participant said *"I don't think that the lamp made me walk more, [but] it made me move more in my workplace."* Later on he was surprised to see how much this small change had increased his number of daily steps. As another example the green participant described the lamp as a good reminder of having been seated for too long. *"Its main effect is to ensure you don't sit still for too long and that you make small movements"*, he replied. Based on his experiences with the prototype, he had tried adjusting his desk so that he could work in a standing position.

Conclusion

This chapter introduced the concept of "Moving Bodies" as a guiding notion for designing interactions in architectural space. We have used this concept as part of an ongoing empirical study on body movement in an office environment and have described our current work on conceptualizing this space and our attempts at designing an artifact whose purpose is to promote movement and interaction within this environment.

As members of the Informatics group within the InPhAct project, we are interested in designing for "Moving Bodies" as interactive elements in social and architectural spaces. Our aim is to use knowledge gained through ethnographic studies to develop concepts and prototype artifacts that will encourage office workers to act as Moving Bodies. Careful thought is required when designing Information Technology to foster movement in workspaces with distinctive architectural and social specifications. The designed artifacts should be effective at provoking "Moving Bodies" and encouraging movement in workspaces without forcing people to move or imposing additional burdens on workers who need to focus on their duties and responsibilities. In this context, it is essential to recall that any Information Technology design will affect its surroundings and space. As demonstrated by the results presented in this chapter, "Moving Bodies" both affect and are affected by physical objects within the architectural space. Some of these objects or artifacts may be static such as the small noticeboard shown in Fig. 6.5, which created a social space shared by those interacting with it. The NEAT lamp and the consequences of its illumination of the ceiling provide a more striking example of the intersection between interaction design and architecture (see Fig. 6.6). As mentioned previously, during the early stages of this artifact's design, we did not think much about how it might interact with other elements of the workspace. The observation of the lamps' effects on multiple workers via their illumination of the ceiling made us reflect on how architecture and interaction design are intertwined. As noted by Wiberg (2015), there is much to explore and investigate in this intersection.

Because workspaces are social spaces, we are interested in exploring the intersection between social interaction design and architecture in future. As we define it, social interaction design relates to sensor-based movement artifacts that are installed in social environments such as meeting rooms or lunchrooms in an office. Like the NEAT lamp, they function as notifiers, but they respond to data on multiple "Moving Bodies" within the social-architectural space rather than a single individual.

References

Atkinson P, Hammersley M (1994) Ethnography and participant observation. Handb Qual Res 1(23):248–261

Barnes RM (1968) Motion and time study; design and measurement of work. Wiley, New York

Bellotti V, Bly S (1996) Walking away from the desktop computer: distributed collaboration and mobility in a product design team. In: Proceedings of the 1996 ACM conference on computer supported cooperative work, ACM, pp 209–218

Benyon D, Turner P, Turner S (2005) Designing interactive systems: people, activities, contexts, technologies. Pearson Education, Edinburgh

Benyon D, Höök K, Nigay L (2010) Spaces of interaction. In: Proceedings of the 2010 ACM-BCS visions of computer science conference. British Computer Society, p 2

Blomberg J, Karasti H (2013) Reflections on 25 years of ethnography in CSCW. Comput Supported Coop Work (CSCW) 22(4–6):373–423

Brown C (2010) Making space, speaking spaces. In: The Routledge dance studies reader, p 58

Camurri A, Hashimoto S, Ricchetti M, Ricci A, Suzuki K, Trocca R, Volpe G (2000) Eyesweb: toward gesture and affect recognition in interactive dance and music systems. Comput Music J 24(1):57–69

Chi D, Costa M, Zhao L, Badler N (2000) The EMOTE model for effort and shape. In: Proceedings of the 27th annual conference on computer graphics and interactive techniques. ACM Press/Addison-Wesley Publishing Co., pp 173–182

Clarke A (2010) Design anthropology. Actar, New York

Corlett EN (1983) Analysis and evaluation of working posture. In: Ergonomics of workstation design. Butterworths, London, p 13

Coyne R (2010) The tuning of place: sociable spaces and pervasive digital media. The MIT Press, Cambridge, MA

Cresswell T (2006) On the move: mobility in the modern western world. Taylor & Francis, New York

Cresswell T (2010) Towards a politics of mobility. Environ Plan D Soc Space 28(1):17

Das B, Grady RM (1983) Industrial workplace layout design an application of engineering anthropometry. Ergonomics 26(5):433–447

Davies E (2007) Beyond dance: Laban's legacy of movement analysis. Routledge, New York

Delaney D (1999) Laws of motion and immobilization: bodies, figures and the politics of mobility. In: Communication au colloque Mobilities, Gregynog Hall, Newtown, Pays-de-Galles (Royaume-Uni)

Doolittle L, Flynn A (eds) (2000) Dancing bodies, living histories: new writings about dance and culture. Banff Centre Press, Banff

Dourish P (2006) Implications for design. In: Proceedings of the SIGCHI conference on human factors in computing systems, ACM, pp 541–550

Fagerberg P, Ståhl A, Höök K (2003) Designing gestures for affective input: an analysis of shape, effort and valence. In MUM 2003: proceedings of the 2nd international conference on mobile and ubiquitous multimedia, 10–12 Dec 2003, Norrköping, Sweden. ACM, Norrköping, Sweden

Fan C, Forlizzi J, Dey AK (2012) A spark of activity: exploring informative art as visualization for physical activity. In: Proceedings of the 2012 ACM conference on ubiquitous computing, ACM, pp 81–84

Forlizzi J, Li I, Dey A (2007) Ambient interfaces that motivate changes in human behavior. In Workshop at Pervasive 2007 designing and evaluating ambient information systems, p 6

Giordano L (1992) Beyond Taylorism: computerization and the new industrial relations. St. Martin's Press, Inc., New York

Goffman E (2012) The presentation of self in everyday life [1959]. Contemporary sociological theory, pp 46–61

Grandjean E, Hunting W, Maeda K, Laubli T (1983) Constrained postures at office workstations. In: Ergonomics of workstation design. Butterworth, London

Grosz E, Eisenman P (2001) Architecture from the outside: essays on virtual and real space. MIT Press, Cambridge

Gunn W, Otto T, Smith RC (eds) (2013) Design anthropology: theory and practice. A&C Black, London

Haggett P (1965) Locational analysis in human geography. Edward Arnold, London

Hammersley M, Atkinson P (2007) Ethnography: principles in practice. Routledge, London

Hazlewood WR, Stolterman E, Connelly K (2011) Issues in evaluating ambient displays in the wild: two case studies. In: Proceedings of the SIGCHI conference on human factors in computing systems, ACM, pp 877–886

Hodgson J (2001) Mastering movement: the life and work of Rudolf Laban. Psychology Press, New York

Jafarinaimi N, Forlizzi J, Hurst A, Zimmerman J (2005) Breakaway: an ambient display designed to change human behavior. In: CHI'05 extended abstracts on human factors in computing systems, ACM, pp 1945–1948

Kvålseth TO (1983) Ergonomics of workstation design. Butterworth-Heinemann, Newton

Laban R, Ullmann L (1971) The mastery of movement. Plays. Inc., Boston

Levine JA (2004) Non-exercise activity thermogenesis (NEAT). Nutr Rev 62(suppl 2):S82–S97

Levine JA, Eberhardt NL, Jensen MD (1999) Role of nonexercise activity thermogenesis in resistance to fat gain in humans. Science 283(5399):212–214

Loke L, Reinhardt D (2012) First steps in body-machine choreography. In: Proceedings of the 2nd international body in design workshop, OZCHI 2012

Lowe JC, Moryadas S (1975) The geography of movement. http://trid.trb.org/view.aspx?id=235072

Luff P, Heath C (1998) Mobility in collaboration. In: Proceedings of the 1998 ACM conference on computer supported cooperative work, ACM, pp 305–314

Maletic V (1987) Body-space-expression: the development of Rudolf Laban's movement and dance concepts, vol. 75. Walter de Gruyter

Martin R (2004) Dance, space and subjectivity, by Briginshaw Valerie. 2001. New York: Palgrave. xviii+ 234 pp., illustrations. $62 cloth. Dance Res J 36(01):181–183

McAlpine DA et al (2007) An office-place stepping device to promote workplace physical activity. Br J Sports Med 41(12):903–907

Moradi F, Wiberg M (2013) Redesigning work – from sedentariness to activeness. Procedia Technol 9:1005–1015

Pallasmaa J (2012) The eyes of the skin: architecture and the senses. Wiley, Hoboken

Pink S (2013) Doing visual ethnography. Sage, Thousand Oaks

Reeves TC, Duncan WJ, Ginter PM (2001) Motion study in management and the arts a historical example. J Manag Inq 10(2):137–149

Rothe K (2012) Economy of human movement: performances of economic knowledge. Perform Res 17(6):32–39

Shephard RJ (1974) Men at work: applications of ergonomics to performance and design. Thomas, Springfield

Stolterman E, Wiberg M (2010) Concept-driven interaction design research. Human Comput Interact 25(2):95–118

Suchman L (1995) Making work visible. Commun ACM 38(9):56-ff

Taylor WC, King KE, Shegog R, Paxton RJ, Evans-Hudnall GL, Rempel DM, … Yancey AK (2013) Booster breaks in the workplace: participants' perspectives on health-promoting work breaks. Health education research, cyt001

Wiberg M (2015) Interaction design meets architectural thinking. Interactions 22(2):60–63

Wodiczko K (1999) Critical vehicles: writings, projects, interviews. MIT Press, Cambridge

Chapter 7
Measuring Interaction in Workplaces

Kerstin Sailer, Petros Koutsolampros, Martin Zaltz Austwick, Tasos Varoudis, and Andy Hudson-Smith

Abstract Interactions in the workplace have long been studied by the architectural research community, however, in the past, the majority of those contributions focused on single case studies. Drawing on a much larger empirical sample of 27 offices, this chapter aims at establishing a baseline of understanding how the physical structure of office buildings shapes human behaviours of interaction. This may form a foundation for the Human-Computer Interaction (HCI) community to investigate the impact of embedded computer technology on human behaviours inside buildings. Methods of data collection included an analysis of floor plans with Space Syntax techniques and direct observations of space usage patterns. Exploring this data, different patterns emerged: interactions appeared unevenly distributed in space; interaction rates as well as preferences for locations varied by industry; spatial configuration appeared to create affordances for interaction, since unplanned interactions outside of meeting rooms tended to cluster in more visually connected areas of the office; in addition, seven different micro-behaviours of interaction were identified, each of them driven by affordances in both the built environment and the presence of other people; last but not least, locations for interactions showed clear time-space routines. The chapter closes with interpretations of the results, reflecting on the problem of predictability and how these insights could be useful for evidence-based design, but also the HCI community. It also gives an outlook on future developments regarding the constant logging of human behaviours in offices with emerging technologies.

K. Sailer (✉) • P. Koutsolampros
Space Syntax Laboratory, The Bartlett School of Architecture, University College London,
140 Hampstead Road, London NW1 2BX, UK
e-mail: k.sailer@ucl.ac.uk

M. Zaltz Austwick • A. Hudson-Smith
Centre for Advanced Spatial Analysis (CASA), The Bartlett School of Architecture, University
College London, 90 Tottenham Court Road, London W1T 4TJ, UK

T. Varoudis
The Bartlett School of Architecture, University College London, Gower Street, WC1E 6BT,
London, UK
e-mail: t.varoudis@ucl.ac.uk

© Springer International Publishing Switzerland 2016   137
N.S. Dalton et al. (eds.), *Architecture and Interaction*,
Human–Computer Interaction Series, DOI 10.1007/978-3-319-30028-3_7

Introduction: Interaction, Space and Architectural Typologies

> Culturally and socially, space is never simply the inert background of our material existence.
> It is a key aspect of how societies and cultures are constituted in the real world, and, through
> this constitution, structured for us as 'objective' realities. Space is more than a neutral
> framework for social and cultural forms. It is built into those very forms. Human behaviour
> does not simply happen in space. It has its own spatial forms. Encountering, congregating,
> avoiding, interacting, dwelling, teaching, eating, conferring are not just activities that
> happen in space. In themselves they constitute spatial patterns. (Hillier 1996, p. 29)

Interaction is one of the key aspects of human life. According to Hillier
interaction is embedded in social and cultural forms, and alongside many other
activities, it forms spatial patterns as an integral part of everyday life (Goffman
1959).

Human-to-human interaction is driven by the spatial setting in which it occurs.
Interaction in digital space, for instance, offers more opportunities for anonymity
than interaction in physical space. Likewise, interaction in urban space offers
more opportunities for anonymity than interaction inside buildings, where one can
expect to meet more like-minded people or even familiar faces. Inside buildings,
interactions are shaped by the type of building (hospital, school, office, museum,
department story, library, etc.), but also by the properties of the layout. Indeed,
it has been argued that buildings have two main functions in this respect (Hillier
and Hanson 1984; Hillier et al. 1984): firstly, they define users by categories: as
soon as we enter for instance a hospital, we assume a particular role as patient,
visitor, nurse, doctor, administrator, cleaner, porter etc. Buildings then transform
our experience of space by granting or inhibiting access and control, not only over
space, but also with regards to the production and reproduction of social knowledge
inscribed in the building. It turns us into visitors with limited access and control, or
inhabitants who define the building and its outputs. Secondly, buildings by virtue
of their spatial layout provide mechanisms for patterns of avoidance or encounter
between the relevant user groups. This aspect of building function has been coined
'the construction of an interface' (Hillier et al. 1984).

Workplaces are interesting cases of buildings to investigate in this interdisciplinary context of Architecture and Interaction for a variety of reasons: firstly,
offices are a building typology characterized by a rather unstructured interface and
subtle role assignments. There are no sharp contrasts between user groups (such
as exist in a hospital), and office buildings do not programmatically limit contact,
hence the detailed spatial configuration and strategic usage choices (for instance
where to put the coffee machine and other attractors) plays an important role in
shaping user behaviours and contact patterns (Sailer 2007). Secondly, they afford
the potential for observational studies and field-testing of real world applications
(Shklovski and Chang 2006) crucial to the field of Human Computer Interaction
(HCI). They also have the capacity to provide a large number of participants for
data collection purposes whilst ensuring high ecological validity of the results – the
extent to which behaviour observed in an experiment reflects behaviour that occurs
naturally. Last but not least, technology has entered the scene and has over the last

decades if not centuries clearly changed the way in which work is structured. This renders them interesting for the wider debate initiated by this book. The bigger picture of the changing landscape of work is relevant, since predictions of the 'death of distance' (Cairncross 1997) have resonated in a lively debate on whether technology has made office buildings obsolete, allowing work to leave the building and (in theory) taking place anywhere anytime, afforded by increased mobility of computing devices such as laptops, tablets or smartphones and the rise in internet connectivity on the go (Rainie and Wellman 2012). While it is unquestionable that technology has changed the way people work, it is equally clear that office buildings are as much needed as ever, evident in the recent renaissance in prestigious architecture projects of large and prominent office buildings, ironically many of them for big technology corporations, such as Facebook (Gehry), Apple (Foster's & Partner), Samsung (NBBJ) and Google (BIG and Heatherwick Studio), to name just a few. Likewise, Yahoo has been in the news in 2013, asking its employees to quit home working and instead return to the office to enable "hallway and cafeteria discussions, meeting new people, and impromptu team meetings (...) [where] some of the best decisions and insights come from".[1] Scholarly research has shown repeatedly that face-to-face interactions allow for rich information exchanges, in particular rapid feedback, high frequency, instantaneous feedback, learning, visual and body language cues, trust, relationship building, socialising and motivation (Nohria and Eccles 1992; Storper and Venables 2004). It was also shown that face-to-face interaction patterns often match digitally-mediated interaction patterns in offices very closely (Sailer et al. 2015), hence the opportunity to overcome physical space offered by technology is not always realized. This embeds our study in the tradition of considering 'situated architectural effects' and the role of technology in everyday life (Fischer and Hornecker 2012).

Against this background, this chapter seeks to explore patterns of human-to-human face-to-face interactions in the workplace mediated by the structure of the physical office layout. Its main research question is grounded in the understanding that interaction constitutes a spatial pattern and aims to discover how interactions are distributed in workplaces, which spatial settings provide favourable conditions for interactions to flourish and to which degree different offices show varying or converging phenomena. This is relevant to the HCI community insofar as it establishes a baseline of understanding of how physical space structures human behaviours in offices. Marshall et al. (2011) proposed that there is a lack of understanding the affordances of space prior to an HCI intervention. Hence, on the foundation of this chapter, future research could test how human behaviour shifts with the impact of embedded computer technology, such as screens and displays in line with HCI relevant research questions.

---

[1] The leaked internal Yahoo memo is documented here: http://allthingsd.com/20130222/physically-together-heres-the-internal-yahoo-no-work-from-home-memo-which-extends-beyond-remote-workers/ (Last accessed: 01 April 2015)

The chapter is structured as follows: section "Architecture and Human Interaction" will provide a brief background of relevant literature and continue contextualizing the understanding of human interactions in physical space in the wider discourse on HCI. Section "Data and Methods" will introduce methodology and the detailed empirical dataset used in this research. Results on locational patterns and the spatial distribution of interaction occurrences in workplaces will be discussed in section "Interaction Hotspots, Locations and Patterns", giving rise to an interpretation of predominant spatial cultures and practices of interaction in offices. Highlighting future work and overall developments in the field, section "Future Work and Developments in the Field" will provide an outlook on where technology might take the world of work and offices, thus building more bridges to bring architectural research and advanced spatial analysis together with the HCI community.

Architecture and Human Interaction

In this context, three relevant bodies of literature are relevant and will be sketched in the following: firstly, scholarly work tackling the question of how to capture interactions in offices; secondly, contributions that highlight the impact of spatial layout on patterns of interaction in workplaces; and thirdly, literature bringing HCI to bear in the context of workplaces and human interaction patterns.

The question of how to capture and measure interaction in the office accurately is an interesting one in the context of this chapter. Traditionally, researchers have relied on methods stemming from the social sciences such as direct observations or spot sampling (Reiss 1971; Bernard 2000), or staff surveys of interaction patterns (Bernard 2000). In recent years, automated methods of collecting interaction data in the workplace have been deployed using sensing systems (Wu et al. 2008; Lopez de Vallejo 2009; Olguin et al. 2009; Brown et al. 2014a, b). Traditional methods of observations and surveys may suffer from problems including validity (Bernard and Killworth 1993), classification errors (in recording ambiguous behaviours such as passive listening), interpretation bias (by respondents completing surveys) (Bernard 2000) or response and recall bias in surveys (Bradburn et al. 1978; Van de Mortel 2008). Still it seems that sensor derived data is far from being as 'objective' as it is often claimed. Interactions are often based on probabilities since not every behavioural instance can be recorded (for instance Olguin et al. 2009 reported a likelihood of 87 % of a face-to-face interaction being captured by their system). Additional issues include accuracy and spatial resolution of the data (the best systems achieve a spatial resolution of the order of a few metres, which can still be insufficient for understanding micro-behaviours within organisations), scalability and affordability, ethical problems as well as calibration issues and context-dependency (certain building materials such as glass and steel may cause interference and reflection). Comparing traditional ways of gathering interaction data in the workplace with sensor derived data typically showed a low correlation (Sailer et al. 2013), highlighting the fact that technical systems cannot yet replace sociological human enquiry. Despite remaining issues with indoor location and interaction sensing (Curran et al. 2011; Li and Becerik-Gerber 2011), this growing field may provide future opportunities for architectural and HCI research to come together.

The second relevant stream of literature regards the impact of workplace layout on social behaviours in general, and patterns of interaction in particular. This has been studied by various scholars over the last decades, with a majority of the contributions coming from the tradition of Space Syntax, which is a method and theory aiming to understand the relationship between spatial configuration (the way spatial elements are interconnected and form part of a wider spatial network), and social behaviours. Research in this domain has found that workplaces with an overall shorter path length in the spatial network (more *integrated* buildings in Space Syntax terminology) showed a higher degree of interaction among staff (Hillier and Grajewski 1990; Toker and Gray 2008) and a higher connectivity between teams (Hillier and Grajewski 1990). Interactions among staff were found to take place predominantly around desks and workstations (Steen et al. 2005; Rashid et al. 2006; Markhede and Koch 2007; Steen 2009); attractors such as water-coolers and photocopiers invited informal interactions especially in integrated locations, but only if they matched an organisation's culture and behavioural norms and respected the need for privacy of conversations (Fayard and Weeks 2007). The importance of paths in the workplace was underlined by showing how interactions often arose out of temporary proximity between people, where one person was on the move and was 'recruited' into a conversation by someone sitting (Backhouse and Drew 1992). In addition, more permanent patterns of proximity between co-workers as measured by the walking distance between their desks was associated with frequency of interaction (Sailer and Penn 2009) but also the structure of interaction networks (Sailer and McCulloh 2012).

Last but not least, research in the HCI field has investigated human interaction patterns in workplace environments. HCI is a young discipline which has developed over the last 30 years. The origins of the discipline are within computer science and cognitive psychology, with influences from sociology, anthropology, ergonomics and design. The multidisciplinary nature of HCI means there are numerous methodological approaches employed to conduct research in the area and ways in which HCI research connects to architectural research relevant to the study at hand. A commonly used framework in HCI research that bridges to architectural research is Hall's proxemics approach (Hall 1966), highlighting how the nature of interactions between people changes with the distance between them. This has been used in HCI to understand both human-to-human, but also human-computer interaction, for instance in an analysis of media facades (Fischer and Hornecker 2012). A particular example of relevant HCI research inside workplaces is the so called mixed reality architecture (MRA) system, which connects office occupants to selected collaborators or colleagues in other locations. Cameras display one location A to a large screen in location B with microphones/speakers allowing an additional audio-connection (if the occupants have chosen to connect, similarly to opening their door in an office). Research in this area proposed that awareness of others and social interactions as well as chance encounters were realized between remote locations in similar ways in which a shared physical space supports face-to-face interaction (Schnädelbach et al. 2006). However, it was also shown that virtual adjacencies between remote locations via an MRA created distinct spatial topologies of a hybrid nature, where configurations changed in a dynamic and rapid way (Schnädelbach 2012). Interestingly, interactions with strangers were not afforded by the system unless people were formally introduced to each other, which highlights the ways in which workplace interactions mediated by screens might differ from face-to-face interactions, where conversations between strangers, for instance at the coffee machine, do happen occasionally. The study of ambient displays in workplaces highlighted that people adapted their micro-behaviour of movement if screens augmented their visual field (Varoudis 2011). It was also shown how ambient displays were able to nudge people's behaviour in workplaces, in this case to increase use of the stairs versus the elevators (Rogers et al. 2010). These approaches pinpoint future research opportunities combining the architecturally motivated research of behaviours with augmentations provided by digital spaces.

In summary, four themes appear relevant for the study of interaction patterns in offices from the perspective of architectural and HCI research: firstly, both research traditions consider the environment as a variable that delivers data on the nature of human interactions. Similarities as well as differences between interactions in physical and augmented reality were observed. Secondly, interactions are framed as part of the user experience, both in physical space (architectural research) and in digital space (HCI). Thirdly, interactions are defined and shaped by the construction of an interface. In architectural research this relates to the way buildings define user groups and systematically facilitate or hinder encounters between the groups by controlling access and visibility. In the case of HCI research, the interface is the connection between human and computer, allowing or hindering user actions and interactions. Fourthly, new research opportunities between architectural and HCI research were seen in understanding how affordances for interaction are structured across physical and digital spaces, but also on a methodological basis in a quest to advance the locational accuracy of sensing systems.

Data and Methods

This paper draws on a large sample of 27 different cases of offices collected by Spacelab, a design and consultancy practice based in London and organized into a Spatial Database during the Knowledge Transfer Partnership Project 'Big data in the office' between UCL and Spacelab. The database (described in more detail in Koutsolampros et al. 2015) contains information on 27 buildings (however, different offices in different locations belonging to the same company have been treated as standalone cases). In total, data from 14 companies across industries such as Media, Advertising, Legal, Technology, Retail and Financial Services was analysed. The cases varied in size, from 400 to 15,000 m^2 of office area and 40–1700 staff.

In each of the cases, the following methods of data collection and enquiry were combined: firstly, structured participant observations of space usage, so called snapshots (Grajewski 1992) recorded and mapped different behaviours (i.e. people sitting, standing, walking and interaction) to their exact location using a tailor-made tablet application. Every area was observed in hourly intervals 8 times per day over the course of a full working week, resulting in a total of 40 observations of each space. This was achieved for 20 buildings. The remaining seven buildings were observed with fewer snapshots (mostly 3 days).

Secondly, the functional allocation of spaces was mapped onto floor plans, showing where open plan and cellular workspaces, alternative workspaces (e.g. breakout spaces), meeting rooms, primary circulation and shared facilities (e.g. kitchens, canteens, tea points) were located. These functional definitions were developed from expert observation of the floor plans and actual space in the course of Spacelab's contracts.[2] Floor plans were also processed in a Space Syntax analysis. Visibility graph analysis (VGA) (Turner et al. 2001) was conducted on eye-level using depthmapX software (Varoudis 2012), which divides the office space into a regular grid (0.45×0.45 m) and determines the number of steps required to establish visibility between any pair of grid points (or pixels); two grid points are defined as one step of depth apart when they are visible to one another. This metric of average mean depth (MD) of visibility path length was used.

Last but not least, visualisations were created that combine two metrics of interest: in the following figures we show the comparison of visual mean depth (an attribute of space) with the observed interaction density (an attribute of the people using the space, and their social and cultural structures). To make the two metrics comparable, interaction was converted from a list of discrete locations where interaction has occurred to a continuous field indicative of interaction rate. To do this, Kernel Density Estimation was employed, a technique utilised extensively in geography (Brunsdon 1995). Thus we are assuming that interaction is generated from space and usage, and varies smoothly across our spaces – that locations close to sites of previous interaction carry a preference for future encounters. While we conceive of the encounter rate as a continuous field, in practice we map it onto the same spatial grid produced by our Space Syntax analyses. The distance function used here is a Kernel Density Estimator with a Gaussian function for the kernel – a kernel density estimator works by convolving each data point with a 'kernel' – typically a Gaussian – and summing the results. In simpler terms, each point is given a 'fuzzy blob' of interaction probability, and where these blobs overlap, they add up and produce a region of higher interaction rate. Conceptually, this allows us to tie together separate interactions which occur close together, and see them as belonging to the same 'place', or locus, of interaction – and to see more clearly how large or intense that locus is. In producing kernel density estimators, the width of the kernel plays a key role – too small, and we fail to link together points into regions

---

[2]It should be noted that, while we have used the categorisation of space based on the organisation's use of their buildings, an unsupervised analysis would also be possible, and from this, cluster analyses or unsupervised machine learning methods (such as Self Organising Maps, originally detailed in Kohonen 1998) could generate those categories organically; this is a subject of ongoing research.

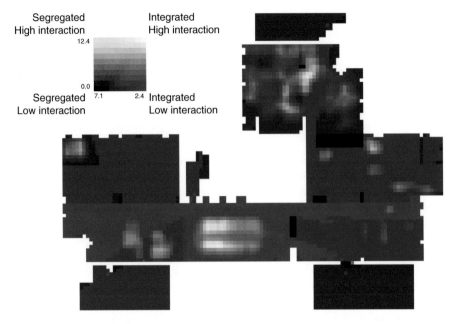

Fig. 7.1 Sample plan with Visual Mean Depth and interaction density overlay; high interaction in segregated areas is coloured in *yellow*, turning to *white* as integration increases; low interaction in segregated areas is coloured in *black*, turning to *blue* as integration increases

of interaction – too large, and all our regions blur together into one giant smudge of interaction. Our kernel size was 1 m, meaning that two interactions which occurred more than 3 m apart would not be grouped into the same locus.

Since both variables (MD and interaction density) are spatial, placing both on the same spatial representation allows for a relational and straightforward interpretation. In order to achieve this layering, a four colour scheme has been selected, as seen in the sample in Fig. 7.1.

Each variable studied is represented by one primary colour, yellow for high levels of interaction and blue for high levels of spatial integration, i.e. low MD and they work additively. When both interaction and integration are low, the pixel will become black; in contrast, when both are high, the colour will turn towards white. The visualisation colour was chosen to be on a colour-blind-safe scale (Brewer and Harrower 2009).

Interaction Hotspots, Locations and Patterns

In this section, we will present results from the analysis of interaction patterns. We will start with the big picture of how interactions are distributed in office space across the sample, but will attempt to dig deeper as we go along. Each new arising question will be applied to a more and more trimmed down data set, where we will use types of industry, types of space, floors and different types of interactions as filters to allow us to move from top level patterns to micro-behaviours, organisational cultures and the impact of time.

The Overall Distribution of Interaction

Interactions are unevenly distributed throughout the different areas of an office building. We know from previous research that the majority of interactions happen near workstations (Steen et al. 2005; Rashid et al. 2006; Markhede and Koch 2007; Steen 2009) and that attractors (such as coffee machines, photocopiers, canteens, etc.) introduce a positive bias to interactions (Fayard and Weeks 2007).

A similar trend emerges from our data. A total of 161,365 people have been observed in our sample. On average, 30.3 % of people (48,893) present in the office are interacting at any one point in time, which renders interactions an important everyday task at work. As seen in Fig. 7.2a, workspaces accumulate the biggest share of those interactions (42.6 % for open plan and 12.6 % for cellular), which means that in absolute figures, the highest number of interactions were observed in workspaces (20,751 and 6056 people interacting respectively). Formal enclosed meeting rooms and shared facilities (such as kitchens, canteens, photocopiers, etc.) account for 23.1 % (11,271 people) and 10.6 % (5153 people) respectively, while circulation and alternative spaces (such as breakout spaces and informal meeting spaces) attract the lowest number of interactions.

However, it could be argued that workspaces make up the majority of area in an office and as such it would be natural for them to attract most interactions. Therefore we divided the number of interactions occurring in the different areas of the offices in our sample as mentioned above by the overall area provided in

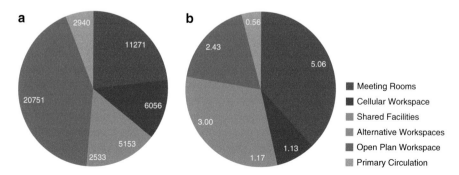

Fig. 7.2 (**a, b**) Interaction (split by type of space it occurs in) across all 27 cases in the sample: numbers of people interacting per observation round as a proportion of all people observed (**a**) and normalised by area provision, i.e. per 100 m^2 (**b**)

each of these categories to understand which of them attracted a disproportionate number of interactions relative to their size; the resulting figures tell us the number of interactions per unit floor area (per 100 m^2). It could be argued that these spaces are interaction hotspots due to their function. Results are presented in Fig. 7.2b, providing a comparison of the interaction intensities of different space categories.

This completely changes the overall picture, since now meeting spaces attract the highest rate of interactions per area (5.06 people interacting per 100 m^2, which equals 38 % of all interactions), followed by alternative meeting spaces (22 % or 3.00 people per 100 m^2). Open plan workspaces now only account for 18 % of interactions (2.43 people per 100 m^2) with cellular spaces hosting another 8 % (1.13 people per 100 m^2). Other facilities and primary circulation make up only one fifth of all interactions. This means that meeting spaces, whether formal or informal, are the places where the highest rate of interaction takes place – clearly an expected result due to the functional programming of these types of areas in the setting of an office. What might come as a surprise is the fact that circulation areas are the least attractive for interactions, which goes against commonly held perceptions. Anecdotally, corridors are often praised as the ideal spot for serendipitous interactions, as the following account from the famous Bell Labs exemplifies: "Traveling the hall's length without encountering a number of acquaintances, problems, diversions and ideas was almost impossible. A physicist on his way to lunch in the cafeteria was like a magnet rolling past iron filings." (Gertner 2012). It might of course be the case that this phenomenon occurs, it is simply not a very predominant pattern overall across our sample.

In addition to the overall spatial distribution of interactions, it is interesting to consider variations across different industries. It could be hypothesized that the distribution, overall occurrence and frequency of interactions varies from one industry to another, depending on their need to exchange ideas, communicate and collaborate. For instance law firms might be expected to have strict rules for handling sensitive data, and might therefore show more proceduralised everyday behaviours. Other companies such as media companies that rely on the quick spreading of information might be expected to tend towards higher levels of interaction due to the need to communicate. Hence we would expect levels of interaction to coincide with the need to coordinate tasks and spread information. We would also expect the locational distribution of interactions to vary by industry.

Despite some relevant variations by industry, the overall distribution of inter-actions across different functional areas remains comparable to the big picture discussed above for the overall benchmark (see Fig. 7.3a, b). Again meeting rooms present themselves as interaction hotspots, however as expected the pattern is not equally pronounced for every industry. Legal firms show the highest preference for formal meeting room interactions, whereas technology companies prefer inter-actions near their workstations in equal measure. Technology firms also show the highest preference for interacting near facilities such as kitchens, canteens, etc. As expected, the average number of people interacting fluctuates by industry (Fig. 7.3b), with companies in the Legal or Media industries showing the most extreme patterns of low levels of interactions (Legal) and very high levels of

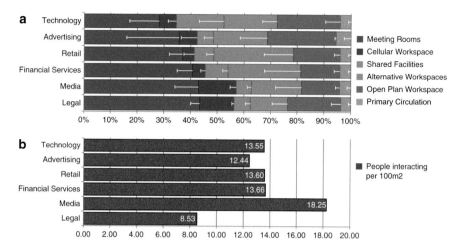

Fig. 7.3 (**a**, **b**) Numbers of people interacting per 100 m², split by types of space and by industry; lines represent standard error (*top*); average number of people interacting per 100 m² per industry (*bottom*)

interaction (Media). This can easily be argued to lie in the nature of the industry and their predominant workflows, as Legal firms tend to deal with sensitive matters, requiring thus a stricter level of privacy and confidentiality, while creative ones, such as those in the Media sector, would encourage interaction as a means to generate new ideas and spread information.

The Configurational Logic of Interaction

But can we pinpoint to specific patterns of interaction that depend on local spatial characteristics? In order to identify such patterns we examine whether interaction systematically relates to visual mean depth. Given that integrated spaces (lower MD) are more connected and more accessible, we would expect these spaces to engender higher interaction rates due to more opportunities for meeting people, as proposed by previous research studies (Hillier and Grajewski 1990; Toker and Gray 2008). This hypothesis would hold true if pixels that belong to segregated areas also exhibit a narrow and lower range of interaction, while pixels in integrated spaces would tend to cover a larger range and higher densities of interaction.

In Fig. 7.4a it is evident that no clear pattern emerges from plotting MD against interaction density. This is not overly surprising, since configuration certainly is not the only force at play. The influence of attractors is crucial here, because different functional areas attract interactions differently due to their programme. Meeting rooms clearly attract interactions disproportionately, as already shown. The same goes for workspaces: someone's desk is a clear interaction hotspot for that person,

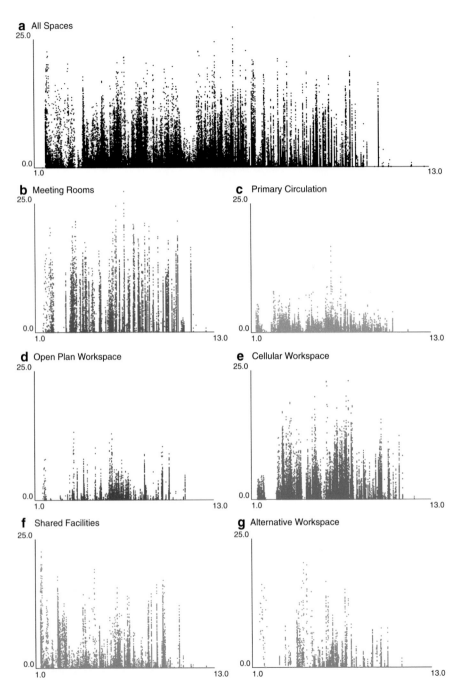

Fig. 7.4 (**a-g**) Scatterplots of visual MD (x-axis) and interaction density (y-axis) for all data in the sample (**a**) (*top row*), and split by type of space: meeting rooms (**b**), primary circulation (**c**), open workspace (**d**), cellular workspace (**e**), shared facilities (**f**) and alternative workspaces (**g**)

since they spend the majority of their time there. In this case we would not expect configuration to matter, since desks are allocated by the organisation. Hence we might expect to see a stronger influence of configuration in certain areas. Therefore the data was analysed separately by the various types of spaces (Fig. 7.4b–g). The fact that the distribution of interaction density appears random in meeting spaces (Fig. 7.4b) and workspaces (Fig. 7.4d, e) is expected due to their strong functional programme, however we would expect that configuration distributes interactions in primary circulation spaces (Fig. 7.4c), shared facilities (Fig. 7.4f) and alternative workspaces (Fig. 7.4g) according to a spatial logic, i.e. higher interaction densities in integrated areas (low MD) and fewer occurrences of interaction in segregated areas (high MD). However, this is not the case. No pronounced patterns of any sort can be found in the distributions. Further research is clearly needed here.

To delve further into the analysis, in the following section we consider three different projects to see if any clearer patterns appear by examining the data per project and per floor. We studied three buildings, chosen to be approximately comparable in size, each having three floors; this should act to rule out size and configuration effects, which could come with varying numbers of floors. The buildings, however, vary in their overall configuration: example A is a completely open plan office, example B combines open and cellular workspaces, while example C is mostly cellularised.

For this analysis, we are plotting all interactions taking place in shared facilities on a single floor of each of the three chosen example buildings against their visual mean depth values. This local analysis floor by floor for attractor-based facilities (kitchen, canteen, photocopiers, etc.) reveals a stronger relationship between spatial configuration and interaction. While the range of MD varies due to the spatial configuration of the overall office, within each example the more integrated areas (i.e. of lower mean depth) tend to attract higher interaction densities. The availability of other such facilities in close proximity is also likely to shape interaction density. A large single space as seen in Fig. 7.5a attracts higher levels of interaction, in contrast to Fig. 7.5b where these facilities are fragmented. In Fig. 7.5c, where these attractors are few and far apart, interaction is even lower. Still, people across all three randomly chosen examples seem to prefer integrated spaces over segregated spaces as a location for interactions. This means attractors show a synergy effect with integration: people could be argued to frequent those facilities based on their attractiveness and function (such as the need for a cup of tea), however, whether they afford interactions in addition to occupancy seems to be a function of spatial integration. More integrated, larger and more clustered facilities seem to support interactions to a higher degree than segregated, smaller and distributed ones. However as the previous analysis illustrated, this effect can only be seen locally on a floor by floor basis and not within the big dataset as a whole.

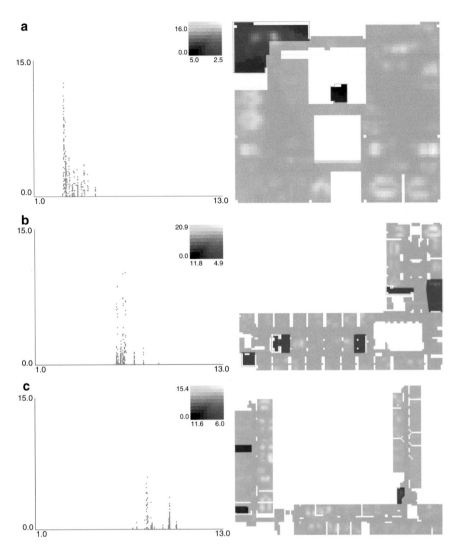

Fig. 7.5 *Left*: Visual mean depth (x-axis) and interaction (y-axis) for pixels in shared facilities for three sample floors. *Right*: Corresponding floor plans with location of facilities highlighted

The Micro-behaviours of Interaction

Since the analysis of localised patterns of interaction seemed fruitful, the next section aims at identifying specific types of interactions in relation to local spatial characteristics. Again, it means delving deeper into the data and exploring details more in-depth than in the previous analysis.

In office spaces, the majority of people interacting coincides with the activity of sitting, either in meeting rooms, workspaces, or in other shared facilities such as canteens. As this imposes predefined locations of interaction in the analysis, the dataset is re-examined taking into account only people standing and interacting. Standing may cause fatigue much faster than sitting and is more dynamic and ephemeral in nature, we thus expect that interactions involving people standing are more likely to be brief. They are also likely to depend to a higher degree on the spatial affordances of the environment, since standing could occur anywhere in space.

In this section we therefore want to identify spatial patterns of brief encounters occurring while people are standing. Therefore, we have plotted interaction densities of people standing on a sample floor plan and highlighted emerging categories of interactions in different colours (see Fig. 7.6), based on affordances and rationales for interaction as present in the environment. These categories were assigned manually for the purpose of this analysis, with plans to automate this in the future.

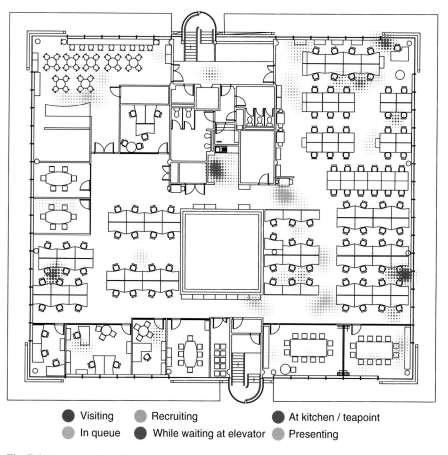

⬤ Visiting	⬤ Recruiting	⬤ At kitchen / teapoint
⬤ In queue	⬤ While waiting at elevator	⬤ Presenting

Fig. 7.6 Hotspots of locations where people stand and interact at the same time

The following seven different micro-behavioural interaction patterns have been identified:

1. *Recruiting*: People standing and interacting in proximity to, or within primary circulation are identified as engaged in the act of being recruited by others into a conversation, a term described by Backhouse and Drew (1992). People walking are in an 'available' state (i.e. not currently focused on work) and are recruited into conversation by their seated colleagues. As this pattern includes people passing-by in a brief conversation, close proximity to the primary circulation perpetuates this behaviour. Interactions like these are considered unplanned, as people passing through may do so at any point in time and will not have planned the interaction in advance. It rather emerges spontaneously based on the opportunity. This pattern is not found in floors which contain cellular workspaces and corridors, since visibility is crucial here.

2. *Visiting*: An interaction between seated and standing people, away from circulation, described by Penn, Desyllas and Vaughan (1999). An example would be someone visiting a colleague by their desk for a discussion or query. The distance usually kept from circulation allows for longer conversations making these interactions most likely planned.

3. *Presenting*: Observed in meeting rooms, these are interactions between a person standing and the rest of the (seated) members of the meeting. This behaviour could be an effect of office culture or the type or size of the meeting taking place. It could also signify the type of meeting and the hierarchy and different roles assumed by presenter and audience.

4. *Standup meeting*: Larger interactions can sometimes be observed taking place in the workspace. They can be brief meetings happening daily in organisations or teams which adopt rapid project development. They may also be quick announcement gatherings, for a team or the whole company. As such, they are considered planned interactions and typically involve larger groups of people.

5. *At kitchen/tea point/photocopy room*: Attractor based interaction pattern, can be found in any floor that contains a functional kitchen/tea point. Spaces like these are considered shared facilities in this analysis and, as seen later on, have peak interaction levels at lunch time. Photocopy rooms work the same way, but used uniformly through the day. As these attractors are usually part of each floor, the interactions within are very likely to be localised to the floor. These spaces, along with canteens all provide proximity for the people interacting, the necessary privacy and social designation with a purpose to afford informal interactions (Fayard and Weeks 2007).

6. *In queue*: Found in spaces with a food service counter, where a queue is formed. These are usually linear, in the same direction as the counter. Given that canteens with seating area and a service counter are usually one per company (as opposed to one per floor) and in some cases attract people from other companies, the interactions identified here are very likely to be more global in scope.

7. *While waiting at elevator*: Another 'waiting' interaction in addition to queuing. This is found in front of elevator doors, most likely by people continuing an

earlier conversation, or people striking up new ones, just because they are forced to wait at the same location. While the spaces where these interactions happen are not likely to have been designated as 'informal interaction spaces', they tend to be away from workspaces and as in queueing, the common target creates the necessary propinquity.

These patterns shed light on rationales and reasons to interact and allow us to identify the effects spatial affordances can have on interaction, in combination with the presence of others and organisational cultures.

The Time-Space Dependency of Interaction

A last piece of analysis that can provide insight into how interaction is distributed in office spaces is in its relationship to time. Since we are interested in the dynamics of interactions over the course of a full working week (see Fig. 7.7), we only take those datasets into account where observations were conducted for this length of time. These 20 cases (out of 27) cover the full spectrum of industries found in the database, i.e. financial services, technology, advertising, legal, media, retail and public sector.

Clear time-space routines become visible in the analysis (as seen in Fig. 7.7a, b), showcasing the daily life of the studied companies and overarching spatial cultures. The overall proportion of people interacting on average (Fig. 7.7a) varies slightly throughout the working week with Wednesday being the most interactive day across all cases and industries represented in this sample. Generally, people seem to interact more in the mornings than in the afternoons. Breaking the results down to the type of space they happen in not only reduces the standard error (Fig. 7.7a, shown exemplary for open plan workspaces), but also reveals more details about the emerging time-space routines. As shown in Fig. 7.7b, interaction levels start high in workspaces each morning and drop towards noon after which they rise again. Friday evening experiences a particular peak in interactions, possibly due to colleagues chatting about their weekend plans, or finalising last bits and pieces of work before breaking for the weekend. Lunchtime has an inverse effect for the facilities category, as it includes canteens, kitchens and other places where people go for lunch and have lots of chats, creating a clear and recurring peak in the pattern. Interaction in meeting rooms and cellular workspaces rises in mid-morning and mid-afternoon, which is the preferred time for meeting bookings. Interactions in primary circulation has varied peaks and troughs, but generally more interactions take place early mornings, at lunch and in the evening, when people are on the move.

These patterns of behaviour emerge in a top-level analysis of a range of different cases, each with its own way of organising space unique to organisational and sector cultures. Our approach has been to explore the data for underlying, generalizable causative structures, but in some cases our results have run into the limitations of the methodology.

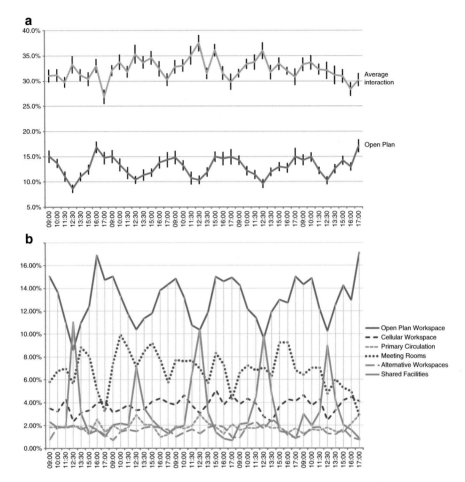

Fig. 7.7 (**a**, **b**) Proportion of people interacting in relation to all people currently in the space, across the week on average and in open-plan spaces; *vertical lines* represent standard error of the means (*top*); breakdown per type of space (*bottom*)

Overall Patterns and the Problem of Predictability

In order to facilitate interaction in offices further and in order to support evidence-based design practices – to apply research to practice and use this in new office design – we would need to solve the problem of predictability: how confident can we be about emerging patterns in a new case from looking at the deviations in existing cases?

It is evident from the analysis presented in this book chapter that predictability is not all that easily established. We can expect some relationships to hold in general, but more often than not, trends are not at all clear, especially those at a higher level.

We have seen for instance that specific types of spaces will tend to attract more interaction than others (meeting rooms versus workspaces), and narrowing this down to industry or time of day strengthens this relationship. Comparisons to visual mean depth have shown that spatial configuration plays a role in affording interactions, but correlations with this metric were only found on a local floor-by-floor analysis limited to specific spaces (shared facilities).

With regards to this type of analysis, we have merely scratched the surface and more research is required to fully understand the phenomenon of interaction in architectural space. While the sample of cases presented here is still growing and will provide a rich set of opportunities for further exploration, it is debatable whether the right type of information has been captured to get meaningful results. Expanding the dataset in both scope and granularity is one approach (see below); and examining a wider suite of space syntax measures may provide more nuanced insight into the effects of space on functional use.

Future Work and Developments in the Field

In this final section, we want to provide an outlook on future work in the field; this will be structured to discuss developments in automated behaviour tracking, which is a growing field of interest and could be seen as one form of human computer interaction; to address implications of our findings for the 'sites of HCI'; and to reflect on implications for Space Syntax research.

Automated Behaviour Tracking

Automated mechanisms for constant monitoring have the capacity to report in much greater temporal detail than the human observations currently employed. Temporal effects were quite pronounced in the data and could offer a wealth of future research opportunities.

Location and behaviour tracking inside buildings is a dynamic and fast-growing field with emerging and rapidly developing:

- New technologies (e.g. using magnetic fields such as https://www.indooratlas.com/)
- New measurement systems (e.g. utilising angle-of-arrival signals rather than received signal strength such as http://quuppa.com/ and http://u-hopper.com/ or mesh capture such as Xbox Kinect);
- New combinations of sensors (e.g. using heartbeat sensors or electroencephalography (EEG) devices, providing geo-located data related to human emotions responses; see for example, Mavros et al. 2012);
- New form factors (e.g. wristbands)

This could add an understanding of additional layers of information, which might create new insights. In recent years, researchers have begun to synthesise sensor data to build models of institutional dynamics (Pentland 2012). Applying this to space usage could be fruitful, since it is by its nature complex, taking place on multiple social, spatial and temporal levels, requiring a nuanced capture of space, time and interactions with the inclusion of human metrics (physiological and psychophysiological) to fully understand it. An even fuller picture of social interaction would require us to go beyond the activity within the office, linking with people's 'digital footprints' in their life outside work – researchers have begun to use social media and/or mobile telephony data to create detailed views of people's general patterns and preferences (see for instance: Noulas and Mascolo 2013).

The move to automated tracking of usage data, however, will require careful evaluations of what is being measured and to which degree this represents the 'ground truth' of life in the office. Technology is not per se objective, following the observation of Kranzberg (1986): "Technology is neither good nor bad; nor is it neutral." (*ibid.*, p. 545). Instead, it is based on its own assumptions, limitations and built-in capacities, so it could be argued that automated logging again creates a representation that might not provide an 'objective' depiction of reality. Constant monitoring already exists in the 'quantified self' movement, but the use of these technologies by employers to monitor employees will undoubtedly raise ethical concerns in a world already sensitive to issues around inequality, surveillance and personal freedoms. The workplace will need to address these issues rapidly – as indeed will the retail, cultural and entertainment sectors that have already started to employ these tools. By capturing and linking this data, and by managing it in reflective, rigorous and ethical ways, we could harness these powerful new techniques in order to understand human behaviours in offices, including face-to-face and human-computer interactions, so that the next generation of office buildings can be adaptive, supportive and enabling human activity and productivity.

Implications for HCI

Our interaction analysis has demonstrated areas where serendipitous interaction is a natural consequence of the building layout; we have also seen spaces and locations which, by their functional assignment, create sociability and interaction opportunities

This knowledge on people's behavioural and spatial preferences in workplace environments can be a useful starting point for new research in the field of HCI. The most obvious bridge from our work to HCI would be to strategically consider the location of technological interfaces, such as screens or installations in order to maximise their impact. For instance knowing that people hardly interact in circulation spaces might mean to reconsider placing an interface that requires interaction away from corridors and closer to shared facilities. Resources (such as networked tablets with voice interfaces, interactive whiteboards or recording and capture apparatus) could be placed close to informal interaction locations. Another possible application of our research might be in devising systems that automatically detect interactions and provide scenarios for intervention. This tension between automated observation and facilitating agency leads to a spectrum of potential solutions, for instance participants might be directed to available meeting spaces, resources or colleagues available for a chat in a kitchen. Knowing that interactions become less prevalent at certain times of the day or week (e.g. Monday and Friday afternoon) could mean to exploit those times for additional suggestions and interventions. Behavioural monitoring and behaviour change interventions are growing fields of research (for instance: Lathia et al. 2013; Efstratiou et al. 2012).

Bringing architectural research and HCI together in this context would mean for architects to embrace possibilities of technology and understand how they can enhance social life in the office and for the HCI community to reflect on the affordances of space. Both fields could be united in their endeavours to understand human behaviours to achieve specific outcomes – a well-used space, or a well-used technology.

Implications for Space Syntax

Furthermore, we can envisage various ways in which our research can push boundaries in the Space Syntax community. Recent contributions have already aimed at methodological innovations that take configurational analysis to the next level by devising methods of visualising and analysing both spatial information and behavioural or organisational aspects in unison. For instance Derix and Jagannath (2014) have combined information of functional allocation (the importance of assets in a bank, for instance) with morphological analysis in a single representation to understand complex relations. Similarly, Kwon and Sailer (2015) have brought behavioural data from where people observe objects inside museum exhibitions and department stores together with a proxemics approach and inter-visibility relations between people. It was shown how different roles emerge (spectators, actors and interactors) and how people in those roles distribute unevenly across space according to spatial configuration. This is highly complementary to the work of Fischer and Hornecker (2012), which classified roles of people in urban encounters in front of media facades (performer, participant, observer) and also worked with a framework of proxemics. In addition, new spatial analysis theories close to core interests of HCI were developed with the intent to unify the understanding of architecture and interaction. Interaction sites, HCI installations, devices or interpersonal interactions form extra layers of 'augmented information' that both spatial analysts and interaction designers manipulate. In Varoudis (2014) and Varoudis and Penn (2015), the core space syntax analysis used in buildings and small scale neighbourhoods, Visibility Graph Analysis, is extended in order to provide a new methodology able to analyse space and interaction information (in extent, any transpatial or spatiotemporal information) as a single systems where relational asymmetries are explicitly expressed in the analysis (space to space, space to device, space to 'interaction data' in this case).

All of these questions at the interface of behaviours, architectural space and technological interventions yield fascinating opportunities for future research. They raise wider and more complex questions with scope for exploration by HCI as well as the architectural research community. We hope that the findings reported in this chapter contribute towards these endeavours in providing a baseline of understanding of the complex interplay between space and human-to-human interactions in the workplace.

Acknowledgments This research was partially funded by Innovate UK under the Knowledge Transfer Partnership Scheme (KTP8978 'Big Data in the Office' by UCL and Spacelab, February 2013 – February 2015).

References

Backhouse A, Drew P (1992) The design implications of social interaction in a workplace setting. Environ Plan B Plan Design 19:573–584

Bernard HR (2000) Social research methods: qualitative and quantitative approaches. Sage, Thousand Oaks

Bernard HR, Killworth PD (1993) Sampling in time allocation research. Ethnology 32(2):207–215

Bradburn NM, Sudman S, Blair E, Stocking C (1978) Question threat and response bias. Publ Opin Quart 42(2):221–234

Brewer C, Harrower M (2009) COLORBREWER 2.0. ColorBrewer: color advice for maps. Accessed 7 Apr 2015. http://www.colorbrewer2.org/

Brown C, Efstratiou C, Leontiadis I, Quercia D, Mascolo C (2014a) Tracking serendipitous interactions: how individual cultures shape the office. In: Proceedings of the 17th ACM conference on computer supported cooperative work & social computing, Baltimore 2531641: ACM, 1072–1081

Brown C, Efstratiou C, Leontiadis I, Quercia D, Mascolo C, Scott J, Key P (2014b) The architecture of innovation: tracking face-to-face interactions with ubicomp technologies. In: ACM international joint conference on pervasive and ubiquitous computing (Ubicomp 2014), ACM, Seattle

Brunsdon C (1995) Estimating probability surfaces for geographical point data: an adaptive kernel algorithm. Comput Geosci 21(7):877–894

Cairncross F (1997) The death of distance: how the communications revolution will change our lives. Harvard University Press, Cambrige, MA

Curran K, Furey E, Lunney T, Santos J, Woods D, McCaughey A (2011) An evaluation of indoor location determination technologies. J Locat Based Serv 5(2):61–78

Derix C, Jagannath P (2014) Digital intuition – autonomous classifiers for spatial analysis and empirical design. J Space Syntax 5(2):190–215

Efstratiou C, Leontiadis I, Picone M, Rachuri KK, Mascolo C, Crowcroft J (2012) Sense and sensibility in a pervasive world. Pervasive Comput, 406–424

Fayard A-L, Weeks J (2007) Photocopiers and water-coolers. The affordances of informal interaction. Organ Stud 28(5):605–634

Fischer PT, Hornecker E (2012) Urban HCI: spatial aspects in the design of shared encounters for media facades. In: Proceedings of the SIGCHI conference on human factors in computing systems, Austin, 2207719: ACM, 307–316

Gertner J (2012) True innovation. The New York Times, 25 Feb 2012

Goffman E (1959) The presentation of self in everyday life. Penguin, Harmondsworth
Grajewski T (1992) Space syntax observation manual (2001 unpublished revised edition: L. Vaughan) 2001 unpublished revised edition: L. Vaughan, London: UCL Bartlett and Space Syntax Ltd.
Hall ET (1966) The hidden dimension. Doubleday, New York
Hillier B (1996) Space is the machine. A configurational theory of architecture. Cambridge University Press, Cambridge. Online at: http://eprints.ucl.ac.uk/3881/
Hillier B, Grajewski T (1990) The application of space syntax to work environments inside buildings: second phase: towards a predictive model. Unit for Architectural Studies, The Bartlett School of Architecture and Planning, University College London, London
Hillier B, Hanson J (1984) The social logic of space. Cambridge University Press, Cambridge
Hillier B, Hanson J, Peponis J (1984) What do we mean by building function? In: Powell JA, Cooper I, Lera S (eds) Designing for building utilisation. Spon Ltd, London, pp 61–72
Kohonen T (1998) The self-organizing map. Neurocomputing 21(1-3):1–6. doi:10.1016/S0925-2312(98)00030-7
Koutsolampros P, Sailer K, Pomeroy R, Austwick M, Hudson-Smith A, Haslem R (2015) Spatial databases: generating new insights on office design and human behaviours in the workplace. In: Karimi K, Vaughan L, Sailer K, Palaiologou G, Bolton T (eds) Proceedings of the 10th international space syntax symposium. Space Syntax Laboratory, The Bartlett School of Architecture, University College London, London, pp 23:1–23:16
Kranzberg M (1986) Technology and history: "Kranzberg's Laws". Technol Cult 27(3):544–560
Kwon SJ, Sailer K (2015) Seeing and being seen inside a museum and a department store. A comparison study in visibility and co-presence patterns. In: Karimi K, Vaughan L, Sailer K, Palaiologou G, Bolton T (eds) Proceedings of the 10th international space syntax symposium. Space Syntax Laboratory, The Bartlett School of Architecture, University College London, London, pp 24:1–24:15
Lathia N, Pejovic V, Rachuri KK, Mascolo C, Musolesi M, Rentfrow PJ (2013) Smartphones for large-scale behaviour change interventions. IEEE Pervasive Comput 12(3):66–73
Li N, Becerik-Gerber B (2011) Performance-based evaluation of RFID-based indoor location sensing solutions for the built environment. Adv Eng Inform 25(3):535–546
Lopez de Vallejo I (2009) Measuring spatial and temporal features of physical interaction dynamics in the workplace [Doctoral Dissertation], Unpublished thesis (Ph.D), University College, London
Markhede H, Koch D (2007) Positioning analysis: social structures in configurative modelling. In: Kubat AS, Ertekin Ö, Güney YI, Eyüboglu E (eds), 6th international space syntax symposium, Istanbul, 12–15 Jun 2007, ITÜ Faculty of Architecture
Marshall P, Rogers Y, Pantidi N (2011) Using F-formations to analyse spatial patterns of interaction in physical environments. In: Proceedings of the ACM 2011 conference on computer supported cooperative work, Hangzhou, 1958893: ACM, pp 445–454
Mavros P, Coyne R, Roe J, Aspinall P (2012) Engaging the brain: implications of mobile EEG for spatial representation. In: Achten H, Pavlicek J, Hulin J, Matejovska D (eds) Digital physicality – proceedings of the 30th eCAADe conference, Prague, Czech Republic, Czech Technical University of Prague, Faculty of Architecture, pp 657–665
Nohria N, Eccles RG (1992) Face-to-face: making network organizations work. In: Nohria N, Eccles RG (eds) Networks and organizations. Structure, form, and action. Harvard Business School Press, Boston, pp 288–308
Noulas A, Mascolo C (2013) Exploiting foursquare and cellular data to infer user activity in urban environments. In: IEEE 14th international conference on Mobile Data Management (MDM), 1:167–76. doi: 10.1109/MDM.2013.27
Olguin DO, Waber B, Taemie K, Mohan A, Ara K, Pentland A (2009) Sensible organizations: technology and methodology for automatically measuring organizational behavior. Syst Man Cybern B Cybern IEEE Trans 39(1):43–55
Penn A, Desyllas J, Vaughan L (1999) The space of innovation: interaction and communication in the work environment. Environ Plan B Plan Design 26:193–218

Pentland A (2012) The new science of building great teams. Harvard Business Review https://hbr.org/2012/04/the-new-science-of-building-great-teams. Accessed 13 Aug 2015.

Rainie L, Wellman B (2012) Networked: the new social operating system. MIT Press, Cambridge, MA

Rashid M, Kampschroer K, Wineman J, Zimring C (2006) Spatial layout and face-to-face interaction in offices – a study of the mechanisms of spatial effects on face-to-face interaction. Environ Plan B Plan Design 33:825–844

Reiss AJ (1971) Systematic observations of natural social phenomena. In: Costner H (ed) Sociological methodology. Jossey-Bass, San Francisco, pp 3–33

Rogers Y, Hazlewood WR, Marshall P, Dalton N, Hertrich S (2010) Ambient influence: can twinkly lights lure and abstract representations trigger behavioral change? In: Proceedings of the 12th ACM international conference on ubiquitous computing. ACM, New York, NY, pp 261–270

Sailer K (2007) Movement in workplace environments – configurational or programmed? In: Kubat AS, Ertekin Ö, Güney YI, Eyüboglu E (eds) 6th international space syntax symposium, Istanbul, 12–15 Jun 2007, ITÜ Faculty of Architecture

Sailer K, McCulloh IA (2012) Social networks and spatial configuration – how office layouts drive social interaction. Soc Networks 34(1):47–58

Sailer K, Penn A (2009) Spatiality and transpatiality in workplace environments. In: Koch D, Marcus L, Steen J (eds) 7th international space syntax symposium, Stockholm, Royal Institute of Technology KTH, 095:01–095:11

Sailer K, Pachilova R, Brown C (2013) Human versus machine – testing validity and insights of manual and automated data gathering methods in complex buildings. In: Kim YO, Park HT, Seo KW (eds) 9th international space syntax symposium. Sejong University Press, Seoul

Sailer K, Pomeroy R, Haslem R (2015) Ten things you might not know about the workplace: insights from an evidence-based design practice. Work&Place (1), 6–9

Schnädelbach H (2012) Hybrid spatial topologies. J Space Syntax 3(2):204–222

Schnädelbach H, Penn A, Steadman P, Benford S, Koleva B, Rodden T (2006) Moving office: inhabiting a dynamic building. In: Proceedings of the 2006 20th anniversary conference on computer supported cooperative work, Banff, Alberta, Canada, 1180924: ACM, pp 313–322

Shklovski I, Chang MF (2006) Urban computing – navigating space and context. Computer 39(9):36–37

Steen J (2009) Spatial and social configurations in offices. In: Koch D, Marcus L, Steen J (eds) 7th international space syntax symposium, Stockholm, Stockholm, TRITA-ARK Forskningspublikation, 107_1–107_9

Steen J, Blombergsson M, Wiklander J (2005) Useful buildings for office activities. Facilities 23(3/4):176–186

Storper M, Venables AJ (2004) Buzz: face-to-face contact and the urban economy. J Econ Geogr 4(4):351–370

Toker U, Gray DO (2008) Innovation spaces: workspace planning and innovation in U.S. University research centers. Res Policy 37:309–329

Turner A, Doxa M, O'Sullivan D, Penn A (2001) From isovists to visibility graphs: a methodology for the analysis of architectural space. Environ Plan B Plan Design 28(1):103–121

Van de Mortel TF (2008) Faking it: social desirability response bias in self-report research. Aust J Adv Nurs 25(4):40–48

Varoudis T (2011) Ambient displays: influencing movement patterns. In: Campos P, Graham N, Jorge J, Nunes N, Palanque P, Winckler M (eds) Human-computer interaction – INTERACT 2011. Springer, Berlin, pp 52–65

Varoudis T (2012) depthmap X: multi-platform spatial network analysis software, OpenSource', 0.30

Varoudis T (2014) Augmented visibility graph analysis – mixed-directionality graph structure for analysing architectural space. In: Fusion, proceedings of the 32nd international conference on education and research in computer aided architectural design in Europe, vol. 2. eCAADe Conferences, Newcastle upon Tyne: Northumbria University, pp 293–302

Varoudis T, Penn A (2015) Visibility, accessibility and beyond: next generation visibility graph analysis. In: Karimi K, Vaughan L, Sailer K, Palaiologou G, Bolton T (eds) Proceedings of the 10th international space syntax symposium. Space Syntax Laboratory, The Bartlett School of Architecture, University College London, London, pp 152:1–152:13

Wu L, Waber B, Aral S, Brynjolfsson E, Pentland A (2008) Mining face-to-face interaction networks using sociometric badges: predicting productivity in an IT configuration task. SSRN [online], (http://ssrn.com/abstract=1130251) available. doi: Accessed 16 Apr 2013

Part III
Going Abstract About the Concrete

Our emerging field both draws on existing theoretical work as explanatory framework and expands and develops new theoretical lenses. Drawing on external theoretical work can be very fruitful when it inspires new departures and when it allows the explanation of otherwise difficult to explain phenomena (e.g. embodiment to explain the theory of space syntax, itself emerging out of observed phenomena). The approach also sometimes bears the risk of perpetuating a misunderstood take on a particular theory. Extending the theoretical work of others and building entirely new theoretical knowledge is then an essential communication medium from the field of Adaptive Architecture with other fields. The authors in this section present their work using theory to explain observed phenomena and their work expanding existing theory to adapt that for the field of human computer interaction.

Memarovic approaches the design of interactive networked public displays through the lens of *Marshall McLuhan's media theories*. This is an interesting approach as media theory is a popular lens applied to the creation and critique of architecture. What becomes apparent despite the use of terms like *figure* and ground or the four laws of media is that the work fundamentally engages with the notion of *place making*. This immediately creates strong links with the chapters by *Luusua* and *Deshpande* at the same time reflecting the chapters by *Moradi*, *Pantidi* and *Scupelli*. It seems interesting that the work from a computer scientist like *Memarovic* centering around social interactions in public spaces, in particular, opportunities for intra- and inter-community interaction should in many ways be readable as a purely architectural work. The fact that Memarovic reaches into the kind of interdisciplinary practices familiar in architectural design reminds us that many of the barriers between architecture and ubiquitous computing are in fact just thin membranes.

Nils Jäger's work seems to sit in that special transitional space between architecture and computation. One of the historical aspects this paper identifies is that ever since the invention of the thermostat, buildings have always sort homeostasis through their very simple nervous systems. Jaeger is interested in the reciprocal interaction between a person and building. The central concrete system here is the exchange of breath. By creating and *adaptive architecture* that reflects the occupants' breathing they show how the architecture through the breathing motion and by reciprocal interaction can change the occupants breathing rate. We seek out buildings that frequently change our mental states. A library for reflection, the café for conviviality. Jäger here seeks a building that at first reflects the user's/occupant's own state, then through its motion sympathizes and finally influences that physiological state that in turn alters mental state. One aspect that is clearly central to this paper is the notion of embodied cognition. Embodiment the notion that thought is not a process which is entirely isolated from the occupation of the space is a theme that we have encountered many times in this book before. Here we are challenged by the notion that the building is also embodied. That its computation is in many ways driven by the occupant. Jäger's work also reflects the notions of adaptive architecture building that is no longer in stasis. While reading his work, I was strongly reminded of Architect Le Corbusier's quote about a house being a machine for living in, except here the house becomes a robot for living in. Jäger's work challenges our notion of occupation "Are we occupying the building all through reciprocal interaction as found in the Exobuilding project or is the building occupying us?"

Chapter 8
Community Is the Message: Viewing Networked Public Displays Through McLuhan's Media Theory

Nemanja Memarovic

Abstract Networked public displays are envisioned to become a new communication medium for the twenty-first century with potentially the same impact on the society as the radio, TV or the Internet. To better understand the capabilities and limitations of such a new medium, we can turn to the field of media theory, and in particular to the work of Marshall McLuhan, who in the 1960s coined the slogan "the medium is the message". In McLuhan's theory, the key to understanding how a medium impacts society is to understand the interplay between the figure – the medium – and the ground – the context in which it operates. In order to understand what processes lead to successful engagement with this new medium we can use McLuhan's "rear-view mirror" metaphor and analyze the causes leading to attachment and engagement with public spaces. McLuhan also put forward the "four laws of media" – the tetrad – to group and describe both a medium's impact on society and its influence on other media. In this chapter I connect McLuhan's media theory – figure and ground, the rear-view mirror, and the tetrad – with research on interactions and processes in public space, in order to better understand why networked public displays are suited to be a communication medium that connects place-based communities and stimulates community interaction.

Introduction

Shopping malls, metro stations, cafes, and streets are just some of the places where we can find public displays. They come in different shapes and sizes, from small displays showing bus schedule at a bus stops, medium ones advertising events in a bar, to entire building facades being turned into a large screen showing the latest brand advertisement. With ever increasing numbers of public displays in urban spaces (Kostakos and Ojala 2013, cf. Fig. 8.1) it is not hard to imagine that these displays will be soon networked through the Internet with each other, thus making

N. Memarovic (✉)
University of Zurich, Binzmühlestrasse 14, CH-8050 Zürich, Switzerland
e-mail: memarovic@ifi.uzh.ch

© Springer International Publishing Switzerland 2016 165
N.S. Dalton et al. (eds.), *Architecture and Interaction*,
Human–Computer Interaction Series, DOI 10.1007/978-3-319-30028-3_8

Fig. 8.1 Public displays are "painting" the urban landscape and are becoming a ubiquitous resource in the urban environments. In this figure we can see them (from the *top left image*) in shopping malls, metro stations, universities, cafes, and shop windows facing the streets

a novel and powerful communication medium – networked public displays. Such a medium could potentially have the same impact on the society as the radio, TV, or Internet (Clinch et al. 2011; North et al. 2013; Ojala et al. 2012). While scenarios that show their potential through highly engaging interactive applications drive the vision of networked public displays (Davies et al. 2012), at the moment these displays are receiving none or little attention (Huang et al. 2008). This is mainly due their non-engaging content in the forms of static images, videos, and/or PowerPoint slides, resulting in the audience expecting to see boring advertisement (Müller et al. 2009).

In order to understand what is it that this medium could be doing and how it could address its audience in this paper I turn to media theory, or more precisely to Marshall McLuhan's media theory (McLuhan 1994). His iconic work is best known for phrases like "the medium is the message", "the user is the content", or "the global village" (at the moment of writing used to describe the impact of the TV on the society, now commonly used to describe the impact of the Internet). Three of the interesting tools he left us for analyzing the impact of media on the society are the figure and ground metaphors that explain the interplay between the *media* and its *context*; the *rear-view mirror* that can be used for understanding of the causes of the processes leading to engagement; and the *tetrad* of "four laws of media" that describe how new mediums interplay with the old ones and impact the society.

In this chapter I extend my previous work (Memarovic et al. 2014) that looked into McLuhan's work and used the figure and the ground and the rear-view mirror metaphors by providing more contemporary examples, and also by looking into the tetrad (McLuhan and McLuhan 1988), in order to present theoretical ground for networked public displays as a communication medium. In the next sections I will first present related work on the history of the networked public displays medium as well as on the works that connected existing theories from social sciences, environmental behavior, and media ecology to explain the effects of public displays. Next I will present a part of McLuhan's media theory that discusses the figure and ground and the rear-view mirror metaphors and the tetrad. I will then "Marshall" and describe networked public displays through the above-mentioned McLuhan's concepts. Finally I will present concluding remarks.

Related Work

Historically speaking the interest in networked public displays has started in the 1980s with the pioneering project *Hole in the Space* (Medien Kunst Netz 2015) that connected two cities, New York and Los Angeles, through a simple video link. The video connection allowed people to glimpse into life on the other side, observing the setting, people, and their interactions (both between the people and between the people and the setting). Additionally this simple video link stimulated direct interactions *between* the people at the two locations and allowed talking and gesturing, warping their settings and creating a new virtual *context* that brought them together. Similarly, the *Hole in the Earth* (Institute for the Unstable Media 2015) and *Telectroscope* (Paul St George 2015) are examples of projects that connected two distant spaces via a video link (Rotterdam and Shanghai in the case of the Hole in the Earth, and London and New York in the case of Telectroscope). Similar installations have been also used to connect locations that are close to each other – a corridor and a room at the end of it – by providing a "sneak peak" of what is happening in the room (Varoudis 2011).

Since the first deployments of networked public displays the work has changed and shifted, due technological advances in computer science and their economical availability, towards creating more multimedia experiences that further blend physical spaces through digital media. For example, people are able to post digital pins and posters to displays (Jose et al. 2013), or post and read classifieds on a public display (Alt et al. 2011a), or express themselves freely by posting photos to a display network via a display-attached camera (Memarovic et al. 2015). Another change from the early days is that today networked public displays would typically have multiple applications running on them (Clinch et al. 2011; North et al. 2013; Ojala et al. 2012), thus providing more ways to connect people within and across public spaces. This progress in the area also prompted new research avenues, e.g., understanding how best to schedule applications on display networks (Elhart et al. 2014), understanding how to entice people to interact with them (Brignull and Rogers 2003), uncovering novel interaction techniques (Alt et al. 2013), or describing the overall challenges in designing, developing, and deploying networked public displays "in the wild" (Memarovic et al. 2013).

Despite all the new research on networked public displays little work has tried to understand *the overall purpose of this new medium from a theoretical stance* (as shown in this and next paragraph). The use of theory in research on networked public displays has been scarce and has mainly focused on its situated aspects and a single public display (Dalton et al. 2013; Ludvigsen 2005; Matthews et al. 2007; Memarovic et al. 2013). In this domain Dalton et al. (2013) have connected the space syntax theory in order to understand people's movement patterns in the space and how best to place a display so it could receive more attention. Memarovic et al. (2013) have also built on the properties of public spaces and human needs in them in order to apply them to public displays. Ludvigsen (2005) has focused on one of these aspects, i.e., social interaction in public spaces according to Goffman (1963), and illustrated how we can design public displays that stimulate it. Matthews et al. (2007) connected activity theory and peripheral displays to explain how we can inform their design by supporting activities that are taking place in a certain space. More recently Memarovic et al. (2012) focused on the networked aspects of the medium and how we can fit it in with the rest of widespread media such as Facebook, Twitter etc. Lastly, Elhart et al. (2014) drew upon system scheduling theory to understand how to schedule applications on this new medium.

The work described in this chapter falls closest to the works of Ebsen (2013) and McQuire (2006) who have connected McLuhan's media theory and how the screen can be used as an artistic material; and investigated the impact of media architecture on the spectator actor roles in public spaces respectively. I complement both Ebsen's and McQuire's work by going beyond the notion of a single screen and by contextualizing McLuhan's theory through the reference to communities. In this way the chapter argues for a vision that shifts from the currently advertisement driven medium and presents a more humane research agenda that connects to people and their needs. The chapter provides the reasoning and motivation for creating applications and content that address place-based communities.

Overall, the work described in this chapter complements the current body of research by motivating the need for the use of networked public displays for community interaction and by showing *why networked public displays are a medium for connecting place-based communities*. This is done by examining the effects of current networked public display systems and connecting them with McLuhan's media theory (McLuhan 1994) and research on social and community interaction in public spaces (Carr et al. 1992).

A Short Introduction to McLuhan's Media Theory

One of the most influential and well-known mass media theories that looks into the long-term societal impacts of medias is the one of McLuhan (1994) that states *"the medium is the message"*. The importance of his work is currently getting more attention and there are even academic conferences that solely analyze the use of his work in understanding the effects of media on the society (Ciastellardi et al. 2011).

According to McLuhan, a key to understanding the impact of a medium on the processes it creates and changes is to *understand the interplay between the figure and the ground*, i.e., the medium and the context in which it operates respectively (Logan 2011). This is different from the architectural stance on figure and ground (Trancik 1986) that is used to analyze how buildings (*figure*) shape the public space (*ground*). For McLuhan one cannot understand the true impact of a medium (*figure*) unless the context (*ground*) in which it operates is not taken into account. For example, if *car* is seen *as a medium* (*figure*) the context in which it operates (literally the *ground*) was influential on the way the car as a medium operates. This is done by amplifying people's social practices in the context: the car allowed faster movement between the suburbs and the city, group movements became more social on a daily basis through carpooling, and the way we think about time also changed as we started to refer to distances in the amount of time necessary to drive to a particular location (Library and Archives Canada 2007).

The importance of understanding the interplay between the figure and ground is best captured with this quote (Molinaro et al. 1987, p. 478):

> My writings baffle most people simply because I begin with ground and they begin with figure. I begin with effects and work round to the causes, whereas the conventional pattern is to start with a somewhat arbitrary selection of 'causes' and then try to match these with some of the effects.

In order to understand the greater impact of networked public displays on the society I will look into the effects documented by prior work on networked public displays and will tie them to the research on the effects of human interactions in and with public space, thus connecting the figure and the ground in a similar manner as McLuhan.

We can also examine the processes happening in public spaces further and understand what causes them, and also what causes human connections with public spaces. By doing so we can create a full picture of *why* people interact in public space the way they do, which in turn can help researchers in integrating these principles into the new medium. For this purpose we can twist McLuhan's *rear-view mirror* metaphor (McLuhan and Fiore 1967, p. 74–75). According to McLuhan people become aware of a medium only when it is overtaken by another medium. For example, the telephone overtook the telegraph and was first thought of as the "talking telegraph"; or the car that was first thought of as a "horseless carriage". McLuhan states that

> We look at the present through a rear-view mirror. We march backwards into the future

which can be seen as a negative thing as we examine new media through the lens of the old one, not fully understanding its potential. This is not far from today's understanding of networked public displays as they are seen simply as digital versions of traditional public notice boards, showing still images, slideshows, and videos. In other words, typically the content of today's public displays would have little or no connection with its ground/context. However, we can put the *rear-view mirror* metaphor into a better use by *looking at the reasons of human interactions in and with the networked public display's ground – the public space*. By backtracking the causes of the interactions in and with public spaces, thus "rear view mirroring" in a way, we can understand the basic principles upon which networked public displays medium should work.

A way to holistically and concisely connect the outcomes of the figure and ground and the rear-view mirror analysis and to describe the boundaries of a medium is through McLuhan' tetrad of *four laws of media*:

1. What processes does a medium amplify?
2. What does it [the medium] make obsolete?
3. What does it retrieve from the past, something that was obsolesced? and
4. What does the medium flip into when it is pushed to the extreme?

For example, Levinson (2004, p. 16) described the radio through the tetrad "Radio, for example, enhanced oral communication across great distances; obsolesced aspects of written communication, such as the newspaper as the leading edge of news delivery; retrieved some of the prominence of oral communication from pre-literate times; and reversed into broadcasts of sounds and images – television." The tetrad has also been used to describe, e.g., the Internet (Sandstrom 2012), augmented reality (Papagiannis 2011), the impact of personal digital assistants (PDAs), or even processes like software testing (Bolton 2007). In the context of networked public displays the tetrad describes the limitations and boundaries of the medium with respect to community interaction (the medium *amplifies* processes that lead to community interaction, which is also a value *retrieved* from the past) and its fit with the rest of the media (as it *obsolesces* other media, and once *pushed to the extreme* becomes a new medium).

"Marshalling" Networked Public Displays

In this section I will analyze the documented effects of networked pubic displays and human interaction in public spaces that lead to them (*figure-ground* metaphor), the reasons why they are happening (*rear-view mirror*), and how the two connect to describe the bigger picture of the medium's impact and its fit with the rest of the media (*four laws of media*).

As mentioned several times throughout this chapter, the key to understanding what a medium does is to understand the context where the medium operates. Public spaces are building blocks of local communities as they provide the ground where local neighbors bump into each other to share the latest news, help with a heavy grocery bag, or just 'hang out'. These activities, in turn, help in creating the common identity:

> When public spaces are successful [...] they will increase opportunities to participate in communal activity. This fellowship in the open nurtures the growth of public life, which is stunted by the social isolation of ghettos and suburbs. In the parks, plazas, markets, waterfronts, and natural areas of our cities, people from different cultural groups can come together in a supportive context of mutual enjoyment. As these experiences are repeated, public spaces become vessels to carry positive communal meanings. (Carr et al. 1992, p. 344)

The next section is written in the spirit of McLuhan's writing and makes an *inventory of effects* (McLuhan 1994) by analyzing documented effects of existing networked public display systems. Also, for each presented case I will look into the processes happening in public spaces that lead to them.

Figure and Ground: Processes in Public Spaces Amplified by Networked Public Displays

Networked public displays can stimulate physical activities and engagement with the space, which in turn can lead to social interaction between passers-by and community members (cf. Fig. 8.2). An example of applications that were able to

Fig. 8.2 An example of how networked public displays can stimulate social interaction between passers-by. In this example the first passer-by is reading a fun fact from the FunSquare application (Memarovic et al. 2013) when another person stops-by and starts interacting

stimulate engagement with the space and people in it is *Communiplay* (Müller et al. 2014) that allows people to play a game where they juggle and bounce balls together through a display network. Another example is *FunSquare* (Memarovic et al. 2013) that stimulates social interaction between passers-by through an obscure/wrapped up information presented on a display, created by matching information from display's vicinity (e.g., the number of people in the space) with information from elsewhere (e.g., the population of Pitcairn Island). The reason why networked public displays are able to stimulate engagement with the space and people in it is because they are stimulating and supporting existing processes in public spaces. One of the most common processes that occurs in public spaces is *social triangulation*, a form of active engagement in the environment, where unusual features in the space, e.g., a sculpture, fountain, or street performance, provide the common ground/theme for people to socialize, which can lead to the notion of belonging to a community (Carr et al. 1992, p. 119). In turn, this also stimulates passive engagement with the environment where people simply observe what others are doing, which can be translated to *the honey pot effect* where seeing people interact with public displays raises interest of passers-by to observe what others are doing as well as to interact with a display.

Exchange and interaction between local community members is another process that networked public displays can stimulate and support (cf. Fig. 8.3). One example of such an application is *Digifieds* (Alt et al. 2011a) that allowed local community members to upload classifieds to a display network. In order to keep the accent on the local community classifieds could be uploaded only through a mobile phone client and when a user is next to a display, or they could be created directly on the display. Also, a classified would be seen only on a smaller part of a display network

Fig. 8.3 An example of how networked public displays can be used for stimulating exchange and interaction through a digital version of a traditional public notice board. In the example above of the Digifieds application (Alt et al. 2011a) a person can see all the classifieds on a display and can upload his content or download a classified ad onto his mobile phone

that was representative of a particular neighborhood. A reason why networked displays are able to stimulate exchange and interaction between local community members is because they represent an improved version of more traditional public notice areas that historically have been used for local community members and neighbors to exchange information and potentially goods (Alt et al. 2011b).

Leaving a mark in the setting and/or decorating a particular space, thus creating history and historical connections with it is another process that networked public displays can support (cf. Fig. 8.4). Within this area *CLIO* project (Ringas and Christopoulou 2013) is a prominent example as it allowed people to upload stories of historical/local relevance for a place in the city of Oulu or Corfu (two separate deployments) in the form of text, pictures, and videos that were shared across a display network. Another and more simple example is the *Moment Machine* (Memarovic et al. 2015) that allows passers-by to take photos and leave them in the urban setting and also share them across the network, thus collecting and creating memories within and across public spaces. *Instant Places' "Pins"* (Jose et al. 2013) that allowed football fans to express their belonging to a community by displaying football club's emblem is another example of an application that allows leaving a mark on a networked public display. Historically, people have been leaving their marks since the beginning of the time, e.g., cave paintings or pictograms or modern city graffiti. Marking of a space in turn creates history and historical connections with it. For example,

Fig. 8.4 An example of leaving a mark in the setting via the Moment Machine application. Application users often took photos and came back to look at them after some time, ensuring they are still there

> The freedom to leave a personal mark on a site, one that can rest within marks of history is one kind of valued modification. The photographs, notes, and flowers left at the Vietnam Memorial in Washington offer a moving image of this kind of transformation. (Carr et al. 1992, p. 223)

Also, the above-mentioned applications – the *Moment Machine* and *Instant Place's Pins* – promote diversity of different communities that thrive in a space through observing the diversity of personally taken photographs or through pins that depict allegiance to a certain group. This is not surprising as Holland et al. (2007) argue that public spaces serve the purpose of promoting "provision of difference" and that they should also cater for the needs of different groups that thrive in them. As they state

> being able to be seen in public and to be able to see different types of social groups may go some way to enabling everyone, and children and young people in particular, to observe difference, and thereby perhaps, promote tolerance for social diversity. (Holland et al. 2007, p. 67)

Also, the *Moment Machine* application and *CLIO* can stimulate greater connections within geographically distributed communities. As mentioned previously, the two applications can aid in recording local events and creating history, which in turn can be moved across spaces (where the recording actually happened). This can be connected to the nature of public spaces that can signal connections within larger societies through connections that *"involves an understanding of the meaning of places beyond the superficial level"* (Carr et al. 1992, p. 222). These connections are developed due historical events that a place symbolizes, e.g., the Washington Monument that signals the sense of togetherness between the US nation, or due actual events that took place at it, e.g., the Boston Common that was a British Camp at a time and also a place for protesting against the war in Vietnam. While currently interactions with such historical public spaces happen only when they are visited (or when people think about them or discuss them), networked public displays would allow more direct interaction with the created content from (potentially) any display. In turn this would make such interactions more concrete and distributed.

Networked public displays can also unite community members to express their opinion about locally relevant topics thus stimulating civic engagement. For example, the *Discussions in Space* application (Schroeter 2012) and *UBInion* (Hosio et al. 2012) allowed local community members to post comments on new architectural changes in the environment and general problems with a city respectively. Similarly to leaving a mark in the setting, also the ability to express one's opinion in public space has been with us since the beginning of time. A prominent example of one such public space is ancient Greek's Agora – a central point in any city where community members would gather to discuss and debate locally relevant topics.

Creating links across space and time is another process that networked public displays support. In this area researchers have mainly investigated the use of real-time video connection to create connection between distant places, e.g., *Hole in Space* connected New York and Los Angeles through a video link. Similar and more recent projects are *Connected Urban Spaces* (Fatah gen. Schieck and Fan 2012),

Table 8.1 Community-space cluster that lists effects of networked public displays

	Within places	Across places
Within communities	Stimulating physical engagement within the environment	Stimulating connections across geographically distributed communities
	Stimulating social interaction	
	Exchange and interaction between community members	
	Leaving a mark in the setting and creating historical connections	
	Civic engagement	
Between communities	Promoting diversity of different communities that thrive in the space	Enriching local life through links with diverse communities

Hole in the Earth, and *Telectroscope*. A more recent example is *Communiplay* that engaged people across spaces in a game where participants from different public spaces were juggling balls together. Some of these experiences of bridging far-away places are similar to the experience of walking in a public space where we see glimpses of connections of our locality with other places, e.g., observing different types of shops in a street ranging from a Chinese restaurant, to a specialized grocery store selling Indian products, to a tailor that makes hand made Italian suits. Networked public displays can go beyond what's currently available in the locality and provide connections with other distant places that are not currently represented.

In Table 8.1 we can see different effects that network public displays produce using community and space as dimensions. The table represents an updated version of the community-space cluster, originally reported in (Memarovic et al. 2011). This table can be used for understanding what effects of networked public displays have been reported, allowing researchers to get new ideas.

The Rear-View Mirror of Public Space: The Basic Principles of the Networked Public Displays Medium

In the section above I have shown the effects produced by networked public displays and human processes that lead to them. Understanding the causes of the processes would be beneficial, as it can lead to the basic principles that the networked public displays medium could be built upon. In order to do so we can use McLuhan's *rear-view mirror* metaphor. The *rear-view mirror* metaphor in our case can be used for analyzing processes happening in public spaces that lead to people's engagement in them and attachment for them. As stated by Carr et al. (1992, p. 20, 223, 233):

> Meaningful spaces are those that allow people to make strong connections between the place, their personal lives, and the larger world [...] By the build up of overlapping memories of individual and shared experiences, a place becomes sacred to a community [...] The freedom to leave a personal mark on a site, one that can rest within marks

of history is one kind of valued modification. [...] The development of meaning is an
interactive process between the space and person that evolves over time, a transactional
process in which user and setting are both impacted. [...] Repeated direct experience is a
requirement for connections to develop.

The above-statements discuss the properties of effective/usable public spaces,
which allow people to engage in them and create connections with them. Good
public spaces are the ones that allow people to engage and create "overlapping
memories of individual and shared experiences" (Carr et al. 1992, p. 20) or allow
them "to leave their mark" (Carr et al. 1992, p. 223). Also, these spaces go
beyond just the local and convey connections with the "larger world". Overall,
engagement with a space and people in it supports the creation of meaning through
"an interactive process between the space and the person" that can impact the
surrounding and sometimes greater community and person's sense of belonging.
Carr et al.'s work point to four important concepts of engagement and creation of
connections and meaning in/with public spaces: creating individual and/or shared
experiences through engagement with the space itself, leaving a personal mark in
the setting, providing greater connections with the larger world, and the need of
"repeated direct experiences" as a requirement for connections to develop. As shown
in the previous section there are existing works on networked public displays that
show how these processes can be amplified through them (through networked public
displays).

For example, stimulating engagement with a space can be seen as stimulating
engagement mediated through a display, thus also creating individual or shared
experiences with it. Existing work has shown that engagement with a place can
be stimulated in different ways, e.g., through whole-body interaction (Müller et al.
2014) or by posing challenging information and stimulating intrigue and curiosity,
which in turn can lead to social interaction between people (Memarovic et al. 2013).

The second concept involves leaving a personal mark in the setting. Current
research has supported this in various ways. For example, this can be done through
lightweight liking of the content (Memarovic et al. 2013) or taking a photo via
a display attached camera and posting it to a display network, thus contributing
to the creation of the community's history (Memarovic et al. 2015). Ringas and
Christopoulou (2013) supported recording a video about a specific location, thus
allowing people to leave their sentiments and marks. Lastly, Schroeter (2012) allow
people to post comments to a public display where a debate on a locally relevant
topic is taking place, this visualizing their opinions.

The third concept shows the necessity for a place to provide greater connections
with the rest of the world, thus showing how it fits in and extends beyond the
locality. Previous work on networked public displays has provided and catered for
this through simple video links (Institute for the Unstable Media 2015; Medien
Kunst Netz 2015; North et al. 2013; Paul St George 2015) or through other
means by extracting information about a place through display-attached sensors
and connecting this place-relevant information with information about other places
outside of the locality (Memarovic et al. 2013).

The fourth, and maybe the most important concept, involves "repeated direct experience" as a requirement for connections to develop. This points out the need for repeated engagement with networked public displays over a longer period of time, arguing for longer deployments in order to make a true impact as a medium.

All these examples show the variety of engagement and impact that networked public displays (*figure*) can stimulate in public spaces (*ground*). In other words, we can connect here the causes of people's interactions in public spaces (that were analyzed through the *rear-view mirror*), the effects that are produced when people interact (the *ground*), and how theses effects are further stimulated through networked public displays (the *figure*). For example, engaging with public displays and leaving a mark in the setting can lead to the creation of awareness of the diverse people that thrive in a public space, as people can observe others interacting with a public display and anyone can use it to leave their mark. If these interactions are recorded somehow, e.g., through photos (Memarovic et al. 2015) or videos (Ringas and Christopoulou 2013) they would contribute to the creation of local history that can be transmitted to other displays in the network. This locally recorded history can then be moved across the displays in the network, affectively transmitting connections across a greater community and signaling the sense of belonging, and at the same time infusing diversity in distant and different places. It would be advisable to record the above-mentioned interactions somewhere on the web or to make backup copies in order to avoid any loss if displays are removed from the setting.

Tetrad or "Four Laws of Media": The Overall Impact of the Networked Public Displays Medium on Other Media and the Society

Another tool that McLuhan left in analyzing media is the tetrad or *four laws of media*. The questions from the tetrad can be used to further understand how a medium operates, by analyzing the processes a medium amplifies, how a medium impacts other media by making them obsolete, what does a medium retrieve from the past – something that was made obsolesced, and ultimately what does a medium turn into when it is pushed into the extreme. For example, Papagiannis (2011) used the tetrad to describe augmented reality as a medium: augmented reality *enhances* information sharing, entertainment and gaming, education, and human vision; it *obsolesces* virtual reality and virtual intangible environments; it *retrieves* tactility, physical engagement, mobility and physical space, and single user looking devices (e.g., stereoscope); and it *reverses* into a window/screen – mediated reality with no identifiable filter, retina projections and no longer being able to distinguish reality from the virtual, brain linked with the visual realms.

To concisely and fully describe how networked public displays impact the society and other media we can look at the processes that were analyzed in the previous two sections also through the McLuhan's *four laws of media*.

What Processes Does a Media Amplify? Networked public displays amplify casual/chance encounters and social interaction between passers-by and local community members (Memarovic et al. 2013; Müller et al. 2014), exchange and community interaction (Alt et al. 2011a), marking the territory and creating historical connections with the locality and local community (Ringas and Christopoulou 2013; Memarovic et al. 2015; Jose et al. 2013), visibility of different social, interest, age and other groups, public debate, links to distant places (Ringas and Christopoulou 2013; Memarovic et al. 2015; Jose et al. 2013).

What Does the Media Make Obsolete? Static "special features" of public spaces such as fountains and sculptures that served the purpose for triggering social triangulation and spontaneous social interaction (Memarovic et al. 2013), analog notice boards (Alt et al. 2011a), physical public decision/discussion meetings (Schroeter 2012), and interactions in the virtual world.

What Does It Retrieve From the Past, Something That Was Obsolesced? The strongest notion that networked public displays bring back from the past is local community interaction and exchange within community members. As pointed by Thompson (2002, p. 68):

> We are thus looking forward to an urban society where, perhaps, more people are living in relative proximity than ever before, but where the regular daily social contact that comes from sharing homes or living in culturally homogenous districts no longer pertains. It is an intriguing prospect – a close-knit society of strangers.

As shown in the above sections *networked displays bring back the accent on local community interaction*. They are also bringing back the notion of a notice board as a tool for local (and in this case also distant) exchange; and graffiti, visual appropriation of the urban space.

What Does the Media Reverse Into When Pushed to the Extreme? TV/ real-time audio-visual connection enhanced with other stimuli that transmit a public space such as smell and noise across the network, a platform used for self-promotion (similar to Facebook) in public spaces, or even something similar to social networking service that creates place profiles and connects places.

Conclusion

With public displays "painting" the urban landscape (Kostakos and Ojala 2013) the vision of networked public displays becoming a communication medium is moving closer to reality. Although this area of research has seen plenty of research, the burning question remains *what is it that this medium should be doing*? After all, displays that we can find in the real world are not living up to the medium's potential and are getting little or almost no attention from the potential audience (Huang et al. 2008), as they expect to see boring advertisement (Müller et al. 2009).

In order to understand what is it that this medium could be doing we can turn to Marshall McLuhan and his media theory that tries to holistically determine the impact of a medium on other media and the society as well. According to McLuhan the key to understanding the impact of a medium is to understand the processes it amplifies that are happening in the context where a medium is deployed, or how he calls it *the interplay between the figure and the ground* (the medium and the context). While in his work he also used the *rear-view mirror* metaphor to describe how we always see a new medium through the eyes of the old one, this metaphor can be used for the analysis of the causes of the processes that lead to the effects produced by the medium. Lastly, McLuhan used the tetrad or four laws of media to describe the processes a medium amplifies, what does it make obsolete, what does it retrieve from the past that was forgotten, and what does a medium turn into when it is pushed to the extreme.

Thus in this work I used McLuhan's media theory to understand the role and purpose of the networked public displays medium: I analyzed processes in public spaces and research on networked public displays through McLuhan's theoretical elements – *figure and ground*, the *rear-view mirror*, and the *tetrad*. This analysis showed that in the core of the processes networked public displays stimulate and support are local communities and community interaction: whether it is stimulating social interaction or exchange between local members or public debate about a locally relevant topic, *local communities are at the heart of the process*. This is due to the ground/context in which networked public displays operate – the public space – and the way they amplify and stimulate processes that have been occurring in it. Also, by examining the public space through the rear view mirror my work has shown the basic principles this medium is built upon: creating individual and/or shared experiences through engagement with the space itself, leaving a personal mark in the setting, providing greater connections with the larger world, and the need of "repeated direct experiences" as a requirement for connections to develop. Lastly, the examination of the networked public displays medium through the four laws of media showed holistically and concisely how this medium fits in with the rest of existing media and how it makes an impact on the society.

Future research can build upon this research and further fill in the community-space cluster and the tetrad by documenting the effects of networked public displays. Researchers can also connect other effects of networked public displays to its causes coming from the ground (the public space). On the other hand, designers and developers of networked public displays applications can look into the basic principles of this medium in order to understand how it operates. Overall, the research presented in this chapter and its approach merges the fields of architecture and Human-Computer Interaction as it shows how researchers can use the knowledge produced by architects (e.g., Carr et al. 1992; Thompson 2002) to explain the impact of human interactions with computers in the public realm.

Acknowledgments This research was funded by Forschungskredit of the University of Zurich, grant no. FK-15-020. I would like to thank Professor Marc Langheinrich and Miss Ava Fatah gen. Schieck for their work on previous versions of the work that is discussed in this chapter.

References

Alt F, Kubitza T, Bial D, Zaidan F, Ortel M, Zurmaar B, Lewen T, Shirazi AS, Schmidt A (2011a) Digifieds: insights into deploying digital public notice areas in the wild. In: Dai Q, Jain R, Ji X, Kranz M (eds) Proceedings of the 10th international conference on mobile and ubiquitous multimedia (MUM '11). ACM, New York, pp 165–174. doi:10.1145/2107596.2107618

Alt F, Memarovic N, Elhart I, Bial D, Schmidt A, Langheinrich M, Harboe G, Huang E, Scipioni MP (2011b) Designing shared public display networks: implications from today's paper-based notice areas. In: Lyons K, Hightower J, Huang EM (eds) Proceedings of the 9th international conference on pervasive computing. Springer, Berlin, pp 258–275

Alt F, Shirazi AS, Kubitza T, Schmidt A (2013) Interaction techniques for creating and exchanging content with public displays. In: Mackay WE, Brewster S, Bødker S (eds) Proceedings of the SIGCHI conference on human factors in computing systems (CHI '13). ACM, New York, pp 1709–1718. doi:10.1145/2470654.2466226

Bolton M (2007) McLuhan for testers. Better Softw 9(10):14–15

Brignull H, Rogers Y (2003) Enticing people to interact with large public displays in public spaces. In: Rauterberg M, Menozzi M, Wesson J (eds) Human-computer interaction – INTERACT 2003. Springer, Berlin, pp 17–24

Carr S, Francis M, Rivlin LG, Stone AM (1992) Public space. Cambridge University Press, Cambridge

Ciastellardi M, de Almeida CM, Scolari CA (2011) Proceedings of the McLuhan Galaxy conference. Collection Shen, Editorial Universidad Oberta de Catalunya, Barcelona

Clinch S, Davies N, Friday A, Efstratiou A (2011) Reflections on the long-term use of an experimental digital signage system. In: Landay J, Shi Y, Patterson DJ, Rogers Y, Xie X (eds) Proceedings of the 13th international conference on Ubiquitous computing (UbiComp '11). ACM, New York, pp 133–142. doi:10.1145/2030112.2030132

Dalton N, Marshall P, Dalton R (2013) Extending architectural theories of space syntax to understand the effect of environment on the salience of situated displays. In: Schilit BN, Want R, Ojala T (eds) Proceedings of the 2nd ACM international symposium on pervasive displays (PerDis '13). ACM, New York, pp 73–78. doi:10.1145/2491568.2491585

Davies N, Langheinrich M, José R, Schmidt A (2012) Open display networks: a communications medium for the 21st century. IEEE Comput 45(5):58–64. doi:10.1109/MC.2012.114

Ebsen T (2013) Material screen: intersections of media, art, and architecture. PhD Dissertation

Elhart LM, Memarovic N, Heikkinen T (2014) Scheduling interactive and concurrently running applications in pervasive display networks. In: Quigley AJ, Boring S, Gehring S (eds) Proceedings of the international symposium on pervasive displays (PerDis '14). ACM, New York. doi:10.1145/2611009.2611039

Fatah gen. Schieck, A, Fan S (2012) Connected urban spaces: exploring interactions mediated through situated networked screens. In: Proceedings space syntax symposium, p 8

Goffman E (1963) Behavior in public places: notes on the social organization of gatherings. The Free Press, New York

Hole in the Earth. http://bit.ly/1exeai0

Holland C, Clark A, Katz J, Peace S (2007) Social interactions in urban public places. Policy Press, Bristol

Hosio S, Kostakos K, Kukka H, Jurmu M, Riekki J, Ojala T (2012) From school food to skate parks in a few clicks: using public displays to bootstrap civic engagement of the young. In: Kay J, Lukowicz P, Tokuda H, Olivier P, Krüger A (eds) Proceedings of the 10th international conference on pervasive computing (Pervasive'12). Springer, Berlin, pp 425–442. doi:10.1007/978-3-642-31205-2_26

Huang EM, Koster A, Borchers J (2008) Overcoming assumptions and uncovering practices. In: Indulska J, Patterson DJ, Rodden T, Ott M (eds) Proceedings of the 6th international conference on pervasive computing (Pervasive '08). Springer, Berlin, pp 228–243. doi:10.1007/978-3-540-79576-6_14

Institute for the Unstable Media (2015) Hole in the Earth. [Online] Available from http://v2.nl/archive/works/hole-in-the-earth. Accessed 10 Apr 2015

Jose R, Pinto H, Silva B, Melro A (2013) Pins and posters: paradigms for content publication on situated displays. IEEE Comput Graph Appl 33(2):64–72. doi:10.1109/MCG.2013.16

Kostakos V, Ojala T (2013) Public displays invade urban spaces. IEEE Pervasive Comput 12(1):8–13. doi:10.1109/MPRV.2013.15

Levinson P (2004) Digital McLuhan. Routledge, London

Library and Archives Canada (2007) Old messengers, new media: the legacy of Innis and McLuhan. [Online] Available from: http://www.collectionscanada.gc.ca/innis-mcluhan/030003-2020-e.html. Accessed: 10 Apr 2015

Logan RK (2011) Figure/ground: cracking the McLuhan code. E-compós 14(3)

Ludvigsen M (2005) Designing for social use in public places. In: Proceedings of designing pleasurable products and interfaces'05, pp 389–408

Matthews T, Rattenbury T, Carter S (2007) Defining, designing, and evaluating peripheral displays. Hum–Comput Interact 22(1–2):221–261

McLuhan M (1994) Understanding media: the extensions of man. MIT Press, Cambridge, MA

McLuhan M, Fiore Q (1967) The medium is the massage: an inventory of effects. Bantam Books, Toronto

McLuhan M, McLuhan E (1988) Laws of media: the new science. University of Toronto, Toronto

McQuire S (2006) The politics of public space in the media city. First Monday, Special Issue #4: Urban Screens: Discovering the potential of outdoor screens for urban society [Online]. Available from: http://firstmonday.org/article/view/1544/1459

Medien Kunst Netz (2015) Hole in space. [Online] Available from http://www.medienkunstnetz.de/works/hole-in-space/. Accessed 10 Apr 2015

Memarovic N, Langheinrich M, Alt F (2011) Connecting people through content – promoting community identity cognition through people and places. In: Proceedings of CIRN community informatics

Memarovic N, Langheinrich M, Rubegni E, David A, Elhart I (2012) Designing "interacting places" for a student community using a communicative ecology approach. In: Rukzio E (ed) Proceedings of the 11th international conference on mobile and ubiquitous multimedia (MUM '12). ACM, New York. doi:10.1145/2406367.2406420

Memarovic N, Langheinrich M, Cheverst K, Taylor N, Alt F (2013) P-LAYERS – a layered framework addressing the multifaceted issues facing community-supporting public display deployments. ACM Trans Comput-Hum Interact 20(3). ACM, New York. doi:10.1145/2491500.2491505

Memarovic N, Langheinrich M, Fatahgen Schieck A (2014) Community is the message: viewing networked public displays through McLuhan's lens of figure and ground. In: Brynskov M, Dalsgaard P, Fatahgen Schieck A (eds) Proceedings of the 2nd media architecture biennale conference: world cities (MAB '14). ACM, New York, pp 30–33. doi:10.1145/2682884.2682891

Memarovic N, Fatahgen Schieck A, Holger SM, Kostopoulou E, North S, Ye L (2015) Capture the moment: "In the Wild" longitudinal case study of situated snapshots captured through an urban screen in a community setting. In: Dan C, Andrea F, Luigina C, David MD (eds) Proceedings of the 18th ACM conference on computer supported cooperative work & social computing (CSCW '15). ACM, New York, pp 242–253. doi:10.1145/2675133.2675165

Molinaro M, McLuhan C, Toye W (eds) (1987) Letters of Marshall McLuhan. Oxford University Press, Oxford

Müller J, Wilmsmann D, Exeler J, Buzeck M, Schmidt A, Jay T, Krüger A (2009) Display blindness: the effect of expectations on attention towards digital signage. In: Hideyuki T, Michael B, Adrian F, Bernheim Brush AJ, Yoshito T (eds) Proceedings of pervasive computing. Springer, Berlin, pp 1–8. doi:10.1007/978-3-642-01516-8_1

Müller J, Eberle D, Tollmar K (2014) Communiplay: a field study of a public display mediaspace. In: Jones M, Palanque PA, Schmidt A, Grossman T (eds) Proceedings of the SIGCHI conference on human factors in computing systems (CHI '14). ACM, New York, pp 1415–1424. doi:10.1145/2556288.2557001

North S, Schnädelbach H, Fatahgen Schieck A, Motta W, Ye L, Behrens M, Kostopoulou E (2013) Tension space analysis: exploring community requirements for networked urban screens. In: Paula K, Gary M, Gitte L, Janet W, Marco W (eds) Human-computer interaction – INTERACT 2013. Springer, Berlin, pp 81–98. doi:10.1007/978-3-642-40480-1_6

Ojala T, Kostakos V, Kukka H, Heikkinen T, Linden T, Jurmu M, Hosio S, Kruger F, Zanni D (2012) Multipurpose interactive public displays in the wild: three years later. IEEE Comput 45(5):42–49. doi:10.1109/MC.2012.115

Papagiannis H (2011) AR storytelling. [Online] Available from: http://bit.ly/1gyV8tu. Accessed 10 Apr 2015

Paul St George (2015) Telectroscope. [Online] Available from http://www.paulstgeorge.com/telectroscope/. Accessed 10 Apr 2015

Ringas D, Christopoulou E (2013) Collective city memory: field experience on the effect of urban computing on community. In: Prinz W, Satchell C (eds) Proceedings of the 6th international conference on communities and technologies (C&T '13). ACM, New York, pp 157–165. doi:10.1145/2482991.2482996

Sandstrom G (2012) Laws of media. Soc Epistemol Rev Reply Collective 1(12):1–6

Schroeter R (2012) Engaging new digital locals with interactive urban screens to collaboratively improve the city. In: Proceedings of the ACM 2012 conference on computer supported cooperative work (CSCW '12). ACM, New York, pp 227–236. doi:10.1145/2145204.2145239

Thompson CW (2002) Urban open space in the 21st century. Landsc Urban Plan 60(2):59–72

Trancik R (1986) Finding lost space: theories of urban design. Wiley, Hoboken

Varoudis T (2011) Ambient displays: influencing movement patterns. In: Campos PF, Nicholas Graham TC, Jorge JA, Nunes NJ, Palanque PA, Winckler M (eds) Proceedings of human-computer interaction – INTERACT 2011. Springer, Berlin, pp 52–65. doi:10.1007/978-3-642-23768-3_5

Chapter 9
Embodied Interactions with Adaptive Architecture

Nils Jäger, Holger Schnädelbach, and Jonathan Hale

Abstract We discuss increasingly behaviour-responsive adaptive architecture from an embodied point of view. Especially useful in this context is an understanding of embodied cognition called 'the 4E approach,' which includes embodied, extended, embedded, and enacted perspectives on embodiment. We argue that these four characteristics of cognition both apply to and explain the bodily interactions between inhabitants and their adaptive environments. However, a new class of adaptive environments now expands this notion of embodied interactions by introducing environment-initiated behaviours, in addition to purely responsive behaviours. Thus, we consider how these new environments add the dimension of bodily reciprocity to Adaptive Architecture.

The Relationship Between Body and Buildings

> The seat cushioned up around me like an enormous white hand, and immediately the walls and ceiling quietened [...] I felt the room shift around me. The ceiling was dilating and contracting in steady pulses, an absurdly exaggerated response to our own respiratory rhythms, but the motions were overlayed by sharp transverse spasms, feed-back from some cardiac ailment. – JG Ballard (2006)

In *A Thousand Dreams of Stellavista*, written in 1962, Ballard describes a strong bodily connection between inhabitants and buildings. In the year 2015, this still sounds like pure science fiction. The mutual bodily interactions of house and occupant Ballard describes, however, are not as futuristic as they may appear. Indeed, our connection to the buildings we inhabit has never been more intimate and direct than now. In fact, the current generation of (experimental) adaptive environments begins to approach Ballard's vision. These environments already

N. Jäger (✉) • H. Schnädelbach
Mixed Reality Laboratory, Department of Computer Science, University of Nottingham, Jubilee Campus, Wollaton Road, Nottingham, UK
e-mail: nils.jaeger@nottingham.ac.uk; Holger.Schnadelbach@nottingham.ac.uk

J. Hale
Department of Architecture and Built Environment, University of Nottingham, Nottingham, UK
e-mail: jonathan.hale@nottingham.ac.uk

© Springer International Publishing Switzerland 2016   183
N.S. Dalton et al. (eds.), *Architecture and Interaction*,
Human–Computer Interaction Series, DOI 10.1007/978-3-319-30028-3_9

indicate the possibility of real-time interactions with their inhabitants, in which both building and inhabitant contribute equally.

One reason for the emerging intimate connections and mutual interactions between buildings and their occupants is the steadily increasing infusion of our built environments with sensors able to monitor our behaviour. However, buildings do not only monitor where we are and what we do, they also begin to respond to our behaviour in a variety of ways. We are already familiar with some of these adaptations from our daily routines, such as automatically changing light levels and regulated temperature as well as air quality, or managed access. Some of these adaptations depend on computing solutions, which enable the link between sensed digital data (e.g., room temperature) and actuators (e.g., automated façade louvers) to achieve the desired response (e.g., consistent temperature).

Physiological Data: Integrating Human and Building

The computationally established connection between sensing and actuating equips buildings with, what in humans we would call, a perception—action loop, making them responsive and adaptive to our behaviour. For example, buildings—or rather their sensors—might be able to perceive expressive behaviour of their occupants, such as their presence or motion, and act upon this perception with expressive behaviour of their own. Examples of such adaptations are described later.

More recently, buildings have also begun to acquire the ability of sensing physiological data of their inhabitants and utilise this particular data stream for actuation, as for example discussed in more detail by Schnädelbach (2011). Physiological data originates directly on and inside our body and includes, for example, our heartbeats, our breathing, or our sweat levels. Through developments in mobile technologies, such as smart phones, smart watches, and other mobile monitoring consumer products, physiological data has become virtually continuously and ubiquitously available. We can personally access this data, use it for our own benefit, and share it with others through social networking platforms. However, physiological data is also potentially available to the built environments surrounding us, as many of the sensor devices are capable of broadcasting live data. The availability of such data enables buildings to adapt in real-time to the core processes operating within our physical bodies. And these real-time responses of buildings to our (expressive or physiological) behaviour can link us through our behaviour with adaptive buildings to an unprecedented degree of intimacy.

Indeed, with this direct physiological link to adaptive buildings, one can imagine how *our behaviour* becomes simultaneously the *behaviour of the building* we occupy. Thus, both our behaviour and that of the building become closely intertwined, and we become essential parts of the building behaviour: as we behave, so does the building. However, we argue that this relationship might also be reversed, such that adaptive buildings may actively influence our physiologies and behaviours.

Some research environments can already assist us in becoming, for example, more relaxed. And this might perhaps become an initial real-world application of bodily interactions with a building. Physiological interactions between buildings and inhabitants may first emerge in healthcare or wellbeing contexts, where they can help their inhabitants achieve, for example, slower and deeper breathing and be more mindful. Once such specialised applications have found acceptance, more general applications in other building types, such as offices and private homes may follow.

While still in its development stages, the next step for adaptive environments will be what a few research environments already offer: to reciprocate behaviour by initiating behaviour on their own.

In the following, we conceptualise the embodied interactions between adaptive environments and their inhabitants, including reciprocal interactions. We (1) define and contextualise the field of *Adaptive Architecture*, (2) introduce and discuss concepts of embodiment (i.e., embodied cognition), and (3) apply a specific approach to embodiment to a number of exemplary adaptive environments that specifically engage the body. This leads (4) to a discussion on the future potential and challenges regarding embodied interactions with adaptive environments.

Adaptive Architecture

Adaptive architecture has been part of our lives longer than static environments have. Nomadic lifestyles required mobile, lightweight structures before humanity developed farming techniques that would enable them to stay in one place. Over the millennia, the increasing wealth alongside increasing availability of resources made it less important for architecture to fulfil multiple functions, as (building) materials (and in some locations space) appeared limitless. However, the currently rising demands on our personal work performance, such as improving efficiency, increasing necessity for multi-tasking, and reduced amount of time to relax, seem to yet again intensify the necessity of adaptive spaces. However now, adaptivity in architectural space is less defined by mobility and more by interactivity with the inhabitants.

Adaptive Architecture, as we use this broad category here, refers to environments that have been specifically designed to adapt to changing conditions. This definition by Schnädelbach (2010) adds to a definition proposed by Brand (1995) who states that all architecture can adapt—or rather can be adapted—given enough time and the right set of tools. Being a sub-category of Architecture, *Adaptive Architecture* itself encapsulates multiple terms, such as Interactive Architecture/Environments (Fox and Kemp 2009; Bullivant 2007), Responsive Environments (Bullivant 2006), Digitally-Driven Architecture (Bier and Knight 2010), Robotic Architecture (Gross and Green 2012), Mobile and Portable Architecture (Kronenburg 2003), or Flexible Architecture (Kronenburg 2007). All these emphasise different adaptations—some analogue, some digital; some audio-visual, some kinetic—to a variety of changing conditions, which include environmental changes, such as temperature, daylight, wind, and seasons (Kontovourkis et al. 2013; Rossi et al. 2012). Human behaviour, including physiological behaviour, plays a significant role as part of these changing conditions.

In the context of this chapter, we focus on architecture that adapts kinetically to human behaviour using sensors (embedded in the environment or worn by inhabitants), actuators, and computing infrastructure (software and hardware). Kinetic adaptations in architecture, for example those actuated through motors, pneumatics or hydraulics are at the core of what we term *Embodied Adaptive Architecture*, as they allow for 'bodily interactions' in a direct and legible way. Such environments translate personal data into motion of architectural components of varying sizes, as large as entire walls (Goulthorpe 2006) or as small as ceiling mounted strings (Jacobs and Findley 2015). In what follows, we will reflect on the concept of Embodiment to begin to frame this work theoretically.

Embodiment

Embodiment is a vital concept concerning the investigation of bodily interactions with behaviour-responsive adaptive architecture as it not only regards the body as part of cognition but situates it firmly in the physical world (see for example Clark and Chalmers 1998; Gallagher 2012; Merleau-Ponty 1964). Because of this universally applicable understanding of the role of the body for cognition, this concept spans multiple disciplines, such as philosophy, psychology, neuroscience, sociology, computer science, and architecture.

In essence, embodied cognition (Calvo and Gomila 2008) rejects the separation of mind and body as proposed by Descartes. His dualistic understanding of cognition has been used in computationalism (or the Computational Theory of Mind), which interprets the brain as a computing machine (cf. for example Putnam 1975). Embodiment on the other hand includes the body as part of the cognitive system. The theory arose out of the phenomenological school of thought created by Edmund Husserl who took as his starting point how the human body perceives and interacts with the world, for example, introduced and discussed by Zahavi (2003). Heidegger, Husserl's student, expanded his teacher's concept of phenomenology and interpreted it as the study of the meaning of Being, leading, among others, to his famous concept of *being-in-the-world* (Heidegger 1978). Being-in-the-world was expanded by Merleau-Ponty who argued that body and world are essentially one and the same through his concept of the *flesh of the world* (Diprose and Reynolds 2008; Evans 2011; Merleau-Ponty 1964). These core concepts of phenomenology are now becoming influential in Embodied Cognitive Science, as illustrated in a number of publications (Gallagher 2005; Shapiro 2011; Pfeifer and Bongard 2006). Thus, this approach argues that cognition emerges from embodiment and, more importantly, the involvement of the active body in the world—navigating, negotiating, and interacting with the world, including physical objects as well as social interactions (Di Paolo et al. 2010; Rowlands 2009; Gallagher and Bower 2014).

The 4E Approach

One approach that synthesises most of the discussion on embodied cognition is the so-called *4E approach* to Embodied Cognition. The 4E approach argues that the physical body contributes significantly to our cognitive processes, which it understands as being *embodied, extended, embedded*, and *enacted*. The following core definitions of the 4Es were derived from Rowlands' (2010b) extensive discussion on the matter.

Embodied

The sequence of concepts starts with *Embodied*, which refers to the manner in which the physicality of the human body is a constituting part of cognition, such as having two eyes for stereoscopic vision. This setup of two eyes at a specific distance to each other allows humans to see and interact with three-dimensional objects, since we can judge their size and distance in relation to us. Simply (but non-trivially) put, embodied cognition depends on the body. Everything hinges upon the body being involved. Gallagher's (2005) work in this context provides more detail on *How the Body Shapes the Mind*, and likewise Pfeifer and Bongard's (2006) *How the Body Shapes the Way We Think*.

Extended

Our body can, through its senses (haptic, gustatory, olfactory, visual, and audial) reach out and extend itself into the surrounding physical world. Thus, *Extended* contributes the notion that some mental processes interact with the environment with the aim of extracting useful information from objects that these contain in a "dormant" fashion. Clark and Chalmers (1998) argue specifically for extended boundaries of the mind, and Clark (2004) explains in detail that the extension of the mind (and body) applies in the context of computing in particular and digital technology in general as both are just another set of tools holistically extending our capabilities.

Embedded

Through the extension of the body into the world, the body becomes *embedded* in a specific spatial context. Being surrounded by the world enables the human body to make use of parts of the environment (by extending itself) in order to reduce mental load on the brain. Haselager and colleagues (2008), for example, explain how the location of the body within an environment helps the brain to make a cognitive task less demanding.

Enacted

Finally, the last aspect of the 4E approach is the *enacted* concept, which refers to the body acting on the world. This acting is an active exploration of the world's physical elements, which Rowlands (2010a, p. 77) describes primarily as exploration with the 'visual modality.' However, despite its recent emergence as a well-defined concept, a large number of publications on enaction, especially by De Jaegher and Di Paolo (see for example De Jaegher and Di Paolo 2007; Di Paolo et al. 2010), argue that enacted cognition consists of much more than visual explorations of the world. Indeed, they build their enactive approach upon the other three 3Es, emphasising the coupling between agents (bodies) and the environment and their embodied interaction. The interaction component, which is the pivotal argument of the enacted thesis, adds the dimension of time to the other three concepts, which are of a spatial nature (see Fig. 9.1).

To summarise, embodied cognition depends on the cogniser's body (embodied). This body reaches out into the world (extended), which puts it in context in the world (embedded). Thus, the body starts interacting with the world (enacted), which includes both people and objects. The latter (enacted) forms the core of embodied interactions with behaviour-responsive adaptive architecture, as we discuss it here.

The four concepts of the 4E approach are interdependent and build upon each other, which make them a connected entity rather than a loose collection from which to freely choose. Indeed, as we will later argue, only in conjunction do these concepts enable truly mutual interactions between environment and inhabitants.

All approaches to Embodiment seem to imply a general consensual view on cognition that accepts most if not all concepts of the 4E approach. Indeed, most of the literature on embodiment appears to subscribe to this view in essence, even if the weighting of the four concepts differs, for example illustrated by Rowlands' (2010a) explicit discussion of the 4Es approach, Wilson's (2002) view on Embodiment, Gallagher's (2005, 2011, 2012, 2014) work, or Clark's views on cognition and the mind (Clark 2004, 2008; Clark and Chalmers 1998).

Fig. 9.1 Sequence and interdependence of 4E concepts including their dimensionality

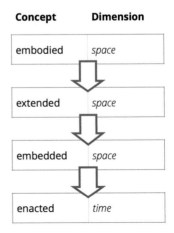

Having introduced key concepts of embodiment and the 4E approach, we now have a better understanding of how we engage with our surroundings. In the following, we introduce examples of behaviour-responsive adaptive architecture, which illustrate how environments can engage our bodies and what specific bodily interactions they facilitate.

Adaptive Architecture That Engages the Body

Thus far, we defined the specific sub-category of *Adaptive Architecture* with which we are concerned as architecture that adapts kinetically to human behaviour using sensors, actuators, and computing infrastructure. In this section, we present and discuss specific interactions with such *Embodied Adaptive Architecture*.

Interactions with adaptive architecture can be classed as *analogue* or *digital* interactions. Both provide distinctly different qualities of experiences for inhabitants.

Analogue adaptive environments always respond directly to inhabitant input. For example, in Steven Holl's Fukuoka Houses (El Croquis (ed) 2003) manually rotatable wall elements change the spatial configuration of an apartment. Here, the activity of the body (pushing a wall panel) corresponds to instant changes in the composition of the physical space.

Digitally-driven behaviour-responsive adaptive environments can offer a greater variety of architectural response. They can, for example, introduce delay into the interaction or create unusual or counterintuitive mappings of data to actuations not usually found with analogue environments. As we show below, many experimental behaviour-responsive environments respond to their users "at a distance." This is an interaction approach contrary to analogue environments, which require inhabitant input in the form of touch. Moreover, digitally-driven adaptive environments can utilise novel data streams for their responses, such as physiological data (heart rate, respiration, skin conductance etc.), presence and proximity, or limb movement (at a distance). Thus, novel data streams enable new forms of bodily interactions between inhabitants and their environments, some of which we introduce now.

Examples of Embodied Adaptive Architecture

To illustrate what kind of bodily interactions are already possible with adaptive environments, we describe a number of exemplary environments, which we classify as belonging to *Embodied Adaptive Architecture* (Table 9.1). These examples range from environments reacting to easily observable (external) behaviour, such as body position, to obscure (internal) behaviour, particularly physiological processes. While external behaviour includes large-scale movements of the inhabitant, such as the movement of limbs (as small as opening and closing a hand and as large as waving with arms) or changes of state of the entire body (posture or position

Table 9.1 Digitally-driven adaptive environments

	Inhabitant Behaviour	Occupancy	Method	Time	Reciprocal
Muscle Tower	expressive	single	kinetic	real-time	—
Dress Room	expressive	single	kinetic	real-time/delay	—
SlowFurl	expressive	multiple	kinetic	delay	—
Sonic Cradle	physiological	single	audial	real-time	—
Open Columns	physiological	multiple	kinetic	delay	—
Breathe	physiological	single	kinetic	offset	—
Lungs [the breather]	physiological	multiple	visual	real-time	—
ADA	expressive	multiple	audial, visual	real-time	✓
ExoBuilding	physiological	single	audial/ visual/kinetic	real-time	✓

changes). Physiological behaviour, on the other side, refers to behaviour occurring directly *on* the body (e.g., electrodermal activity) or *inside* the body (e.g., heartbeat, respiration). In both cases, the environments discussed here utilise these external or internal behaviours of their inhabitants to respond in kinetic, audial, or visual ways. An additional aspect of the examples of adaptive environments on which we focus is their *continuous interaction* with their occupants as long as occupants are inside or close to the environment.

Muscle Tower

The first adaptive environment, *Muscle Tower* (Oosterhuis 2004), is part of the so-called *Muscle Projects* (Oosterhuis and Biloria 2008) designed by the research group Hyperbody at TU Delft. This tall, open structure engages one passer-by at a time as it leans and bends towards the moving person. The structure is made from aluminium tubes and pneumatic muscles. It twists, bends, and leans towards nearby human bodies, following their motion path as if turning its neck. This "life-like" response integrates the body of the passer-by in the interaction with architecture. Through their interaction, both artefact and human create an emerging symbiosis, virtually locking both in the interaction. Naturally, the passer-by can break the interaction at any time, by stepping outside of the sensor range while the same is true for Muscle Tower if it switches off. The passer-by has control both over the duration of the interaction as well as the motion of the tower.

Like other projects in the Hyperbody portfolio (e.g., Interactive- Wall, Bamboostic, Interactive Curtain), Muscle Tower affords immediate bodily interaction with a physical environment or components thereof. It shows the feasibility of the integration of kinetically adaptive components into architectural structures at varying scales. Furthermore, it indicates how inhabitants of interactive architecture might temporarily engage with such kinetic features and then transition into another space with possibly another set of features.

Dress Room

Similar to Muscle Tower, Dress Room by Vallgårda (Vallgårda 2014) responds to the location/position of an inhabitant, measured through pressure sensors integrated into the floor. Dress Room is an adaptive rectangular room made of white fabric 'walls' intended to merge the categories of architecture and clothing. The fabric walls hang inside a larger steel frame. Eight pneumatic pistons actuate (pull or push) the wires from which the fabric hangs. Depending on the position of the user, different pistons are activated or turned off, causing the walls of the white room to collapse and expand in response.

Dress Room was primarily tested with one dancer who perceived the room as intimate and motivating motion. The intimacy apparently emerges out of a phase of getting to know the responses of the space through active exploration, something that is also apparent in the Muscle Projects. The increasing familiarity with Dress Room seemed to have encouraged the dancer to become more expressive within the space, especially to repeat previously enjoyable responses of the room. Through her motion, she describes to have created a form of dynamic interaction with the room. It is currently unclear how this interaction between room and user/dancer develops over time, especially in light of the fabric swaying back forth after a single actuation. No further study presently exists, which could explore other aspects of interaction with this space, such as multi-occupancy.

SlowFurl

Also reacting to the presence (and position) of its inhabitants, *SlowFurl* (Vindum 2009) consists of a plywood sub-structure supporting a large fabric skin. This structure forms one entire wall of an exhibition space. The fabric reacts to the presence of multiple inhabitants on a 'deep timeframe.' SlowFurl engages inhabitants continuously but through a delayed or time-shifted response: inhabitants perceive very subtle changes in the constitution of the wall as the traces of the presence of previous occupants of the space.

The actuations of SlowFurl do not replay the behaviours of previous users in the same timescale as they were performed but respond more slowly. Thus, the way in which current occupants of the space relate to their predecessors is far removed from an immediate, legible experience of other people. Because no user study has been published, it is difficult to understand how occupants of the space relate to SlowFurl and the previous inhabitants of the space. However, due to the lack of direct feedback to one's own movements, it might be difficult to relate to the movements or presence of predecessors, as there is no indication of the effects of presence other than a cognitive engagement with a description of the operation and function of SlowFurl. Thus, while SlowFurl also responds to bodily behaviour, the delay appears to deny an 'intuitive' bodily interaction with it.

OpenColumns

Marginally more direct in its response to inhabitant behaviour compared to Slow-Furl, *OpenColumns* (Khan 2010) is a multi-user environment primarily exploring the use of polyelastomeres in architecture. The ceiling-mounted columns respond to variations in carbon-dioxide levels in interior spaces. These levels change depending on the number and location of people exhaling—carbon dioxide is a product of exhalation. Once the carbon-dioxide saturation of the air in one area of the room reaches a pre-defined threshold, a mesh column (or multiple) deploys and slowly drops from the ceiling. In the process of lowering from above, the columns cause groups of people congregating below them to disperse and regroup elsewhere.

The columns operate slowly, so that a connection between inhabitant behaviour and architectural response is difficult or impossible to determine purely through the interaction. Furthermore, no study of the experiences of users has been published so far. However, one can speculate that it would take a significant amount of time for inhabitants to make a connection between their breathing and the behaviour of the columns.

Breathe

While also partially using a delayed response, *Breathe* by Jacobs and Findley (2015) is a tent-like environment that responds to and records the breathing of the current inhabitant while simultaneously replaying the recorded breathing of the preceding inhabitant. Two sets of coloured strings sway based on the live (one colour) and the recorded (other colour) breathing of the previous inhabitant. Breathe provides a time-shifted multi-user experience where the current inhabitant experiences her own breathing as well as the breathing of the previous inhabitant. Thus, the environment offers both real-time and time delayed feedback to its inhabitants, enticing inhabitants to synchronise their breathing with their predecessor in the space.

In some sense, Breathe is a dual-user environment with one person absent. This interaction offset in time raises questions about the traces people leave in space, for example. It enables users to try and envision the other person breathing and match their own respiratory behaviour to that of the previous occupant. Thus, the environment effectively enacts a running (or rolling) embodied history of its users while providing real-time feedback to the current inhabitant who subsequently turns into a historic breather to the next occupant.

Sonic Cradle

Moving from delayed responses to real-time feedback, the single-user adaptive sound environment Sonic Cradle (Vidyarthi et al. 2012) also responds to its inhabitant's respiration. It is intended to induce a state of mindfulness in its user. In a completely dark chamber, the user wears a respiration sensor and sits in a hammock-like contraption. The breathing pattern affects an adaptive sound environment, which blends sounds depending on the breathing frequency and amplitude. An exploratory study found that the level of perceived control strongly influences the experience of participants. During the design stages, some participants experienced a lack of control over the adaptive soundscape as they 'summoned' more than three sounds. As the authors point out, lack of perceived control may cause stress. Thus, the authors modified Sonic Cradle in the next design stage to prevent this loss of control from happening.

While Sonic Cradle focuses on mindfulness, an inwardly looking self-awareness, it does extend the user's body to become part of the emerging soundscape, which at the same time becomes a modulating part of the user's body. Thus, Sonic Cradle blends inhabitant body and environment through real-time audio feedback.

Lungs [the Breather]

Also providing real-time feedback, *Lungs* [the breather] (Guerra et al. n.d.) is an interactive exhibition. It is set in a dark room around a rectangular pool of white paint onto which adaptive video animations are being projected. Fitted with respiration sensors, four people sit on the floor around the edges of the shallow projection pool and breathe. Their breathing patterns affect the adaptive video projections. The interaction with Lungs [the breather] is perhaps less immersive than that with Sonic Cradle as the users' breathing affects a clearly delineated two-dimensional video projection rather than an immersive soundscape. However, it does provide the opportunity to physiologically connect to and interact with other co-present users. While Lungs [the breather] is a rare example of shared (real-time) biofeedback, no study has been published of its effects on users or their experiences of this installation.

Reciprocating Environments

The environments we reviewed so far respond to their inhabitants either in real-time or with varying degrees of delay. Especially those environments allowing real-time bodily interactions establish a special bodily relationship between themselves and their users by blurring the boundaries between physical surroundings and inhabitant. They draw inhabitants temporarily into a continuous interaction. However, a different kind of interaction is also possible, which extends beyond responsive behaviour and introduces proactive environmental behaviour, which we term reciprocal behaviour. This is autonomous environmental behaviour based on responses to inhabitant behaviour. So far, these environments are very rare, but they may point toward a new direction for adaptive environments.

Ada: Intelligent Space

The interactive exhibition *Ada: intelligent space* (Eng et al. 2003; Bullivant 2005) accommodates multiple people. It consists of interactive floor tiles that light up in a variety of colours, for example, in response to visitors stepping on them. Additionally, Ada features large video screens and responsive sound systems. The intention of the design of Ada was to make inhabitants believe that they interact with 'an artificial organism' (Eng et al. 2003, p. 4156).

It engages visitors directly by, for example, enticing them to play games with it, such as drawing outlines around what Ada perceives to be a group of people or tracing the steps of individual visitors through the space. While numerous interactive features are intended to suggest intelligence, none of them is kinetic, as they are not physically but visually and sonically actuated.

ExoBuilding

The ceiling-mounted, tent-like space ExoBuilding (Schnädelbach et al. 2010) was originally designed for a single-user in order to test the concept of mapping physiological data to an architectural space. Jersey fabric stretches over a thin aluminium tent pole attached to two independent servomotors, which in turn are suspended from the ceiling. A video projector projects a circular blue graphic onto the centre of the fabric and large speakers both play sound and cause the floor to vibrate. Physiological data is directly measured on the occupant and used to drive all actuations in real-time. ExoBuilding embeds the occupant into its own structure and behaviour by using the direct physiological coupling achieved through bio-sensing technology.

Originally, ExoBuilding responded to respiration in form of a kinetic actuation of the entire structure. It sonified the inhabitant's heart beat and adapted the projection of a graphic based on the inhabitant's skin conductance. Since its conception,

ExoBuilding has sparked a research programme around the effects of behaviour-responsive adaptive architectural spaces on their inhabitants. A first controlled study (Schnädelbach et al. 2012) found that participants significantly reduced their respiration rate when ExoBuilding was providing biofeedback. When ExoBuilding was moving automatically at a slow, steady pace emulating a slow breathing frequency, participants did not show this significant effect. The same held true in a condition where ExoBuilding did not move at all. We are currently in the process of testing whether ExoBuilding can guide its inhabitant toward physiological behaviours unintended by him or her. Initial tests indicate that ExoBuilding may be able to deliberately and predictably change the respiratory behaviour of its inhabitant by manipulating the control relationship between itself and the occupant. This form of interaction—inhabitant having input into environment and environment having input into inhabitant behaviour—hints at opportunities for reciprocal interactions between our environments and us.

Summary of Reciprocal Interactions

Both Ada and ExoBuilding indicate the potential for environments to actively engage their inhabitants either in overtly playful bodily interactions or to potentially support their physiological behaviour. In order to understand more closely how such bodily interactions function and how they already relate and apply to the presented projects, we will now discuss how the *4E approach* forms the basis for interactional reciprocity in this context. Building on this foundation, we then propose the adoption of an interpersonal interaction model, which promises to be highly relevant for the future of investigations of *Embodied Adaptive Architecture*.

The 4Es: Basis for Interactional Reciprocity

Having described the interactions between inhabitants and a number of exemplary adaptive environments as well as the principles of embodiment including the 4E approach, it is now time to discuss how these embodied interactions with the adaptive physical world in which they occur build the foundation for an emerging kind of interaction with adaptive environments: reciprocal interaction.

To be able to apply the 4E approach to *Adaptive Architecture* and vice versa, we reiterate that the 4Es are an attempt to explain *cognition* by relating cognitive processes to the body, which itself relates to the environment. In support of the argument of such an environment-body relationship, Clark and Chalmers (1998) argue that the body deliberately extends into the environment, which itself is part of cognition. Similarly, proponents of the more recently developed research field of enactivism (De Jaegher and Di Paolo 2007; Di Paolo et al. 2010; Fuchs and De Jaegher 2009; McGann et al. 2013) emphasise the coupling between environment and human agent, where the (static) environment can already distinctly modulate human behaviour and cognition.

As we illustrate in the next section, the digital means now being employed to create real-time adaptive environments directly engage with the 4Es. They facilitate embodiment, extension, embeddedness, and enaction between building and inhabitant and, thus, transform the built environment from a static to an active component in our lives. And this transformation increases the potential of (the now adaptive) buildings to modulate human behaviour and cognition significantly.

Starting with the first E, *embodiment*, all the previously described examples of adaptive environments relied on the body as a constituting part. In other words, the inhabitant's body is key to creating *Embodied Adaptive Architecture*, as without it, the environment would be no more than a static artefact. The connection or link between environment and body occurs through sensors either integrated into the environment or worn by inhabitants as well as actuators and software platforms coordinating both and facilitating interactions between environment and inhabitant body. Because of the body interacting with it, *Embodied Adaptive Architecture* becomes an interactive system in which occupant and environment (may) become interdependent. Indeed, our own studies indicate that some inhabitants temporarily relied on environmental cues (motion of ExoBuilding) for the pacing of their own respiratory behaviour. Thus, the directionality of embodiment was reversed for these participants, such that the environment (temporarily) became a constituting part of their physiological behaviour.

The interactive system of interdependent agents relies on inhabitants to *extend* their bodies into the environment. For example, participants using ExoBuilding have described their experience as inhabiting their own (but very large) lungs reflecting their breathing behaviour. This illustrates a literal physical extension, such that the inhabitant perceives his or her own body to be larger than it is in reality. Similar to *embodiment*, this extension also operates in reverse: the environment extends beyond its physical limits into the body of its inhabitant. This can, for example, also be seen in the interactions between *Muscle Tower* and a passer-by: the person extends their body into muscle tower, which translates the motion of the person into a twisting and bending behaviour. By doing so, it may trigger the person to alter their behaviour (walk in a different direction), which can be seen as the tower extending into the body of the passer-by. Thus, the mutual extension might lead to a temporary choreography between environment and human.

Through the previously described extension into the adaptive environment, the body becomes *embedded* in it. Being surrounded by, for example, what feels like a large set of lungs, enables self-monitoring of a kind otherwise not possible. This embeddedness has helped inhabitants of ExoBuilding to breathe more slowly and regularly because it made them more aware of their own behaviour. A similar relationship between environment and occupant can be observed in *Breathe*, where the single inhabitant is both embedded in her or his own physiology (one set of strings reflects their own breathing) but can choose to embed himself/herself into the breathing of another person (reflected by the other set of strings playing a recording of the previous visitor) by matching their predecessor's breathing rhythm.

In this case, the predecessor becomes also embedded in the current inhabitant's body through the matching of both behaviours.

Finally, *enaction* describes the active, on-going process of interaction between inhabitant and environment. Whereas the previous three concepts relate mainly to space, the enacted concept introduces the dimension of time. This is particularly central to biofeedback environments, as only continued engagement with them has beneficial effects, such as increased relaxation. Through continuous, and perhaps even repeated, interaction with a biofeedback environment, inhabitants gain experience and skills that allow them to improve their health.

Embodied Adaptive Architecture

With the description and application of the 4Es, we have shown how these four concepts of embodied cognition underlie the principles of bodily interactions with adaptive environments. They explain how body and environment are linked in an embodied, extended, embedded and enacted fashion. We discussed how the 4Es apply bi-directionally, such that both agents (human and environment) might, for example, equally embody each other. Especially through the fourth, time-based dimension of enactment, the mutual applicability of the 4Es becomes evident. Until now this kind of bi-directional relationship—or reciprocity—between inhabitants and adaptive space has not been described in terms of their bodily interaction.

In what follows, we present a first sketch of a model that draws on work in psychology to illustrate embodied reciprocal interactions between buildings and people, before concluding with a set of challenges that architects and interaction designers will face when applying the presented work.

Reciprocity Between Buildings and Inhabitants

The intentionally reductionist setup of ExoBuilding allows a clear analysis of the required 4E setup to achieve behavioural reciprocity from the environment. First, respiration and heart rate sensors establish a 'hardwired' physiological coupling between inhabitant and structure. Thus both embody each other. Through this same link and the ensuing respiratory behaviour reflected in ExoBuilding's motion, the inhabitant is embedded in and extends toward ExoBuilding (and vice versa). The physiological link (and ExoBuilding's enactment of the inhabitant's data) allows both to interact on a bodily level as long as this coupling is active. While the default assumption is that the inhabitant controls every motion of ExoBuilding, it seems also possible to reverse this relationship during the interaction. We have designed it such that ExoBuilding can now subtly take over the initiative and start dominating the interaction without its inhabitant noticing. Our initial observations of reciprocal interactions with ExoBuilding suggest that the environment appears to lead some inhabitants to unknowingly adjust their own behaviour to that of ExoBuilding.

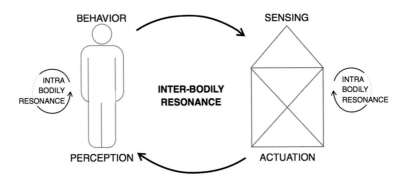

Fig. 9.2 Model of inter-bodily resonance (Adapted from Froese and Fuchs 2012)

This seems to occur on a pre-cognitive, purely physical level by guiding inhabitants to a different respiratory frequency. Another relevant example for such reciprocity is ADA, which was designed to engage occupants cognitively through various games and inferences of their behaviours. Ada drew visitors into games, for example visually suggesting walking routes through the space.

In human interactions, behavioural reciprocity is a common mode of communication. This can occur on many levels, of which the physical bodily level is the most relevant here. When we communicate with others, communication flows in both directions. It is natural that the interacting partners take turns leading or dominating the interaction, which might occur cyclically—in phases. We argue that a similar form of mutual interaction is now possible between adaptive environments and their inhabitants. One concept that can explain such an interaction is that of inter-bodily resonance, originally developed for inter-personal interaction.

The model of *inter-bodily resonance* by Froese and Fuchs (2012) describes the interaction between two human partners (A and B) as continuous behavioural micro-adjustments between the two. These micro-adjustments are based on the bodily expressions of the respective other partner. As Froese and Fuchs elaborate, Partner B senses expressions of Partner A through his/her body, resulting in partner B's physically expressing reactions to the perceived emotional state of Partner A, who also perceives and physically reacts to Partner B's expressions. Thus, a form of bodily resonance emerges between the two interaction partners. The continuously adjusting, cyclical interaction between the partners describes a phenomenological and embodied feedback loop between and within two individuals. Both individuals share inter-bodily resonance between them.

In our view, this model applies in an adapted form to the context of *Adaptive Architecture* (see Fig. 9.2). But instead of having two human interaction partners, one of the partners introduced by Froese and Fuchs is substituted by the environment. As Fig. 9.2 depicts, the human body expresses behaviour, which the environment senses. The sensed data, then either directly or in processed form, becomes the driver for an actuation of the environment. The human can then perceive this actuation through their bodily senses and the cycle starts anew.

Further supporting the link of this model to the 4E approach—in addition to the enacted dimension—, Froese and Fuchs explicitly describe inter-bodily resonance also as a form of extending each other's body such that the actions of one are reflected in the responses of the other. The same extension applies to human-environment interactions: through the feedback cycle of inter-bodily resonance both human body and environment extend each other by reacting to and reflecting the other's behaviour. Moreover, this specific form of interaction also reflects the remaining 'Es' of the 4E approach. Both interaction partners (human and environment) are embedded in the interaction, as they continuously respond to each other. This also means that they enact their interaction through their body, be it the human or the environmental body.

In summary, the engagement in the other's bodily behaviour through inter-bodily resonance sets the stage for a potential interactional and continuous choreography between environment and inhabitant. As our understanding of bodily interactions with adaptive spaces increases, these continuous interactive engagements will become more complex and diverse.

Future Challenges

At this point, we propose the presented model of reciprocal interaction between building and inhabitant, primarily drawing on our review of background work and direct experience with a series of experiments using ExoBuilding as vehicle to explore this space. Making this work applicable by architects and interaction designers alike presents a number of challenges that we will briefly address below.

Research Challenge

Through further research, we need to address the validity of the model, which we have begun through additional experimental work with ExoBuilding. We will be considering novel bodily interaction methods, which make use of the theoretical concepts introduced here. Such explorations may also include appropriate (potentially novel) materials and adaptation methods. This would link into our observed more general lack of evaluations of existing adaptive environments in terms of their embodied interactions. Both quantitative and qualitative approaches to study the physiological and psychological effects of embodied interactions with adaptive environments will greatly advance our understanding of the relationship between human body and adaptive space.

The starting point might be to investigate how individual occupants of adaptive spaces interact with the structure, such as research of Sonic Cradle and ExoBuilding already suggests. New research avenues will emerge from investigations with multi-occupancy settings in adaptive environments. Not only will it be of interest how multiple inhabitants interact with the adaptive space but also how they interact with each other. Addressing multi-occupancy scenarios in *Embodied Adaptive*

Architecture requires either modification of existing environments or the design of new prototypes. To this extent, we are currently exploring both design strands. We are exploring how ExoBuilding can accommodate multiple inhabitants, for example in meditative practices, such as yoga. We are also at present evaluating a recently developed multi-user prototype, which is able to provide biofeedback to two inhabitants simultaneously and independently but has been designed to expand in the future.

Professional Challenge

Embodied interactions with adaptive architectural spaces seem already suitable for a number of specific contexts, such as therapy rooms. It is crucial to test adaptive environments in real-world settings with real users to delineate possible application areas. With this in mind, it will be important to establish a dialogue between architectural design professionals who design healthcare and wellbeing spaces and interaction designers, who are increasingly concerned with salutogenic design. This dialogue needs to have a particular focus on the relative benefits and drawbacks of the possible reciprocal mappings that can be established between inhabitants and buildings. Information exchange with such professionals might benefit both the design of healthcare and wellbeing spaces as well as our theoretical understanding of how rehabilitation and wellbeing is already built into the architectural fabric and how this might be enhanced through interactive features enabling enactive embodiment in such spaces. Such engagement with the profession of Architecture and Interaction Design may also eventually lead to applications of *Embodied Adaptive Architecture* in other building types, such as office buildings.

Conclusion

Understanding the embodied nature of interactions with adaptive environments will enable the design of new and inspiring physical interactions with the built environment. These interactions will not rely on suggestions of humanoid abilities of a given space. Instead, they will utilize the 'configuration' of the human body (including pre-cognitive and rational responses) to engage with inhabitants.

Thus, we think that both the 4E approach as well as the concept of inter-bodily resonance could become a driving force in the design process of new adaptive environments that (pro)actively or mutually interact with their inhabitants. By sensing user behaviour, be it expressive or internal behaviour, adaptive environments, or better the algorithms operating them, could identify ways in which they might most effectively interact with users. They might even be able to influence inhabitant behaviour through minimal changes in the kinetic expression of architectural behaviour. Inhabitants would sense these minimal changes through their bodies and unconsciously perform micro-adjustments of their own behaviour potentially resulting in physiological and psychological benefits. Thus, embodied interactions with behaviour-responsive architectural spaces may animate the built environment around us with new behaviours and connect us literally and figuratively to the spaces we inhabit.

Acknowledgements This work was supported by EPSRC Grants EP/P505658/1 and EP/M000877/1 as well as the University of Nottingham via the Nottingham Research Fellowship 'The Built Environment as the Interface to Personal Data'.

References

Ballard JG (2006) The thousand dreams of Stellavista. In: The complete short stories. Harper Perennial, London, pp 414–435

Bier H, Knight T (2010) Digitally-driven architecture. Footprint 6:1–4

Brand S (1995) How buildings learn: what happens after they're built. Penguin Books, London

Bullivant L (2005) 4dspace: interactive architecture (Architectural Design). AD 128

Bullivant L (2006) Responsive environments. Victoria & Albert Museum, London

Bullivant L (2007) 4dsocial: interactive design environments (architectural design). In: Castle H. (ed) Wiley. Available at: http://onlinelibrary.wiley.com/doi/10.1002/ad.v77:4/issuetoc

Calvo P, Gomila T (2008) Handbook of cognitive science. Elsevier, Oxford

Clark A (2004) Natural-Born Cyborgs: minds, technologies, and the future of human intelligence. Oxford University Press, Oxford

Clark A (2008) Supersizing the mind: embodiment, action, and cognitive extension. Oxford University Press, Oxford

Clark A, Chalmers D (1998) The extended mind. Analysis 58:7–19. doi:10.2307/3328150

De Jaegher H, Di Paolo E (2007) Participatory sense-making. Phenomenol Cogn Sci 6(4):485–507

Di Paolo EA, Rohde M, De Jaegher H (2010) Horizons for the enactive mind: values, social interaction, and play. In: Enaction. MIT Press, Cambridge, MA, pp 33–88

Diprose R, Reynolds J (2008) Merleau-Ponty: key concepts, Acumen, Durham, GBR

El Croquis (ed) (2003) Fukuoka Housing. In: Steven Holl 1986–2003. El Croquis, Madrid, pp 146–159

Eng K, Babler A, Bernardet U et al (2003) Ada – intelligent space: an artificial creature for the SwissExpo.02. ROBOT-03, Taipei, pp 4154–4159

Evans F (2011) Chiasm and flesh. In: Diprose R, Reynolds J (eds) Merleau-Ponty. Acumen Publishing, Durham, pp 1–10

Fox M, Kemp M (2009) Interactive architecture. Princeton Architectural Press, New York

Froese T, Fuchs T (2012) The extended body: a case study in the neurophenomenology of social interaction. Phenomenol Cogn Sci 11(2):205–235

Fuchs T, De Jaegher H (2009) Enactive intersubjectivity: participatory sense-making and mutual incorporation. Phenomenol Cogn Sci 8(4):465–486

Gallagher S (2005) How the body shapes the mind. Oxford University Press, Oxford

Gallagher S (2011) Strong interaction and self-agency. Hum Ment 15:55–76

Gallagher S (2012) Phenomenology. Palgrave Macmillan, London

Gallagher S, Bower M (2014) Making enactivism even more embodied. Avant 5:232–247. doi:10.12849/50202014.0109.0011

Goulthorpe M (2006) HypoSurface – press release. In: hyposurface.org. http://www.hyposurface.org/content/pdf/PressRelease.pdf. Accessed 10 Feb 2015

Gross MD, Green KE (2012) Architectural robotics, inevitably. Interactions 19(1):28–33

Guerra LC, Todoroff T, Sebti Y (n.d.) Lungs [the breather], Brussels, Belgium. Available at: http://thebreather.org/index.php?page=about_en

Haselager P, van Dijk J, van Rooij I (2008) A lazy brain? Embodied embedded cognition and cognitive neuroscience. In: Handbook of cognitive science. Elsevier, Oxford, pp 273–290

Heidegger M (1978) Basic writings from 'Being and Time' (1927) to "The Task of Thinking" (1964). Taylor & Francis, Abingdon

Jacobs M, Findley J (2015) Breathe. sonicribbon.com. Available at: http://www.sonicribbon.com/sonicribbon/breathe/. Accessed 9 Feb 2015

Khan O (2010) Open columns: a carbon dioxide (CO_2) responsive architecture. ACM, New York

Kontovourkis O, Phocas M, Tryfonos G (2013) Prototyping of an adaptive structure based on physical conditions. Int J Archit Comput 11(2):205–226

Kronenburg R (2003) Portable architecture: design and technology, 3rd edn. Birkhäuser, Basel

Kronenburg R (2007) Flexible: architecture that responds to change. Laurence King Publishing, London

McGann M, De Jaegher H, Di Paolo E (2013) Enaction and psychology. Rev Gen Psychol 17(2):203–209

Merleau-Ponty M (1964) The primacy of perception and other essays on phenomenological psychology, the philosophy of art, history and politics. Northwestern University Press, St. Evanston

Oosterhuis K (2004) Muscle tower II: an interactive & kinetic tower. TU Delft 4:55

Oosterhuis K, Biloria N (2008) Interactions with proactive architectural spaces: the muscle projects. Commun ACM 51(6):70–78

Pfeifer R, Bongard J (2006) How the body shapes the way we think. MIT Press, Cambridge, MA

Putnam H (1975) Mathematics, matter, and method. Cambridge University Press, London

Rossi D, Nagy Z, Schlueter A (2012) Adaptive distributed robotics for environmental performance, occupant comfort and architectural expression. Int J Archit Comput 10(3):341–360

Rowlands M (2009) Enactivism and the extended mind. Topoi 28(1):53–62

Rowlands M (2010a) Chapter 3: The mind embodied, embedded, enacted, and extended. In: The new science of the mind. MIT Press, Cambridge, MA, pp 51–84

Rowlands M (2010b) The new science of the mind. MIT Press, Cambridge, MA

Schnädelbach H (2010) Adaptive architecture-A conceptual framework. In: Media city: interaction of architecture, media and social phenomena, Weimar, pp 523–556

Schnadelbach H (2011) Physiological data in adaptive architecture. International Adaptive Architecture Conference, London, pp 1–15

Schnädelbach H, Glover K, Irune AA (2010) ExoBuilding: breathing life into architecture. NordiCHI 2010, Reykjavik, pp 442–451

Schnädelbach H et al (2012) ExoBuilding: physiologically driven adaptive architecture. ACM Trans Comput Hum Interact 19(4):1–22

Shapiro L (2011) Embodied cognition. Taylor & Francis, Abingdon

Vallgårda A (2014) The dress room. In 8th Nordic Conference on Human-Computer Interaction Fun, Fast, Foundational – NordiCHI '14. ACM Press, New York, NY, USA, pp 618–627

Vidyarthi J, Riecke BE, Gromala D (2012) Sonic Cradle: designing for an immersive experience of meditation by connecting respiration to music. In the Designing Interactive Systems Conference. ACM, New York, NY, USA, pp 408–417. Available at: http://dl.acm.org/citation.cfm?doid=2317956.2318017

Vindum K (2009) Bevægelig arkitektur i bevægelse: Slow Furl, en interaktiv ruminstallation udviklet og designet af arkitekterne Mette Ramsgaard Thomsen og Karin Bech. Arkitektur M

Wilson M (2002) Six views of embodied cognition. Psychon Bull Rev 9(4):625–636, Available at: http://link.springer.com/article/10.3758/BF03196322

Zahavi D (2003) Husserl's phenomenology. Stanford University Press

Part IV
Activating Spaces

Strands in both architecture and computing approach development through making. Architects make spatial prototypes to explore future ways of inhabiting our environments, this can be physical or digital prototypes. Computer Scientists frequently make prototypes of underlying infrastructure, interaction mechanisms or physical computing. Both disciplines now produce spatial prototypes that embed computing to better understand our interaction with each other, artefacts and the environment when those are augmented with computation. The authors in this chapter discuss their work to understand interaction in architectural space through the development of prototypes and their study.

Bolbroe complements Jäger's work and introduces an architecture unlike that you might have never seen. The Weiser vision seeks to augment traditional buildings with digital technology that merges the digital with the physical. This vision presumes that architecture is a static thing. Bolbroe's work shows that Architecture is not a passive subject but a highly dynamic and engaged one. Bolbroe discusses numerous digitally enhanced visions of non-static Architecture, Adaptive Architecture. Here the question becomes how does one design when the subjects of architect's notation – the static location of walls and items cannot be assumed. Bolbroe's work seems to reach into Computing and pull out the interactive scale prototype that is termed relational prototyping. Bolbroe also tries to abstract out concerns into a framework consisting of Temporality, Memory, Learning and Emergence as a way of guiding Architectural practice.

Krietemeyer's chapter Interactive Design Frameworks introduces the problems of exploring the design potential for responsive and adaptive facade systems. The objective, in this case, was to create what is referred to as the triple ecology vision that is the merging of intertwined registers of social mental and environmental ecologies. Krietemeyer argues that to design adaptive architectural facades something that could have a considerable impact on the energy consumption of a building it is necessary for architects and interaction designers to work with interactive simulations. For those outside architecture, it may be interesting to understand that the notion of at scale prototyping and building is very foreign to the architectural design experience. Architecture typically deals with scale models, drawings and other renderings of future buildings. Part of the training of architecture is to deal with these relatively abstract materials. So it is therefore very significant that a researcher from the field of architecture is suggesting the need to have facilities that allow designers to experiment with potential facade designs like a physical prototype. This prototype approach is very common in the world of computing. It seems significant that both areas appear to be converging on a similar mode of operational design when dealing with complex behavioral technology.

"The distinction between physical and virtual is increasingly blurred" says **Bier** and this could be a good sentence describing the book. Ending the trio of papers this paper reminds us that buildings are becoming computational entities as computational entities are becoming buildings. This text reminds the reader of some of the converging forces that are not apparent in other works. One such example is the rise of local digital custom fabrication that is replacing the era of mass production. For while a Georgian time traveler would not recognize our ability to manufacture machines or clothes, the production of buildings would be familiar, still highly driven by hand craft and skilled artisans. Combining 3D printing robots at scale offers a new future driven for Bier by robotic architecture.

For this it is not enough to design, it is necessary to create 'meta-designs'. Meta-designs create new problems, the architect is no longer the creator, but a co-creator together with clients, occupants and non-human agents. They all become part of this process. Notions such as copy, original, reproduction all become blurred challenging ideas such as 'quality', 'creativity' so central to modern western design practice. *Bier* also identifies a second force that of the environment and crafts a robotic building which responds by adaption and reconfiguration as mentioned by *Krietemeyer's* and *Bolbroe's* chapters. What we gain here is a design practice in evolution not only to the affordances of digital buildings and digital construction but to digitally augmented design and containment of computational facilities. For any designer of software, it is informative to see the co-evolution that architecture is making both in responses to and by the implementation of digital equipment.

Chapter 10
Mapping the Intangible: On Adaptivity and Relational Prototyping in Architectural Design

Cameline Bolbroe

Abstract In recent years, new computing technologies in architecture have led to the possibility of designing architecture with non-static qualities, which affords the architectural designer with a whole new opportunity space to explore. At the same time, this opportunity space challenges both the principles governing the design of architecture as well as the agency of and the methods at hand for architectural professionals since architecture is traditionally contained in a paradigm of permanence. This essay focuses on a sub-domain of non-static architecture, namely adaptive architecture. Through an investigation into contemporary architectural discourse supported by examples from practice, I frame a shift in attention from the architectural object alone to the act of inhabitation. Further, I argue that the act of inhabitation is a process of negotiation and exchange between the architectural object, the inhabitant and the environment. Consequently, I discuss four aspects of adaptivity in architecture, namely temporality, memory, learning and emergence as an organizing hierarchy, which form the basis for further unpacking adaptivity. Finally, in order to facilitate this further unpacking, and as a response to meet the challenges of designing with adaptivity in architecture, I propose a particular method specifically tailored for adaptive architectural design. The method, relational prototyping, is founded on the idea of inhabitation as an act. Relational prototyping adapts techniques from performance to construct a full-scale prototyping genre, which equips and capacitates the architectural professional with a means to explore and operationalize adaptive qualities of architecture such as temporality, memory, learning and emergence.

C. Bolbroe (✉)
Adaptive Environments, IT University of Copenhagen, Rued Langgaardsvej 7,
DK-2300 Copenhagen, Denmark
e-mail: camb@itu.dk

© Springer International Publishing Switzerland 2016
N.S. Dalton et al. (eds.), *Architecture and Interaction*,
Human–Computer Interaction Series, DOI 10.1007/978-3-319-30028-3_10

Introduction

Until recently, architecture as a design field has been dominated by the design principles of permanence and the static. However, in recent years, the introduction of new computing technologies in architecture has led to the possibility of designing architecture with non-static qualities. With the rise of new maker, manufacturing and robotic technologies and readily available off-the-shelf hardware as well as the prospect of new types of software, new opportunities have literally landed in the hands of architectural professionals who wish to explore this kind of architecture. It has become practically possible for the architectural professional to actually experiment with design propositions and design thinking relating to non-static architecture.

Several scholars and practitioners are focusing on the domain and are attempting to describe the specific qualities of these types of architecture using terms such as responsive, interactive, smart and adaptive to mention but a few. Many of the underlying ideas of these terms are not novel at the core, but surfaced during the 1960s, were developed through the 1970s and 1980s, after which interest declined in the 1990s. Today, the area is receiving renewed focus due to the technological advancements and increased availability of technology we are currently experiencing within the field of architectural design. The field, encompassing various types of non-static architecture, is still maturing and is far from being exhaustively explored. Therefore, there is a need to further develop notions of design and design practices, both theoretically and experimentally, which specifically privilege non-static architecture. As Kolarevic suggests, "*change in architecture is far from being adequately addressed or explored theoretically, experimentally, or phenomenologically*" (Kolarevic 2009, p. 1). Consequently, we need to consider, discuss and refine design concepts specifically related to non-static architecture. Importantly, since today the majority of design methods available for the architectural professional privilege principles of permanence, we need to extend the methodological catalogue to include methods specifically tailored for the design of non-static architecture.

This chapter specifically focuses on adaptive architecture within the domain of non-static architecture and, therefore, critically examines the discourse on contemporary architecture relating to adaptive aspects of architecture. I seek to contribute to an account of adaptivity in architecture through an in-depth, pragmatic, but not exhaustive, exploration of the qualitative aspects underlining the discourse. Subsequently, with a starting point in a set of specific adaptive architectural characteristics, I propose a design method – relational prototyping – specifically tailored to designing with adaptivity as part of an architectural design process.

From Static Architecture to Non-static Architecture

When we were having a book printed in France we complained about the bad alignment. Ah they explained that is because they use machines now, machines are bound to be inaccurate, they have not the intelligence of human beings, naturally the human mind corrects the faults of the hand but a machine of course there are errors. The reason why all of us naturally began to live in France is because France has scientific methods, machines and electricity, but does not really believe that these things have anything to do with the real business of living." [sic] (Stein 2003, p. 8)

Being an intellectual patron in the aftermath of the industrial revolution, Gertrude Stein noticed a confrontation between the machine and the individual, where conflicts around inaccuracy, intelligence, errors and faults challenged the relation to the human being. Today, her reassurance that machines – technology – have nothing to do with the real business of living is problematic because it is hard to neglect the fact that technology is playing an increasingly significant role in our everyday lives. For architecture, technology is also being increasingly directly embedded into our inhabited environment. This development has implications not only for architecture as a built expression, but also the practice of designing architecture (Terzidis 2006).

However, we cannot simply move to France and reject the challenges that follow the introduction of new technologies in architecture, as Gertrude Stein wittily suggested in relation to the publishing industry. It becomes important to position technology and the implications it has for architecture in a meaningful relationship to those inhabiting architecture. Specifically for the architectural professional, it becomes relevant to embrace technological developments and ask how architects can design in such a way that technology can support a meaningful *lived* relationship between architecture, inhabitant and environment.

Efforts to understand and meet the challenges such as the one posed in Gertrude Stein's statement, have been made repeatedly across architectural communities. The idea that architecture is not only a static and permanent expression, but that it also operates in a relationship with its surroundings, is a strand of thinking that can be traced back in time.

Non-static elements in architecture have always been present in the sense that the inhabitant remodels her physical surroundings through the process of inhabitation: maybe adding a shed or tearing down a wall, the village changes over time to meet new demands while general wear and tear affects the appearance of the built environment. Furthermore, for a long time, the nomadic way of life was, and still is, a common way of inhabiting spaces in environments that continuously change through mobility (Kronenburg 2007).

An early example of an inclusive conception of architecture can be traced in the extended meaning of the house, or *domus,* found in classical Greece and Rome (Brand 1997). This conception not only considers the mere material expression of architecture, but actively includes the inhabitant as well as more ephemeral qualities: "*People and their dwellings were indistinguishable: domus referred not only to the walls but also to the people within them. Evidence for this is found in inscriptions and texts, in which the words refer now to one, now to the other, but most often to both at once, to the house and its residents envisioned as an invisible whole. The architectural setting was not an inert vessel; the genius of the domus, honored by a cult, was the protector of both the place and the people who lived in it."* [sic] (Thébert 1987 p. 407). From this quote, we can clearly gather that architecture not only referred to the materials that constituted the physical space such as bricks and mortar, but also to the dynamic human aspects of people inhabiting their houses – moving around, having daily routines and engaging with one another – to such an extent that it was perceived as one entity.

In 1954, Walter Gropius described, although slightly ephemerally, an architecture, which embodies, *"the flow of life"* as well as touches upon the notion of the unpredictable and uncertain by architecture achieving the, *"flexibility to absorb dynamic features"* (Gropius 1954, p. 178). Likewise, Zuk and Clarke expressed a similar interest when stating, *"our present task is to unfreeze architecture, to make it a fluid, vibrating backdrop for the varied and constantly changing modes of life. An expanding, contracting, pulsating, changing architecture would reflect life as it is today and therefore be part of it"* (Zuk and Clarke 1970, p. 3).

Altogether, we can begin to trace a type of architecture framed around an interest for how humans and the environment interact with and change the properties of inhabited spaces. Architecture is even proposed as a backdrop, as Zuk and Clarke explain: something that no longer presents itself as a centerpiece, but instead supports the changing activities, preferences and experiences of humans. Seen from this perspective, the architectural professional has to move beyond the mere consideration that there are dynamic capacities *external* to architecture and to instead incorporate these capacities as *internal* constituents of architectural space. Architecture exists, in this framework, in a constant exchange with the inhabitant and the environment.

Similar approaches to architecture can be found in the works of several scholars. Significantly Christopher Alexander, inspired by biological systems, applied the metaphor of growth to the genesis of architecture (Alexander et al. 1977). In relation to Thebert's account of the ancient holistic notion of the house, Gropius's inclusion of dynamic aspects and Zuk and Clarke's idea of absorption, applying the metaphor of growth to architecture is again indicative of a mode of thinking where architecture is not only perceived as a purely static material expression. Instead it holds the capacity to change over time and adapt to changing conditions in the environment and the inhabitants' activities.

A radical proposition of a consequence of the stream of thinking outlined above is that it becomes problematic if we mostly perceive architecture in terms of its material expression and, therefore, try to shape it through our *anticipation* of what will suit future. As Stewart Brand polemically puts it, *"All buildings are predictions. All predictions are wrong"* (Brand 1997, p. 178). However, the fact that it is difficult or maybe even impossible to predict does not mean that we should care less about the unpredictable or the uncertain. Perhaps rather the opposite.

Adaptivity in Architecture

Moving on from the idea that architecture is a physical, material expression that involves the capacity to change over time in an exchange with the environment and the inhabitant, we shall examine how conceptualizations of this form of architecture have been expressed in more recent contemporary architectural discourse.

Adaptivity in architecture is one among several terms describing non-static qualities. Yet, the description and framing of non-static architecture varies between different architectural communities, as well as from scholar to scholar (Schnädel-bach 2010). A somewhat diverse range of terms relating to adaptivity is therefore in use including (but not exhaustive): moveable, adaptable, flexible, kinetic, dynamic, fluid, reactive, responsive, interactive, smart and built-in intelligence. Moreover, many of the terms are used interchangeably to describe qualities that may, in fact, be different from one another. For example, reactive and responsive may be used interchangeably to describe particular qualities of change in an architectural proposal, even though there may be a difference regarding the specificity and even content which the terms are meant to describe. Acknowledging this diversity, I concentrate on the notion of adaptive architecture.

As a starting point, my proposal for an overarching idea of adaptivity can be attributed to definitions of adaptivity originating in evolutionary biology (Bonner 1988). I draw upon two explanations of adaptivity. First, according to Herbert Simon (1996), adaptation demands a relationship between artifact and environment as well as a relationship between the purpose (or goal) or the character of the artifact and the environments that embraces the artifact. Subsequently, the consequence of adaptivity, referred to as adaptation, cannot be attributed to any single entity in isolation. As we can see, this definition is in line with the strand of thinking we encountered previously, namely that architecture can be perceived as a compound that consists not only of architectural materiality, but also the surroundings and the people occupying a space. A similar concept of adaptivity can be found in the fifth application of the definition of adaptivity from Henderson's Dictionary of Biological Terms, *"Any trait that can confer some advantage on an organism and thus is maintained in a population by natural selection. Traits can only be defined as adaptive with reference to the environments pertaining at the time, as a change in environment that can render a previously adaptive trait non-adaptive, and* vice versa." (Lawrence 2000). Across the two definitions of adaptivity, we see a framing that contains both the environment and the organism. Furthermore, the definitions stress the exchange, which takes place between the organism and the environment.

As previously mentioned, some of the terms in use in the discourse may fall under the definition of adaptivity through the evolutionary biological lens, whereas other terms fall outside this definition. For example, moveable, flexible, kinetic and adaptable fall outside the definition of adaptivity as they have a strong focus on the architectural object and do not specifically include the inhabitant or the environment. Some are mostly figurative such as dynamic and fluid since we do not know exactly what this dynamism and fluidity mean other than 'something is changing'. And finally, terms such as responsive, interactive, smart and intelligent are slightly ambiguous in that there is some sort of connection between the architectural object itself and an outer world. Still, if and how there is exchange activity between an environment *and* an inhabitant simultaneously is unclear. For example, there are several cases where structures referred to as responsive, display trigger-response activity such as automated roller blinds responding to temperature, which typically respond to selected environmental data and less so, if at all, to the inhabitant.

We shall now examine the concept of adaptivity in more detail.

Architecture as an Act

As identified in the notion of adaptivity rooted in evolutionary biology; adaptivity entails a continuous change. Not only does *change* occur as an isolated process, but it also involves an *exchange* between architectural materiality, inhabitants and the environment. Consequently, as indicated by van Hinte (2003) and Allen (2008), it may prove a worthwhile strategy to not only perceive of architecture as a product, but also as a process. This principal change entails a shift in the conceptualization of the architectural object. Not only does the object acquire new features, but it also means that we have to expand our understanding of the object.

To help navigate the definition space of the adaptive architectural object, approaches taken in more recent strands of posthumanist philosophy, such as new materialism, provide a basis for a non-dualistic understanding of the architectural object The object in this sense is, therefore, not purely bound to the object as an enclosed entity, which is *different from* (a negative difference) other entities. Instead, the object becomes continuously different *in itself* (a positive difference) (Dolphijn and van der Tuin 2012; Braidotti 2013).

Let us pragmatically examine a house as an architectural object from this point of view. We are living in a physical, material world where there is, among many other things, such a thing as a house. In the house, a family live, they are the inhabitants. And the house is located, for example, on a hillside which we may call an environment. The posthumanist would not define the house as an enclosed entity with an essence as did Plato and Aristotle. He or she would rather acknowledge the house because we can see it and touch it and in general experience it with our senses, while at the same time perceive it as a continuum and a multiplicity (Ballantyne 2007; DeLanda 2002). We can say that essences are replaced by constant flows of matter in exchange (Deleuze and Guattari 2004). Thinking about the house, the family living in it and the hillside, where the house begins and where it ends now becomes an interesting question since it has now become a flow. What then makes the house a house? Is it the bricks and mortar and how it is put together? Is the house more 'housy' when someone is living in it? Is the house less 'housy' if it floats around in pitch-black emptiness (Ingold 2010)? The answer is strangely that the house is all and nothing at the same time, it does not really begin or end – it becomes – and instances of this continuous *process of becoming* are what we can momentarily discuss as houses in relation to what it is embedded in and how it is acted upon. However, in a material world, we also have to be a little practical. If we look at something together at the same time and would like to have a meaningful conversation about it, we have to agree on how to contain that thing. Even if it is for only a moment and even if we know that in the next second, the thing will perhaps become something else. We have to draw an imaginary boundary around it that we can agree on and share.

From this context, we can approach adaptive architecture, elaborating on Schnädelbach's (2010) definition of adaptive architecture, as: an architecture where equal attention is paid to the architectural object, the inhabitant and the environment as well as the negotiation and exchange going on in the relationship between the architectural object, the inhabitant and the environment.

Now, let us dig a little deeper into what is at stake in this relationship between the architectural object, the inhabitant and the environment. We are going to engage with an example from Bateson's *"Steps to an Ecology of Mind"*. Here, Bateson describes the characteristics of a healthy ecology of human civilization using the notion of flexibility. Being a component of human civilization, architecture can be inscribed into his conceptualization. With a simple, yet eloquent story about a man on a wire, Bateson explains:

> *To maintain the ongoing truth of his basic premise ('I am on the Wire'), he must be free to move from one point of instability to the other,* i.e. *certain variables such as the position of his arms and the rate of movement of his arms must have great flexibility, which he uses to maintain the other more fundamental and general characteristics. If his arms are fixed or paralyzed (isolated from communication), he must fall.* (Bateson 1987, p. 503)

In this example, the man on the wire needs flexibility to achieve stability. This stability *becomes*, in his persistent negotiation with an unstable system in order to acquire a stable and meaningful outcome, namely to walk the wire from one point to another. The tightrope walker, therefore, needs a sensibility towards a kind of stability that not only incorporates the wire alone. In other words, he must engage with a sensibility that reaches beyond the wire at the tip of his toes to his extended environment to be able to make a successful journey – or a controlled fall, for that matter. He must sense the grip of his feet, the way in which he can turn his bodily movements into balance, how he and the wire respond to wind speed as well as perhaps his previous experience with tightrope walking, his state of mind in a potentially precarious situation, and so on. We can say that the *act* of walking the wire becomes stable rather than the material and structural form of the wire alone.

By inscribing architecture into Bateson's "healthy ecology", we can compare the act of walking the wire to that of inhabiting. We could perhaps even say that the tightrope walker inhabits the wire. But, as we established, he can only do so if he is willing to consider qualities other than the pure materiality and form of the wire itself. While the act of walking the line requires flexibility to accommodate instability, inhabiting architecture, likewise, requires flexibility to accommodate instability. Moreover, the *act* of inhabiting, specifically because it has a meaning, becomes the new stability, which potentially allows freedom to change. The primary preoccupation is then less on the architectural object itself, e.g. a dining room, and more on the act of dining which may play out in a variety of scenarios and, thus, potentially requires many different dining rooms. Imagining our man on the wire, he can walk the wire in numerous ways, as long as he is able to respond meaningfully to the changing conditions that surround him. Seen through this lens, there is a requirement of instability to find stability and further, from a purely architectural point of view, the notion of architecture shifts from being primarily focused on the object, to becoming more focused on the act.

For technology-saturated architecture, and significantly adaptive architecture, a shift in attention from the object to the act may prove to be of particular value because it is hard to refuse to look beyond the architectural object itself. I suggest that this specific attention can help unfold the particulars of adaptivity that lie within the relationship between the architectural object, the inhabitant and the environment. What these may be, I explore next.

Four Aspects of Adaptivity

There are four aspects that I would particularly like to draw attention to and discuss in relation to adaptivity in architecture: Temporality, memory, learning and emergence. These four aspects have been areas of interest that, to varying degrees, have occupied the minds of architects throughout time even before information technology entered the architectural arena. They are, therefore, not new as such. However, they are important to discuss because they have gained greater prominence due to the increased use of information technology in architecture. That is, as previously noted, information technology currently shifts from being primarily *external* to architectural materiality to becoming *internal* to architectural materiality. In the following, I elaborate on these four qualitative aspects in relation to contemporary architectural discourse and selected examples from the practice of architecture. We are also going to stick around our man on the wire for a little longer.

In an adaptive architectural context, Bateson's healthy ecology, as we encountered previously, urges us to dig a little further into what is happening during the act of walking the wire. Because the situation is constantly changing and, therefore, also changes the relationship between the wire, the tightrope walker and the environment, it becomes interesting to explore what happens over the course of time between instances of change and at thresholds. There are two scenarios that are easy to imagine. Either the man successfully completes the journey across the wire or he falls. His journey, regardless of the outcome, has a speed, duration and perhaps a rhythm. In both scenarios, we can equally say that he moves in a state between two thresholds, specifically the point at which he begins his journey and the point at which he ends his journey. We can express the differences between the two scenarios with qualitative temporal descriptors. In the scenario where he successfully completes the journey, both the speed and the rhythm are more stable, the duration is longer and the thresholds occur with a specific distance relative to the anchoring points of the wire. In the scenario where he falls, however, the speed patterns of the tightrope walker, and perhaps also the wire and the environment, are more inconsistent: perhaps he makes rapid movements with his arms just before he falls in an attempt to regain his balance, or perhaps the wind speed changes suddenly and makes the wire sway. The rhythm is definitely broken at the exact point where he falls and the second threshold will, therefore, occur at another distance from the anchoring points of the wire. In between the scenarios of the full journey and the fall, there are, of course, a large number of potential outcomes, each with different temporal qualities.

In contemporary architecture, there is an increasing amount of work and experiments, which contain temporal qualities like the ones in the tightrope walker example. For example, the display system, HypoSurface, developed by Mark Goulthorpe and tdECOi architects in collaboration with MIT (2003), which features physical movement directly in the screen surface. The display surface is controlled by high-speed pneumatic pistons which actuate triangular panels on the surface causing a broad variety of motion patterns to ripple across the screen based on pre-defined inputs. Another, less recent, example is Jean Nouvel and Architecture-Studio's Institut du Monde Arabe in Paris, with its 240 photosensitive façade mounted apertures controlling the amount of light and heat entering the building (Nouvel 1987). Many other examples have been described in the literature on kinetics and responsivity in architecture (see, for example, Moloney 2011; Bullivant 2006). Common to many of these examples is the fact that temporal aspects are directly embedded in the structures by means of technology. Likely, we cannot call HypoSurface and Institut du monde Arabe adaptive according to the definition since HypoSurface mainly concentrates on the relationship between the surface and the person experiencing it, while Institut du Monde Arabe primarily links environmental data to the actuation of the façade. Nevertheless, they both contain temporal qualities like many other kinetic and responsive structures shared with adaptive structures. If we want to design architecture with adaptive qualities, we need to actively consider temporal design parameters just like we consider qualities such as proportion and scale.

In summary, temporality becomes a design parameter, internal to architecture, which directly affects the functionality, expression and experience of architecture. In developing specific temporal descriptors, we can begin to investigate, unfold and design with temporal qualities.

Along with HypoSurface and Institut du Monde Arabe, we can find related examples in the recent development of many so-called smart materials whose properties change depending on, e.g. moisture, stress, electrical fields and so on. But what kinds of change do they typically express? Unlike the ecology in the story of the man on the wire, it is possible to predict how the smart materials, HypoSurface and Institut du Monde Arabe respond in isolation. We do not know exactly when the filigree-like apertures of Institut du Monde will retract, but we know that they will do so when a certain temperature threshold has been reached. What if we, like Gropius, are interested in, "the flexibility to absorb dynamic features" (Gropius 1954, p. 178)?

And what if the employees of Institut du Monde Arabe have different preferences for the amount of sunlight which bathes their office spot? In this case, two concepts are interesting, namely memory and learning.

Let us have a look at our tightrope walker once again. To achieve the skills of walking a wire, he must be able to remember and learn. In the beginning, he is a novice. Perhaps he begins his training walking on chalked lines on the asphalt, his head up, knees slightly bent, his arms stretched out and flexible. He closes first one eye, then the other, until he can balance with both eyes closed. He needs to remember the way in which his body responds to balance, motion and wind. And if he practices enough, he might one day feel safe and able to walk a wire suspended high above the ground.

Bateson probably did not imagine the wire as a piece of adaptive architecture infused with advanced technology. But, if we were to play the mind game of imagining that a piece of steel wire was adaptive, we could assign it a set of new properties. Perhaps it would respond to wind speeds in order to change the stress properties of the wire on the fly. Still, little would our tightrope walker benefit from this new kind of wire, if we did not consider his particular way of moving his body to stay in balance. To him, the wind responsive wire might just as well feel like a wire with new properties, similar to the difference he experiences when walking a slack line and a steel wire. The goal, as we remember, is not the materiality and form of the wire itself, but the act of walking the wire. Therefore, we would need the wire to be able to register, remember and learn an extensive context in direct exchange with the tightrope walker's interaction with the wire and the environment.

Like the scenario with an adaptive wire having a memory and learning capacities, Tristan D'Estree Sterk (2006) considers what he calls levels of control in architecture. He defines three levels of control, where the third level, the hybridized level, is particularly relevant. The hybridized level enhances architecture with a capacity to actively adapt to a change in patterns of occupancy: "*the hybridized model can also be used to produce responses that have adjustable response criteria, achieving this by using occupant interactions to build contextual models of the ways in which users occupy and manipulate space*" (Sterk 2006). Even though he is not explicit about memory, the consequence of Sterk's proposal must be that the adjustable response criteria contained in the contextual model are stored in some form of memory, either in relation to the space or directly embedded in the materials that form the space. Still, exactly how this contextual model is created, we are curiously left to wonder. Usman Haque speculates a little further and introduces the notion of an architecture that has the capacity to transform. But, not only does it transform based on a contextual model, as Sterk (2006) suggested, it transforms as a consequence of learning from the inhabitant. The goal for Haque is, therefore, "*a model of interaction where an individual can directly adjust the way that a machine responds to him or her so that they can converge on a mutually agreeable nature of feedback: an architecture that learns from the inhabitant just as the inhabitant learns from the architecture*" (Haque in Fox and Kemp 2009, p. 80). The idea that architecture can learn once again urges us to focus on architecture as an act which is played out *between* the inhabitant, the architectural object and the environment because information exchange is necessary for learning to take place. Haque articulates it through the metaphor of the conversation, "*A truly interactive system is a 'multiple loop' system in which one enters into a 'conversation': a continual and constructive information exchange*" (Haque in Fox and Kemp 2009, p. 80).

Subsequently, we can begin to ask how to build such systems as Kolarevic suggests when he situates the construction of Paskian systems,[1] which are presumably similar to Sterk's contextual models, as a main challenge in the field (Kolarevic 2014). How exactly do such systems function? What should a contextual model contain and what does a conversational 'multiple loop' system produce in practice?

Kolarevic identifies the purpose of such systems as enabling the design of an architecture that avoids boredom and retains a high degree of novelty (Kolarevic 2014). Similarly, although less specific than Kolarevic, Terzidis (2006) argues that an agile architecture with unpredictable and uncertain properties may be of great importance exactly because it may suggest change, anticipation and liveliness in architecture.

I, however, want to direct attention towards the notion of emergence, which is a process through which the architect might consider working with the agility of which Terzidis speaks. Relative to the definition of adaptivity originating in biology, emergence is a process whereby larger patterns and entities arise through interactions among smaller or simpler entities that themselves do not show such properties. With emergence, agility *may* arise or change as a result of exchange between the architectural object, the inhabitant and the environment. A result of emergence might be novelty or liveliness, but not necessarily. A result of emergence might be boredom, but again, not necessarily. Importantly, approaching architecture from an emergent point of view, we are not locked into a situation where we perhaps misguidedly build in pre-defined values such as novelty and, thereby, hamper adaptivity. Since we may be wrong when we try to predict future needs, if we listen to Brand, 'anti-boredom' becomes a less interesting objective because we do not know if a future need actually does involve boredom. Rather than striving for static objectives such as 'anti-boredom' or novelty as such, I believe we need to pay attention to the act of inhabiting architecture as an emergent process in order to make full use of the uncertainty and unpredictability that Terzidis considers to be of such importance. And intriguingly, he announces that it may very well, "*challenge the very nature of what architecture really is*" (Terzidis 2006, p. 37). Paying a final visit to our man on the wire, I suggest we help him to engage with the wire in precisely the manner he finds the most useful, and allow the wire to be just as boring or novel as it happens to become, while he does so.

Seen in the light of this discussion, there is of course a long way to go before we arrive at architecture with memory and learning capacities and that

---

[1] A Paskian system refers to a cybernetic system. Gordon Pask was one of the early proponents of cybernetics, specifically contributing with the notion of second order cybernetics. Such systems include levels of feedback beyond achieving a goal and, therefore, also embed interactions from, e.g. human participants in the system (Negroponte 1975).

ultimately display emergent properties. We have only just begun our expedition to explore adaptivity. Therefore, we need to devise ways in which we can gain deeper and better-informed insights into the acts of inhabitation and the exchange and negotiation in relationship between architectural objects, inhabitants and the environments.

The process of designing architecture typically involves means of exploring ideas and concepts in representational media, before the physical manifestation of a building stands on site. For adaptive architecture, we also need to develop methods through which the architectural professional can explore, refine and work with the particulars of adaptivity in architecture. The second and following part of the chapter is, therefore, devoted to practical experiments with adaptivity.

Relational Prototyping

The architectural design methods at hand today typically privilege the permanent and the static over the dynamic. With the introduction of adaptivity and the previously outlined qualitative aspects of adaptivity, the prevailing design methods that an architect makes use of are, therefore, challenged when it comes to understanding non-static qualities. Unlike, for example, time-based art forms such as filmmaking, performance and music; architects are typically not used to or trained to work with non-static design qualities.

Stan Allen suggests that the concept of *notation*, inspired from the domains of music and choreography, can be adopted and tailored as an architectural design method to enlarge the catalogue of techniques available to the architectural professional and support time-based qualities in architecture (Allen 2008). In line with van Hinte's suggestion to look at architecture as a process rather than a product, Allen argues for the adoption of notation while he explains, "*The use of notation marks a shift from the production of space to the performance of space*" (Allen 2008, p. 60). Supportive of Allen's position and extending the idea to, "the negotiation of space through the performance of space", I see a constructive approach in actively *engaging* with the performance of space; the performance of space then becomes a process of space-making that is conductive of the constitution of space in an ongoing negotiation between the inhabitant, architectural object and the environment. A strategy to inform the production of space through the performance of space is, therefore, to look to fields where performative techniques are already well-established.

I propose an explorative design method, relational prototyping, which is specifically devised to support design attempts with adaptivity in architecture. It consists of three components in relation to the definition of adaptive architecture; the prototype, the participant and the scenario and it proposes a way in which to explore their mutual negotiation and exchange, as means of acts supported through performative techniques. Before I go into detail regarding the performative techniques, I first examine the components that are elementary to relational prototyping.

Components in Relational Prototyping

We zoom in a little to have a more specific look at the components in relational prototyping: the object, the inhabitant and the environment. Preliminarily, we can grasp the object as an assembly of materials including computational capacities, the inhabitant as the person or persons inhabiting a space, and the environment as the matter the inhabitant and the object is embedded in. These three terms are, in this context, inscribed into a domain of architecture, although other design domains could potentially be included. This means that when I speak of the object, I refer to an architectural object. This kind of object could of course, in principle, include a whole range of physical qualities, it could be anything from a door handle to a whole building, and it could include models and other work-in-progress objects. In the following, the object of reference is a specific object; namely a particular kind of prototype. The inhabitant refers to participants in a particular situation and the environment is typically established as the framed surroundings in which the participant and the prototype are staged.

Each one of them plays a single role, in themselves, so that it becomes pragmatically possible to discuss and explore the agency, the meaning and the character of each. On the other hand, we should bear in mind that it may not be easy, or even helpful, to very narrowly delimit the definition of either the inhabitant, the object or the environment, since adaptivity entails change over time and, thus, a continuous reframing of the boundaries of each – as we saw in the section on adaptivity – to allow for, for example, exchange and negotiation.

Exchange and negotiation, which we can frame as *relations*, is just as much of interest as the components themselves because this is where it is possible to explore what is going on *between* the inhabitant, the object and the environment. The combination of the inhabitant, the object and the environment, observed over time, therefore, also constitutes environments in themselves to which we can ad new inhabitants and new objects. The notion of the environment, the inhabitant and the object are, therefore, to be considered as placeholders. They are placeholders so that we can still point to a specific object and talk about it, while keeping open discussions about the exchange and negotiations going on between the environment, the inhabitant and the object, which constantly re-inform each. This idea is aligned with Herbert Simon's definition of adaptation, which says that the outcomes of adaptivity cannot be attributed to any single entity in isolation. Adaptation demands a relationship between object, inhabitant and environment as well a relationship between the purpose (or goal) or the character of the object and the environments that embrace the object in relation to the inhabitant (Simon 1996).

In the following practice examples, the notion of the object is framed as a particular form of prototype, the inhabitant as participants and finally the environment as a specific scenario. Altogether they populate performative situations, *acts*, where it is possible to explore their mutual relationships in aspects of time, learning, memory and emergence.

The background for the following explanation of the components in relational prototyping is based an explorative practice underlining the development of relational prototyping. I developed several batches of prototypes with different time-based qualities and tested them with the application of performative techniques to structure the engagement between prototypes and participants in varying contexts that formed different scenarios.

Object: The Prototype

If we want to open up for the possibility of exploring adaptivity as an integrated part of an architectural design method, we must enable a mode of designing where we gain access to adaptive qualities. Not disputing the relevance of traditional representational design methods such as the scale drawing and the scale model, the choice of scale here needs to be the full-scale (see Fig. 10.1). The choice of the full-scale makes it possible to study aspects that would otherwise be hard to access. The full-scale lends a direct focus on the exchange occurring in the relationship between the inhabitant, the object and the environment in real time and at the true order of magnitude. A banal but important observation is that it is hard, if not impossible, to engage physically with our bodies in a scale model or to investigate real time actions in a drawing. Even many simulation strategies designed to predict movement patterns and so on, still do not give us the opportunity to gain an insight into what happens with the human body and how we experience the engagement with a particular architectural situation. Therefore, the prototypes must be physical objects interpreted as being in full-scale relative to the human body.

The prototypes, exemplary for relational prototyping in this context, are technology-equipped entities with the capacity to move in response to people engaging with them or other obstacles in the environment. They have a variety of sensors mounted in their skins to facilitate interaction, as well onboard microprocessors for memory storage, exchange of information and communication between the prototypes. Additionally, I have been working with various forms of external technologies in conjunction with the prototypes such as ultrasound tracking systems, video and sound recordings and live visualization feedback (see Fig. 10.2).

For relational prototyping, the prototype requires a specific understanding because the prototypes as objects become part of an exchange situation with an extended environment. They are not, therefore, objects in a representational sense as the drawing usually is. This means that they are not to be deliberately interpreted as specific architectural elements such as simple wall objects or the like. That said, I am aware that it is not fully possible, or desirable, to avoid personal interpretation and association, but by adopting this approach, I strive instead to create an open-endedness in the physical appearance.[2] The prototypes are, therefore, deliberately,

---

[2]In fact, the prototypes are indeed interpreted. Preliminary results reveal that the objects are typically assigned, e.g. the character of furniture, walls, doors, animals and people. However, the spectrum of interpretation indicates that there is, in fact, an open-endedness rather than reoccurring specific interpretations.

Fig. 10.1 © Cameline Bolbroe. Responsive prototypes in action in two different environments. These prototypes respond to motion in their vicinity via ultrasound sensors. When participants trigger the sensors, the beams move around via embedded motors. The beams have varying motion patterns so that three of them move around a pivot point at one end, whereas the other two move transitionally

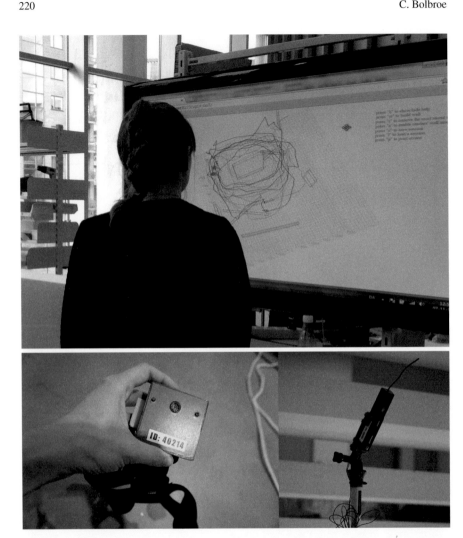

Fig. 10.2 © Cameline Bolbroe. Example of an external technology generating live visualizations of movement patterns in an environment. Ultrasound trackers (*lower left*) can be placed on prototypes and on the bodies of participants. Position data are then transmitted via ultrasound receivers (*lower right*) and visualized in real time as a 3D map of the participants' movements in space. Also, the geometries of various prototypes can be grabbed via the trackers and shown in relation to the movement patterns on the screen

and to varying degrees, constructed as simple geometrical objects with embedded technology that gives them the capacity to move (and potentially otherwise engage through sound, haptic responses, visual cues and so forth) in relation to participants and the environment. They are stripped of stylistic or ornamental features in an attempt to establish a focus on '*action*' rather than appearance and potential personal associations. In this sense they are open, abstract physical entities in line with the concepts that artists in the domain of minimal art, such as Donald Judd, Sol Le Witt and Robert Morris, have been pursuing (Schmidt 2007).

When working with prototypes that are intentionally constructed to be active, responsive and ideally adaptive, we can begin to explore the four qualitative aspects explained previously: temporality, memory, learning and emergence. Here the quadrille of aspects helps identify in which domain change is having an impact or is receiving particular attention. For example, the prototypes actively respond to the participants in real time, through motion, which radically changes the experience of spatial constitution. The time aspect now becomes physically present directly in the actions of the prototypes as an expression of their fluctuating positions in space. Qualities such as the timing, the speed, the character and duration of the motion in the prototypes, affect how participants experience the prototypes and, thus, how they choose to interact both with the prototypes and one another. If we add memory and learning to the equation, we can start to learn which action parameters should be stored in the memory and which ones should be discarded. We can observe how participants engage with the prototypes to achieve a specific character in motion or position that they might be interested in saving and retrieving for future needs. And we can observe how this particular kind of engagement constitutes spatial configurations, which we did not anticipate or design beforehand.

Inhabitant: The Participant

In performance, the body is the primary device for directly engaging in relation to an environment. The expert performer is trained to use her body as an active tool, in structured ways, in relation to her environment and other performers (Søndergaard and Petersen 2011). With performative techniques, it is possible to stage specific situations over time and enquire into the relational aspects using our bodies directly as explorative devices (see Fig. 10.3).

In performance theatre, the expert performer is typically the most prominent type of performer. Outside a theatre situation, the choice of participants can shape the outcome of the explorations in various desirable directions and can provide an insight into different approaches taken by different types of participants; perhaps because they have smaller bodies (children) or because they have different professional backgrounds (dancers, musicians, architects). For example, the architect has a developed and more readily available vocabulary with regards to space that can be activated through a performative engagement. In scenarios like these, the participant, say, the architect goes through several performative sessions to condense both an enactment and a verbalization of the situation. When using non-expert performers, which is both possible and relevant, expertise from domains other than performance theatre can be explored. As Søndergaard and Petersen explain, when framing the researcher as performer, "*the researcher is involved in generating her own experiential accounts, both observing and performing the experience, and the evidence emerges as a consequence of that enactment*" (Søndergaard and Petersen 2011, p. 83]. Again we can use the four qualitative aspects, temporality, memory,

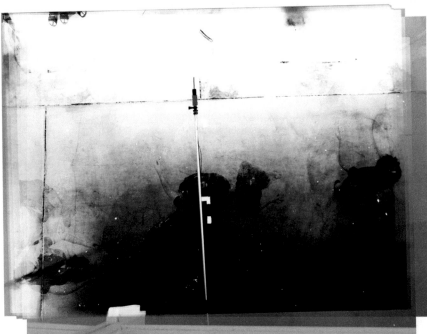

Fig. 10.3 © Spaces in experience cluster/Jessica Lai. Participant in performance session enacting two different rule-sets. Ultrasound trackers are positioned on top of the participant's head and in his hands. The little red ultrasound receiver can be seen in the middle of the image at the end of the grey pole. Spaces in Experience Cluster, Smartgeometry, Hong Kong, 2014

learning and emergence as an organizing hierarchy for inquiry. Through the actions between the participant and prototype, and depending on the choice of evidence we might wish to collect during the session (e.g. interviews, video recordings, tracking, etc.), we can, e.g. explore which characteristics gain prominence over time and how perhaps certain action patterns emerge as a result of a specific engagement.

Environment: The Scenario

The notion of the environment, as we have previously encountered in the example of Bateson's man on the wire, constitutes everything which is not the man or the wire, i.e. all the fluctuating elements surrounding him that might affect his journey on the wire. The man on the wire engages directly in a 1:1 relationship with not only the wire, but also the environment. In theatre or in a performance situation, the environment in which the performer performs is also typically a full-scale environment. The performer engages in a time-based, 1:1 relationship with a particular environment that can either be designed and take place on a stage, or it can take place in an everyday setting, for example a train station or in a mall (Schechner 2003, 2006).

The combination of full-scale prototypes and everyday or staged environments supports a grounding of the body *in* the environment and in direct relation to the prototypes, which is different from many traditional modes of development which define architectural design practice (i.e. sketches, drawings, models) (Evans 1997; Allen 2008; Plowright 2014). The characteristic of the performance as an event that takes place in a full-scale environment is, therefore, relevant because we can then situate the human body over time in relation to the prototypes and directly in the environment.

The environment in relational prototyping pragmatically refers to everything which is not the prototypes or the participants. It is a location or a site that we choose in which we conduct our explorations with a set of prototypes and participants. When choosing a location or a site, it is helpful to consider the complexity of the location in relation to what we are interested in exploring. For rehearsal situations or to facilitate a particular focus, it may be desirable to begin with less complex locations. For example, an indoor environment might involve fewer unknown factors making it easier to establish a shared and clear focus, especially if we are working with participants who are not trained performers (see Fig. 10.4).

The Act: Performative Techniques

When we want to investigate the negotiations and exchanges occurring in an adaptive situation, we need a structure that can help direct our focus towards the qualities that we are interested in exploring, e.g. temporal aspects or emergent

Fig. 10.4 © Cameline Bolbroe. Trained performer interacting with a set of prototypes, here in the form of a number of cardboard props. In the upper image, he is rehearsing in an indoor environment with lower complexity. He repeats the session in an outdoor environment, increasing the complexity of the session. In the lower image, he is lying on a bicycle lane

aspects. In a scenario with a set of prototypes and a number of participants, these aspects can be structured through a set of rules and a set of roles of engagement (Søndergaard and Petersen 2011). Through the rules of engagement, the participants are actively guided to use their body in particular ways relative to the prototypes, other participants and the specific scenario. All participants are, furthermore, assigned specific roles that will help them obtain a condensed form of awareness that we can use to refine our conceptualization of adaptivity. The rules and the roles are relevant as one of the founding figures of performance studies, Richard Schechner puts it, because it is our interest to *"investigate what the object does, how it interacts with other objects or beings, and how it relates to other objects and beings"* (Schechner 2006, p. 30).

The four roles of Meyerhold's performance quadrialogue: *sourcers, producers, performers and partakers* give us a framework for structuring our exploration (see Fig. 10.5). From the performance terminology used by Meyerhold, I have extrapolated the four roles to a more general framing as a set of observational positions: *organizational, directive, active and reflective*. The organizational position, which Meyerhold calls 'the sourcers', denotes the person who initially established or orchestrated the environment. In practice sessions, this role is left out since it typically has no direct function here. The directive position denotes the participant who guides the situation and provides a rule set for the active position to enact. In Meyerhold's terminology, this is 'the producer'. The participant in the active position, which Meyerhold calls 'the performer,' follows and acts out the rules. Lastly, the reflective position finally provides an overview of the situation with a focus on the relationship between the three other observational positions, which Meyerhold calls 'the partaker' (Meyerhold 1969).

During practice sessions, the participants take on the three active observational positions in turn, namely the directive, the active and the reflective. Each position enables a certain focused attention towards the situation through rules evoked from the directive position. As Søndergaard and Petersen describe, *"the rules can arrange moments of refined analytic presence for the researcher and bring a particular focus on the matter of investigation"* (Søndergaard and Petersen 2011 p. 83–84). A scenario experienced from the active position is different from the scenario experienced from the directive position. For example, while the active participant might focus on a particular prototype, the directive participant may focus on actions that will trigger the active participant to focus on a different prototype. When rehearsed over time, the combination of shifting observational positions and rules qualify a heightened awareness of the overall situation known as the extra-daily state within performance (Barba and Savarese 1995). This means that, through rehearsing, we can model the participants' physical and mental presence to accommodate a particular awareness of particular situations, which is more focused than that of an everyday situation.

In summary, relational prototyping is a speculative sketching practice particularly suited for the exploration of adaptivity in architecture in that it enables an inquiry into the negotiations and exchanges particular for adaptive qualities. It is orchestrated around three specific components, the prototype, the participant and the scenario, and a guiding structure, which is a set of roles and rules of engagement.

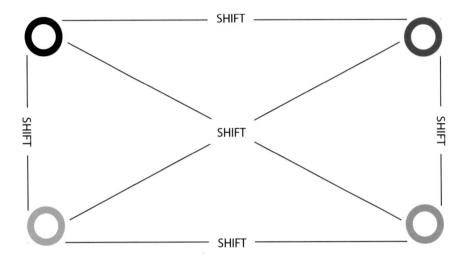

ORGANIZATIONAL (sourcers)
authors, composers,
dramaturges, etc.

(producers) **DIRECTIVE**
directors, conducters,
designers, etc.

SHIFT

SHIFT

SHIFT

SHIFT

SHIFT

ACTIVE (performers)
participants, ect.

(partakers) **REFLECTIVE**
observers, spectators,
audience, ect.

Fig. 10.5 © Cameline Bolbroe. An adaptation of the performance quadrialogue (Meyerhold 1969)

The Potential of Relational Prototyping

The motivation behind relational prototyping is, along with traditions in the architectural field, to establish a sketching environment which is specific to the particular problems involved in adaptive architecture. It is a speculative sketching environment that enables a position of theoretical and methodological rigor, which opens up for otherwise ephemeral adaptive qualities. Relational prototyping aims to access and unfold relational accounts through engagement in actual situated contexts.

Relational prototyping is devised specifically to enable an enquiry beyond the classical notion of the architectural object to, thus, also incorporate an active attention towards the inhabitant and the environment. Relational prototyping facilitates a specific focus on the relational aspects of inhabitation under dynamic, fluctuating conditions.

The four qualitative aspects: temporality, memory, learning and emergence form here the start of an organizing structure for further explorations. While I have framed already existing patterns of interest in current discourse as temporality, memory, learning and emergence, the role of relational prototyping is also to promote a further unpacking of these qualitative aspects as well as other potential, as yet, hidden aspects.

My explorations so far indicate that there are, in fact, many more potential interesting aspects that can be extracted from practices involving relational prototyping, while each of the four qualitative aspects can also easily be expanded with a set of sub-aspects. For example, temporality entails a whole subset of qualities that may be of interest to the architectural professional either as deign parameters or points for consideration in a design process. Concepts such as speed, duration, pulse and pitch are, of course, not new concepts, but how they specifically relate to, unfold and influence adaptivity in architecture is an area that needs further research. Additionally, depending on the architectural material, or whether the aim is to develop software, to qualify human narrativization, experience or something else, the rules of engagement should be crafted specifically for the task at hand. Relational prototyping is, therefore, a method that invites the architectural professional to further investigate and qualify a broad range of aspects in relation to adaptivity in architecture.

Conclusion

Assuming that we are not all going to move to France to avoid engaging with the challenge of integrating technology as part of the real business of living as Gertrude Stein wrote in 1940, the intention of this chapter has been to equip the architectural professional with a framework and tools to address this challenge.

Until recently, architecture, as a design field, was governed by the design principles of permanence and the static. Today, technological developments are driving the idea of architecture characterized by persistent transformation, which has prompted the architectural professional to address the unique opportunities and challenges that non-static architecture, specifically adaptive architecture, introduces to architectural design.

I have discussed and analyzed the discourse of non-static architecture, specifically relating to adaptive architecture. Based on the discourse and through the presentation of additional examples from the practice of architecture, I have identified a shift in attention in architecture: from the architectural object in isolation to the enactment of the relationship between the architectural object, the inhabitant and the environment. I have mapped out four qualitative aspects of adaptivity, namely temporality, memory, learning and emergence, which provide an operational structure that further specifies adaptivity in architectural design. The operational structure forms the basis for research which seeks to explore what the aspects of temporality, memory, learning and emergence entail for architectural design.

As a response to the new opportunities that reside in adaptivity in architectural design, and with a foundation in the four qualitative aspects of adaptivity, I have tailored a method specifically for designing with and exploring adaptive qualities in a design research process. The method, relational prototyping, utilizes techniques from performance to devise a full-scale prototyping genre, which equips and capacitates the architectural professional with a means to explore, operationalize and advance the understanding of the adaptive qualities of architecture.

References

Alexander C, Ishikawa S, Silverstein M, Jacobson M, Fiksdahl-King I, Angel S (1977) A pattern language. Oxford University Press, New York

Allen S (2008) Practice: architecture, technique and representation. Routledge, New York

Ballantyne A (2007) Deleuze for architects. Routledge, London

Barba E, Savarese N (1995) The secret art of the performer. Routledge, London

Bateson G (1987) Steps to an ecology of mind. John Aronson Inc., London

Bonner JT (1988) The evolution of complexity. Princeton University Press, Princeton

Braidotti R (2013) The posthuman. Polity Press, Cambridge

Brand S (1997) How buildings learn: what happens after they're built. Weidenfeld Nicolson Illustrated, London

Bullivant L (2006) Responsive environments – architecture, art and design. V&A Contemporary, London

DeLanda M (2002) Deleuze and the use of genetic algorithm in architecture. In: Leach N (ed) Designing for a digital world. Wiley, London

Deleuze G, Guattari F (2004) A thousand plateaus. Continuum, London

Dolphijn R, van der Tuin I (2012) New materialism: interviews & cartographies. Open Humanities Press, Ann Arbor

Evans R (1997) Translations from drawings to building and other essays. Architectural Association, London

Fox M, Kemp M (2009) Interactive architecture. Princeton Architectural Press, New York

Goulthorpe M, Shpiner S, Allen CW (2003) Hyposurface. http://www.hyposurface.org/. Retrieved: 2 Mar 2015
Gropius W (1954) Eight steps toward a solid architecture. Reprinted in architecture culture. (1993) Ockman J (ed) Rizzoli, New York
Ingold T (2010) Bringing things to life: creative entanglements in a world of materials. NCRM working papers series. University of Aberdeen, ESRC National Centre for Research Methods
Kolarevic B (2009) Exploring architecture of change: ACADIA 09:Reform
Kolarevic B (2014) Outlook 2014. In: Kretzer M, Hovestadt L (eds) ALIVE. Advancements in adaptive architecture. Birkhäuser, Basel
Kronenburg R (2007) Flexible: architecture that responds to change. Laurence King, London
Lawrence E (ed) (2000) Henderson's dictionary of biological terms. Prentice Hall, Edinburgh
Meyerhold V (1969) Meyerhold on theatre (Trans and ed. Edward Braun). Hill & Wang, New York
Moloney J (2011) Designing kinetics for architectural facades. State change. Routledge, New York
Negroponte N (1975) Soft architecture machines. MIT Press, Cambridge
Nouvel J (1987) Institut Arabe du Monde. Paris. http://www.jeannouvel.com/en/desktop/home/#/en/desktop/projet/paris-france-arab-world-institut1. Retrieved: 16 Feb 2015
Plowright P (2014) Revealing architectural design. Methods, frameworks & tools. Routledge, London
Schechner R (2003) Performance theory. Routledge, London. Revised Edition
Schechner R (2006) Performance studies – an introduction, 2nd edn. Routledge, New York
Schmidt U (2007) Minimalismen Æstetik. Museum Tusculanums Forlag
Schnädelbach H (2010) Adaptive architecture – a conceptual framework. In: MediaCity: interaction of architecture, media and social phenomena
Simon H (1996) The sciences of the artificial, 3rd edn. The MIT Press, Cambridge
Søndergaard K, Petersen K (2011) Material evidence as staged experientiality. In: Beim A, Thomsen, MR (eds) The role of material evidence in architectural research. The Royal Danish Academy of Fine Arts, Schools of Architecture, Design and Conservation
Stein G (2003) Paris France. Personal recollections. Peter Owen Publisher, London
Sterk T (2006) Responsive architecture: user-centered interactions within the hybridized model of control. In: Games and match II: on computer games, advanced geometries and digital technologies. Episode Publishers, Rotterdam
Terzidis K (2006) Algorithmic architecture. Architectural Press, Oxford
Thébert Y (1987) Private life and domestic architecture in Roman Africa, vol 1, A history of private life, 5 vols. Harvard University Press, Cambridge, p 407
van Hinte A (ed) (2003) Smart architecture. 010 Publishers, Amsterdam
Zuk W, Clarke R (1970) Kinetic architecture. Van Nostrand Reinhold, New York

Chapter 11
An Interactive Simulation Environment for Adaptive Architectural Systems

Bess Krietemeyer

Abstract Current architectural design methods for visualization and analysis of the relationship between energy flows, building demands, and occupant control remain limited because existing software tools and virtual reality environments are not yet integrated into a seamless feedback loop. This chapter presents the development of an interactive visualization and simulation environment that combines real-time energy analysis with hybrid-reality techniques to support user interaction with adaptive architectural systems and spaces. It argues for a combination of a new material testbed, hybrid reality visualizations, and energy simulation to create a design tool for architects and end-users to experience and develop the many performance possibilities of adaptive systems. Using an Electroactive Dynamic Display System as an adaptive facade testbed, an interactive simulation environment examines the impacts that adaptive architectural facades have on a building's energy performance and spatial effects. As a result of the experimental simulations with large-screen projections and virtual reality technologies, new criteria related to user control and comfort are informing the material and physical prototyping of emerging adaptive facade systems. For designers integrating next-generation adaptive architectural systems into buildings, interactive simulation environments are necessary to anticipate the fundamentally new environmental, social, and spatial implications of their dynamic and responsive potential. This research is producing a design decision-making tool for both visualizing and measuring the architectural and environmental impacts of multi-user interaction with adaptive architectural systems. In the process, an iterative co-design process emerges between fields of architecture, materials science, and human-computer-interaction that informs each in multidimensional ways.

B. Krietemeyer (✉)
School of Architecture, Syracuse University, 201 Slocum Hall, Syracuse, NY 13244, USA
e-mail: eakriete@syr.edu

© Springer International Publishing Switzerland 2016
N.S. Dalton et al. (eds.), *Architecture and Interaction*,
Human–Computer Interaction Series, DOI 10.1007/978-3-319-30028-3_11

Introduction

Opportunities for Adaptive Architectural Systems

In the context of sustainable building design, novel material innovations are shifting the performance capabilities of building envelopes towards adaptive systems that can respond to the changing energy demands of buildings while addressing to occupant preferences for comfort and control (Krietemeyer et al. 2015). Adaptive architectural systems include building skins or surfaces that can mechanically, electrically, or chemically alter their state to adapt to changing external or internal stimuli, such as outside temperature, sunlight, or building inhabitants (Schnädelbach 2010). In contrast to fixed all-glass building facades, where uncontrollable solar gains and little consideration for occupant control were the result of architectural ideologies of the twenty-first century, emerging glass building facade technologies maintain a different focus. Smart films and shading devices are incorporated into glazed facade systems to combat incoming solar energy (Baetens et al. 2010), and adaptive facade systems are increasingly focused on user control for better privacy, thermal comfort, views, and visual effects (Loonen et al. 2013) (Fig. 11.1).

The degree to which user control has been integrated into building envelopes has changed over time. While the early 1900s made use of Venetian blinds for solar shading and privacy, this common shading device allowed for a range of visual variation with which occupants could individually control the amount of diffused light and views at windows. In contrast to this variation, all glass curtain wall systems of the mid-twentieth century no longer controlled incoming solar radiation at the building facade; instead, mechanical cooling systems were used to

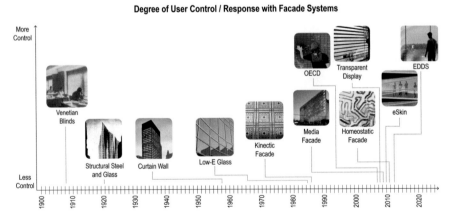

Fig. 11.1 Examples of building facade systems illustrating the trajectory towards adaptive architecture and increased degrees of user control over the building facade's appearance and behaviors

maintain a consistent level of indoor thermal comfort despite changes in weather or occupant preferences. As a result, minimal control was available to building inhabitants for modifying views, daylight, or glare within the perimeter glazing areas of the building. Conventional building systems created a homogeneous indoor environmental standard for visual comfort, a sociocultural construct of modernity that has in turn led to occupant dissatisfaction and overall decrease in well-being (Shove 2003). With the energy crisis of the 1970s, the excessive use of mechanical building systems generated a greater awareness of energy use, thus spurring the development of glazing technologies and facade shading devices to combat unwanted solar gains. Glazing technologies such as tinted or Low-E glass are aimed at mitigating solar energy and were engineered to block heat gain and reduce glare. However these glazing technologies do not necessarily solve issues associated with the lack of individual control since they are typically fixed tinted glazing systems applied around the entire building. They still face limitations with visual discomfort. As new materials have been integrated into building facade systems, the performance criteria driving their design have expanded to include both solar control and increased user control over the facade's appearance and behaviors.

Numerous contemporary design research projects and installations demonstrate ways in which intelligent materials and building technologies could alter the relationship between the user, building system, and interior and exterior space. Interdisciplinary research groups are investigating responsive architectural materials and environments along with ways in which building technologies can incorporate a range of inputs into their dynamic response. The Material Dynamics Lab at the New Jersey Institute of Technology experiments with the integration of electro- and thermo-responsive smart materials for systems like the Homeostatic facade that can adapt to their local environment (Decker 2013). Similarly, collaborators in interactive and responsive design at the Swiss Federal Institute of Technology (ETH) in Zurich explore organic kinetics in architectural applications using electroluminescent screens, electroactive polymers, and flexible audio panels to generate emotive and responsive environments (Kretzer et al. 2013) The Sabin Design Lab at Cornell explores the integration of passive materials, sensors, and imagers into responsive building eSkins (Sabin 2015). The Center for Architecture Science and Ecology (CASE) at Rensselaer Polytechnic Institute is developing Electroactive Dynamic Display Systems (EDDS) to address energy performance goals of building facades while simultaneously allowing for a range of information patterning and user control (Dyson et al. 2013). Each design research group investigates various material prototypes for high-performance building envelopes that can respond to a range of stimuli. The ability to scale up these physical prototypes and integrate their behaviors with other building sensing and control systems is a critical step in determining their feasibility and overall performance relative to balancing quantitative and qualitative criteria. Systems like the EDDS offer many opportunities for user engagement and control over the environmental, visual patterning, and spatial effects. Because of the multivariate parameters, it is necessary to digitally simulate the numerous possibilities to understand the energy performance impacts before investing in the physical prototyping phase of research.

Until recently, there haven't been building envelope materials and technologies that have provoked the engagement of occupants to the degree that they offer now. For the EDDS and many of the featured projects and research groups, emerging material breakthroughs are redefining the meaning of performance for building envelope technologies, transforming their role as static and sealed enclosures to fluctuating membranes mediating energy and information. Novel building envelope systems being explored by architectural designers are becoming increasingly legitimized in the building science community by their ability to address quantitative energy performance benchmarks. At the same time they are challenging traditional architectural notions of boundary and space, physics and energy, experience and perception, and author and interpreter. The remarkable material malleability and responsiveness of new systems will transform buildings from fixed enclosures to flexible interfaces that effortlessly capitalize on local environmental flows while inviting a participatory dialogue with the people who reside in their presence. It is critical that the architectural design, simulation, and prototyping methods are able to adequately consider occupant interaction with responsive building skins. Furthermore, occupant interaction should be understood as integral to methods for predicting the energy performance of adaptive architectural systems.

Computational Design Tools for Adaptive Architectural Systems

There are several different methods for the design, prototyping, and simulation of novel building envelope systems. In the case of systems like the EDDS and others mentioned above, physical prototypes are a necessary step in the research process for measuring quantitative performance metrics such as electromagnetic response, cycles of durability, and fabrication feasibility. Yet relying solely on lab-scale prototypes during the design and development phase risks overlooking valuable qualitative characteristics that could more effectively be examined at various scales, such as visual comfort, perception, interactivity, and control. Since physical prototyping can be costly, time consuming, and limited in scale, computational simulations are often used in the design process to visualize the architectural or daylighting effects and to measure the predicted energy performance of these adaptive systems. Simulations also provide exciting opportunities to visualize and test the interactive potential of adaptive systems.

3d computational modeling, simulation, and energy analysis tools typically utilize a linear workflow in which a design option for a building facade is modeled in one software for visualization and then imported in a separate program for analysis. The designer must manually manipulate the building geometries and parameters, export the fixed model, and then analyze the design separately in simulation software to test for building energy impacts (Lagios et al. 2010). The disconnected workflow makes it challenging to test various configurations of adaptive systems quickly and according to both external and internal stimuli.

One recent approach that utilizes the parametric modeling tool DIVA for Rhino builds on the linear method of exporting a model for energy analysis through direct links to EnergyPlus and Radiance for a seamless daylighting simulation workflow. This method allows the rapid visualization of daylight and energy impacts from an architectural design model where users can easily test multiple design variants for daylight and energy performance without manually exporting to multiple softwares (Jakubiec and Reinhart 2011). While this simulation workflow speeds up the daylighting analysis process and integrates occupant comfort models to determine the status of shading systems such as venetian blinds, it lacks real-time capabilities for analyzing the impacts of more complex adaptive facade systems according to both internal and external stimuli. This real-time analysis is essential for understanding how adaptive architectural systems respond simultaneously to fluctuating environmental flows and variable occupant preferences, which can often pose conflicts with regard to desires for views, privacy, daylight, and the need to mitigate solar heat gain.

Another method to a building energy simulation for adaptive facades aims to quantify their long-term impact on building performance using genetic algorithms for multi-objective optimization. This method supports the need for simulation tools that analyze the energy impacts of adaptive conditions on a long-term basis and allows for visualization of trade-offs between two or more conflicting design objectives. It argues that seasonal facade adaptation is a more practical and reliable approach than facades that change on a higher-frequency basis (Kasinalis et al. 2014). The approach fills gaps in the field of dynamic simulation frameworks through the integration of multi-objective algorithms; however it does not yet support exploration of adaptive systems that could respond immediately and simultaneously to a range of occupant comfort needs, instead privileging longer-term external response.

Existing energy simulation frameworks remain somewhat limited to basic pre-defined inputs and do not always accommodate analysis at various spatial or temporal scales. Further, they do not include real-time visualization and spontaneous interaction with the inhabitants as factors to the energy analysis. Standard building simulation tools are lack dynamic, geometric and material complexity, and are unable to incorporate realistic occupant behavioral models. These limitations lead to evaluation methods that treat external environmental response and internal occupant response as separate performance goals (Fabi et al. 2011).

Immersive virtual reality (VR) environments offer alternative methods for visualizing adaptive architectural systems and for incorporating human behavior models, or real-time user interaction, for experimental testing. One example is a cave automatic virtual reality environment (CAVE), where flat panel displays or projections are directed on multiple interior surfaces of a room-sized cube. A CAVE provides true-stereo 3D and can be used to visualize large datasets of information in a 3d interactive and immersive way. CAVE systems support groups of users in a high resolution 3d shared immersive setting, but they are expensive and require a substantial amount of physical space, supporting infrastructure and hardware. Smaller VR visualization devices such as the head-mounted display (HMD) create a similar VR experience that is less expensive and more mobile than a CAVE. HMD devices allow stereo viewing through small monitors mounted in front of each eye and head tracking hardware for 3D immersion.

Various scales of CAVE and VR HMD technologies are becoming increasingly popular visualization tools for the architectural profession (Kim et al. 2013). Although most of the research related to immersive simulation has been conducted in fields other than architecture, it can have a direct parallel and can be used to advance the work in immersive building simulation. Potential applications include the post-processing of Computational Fluid Dynamics (CFD) Data, building and data representation, building performance visualization, and immersive visualization for structural analysis (Malkawi 2003). An early example of a fully immersive CFD visualization enabled users to visualize various building thermal analysis data using a CAVE. Users could change the space parameters such as window size or materials and visualize the resulting thermal conditions. This study was one of the first aimed at building a system that allows a user to perceive different environmental factors in a three-dimensional space (Malkawi and Choudhary 1999). Various combinations of VR environments for architectural applications have been explored over the last decade, such as wearable systems for the design process, mixed reality systems for archiving historical building information, augmented reality systems on construction sites, and integration of mixed reality in education and design studios (Wang and Schnabel 2009). Architectural researchers and practitioners continue to explore opportunities for evaluating designs, improving 3D models, facilitating remote collaborative design, and studying human preferences in virtual environments that represent real-world settings. One application of a VR HMD for studying human preferences in architectural applications creates an Immersive Virtual Environment (IVE) to understand the relationship between human comfort, daylighting, and lighting controls in an interior space. The IVE provides flexibility in creating environments with different control settings and in evaluating end users' behavior and preferences given different design and operation scenarios (Heydarian et al. 2015). Similar to the aims of the research presented in this chapter, the IVE design process seeks to ensure that architectural proposals not only meet the end-users' preferences but also encourage more energy efficient behaviors.

With the integration of new adaptive material technologies and virtual reality systems into architectural design, questions of design authorship and agency are raised: what types of information patterning will be expressed on and within buildings, and who will curate this information? How can a building envelope system move beyond an automatic response to external forces and instead engage in an interactive dialogue between external and internal stimuli—between itself, energy and people? The interactive simulation environment presented in this chapter combines new material technologies, hybrid reality visualization systems, and energy simulation software into a design tool for architects and end-users to experience the many performance possibilities of adaptive systems.

Objectives

Visualizing the energy performance of adaptive architectural facade systems is important for understanding their architectural effects and energy performance. However, current methods for visualization and analysis of the relationship between energy flows, building demands, and occupant control remain limited because commercial software tools and virtual reality environments are not yet integrated into a seamless feedback loop. In order to keep pace with rapidly advancing research towards responsive building envelope technologies on multiple fronts, new design tools are needed to address the multiscalar complexity and socio-cultural performance possibilities inherent within emerging material behaviors. For designers integrating next-generation adaptive architectural systems into buildings, interactive simulation environments are necessary to anticipate the fundamentally new environmental, social, and spatial implications of their dynamic and responsive potential. This is particularly important in response to inevitable conflicts between user control, aesthetic desires, and environmental performance criteria.

The following sections of this chapter present the development of an interactive visualization and simulation tool that combines real-time energy analysis visualizations with hybrid reality techniques to support user interaction with adaptive architectural skins and systems early in the design process. Computational algorithms and virtual reality visualization tools are integrated into a simulation environment for real-time interaction and analysis of adaptive architectural systems and their impacts on energy performance. Using the EDDS as a facade testbed system, the goal is to utilize the interactive simulation environment as a design tool that informs the physical prototyping of novel architectural facade systems. Developing computational simulation tools to support new facade material opportunities such as the EDDS is a critical step concurrent to ongoing physical prototype developments.

The challenges that this approach begins to address are threefold: first is the ability to design adaptive facade systems according to unpredictable environmental and human inputs simultaneously; second is the ability to integrate human perception and behaviors into the evaluation and decision-making process based on the various degrees of observation and interaction that can be experienced at full-scale; third is the ability to visualize and experience the architectural effects and dynamic potential of emerging material systems like the EDDS that aren't physically scalable at this point in time, particularly in generating synergistic relationships between the human desires and environmental response. Critically, this research is producing a design decision-making tool that both measures and visualizes dynamic architectural conditions while receiving real-time energy feedback based on users' engagement. In the process it establishes exciting opportunities for the fields of architecture, materials science and engineering, and human-computer-interaction to inform each other in multidimensional ways.

Methodology

Constructing Hybrid-Reality Simulations for Interactive Design

The setup for the simulation environment uses multiple digital projectors, sensors, large flexible screens, VR displays, and customized algorithms for interactive design. This approach uniquely utilizes a combination of digital projection and VR display technology as a hybrid method for experiencing and interacting with the full-scale effects of dynamic facade systems like the EDDS. The approach is considered hybrid since it combines a large-screen semi-immersive projection environment with a fully immersive VR environment using a head-mounted display (HMD) (Fig. 11.2).

The purpose of the large-screen projection is to create a full-scale visualization of an adaptive facade system where multiple users can experience and modify its behaviors. The physical setup supports the visualization and interaction with the facade's dynamic patterning, changing views to the exterior, and ambient daylight and shadows within the space. Similar to a CAVE, the large-screen projection environment uses digital projectors and sensors for position and perspective tracking. Two projectors are used to simulate the facade and its daylighting effects: one rear-projection throws an image of the simulated facade onto a large flexible screen, and a second ceiling-mounted projector throws an image of the daylighting and shadow effects onto the floor. Kinect motion and infrared sensors located in the corner of the screen and connected to a desktop computer track the physical positions and gestures of users as they interact with the dynamic facade systems' behavior.

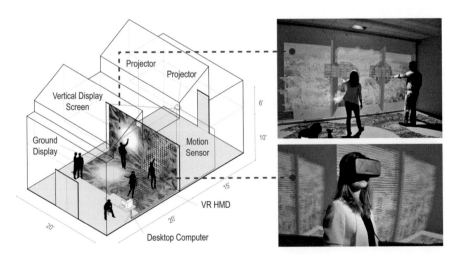

Fig. 11.2 Diagram illustrating the hybrid-reality simulation setup at the Interactive Design and Visualization Lab at Syracuse University. Users can interact with the large-screen projection (*top right*), or use the VR HMD to view architectural design proposals (*bottom right*)

Projectors and sensors are wired to one desktop computer. This type of environment provides a collaborative design space with real-time visual and analytical feedback unlike standard 3d architectural modeling tools. The setup is more adaptable and cost-effective than a standard CAVE and can be installed in most spaces using one or two projectors without the need for specially designed rooms and extensive infrastructural support. The flexible fabric projection screen stretches across large room widths and heights without the spatial restrictions of typical CAVE systems, and can be adapted to different architectural offices or studios for designers and clients to visualize architectural proposals.

The purpose of incorporating the VR HMDs is to create additional flexibility and full immersion for interactive, multi-user design at a range of architectural scales. The integration of HMD devices like the Oculus Rift, combined with motion sensors and the gaming engine Unity3d, offers a number of exciting possibilities for the design process. First, a user can visualize, meander, and interact with a dynamic building system or architectural space in a completely immersive 3d visual environment without concerns for the physical lighting or spatial requirements. Depending on the extent of the modeled environment, the boundaries are essentially limitless, whereby one can explore multiple scales of architecture within the virtual environment. Second, with a state-of-the-art combination of VR HMDs and motion sensors, an interactive design concept developed by collaborators Noirflux (2015), users wearing the Oculus Rift can physically walk around while viewing their virtual environment through the headset. This physical movement reduces the effects of simulator sickness, which is caused by the visually-induced perception of self-motion when the body isn't actually moving. Third, the large-screen projection can display the view from the Oculus Rift, or display supplemental environmental information that can be accessed by a group simultaneously. Further possibilities for collaborative, remote architectural and urban simulation are discussed later in the chapter in ongoing work.

The simulation software uses VVVV, a live-programming environment for quick prototyping and development. VVVV is designed to integrate large datasets and media environments with physical interfaces and real-time motion graphics, and audio and video that can interact with many users simultaneously (VVVV 2015). In our interactive design simulation, VVVV provides an immersive visualization platform and graphical user interface (GUI) for 3d architectural modeling software tools such as Rhinoceros and Grasshopper. By importing 3d geometric data into VVVV, architectural designs and their energy performance analyses can be viewed and experienced in a dynamic way either through web/App-based user interfaces or through VR HMDs (i.e. Oculus Rift, Google Cardboard, etc.). Users can visualize and interact with a simulated architectural space or adaptive facade system and experience both exterior and interior conditions for any 3d geometry at multiple scales. Alternative dynamic facade materials, geometries, and building designs can be imported and viewed interactively, which is enormously beneficial for architects testing different design proposals in various climate and site scenarios.

Gestural Interactions for Controlling Facade System Behaviors

Users can interact with the simulation in one of three ways: the first is through a custom graphical user interface (GUI), which is accessible through a monitor, the second is through gestural interaction with the large-screen, and the third is through gestural interactions with the Oculus Rift. The GUI provides access to modify the parameters of the simulation, such as the geographic location, solar position, material composition, and library of facade patterns and user interactions. It also provides access to a user's point cloud position data, which is recorded for data collection on user's interactions. Both the Oculus Rift and the large screen and motion sensors allow users to interact with the simulation through position and perspective tracking, as well as through gestures that change the pattern or visual effects of the facade's behaviors.

The facade's dynamic behaviors include opening locally for viewing portals, closing for personalized privacy screens, and morphing into customized pixilated patterns or animated videos across the facade. The motion sensors and customized algorithms identify a user's presence by creating a point cloud, and then locate an individual's head, hands, feet, and body for gestural interaction. Users can swipe their hands and arms left to right or top to bottom to change the appearance of the facade, or they can use both hands simultaneously to switch the pattern, portal, image, or animated effect they wish to see on the facade. Personalized images or videos can be 'uploaded' to the facade as pixilated versions, creating dynamic shadow effects on the interior, and individualized expressions along the exterior of the facade. Combined, the simulation environment creates a full-scale interactive visualization of an adaptive building facade system and its perceived effects on views to the exterior as well as daylighting and thermal conditions (Fig. 11.3).

Point cloud data viewed through the GUI on the monitor anonymously records gestural interactions in order to analyze the tendencies and degrees to which users modify and adapt to a dynamic systems' behavior (Fig. 11.3). This data is currently used in several ways: one is to observe how quickly users adapt to the gestural control settings. This allows us to identify which gestural interactions are most intuitive. Another is to examine how adaptive building envelope systems negotiate potential conflicts between groups of users (i.e. how to program the facade to adapt to different user gestures within the same area). Lastly it is to program and test how a facade adapts to users' control preferences while still meeting energy performance goals for reducing unwanted solar heat gain.

Moving beyond typical architectural modeling and analysis tools, users of our hybrid reality simulations have the ability to interact with and modify adaptive building skins while receiving measured feedback as to their predicted energy and daylighting performance. There are multiple ways to receive energy performance feedback. The first is by viewing performance data related to the glazing assembly's ability to mediate solar heat gain and daylight. Users can hold up their arms to trigger a pop-up data panel that displays real-time measured energy performance feedback of the glazing at that specific frame rate (Fig. 11.4, left). Numeric values representing visible transmittance (Tvis), U-value, and solar heat gain coefficient

Fig. 11.3 Multiple users can simultaneously interact with the dynamic facade simulation (*top row*). Point cloud data allows designers to document and record positions and gestural interactions with a dynamic systems' behavior (*bottom row*)

Fig. 11.4 A pop-up data panel displays real-time performance values for the adaptive facade system (*left*). The large-screen simulation environment displays a full-scale analysis map on the floor in colors representing daylighting or heat gain (*right*)

(SHGC) are calculated for the building envelope assembly and visualized in real-time through dynamic charts that continuously update as the patterns shift based on solar position, pattern changes, and privacy or viewing portals. Another method for real-time energy performance feedback includes a full-scale daylighting analysis map that is displayed on the floor of the simulation environment (Fig. 11.4, right). This allows the user to interact with the facade and be semi-immersed in a dynamic pseudo-color analysis showing illuminance levels. For the first time, users of the simulation environment—especially architects and engineers—get an interactive and immersive experience of performance data that is typically only viewed as graphs, image stills or an animation through a computer monitor. Instead, the real-time full-scale daylighting analysis creates a stronger and more intuitive connection between the design and data analysis workflow, simultaneously folding in user input directly into the process.

Experimentation with User Interactions and Energy Performance

Initial experiments with participants examined the ability of the dynamic building envelope to negotiate its response for both solar tracking and user preferences for certain patterning effects or views. Using the EDDS as a facade testbed, these studies tested the ability of the simulations to allow for the design of system behaviors that matched glazing energy performance goals without compromising the dynamic visual effects designed by individual users (Krietemeyer et al. 2015). In the process, individual participant designs overlapped with others' preferences for viewing portals, privacy screens, or sunshades, which materialized or disappeared based on one's proximity to the simulated facade. When environmentally-responsive patterns were combined with participant interactions, an unanticipated series of optical effects, or biomorphic expressions, emerged at the intersection of human desires, material behaviors, and energy flows (Fig. 11.5). The interactive simulation as an open platform for participation and observation demonstrated how moments of collective ideation and design enabled participants to extend individual knowledge and contribute to a spatial assemblage that produced unexpected outcomes through localized inputs. As a result, the blended outcome of multiple participant designers satisfied a range of performance demands, both in terms of environmental performance and aesthetic effects. Participant feedback of designs further demonstrated a collective preference for hybrid visual effects that allowed for interrupted interactivity, regardless of the final blended appearance (Krietemeyer et al. 2015).

Fig. 11.5 When environmentally-responsive patterns (*top*) are combined with participant interactions, an unanticipated series of optical effects emerge (*bottom*) at the intersection of human desires, material behaviors, and energy flows

Another series of experiments investigated the impacts that multiple users interacting with the same dynamic facade had on a building's energy consumption. Algorithms and customized scripts were developed to link the interactive simulations to the energy simulation software EnergyPlus, which is an open source building energy modeler available through the U.S. Department of Energy to calculate a building's energy consumption. The goal was to understand the environmental impacts that multi-user interaction with the facade had at the scale of an entire building. The EDDS dynamic facade was again used as a material testbed for the interactive energy performance simulations. First the EDDS was programmed to respond to changing solar positions to provide adequate shading to maintain a certain level of daylight and heat gain on the interior. Next, the EDDS was programmed to adapt or 'compensate' its surface patterning in order to respond to users' desires for views or other visual effects while still maintaining the required solar control or daylighting levels on the interior. For example, the EDDS adjusted its pattern density as users engaged or 'interrupted' the default solar tracking state of the system. The resulting pattern configurations were then translated to glazing information that was integrated with the EnergyPlus software to measure the impacts of user interactions on the heating, cooling, and lighting loads of a whole building (Krietemeyer and Rogler 2015) (Fig. 11.6).

Results were measured as values for daylighting and heat gain and were visualized as an analysis map on the floor of the full-screen simulation environment. An optimized facade baseline pattern was programmed to block out direct sunlight

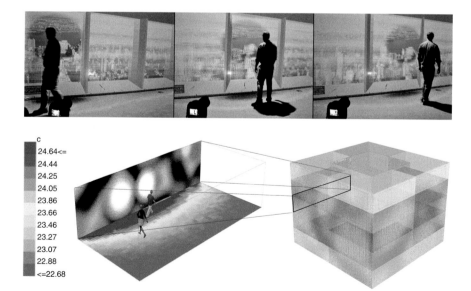

Fig. 11.6 Methods for real-time feedback incorporate full-scale daylighting analysis maps into the simulation environment (*top row*), which are then linked to a whole-building modeler to measure energy consumption (*bottom row*)

to reduce solar heat gains within the interior space. Then facade adaptability was introduced through the option of user-controlled viewing portals, whereby motion sensors tracked users throughout the simulation space and the facade simulation opened or closed based on proximity to the screen. This user interaction caused a deviation from the optimal baseline pattern and an increase in daylighting and heat gain levels. In order to adapt to both the users' positions and to the performance goals for controlling heat gain, the facade's response was programmed to redistribute its pattern so that viewing portals were provided but the facade still blocked out the necessary percentage of incoming solar radiation. The results of one interior space with the adaptive facade were then multiplied and simulated within a larger building model to measure the effects on an entire building's energy consumption.

The computational workflow between interactive simulations and building energy performance software examined how adaptive facade systems can reduce a building's energy consumption while simultaneously responding to occupant interactions and overrides. Preliminary analysis results demonstrated that systemic compensation for occupant interaction with the EDDS had positive impacts on the daylighting and thermal performance of a building (Krietemeyer and Rogler 2015). They also demonstrated the ability of the interactive simulations to visually scale up a dynamic building skin system, to experience and measure its daylighting performance, and to simulate its ability to compensate for multi-user interactions in order to meet goals for both occupant desires and environmental response.

In sum, current experiments combining hybrid-reality simulations and energy analysis software examine the ability of an adaptive architectural facade system (the EDDS) to negotiate potential conflicts between external and internal demands. In order to understand the implications of this methodology and its implementation in related design fields, it is important to discuss the benefits and challenges of hybrid reality simulations and ongoing work in adaptive architecture.

Discussion

Benefits and Challenges with the Hybrid-Reality Simulations

Hybrid-reality interactive simulation methods provide support to the research and development process on several levels. Simulations are critical for understanding the impact on energy and information performance from user interaction and behavior patterns, as well as on overall system performance. Dynamic decision-making design tools and shared visualization spaces are crucial for the growing field of adaptive and sustainable architecture where visual real-time communication is the primary tool for collaborating across disciplines and with clients. By constructing immersive visualization environments that simulate the responsive behavior of intelligent materials at full scale for multi-user interaction, the feedback and analysis can inform the physical prototyping process with valuable user input early on. This significantly reduces risks associated with physical prototyping new material technologies in the research and development phases while allowing for an iterative co-design process to occur between material and computational experimentation.

There are exciting areas for ongoing work that aim to address current challenges with the hybrid-reality simulations, namely those that focus on structured human factors empirical studies with the interactive simulations and physical prototypes, accurate calibration of the computational simulations with physical material prototype performance, and advancement of algorithms for more precise energy analysis at the system and building scales. Computational work is important in the development of algorithms for an entire building management control system, which will streamline communication between different spaces and types of building systems to maintain optimal energy performance.

The methodology must include the calibration of more precise material spectral properties of the physical prototypes with the computational simulations. The energy analysis methodology currently simplifies the material properties and dynamic range of movements to accommodate the limitations of the whole building modeler, EnergyPlus. The parallel development of the physical material prototypes with the interactive simulation is pushing widely used software like EnergyPlus to support higher resolution characterization of emerging materials into its tool palette. Finally, exposing the simulation methods to a wider audience is important for incorporating diverse user feedback.

Ongoing Work: Expanding Audiences and Scales

Advancements in physical prototype testing, computational development, and human factors studies all present important yet distinct areas for ongoing work that will inform each other in significant ways. The interactive simulations provide an interdisciplinary framework within which seemingly disparate areas of study can co-exist and where collaborative innovation is fostered. One of the challenging elements of this collaborative work that aims to address user needs, preferences, and desires is to include a diverse range of user input into the design and testing process. This involves increasing access to these tools and environments to remote locations and to the public in order to expand audiences and scales.

The hybrid use of large-screen projection and VR HMDs creates a flexible virtual design space for collaboration. The increased mobility and freedom from physical spatial constraints provides opportunities for designers and users to collaborate from different geographic locations for remote interdisciplinary design using HMD devices such as the Oculus Rift. With the Oculus Rift, challenges of multiuser perspective tracking can also be addressed, whereby multiple people could be wearing an Oculus Rift and occupying the same virtual space, much like a shared gaming environment. In a shared virtual environment, users can simultaneously interact with adaptive building envelope systems and spaces and still receive the same

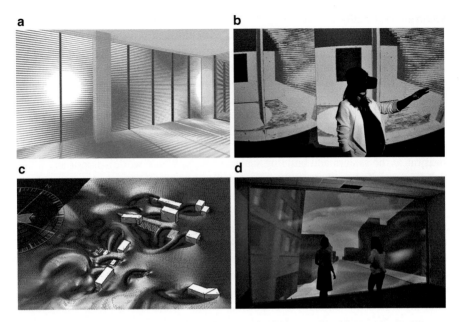

Fig. 11.7 Preliminary examples of user interactions with simulated energy flows at the building facade and urban scales: **a** Simulation of facade's energy flows from the interior perspective, **b** User interacting with the facade simulation using a combination of the large-screen projection and the Oculus Rift VR HMD, **c** Simulation of urban energy flows from an aerial perspective, **d** Two users interacting with the urban energy flows through the large-screen simulation environment using the hybrid-reality environment

real-time measured energy performance feedback of ambient lighting or thermal flows, visualized as three-dimensional pseudo-color matrices or computational fluid dynamic analyses. Unlike many typical architectural applications of HMDs, users have the ability to gesturally interact with the adaptive facade system and could potentially engage in a learned dialogue between the material, energy flows, and other people in the same virtual space. Because of the limitless scale of virtual worlds such as Unity3d, a multitude of architectural proposals can be designed and explored at the building skin, building, or urban scales. As the simulation environment is further developed to support interaction at multiple scales, users will have the opportunity to modify not only the behavior of dynamic systems, but also participate in designing and interacting with energy flows across the facade, building, and city (Fig. 11.7).

There are several aspects of this methodology to consider relative to designing, analyzing, and observing user interaction with adaptive architectural systems in real-world settings. Social behaviors and preferences for interacting with dynamic building systems are likely to differ in real-world settings versus those that are simulated in a laboratory. Exposing the interactive simulation methods to a wider audience and in different locations will be important for getting diverse user feedback, especially to better understand the various tendencies and preferences of people when engaging emerging systems for the very first time or over long periods of time. Our ongoing work includes designing algorithms for various degrees of interaction with dynamic systems, buildings, and cities that can be demonstrated and tested outside the lab and in the broader public realm – through public exhibitions, museum installations, and facade testbeds.

Moving forward, improved computational methods and sensing algorithms for multiuser interactivity will also generate opportunities for more comprehensive participant experiments that explore a greater range of human factors issues. The integration of alternative sensing technologies for multi-modal interactions can heighten the perceptual experience and learned capabilities of the building system or environment, such that a dialogue continually takes place between multiple users, responsive architectural systems, and energy flows. For interactive artist Usman Haque, accounting for underspecified and observer-constructed goals enables the collaboration and convergence of shared goals in connecting with our environmental systems (Haque 2007). In the context of highly-responsive building envelope systems that are open to the inputs and preferences of many different people from diverse backgrounds, this convergence could result in an unanticipated performance between extremely complex and dynamic systems. What's critical is that criteria for ecological design enables multiple readings, interpretations, and degrees of user engagement, and that these methods are exposed to a wider audience, where people become players in the development of these systems. Regardless of the enabling technologies for these emergent interactions and assemblages of knowledge space, it seems inevitable that maintaining degrees of choice in the ways that people participate, engage, and observe the aspects of environmental performance will be essential in developing the criteria for responsive architecture.

Adaptive Architecture: Toward User Empowerment

Simulation environments that support interaction with adaptive building materials and envelope systems enable sustainable architectural design practices to expand beyond energy performance criteria to include multiuser desires for diverse comfort preferences, degrees of interaction, and overall aesthetic effects. In the case of the EDDS and many adaptive architectural skins and systems in development, energy performance goals of modulating light and heat have the opportunity to blend into extensions of human performer, expressing emotion and desire, whereby one's decisions fluctuate according to ambient energy flows or the interactions of other people with the system. In this case user empowerment comes with degrees of participation that adapts with the material and computational developments. Personal preferences, needs, and ideas might evolve based on their exposure to the technology and to exposure of others' choices. In architectural discourse on sustainable design, the focus no longer needs to associate an architectural design intention with either energy-driven or aesthetically-driven criteria, but rather adaptive building skin systems such as the EDDS offer a both/and condition, where environmental mediation is an expression of user empowerment and interactivity at multiple scales. In the process of expression, individual and collective identities emerge for a diversified experience that is at once sustainable and empowering.

The authoritative role of the designer or architect becomes ambiguous as primary author and instead is transformed into a choreographer of material, energy, and information. Within the simulation, certain material parameters are pre-assigned by the architect, but the behaviors and visual outcomes are a result of a negotiation between solar- and occupant- responsive interfaces, atmospheres, and effects. Design agency is not limited to the intentional actions performed by a system or by people; instead it embodies people, material responses, and energetic flows, and the architectural outcome is temporally emergent. The interactive simulation environment allows us to stage dances of agency as a way of exploring how we get along with these new materials, our environment, and with each other. Performance criteria don't rely solely on quantitative benchmarks, but rather are an entanglement of qualitative and quantitative characteristics, human, and non-human agents. Variability, choice, and learning from the architecture and from each other could lead to greater occupant satisfaction while reducing energy consumption in buildings. Introducing individual agency—and perhaps most importantly, various degrees of engagement—to the expression of the architecture expands design opportunities for building-integrated energy performance and for redefining cultural expectations for environmental comfort.

Impacts on Materials Science: Criteria for Material Behaviors

In returning to the iterative co-design process introduced in the Discussion section, the design feedback loop between experimental physical prototypes and the interactive simulation environments are especially important in the context of the EDDS prototype development. For example, as a result of the interactive architectural simulations of the EDDS micro-scale material assembly, a new set of architectural criteria embodying environmental and user-driven performance is pushing for far greater adaptability of these materials at the nanoscale. Current research at CASE/Rensselaer is focusing on multifunctional nano-structured materials for energy harvesting and environmental mitigation at the facade, but with an increased emphasis on user interaction, environmental comfort, and information display (Thomas et al. 2015). Nano-material prototypes are now considering criteria for user interaction, environmental comfort, and information display alongside criteria for energy harvesting and mitigation. This expanded set of criteria was introduced during the research process because of the possibilities discovered through interactive simulations.

Based on these material innovations we will increasingly be able to program precise mechanical, electrical, and optical behaviors of materials to respond to a range of environmental inputs, building demands, and physiological needs and individual desires. This multiscalar approach is leading to technical strategies for solar tracking and spectral selectivity for improved glazing performance, and it's also leading to design strategies that amplify the potential for variable patterning, information exchange, and biomorphic expression of buildings. Environmental and aesthetic criteria at the building scale are informing the design and engineering of new material behaviors at the micro and nanoscale. An extension of the research at the Interactive Design and Visualization Lab aims to develop simulations that support the higher resolution characterization of systems like the EDDS. This is a primary example of how the development of the simulations alongside the testing of multi-scalar physical prototypes is creating an iterative co-design process between physical and computational experimentation.

Impacts on Human-Computer-Interaction: A Co-design Research Process

In designing environmental building envelope systems, engaging both energy metrics and user experience approaches what Felix Guattari has referred to as a "triple ecological vision" (Guattari 1989), merging the intertwined registers of social, mental, and environmental ecologies. Self-determination and individual conceptions of personal preferences for environmental quality and visual effects cannot be disregarded or relegated as secondary to energy performance benchmarks. Previous attempts have approached the building envelope technocratically as an isolated problem to be solved. The false dichotomy established between energy performance and user engagement is one which must be challenged. By testing new material innovations and interactive design tools in action and according to broader audiences, a more encompassing vision of ecology is possible.

Advancing immersive and interactive simulation environments for emerging architectural materials and technologies could provide radically new interdisciplinary opportunities at the intersection of architectural design, materials science and human-computer-interaction. The ability to experience and test dynamic visual, aural, or haptic perception within shared physical environments entails an inherent exploration into the social organization and politics of space. Combining innovative design processes into synthetic testing environments that utilize distributed interactive computing and/or big data allows for architects, computer scientists, and interaction designers to participate in the making of multifunctional material behaviors. Simultaneously this allows them to explore the ecological, spatial, and social implications of these compositions through immersive experimentation.

Future developments in adaptive building technologies and spaces will continue to inform the need for new computational design and interactive prototyping methods for predicting the technology's performance according to a range of architectural, social, and environmental criteria. By focusing on the spatial and cultural potentials at the intersection of human desires, material behaviors, and energy flows, material technologies and human-computer-interaction (HCI) methods will support broader visions of sustainable architecture and ecological design. HCI methods will be especially important in the increased use of VR as an effective and usable design, visualization, and analysis tool. Within the built environment HCI research can facilitate interactions between users and VR systems and support iterative prototyping and testing outside of lab environments to figure out the best way to build user-friendly interfaces (Kim et al. 2013).

Through the co-development of hybrid physical-computational design simulations, the formation of individual identity simultaneously occurs for both the designer and end-user through the process and product. This approach, however, cannot be achieved by architectural designers alone. Experts in HCI can contribute significantly to the systemic, analytical, and navigational knowledge as it relates to the interface design and user experience with emerging technologies that typically don't fall within the architectural material palette. Because of these different approaches, the collaboration of architects and HCI designers can have profound impacts on how the simulation parameters and workflows are organized, defined, and implemented within our built environment in environmentally and culturally productive ways.

Rather than solely operating in isolated vacuums, each field engages each other's methods of research. Whereas the sciences typically decouple variables allowing for the testing of hypotheses, architectural design processes focus on simulating complexity (Latour 2008). Unlike the premise of the scientific method and its rational procedures, architectural design is not linear. Creative processes between multi-disciplinary researchers and methods are messy, iterative, and informed by sometimes illogical choices. Inevitable conflicts ensue in the exchange of ideas and the negotiation of value systems. Despite these challenges, the combined team of faculty members, students, professionals, and end-users disrupt traditional hierarchies of contribution and credit, allowing for a transparent exchange of ideas found typical in architectural design. The presumed boundaries of these knowledge spaces reveal themselves to be porous and transmissible. This collaboration demonstrates that the entanglement of sociological factors, while typically characterized as barriers, can be catalyzing rather than paralyzing constituents in the production of a synergistic co-design research process. They can generate constructive tensions and pivotal moments within the 'messy' production of shared knowledge space (Turnbull 2009). Critically, this work demonstrates that access, experimentation, and observation within a shared space—physical or virtual—is necessary to expose each other to alternative methods, to identify overlaps in research, and to invite new design methodologies that expand beyond typical disciplinary boundaries.

Acknowledgments Contributors to the interactive simulation environment include Bess Krietemeyer, Lorne Covington/Noirflux, Anna Dyson, Samuel Seifert, James Krietemeyer, Neil Katz, Satoshi Kiyono, Brandon Andow, Kurt Rogler, Amber Bartosh, Xuhao Wu, and Fenqi Li. The research is currently supported by the Syracuse Center of Excellence in Environmental and Energy Systems (COE), the Syracuse University School of Architecture, and the Milton J. Rubenstein Museum of Science and Technology (MoST). This research has been supported by Rensselaer Polytechnic Institute, the Experimental Media and Performing Arts Center (EMPAC), SmartGeometry/Bentley Systems, and the New York State Energy Research and Development Authority (NYSERDA).

References

Baetens R, Jelle BP, Arild G (2010) Properties, requirements and possibilities of smart windows for dynamic daylight and solar energy control in buildings: a state-of-the art review. Sol Energy Mater Sol Cells 94:87–105

Decker M (2013) New material compositions. In: Ng R, Patel S (eds) Performative materials in architecture and design. University of Chicago Press, Intellect, Chicago, pp 61–79

Dyson A, Krietemeyer B, Stark P (2013) Electroactive Dynamic Display Systems (EDDS). In: Lorenzo-Eiroa P, Sprecher A (eds) Architecture in formation. Routledge, New York, pp 150–155

Fabi V, Andersen RV, Corgnati SP, Olesen VW, Filippi M (2011) Description of occupant behaviour in building energy simulation: state-of-the-art and concepts for improvements. In: Proceedings of the 12th conference on building simulation, International Building Performance Simulation Association (IBPSA) Sydney, Australia, 2011

Guattari F (1989) The three ecologies (trans: Turner C). New Formations 8:131–48

Haque U (2007) The architectural relevance of Gordon Pask. Archit Des 77:54–61

Heydarian A, Carneiro JP, Gerber D, Becerik-Gerber B (2015) Immersive virtual environments, understanding the impact of design features and occupant choice upon lighting for building performance. Build Environ 89:217–228

Jakubiec JA, Reinhart C (2011) DIVA 2.0: integrating daylight and thermal simulations using Rhinoceros 3D, DAYSIM, and EnergyPlus. In: Proceedings of building simulation, Sidney

Kasinalis C, Loonen RCGM, Costola D, Hensen JLM (2014) Framework for assessing the performance potential of seasonally adaptable facades using multi-objective optimization. Energy Build 79:106–113

Kim MJ, Wang X, Love PE LIH, Kang SC (2013) Virtual reality for the built environment: a critical review of recent advances. J Inf Technol Constr 18:279–305

Kretzer M et al (2013) Actuated matter. In: Ng R, Patel S (eds) Performative materials in architecture and design. Intellect, University of Chicago Press, Chicago, p 213

Krietemeyer B, Rogler K (2015) Real-time multi-zone building performance impacts of occupant interaction with dynamic facade systems. In: Proceedings of the 33rd annual international conference of the Association for Education and Research in Computer Aided Architectural Design in Europe (eCAADe) Vienna, Austria, 2015

Krietemeyer B, Andow B, Dyson A (2015) A computational design framework supporting human interaction with environmentally-responsive building envelopes. Int J Archit Comput (IJAC) 1(13):1–24

Lagios K, Niemasz J, Reinhart C (2010) Animated building performance simulation (ABPS) – linking rhinoceros/grasshopper with radiance/daysim. In: Proceedings of SimBuild 2010, New York City, 2010

Latour B (2008) A cautious Prometheus? A few steps towards a philosophy of design (with special attention to Peter Sloterdijk). In: Networks of design meeting of the design history society. Cornwall. Available via: http://www.bruno-latour.fr/sites/default/files/112-DESIGN-CORNWALL-GB.pdf. Accessed Aug 2015

Loonen RCGM, Tricka M, Cóstola D, Hensen JLM (2013) Climate adaptive building shells: state-of-the-art and future challenges. Renew Sust Energ Rev 25:483–493

Malkawi A (2003) Immersive building simulation. In: Malkawi A (ed) Advanced building simulation. Spon Press, New York, pp 220–244

Malkawi A, Choudhary R (1999) Visualizing the sensed environment in the real world. J Hum-Environ Syst 3(1):61–69

Noirflux: Art in Interaction (2015) www.noirflux.com. Accessed August 2015

Sabin J (2015) Transformative research practice: architectural affordances and crisis. J Archit Educ 69(1):67

Schnädelbach H (2010) Adaptive architecture – a conceptual framework. In: Proceedings of MediaCity 2010, Weimar, Germany, 2010

Shove E (2003) Comfort, cleanliness and convenience: the social organization of normality. Berg Publishers, Oxford

Thomas AV, Andow BC, Suresh S, Eksik O, Yin J, Dyson AH, Koratkar N (2015) Controlled crumpling of graphene oxide films for tunable optical transmittance. Adv Mater 27(21):3256–3265

Turnbull D (2009) Working with incommensurable knowledge traditions: assemblage, diversity, emergent knowledge, narrativity, performativity, mobility and synergy. Available via: http://thoughtmesh.net/publish/279.php?space#conclusionassemblage. Accessed Aug 2015

VVVV-A Multipurpose Toolkit (2015) www.vvvv.org. Accessed Aug 2015

Wang X, Schabel MA (2009) Mixed reality in architecture, design and construction. Springer, New York

Chapter 12
Robotic Building as Physically Built Robotic Environments and Robotically Supported Building Processes

H.H. Bier and S. Mostafavi

Abstract The development of concepts and practical applications for Robotic Building (RB) is based on an understanding of buildings from a life-cycle perspective with respect to their socio-economical and ecological impact. This implies developments of interactive building components, which respond to users needs in ever-changing environments and requires seamless, numerically controlled and robotically supported design-to-production and operation chains enabling implementation of robotic building components from conceptualisation to use. RB implying both, physically built robotic environments and robotically driven building processes as developed more recently at Hyperbody, which is a research group at the Technical University Delft, is presented and discussed in this chapter with the aim to evaluate results and identify potential developments for the future.

Introduction

As more recently defined and experimentally developed at Hyperbody, which is a research group at the Technical University Delft, Robotic Building (RB) implies both physically built robotic environments and robotically supported building processes (Bier 2013). Physically built robotic environments are performative, adaptive physically built spaces partly incorporating sensor-actuator mechanisms that enable buildings to interact with their users and surroundings (inter al. Eastman 1971; Fox 2009; Bier and Knight 2010) in real-time. These require design to production and operation chains that may be (partially or completely) implemented by robotic means. Hyperbody's development of concepts and practical applications for RB, leading to the emergence of performative building components that are responding to individual needs in ever-changing spatial and environmental conditions, is based

H.H. Bier (✉) • S. Mostafavi
Department of Architectural Engineering & Technology (AE&T),
Faculty of Architecture/AE&T/Hyperbody, TU Delft/BK, Julianalaan 134,
2628 BL Delft, The Netherlands
e-mail: h.h.bier@tudelft.nl

© Springer International Publishing Switzerland 2016
N.S. Dalton et al. (eds.), *Architecture and Interaction*,
Human–Computer Interaction Series, DOI 10.1007/978-3-319-30028-3_12

on understanding buildings from a life-cycle perspective with respect to their socio-economical and ecological impact.

The assumption is that performances ensuring customisability, reconfigurability and adaptation of building components offers solutions for dealing with societal urgencies as for instance: Robotic building components (such as wall-, floor-, ceiling-, and skin-components) may offer solutions for dealing with the rapid increase of population and urban densification, as well as the contemporary inefficient use (25–50 %) of built space by introducing spatial reconfiguration, which is enabling multiple, changing use in reduced timeframes. The inefficient use of space is due to the mono-functional use of space for either work or leisure and the speculative urban development leading to, for instance, 6 million m^2 empty office buildings (Remoy and van der Voordt 2014) in Netherlands.

Furthermore, distributed, embedded, robotic energy- and climate-management systems, which employ renewable energy sources, such as solar and wind power, may reduce architecture's ecological footprint while enabling a time-based, demand-driven use of space.

In order to achieve these goals, building components are designed to respond at the material or componential level to changing conditions. For that purpose seamless, numerically controlled (NC) and robotically supported design to production and operation chains are developed and employed. These enable implementation of performative building components and buildings from conceptualisation to use by employing modelling, simulation, prototyping, and production environments that are facilitating communication and exchange between experts (from different disciplines) and machines.

Background

Physically built robotic environments and robotically supported building processes exploit the generative potential of NC approaches wherein interactions between (human and non-human) agents and their (virtual and physical) environments have emergent properties that enable proliferation of hybrid architectural systems.

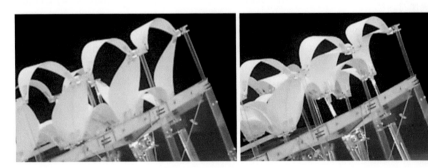

Fig. 12.1 Hyperbody MSc 4 project (2012) featuring interactive skin components employed for ventilation purposes

Such hybrid architectural systems require a holistic approach implying an understanding of the parts of a system in the context of their relationships with each other and with other systems. Furthermore, they require the study of the communication and control of regulatory feedback between natural and artificial systems with focus on interaction between robotic devices and humans.

In this context, robotic devices are programmed to carry out a variety of tasks related to spatial or sensorial transformation. These devices are either autonomous or semi-autonomous and operate individually or collectively as swarms of robots. While individual robots may be quite simple, the emergent behavior of swarms is increasingly complex as it implies that local interactions between robots lead to the emergence of global behavior. Such robotic swarms are relevant for architectural applications not only because of their ability to operate as distributed systems but also because of their capacity to be more resistant to failure since the swarm can operate even when several individual robots fail.

Even if diverse in application ranging from indoor climate (Fig. 12.1) to spatial (Fig. 12.2) reconfiguration, all RB robots have a mechanical part that is allowing them to complete an assigned task, an electrical part, which powers and controls movement (through actuators e.g. motors), sensors measuring temperature, position, and/or energy status, and actuators enabling them to perform operations. They also contain some level of computer programming that enables a range of behaviors from simple to high-level artificial intelligence, which allows semi-autonomous or autonomous interaction.

RB robots exhibit behaviors ranging from responsive to interactive in order to implement tasks of physical and sensorial reconfiguration. Such behaviors build

Fig. 12.2 Interactive Wall developed by Hyperbody in collaboration with Festo responds to people's movement (2009)

upon principles of cybernetics formulated already in the first half of the twentieth century (Wiener 1948), which were basis of today's practical robotics. Autonomous robots were, however, built only in the second half of the twentieth century.

The first electronic autonomous robots exhibiting complex behavior employed analogue electronics simulating brain processes and were built by Walter 1948. Walter's robots used circuits connecting two sensors to two motors. One sensor was a photocell connected to the driving and steering motors and the other sensor was a contact switch that indicated when the robots bumped into an obstacle and prompted the robots to change direction. This simple set-up allowed the robots to move around and autonomously, find the outlet for recharging batteries, which demonstrated that complex behaviors could emerge from a simple structure based on neural-like circuit designs (Walter 1951).

At the time Walter employed analogue electronics, Turing was exploring with mental processes in terms of digital computation, and a decade later patented the first digitally operated and programmable robot, which was an industrial robot. This robot was supposed to implement repetitive or dangerous tasks in industrial manufacturing and assembly lines.

Today industrial robots are used in a wide range of production processes and more recently architectural research and practice teams started to explore their potential for architecture. Gramazio and Kohler (inter al. Kohler et al. 2014) and Menges (inter al. Krieg and Menges 2013) employ industrial robots for developing 1:1 prototypes that explore the potential of robotic production in architecture. Similarly, Hyperbody develops 1:1 prototypes but focuses on the building and building process in a holistic way looking at the complete design to production and operation chain. RB does not separate the design to production process from operation; the opposite, it integrates operation from the early stages of design. It, furthermore, employs industrial robots with customized end-effectors in design to production processes and embeds customized robotic devices into robotic buildings.

Robotic building components exhibit behaviours that follow simple rules in order to satisfy climatic or spatial requirements and build collectively a dynamic, *intelligent* environment (inter al. Oosterhuis 2010). For that purpose, components are tagged and incorporate information regarding their design, material, structure, production, and operation. Furthermore, they are equipped with sensors and actuators that enable them to not only perceive but also act on their surrounding environment. This ability to act may imply physical (such as geometrical, material, or sensorial) transformation.

Robotic Building (RB) has been developed as framework for investigating applications of robotics to performative architecture (Figs. 12.1. 12.2, 12.3, 12.4, and 12.5) and the required design-to-production and operation processes (Figs. 12.6 and 12.7) enabling the implementation of such architecture.

Reconfigurable, robotic environments incorporating digital control namely sensor-actuator mechanisms that enable buildings to interact with their users and surroundings in real-time (Bier and Knight 2010) through physical or sensory change and variation require multi-disciplinary research with respect to architectural design and engineering of reconfigurable, robotic systems employing additive-subtractive and folding principles, materialisation research for rapid numerically controlled (NC) and robotic fabrication and assembly as well as sustainable operation in-situ. In this context, robotic buildings have been envisioned as a componential, spatially and sensorially self-adjustable system.

In general terms, application of embedded robotics in architecture has been identified as relevant for areas dealing with (a) health, demographic change and well being, as well as (b) sustainable climate control and energy management. For each of these areas, robotics may be employed as follows:

(a) Robotic spatially reconfigurable building components (such as ceiling-, floor-, wall-, and skin-components) support daily life activities offering solutions for dealing with rapid increase of population and urban densification as well as improve contemporary inefficient use (25–50 %) of built space.

   Similarly to Rietveld's house from 1924 and contemporary Chang's transformer home (Gardiner 2009), RB explores possibilities to improve efficiency of space use through spatial reconfiguration. In addition, RB incorporates interactivity into building components transforming the initial one-way communication into a two-way communication or dialog between building and user.

   In principle, application of embedded robotics in architecture allows for downtime (referring to time periods when the system, in this case the building, is non-operational) to be reduced through physical reconfiguration. This is accomplished through advancement of intelligent collective behaviour systems so that several autonomous building components operate in cooperation in order to accomplish major reconfiguration and adaptation tasks. As earlier indicated, the goal is to address societal issues such as inefficient use of built space (25–50 %) and urban densification by increasing up to 50–75 % the 24/7 use of built space through changing and multiple uses in reduced timeframes.

(b) Robotically supported sun and wind energy production devices embedded in building components enable sustainable energy generation, while distributed climate control allows improving indoor climate. Climate control, material- and energy-efficiency are implemented not only on building and component but also on material level, implying that active and passive systems are combined.

In both cases, the aim is to address energy-efficiency and sustainability aspects as well as building life cycle, operating costs, and human well being aspects from the very beginning of the design.

Physically Built Robotic Environments

Robotic Environments build up on knowledge in Non-standard and Interactive Architecture (NS&IA) developed at Hyperbody TU Delft (www.hyperbody.nl) and Kinetic Design at MIT. It systematically advances this knowledge since 2012 by developing with MSc 4 students (2012) interactive indoor climate regulating systems (Fig. 12.1) and prototypically developing with MSc 2 students (2013) spatially reconfigurable, multimodal systems (Fig. 12.3). The Multimodal Apartment experiments (http://multimod.hyperbody.nl) have proven, as in case of the Pop-up Apartment (Fig. 12.3), that spatial reconfiguration can optimize 24/7 use of built space, while the climate control related investigation has shown that integrating distributed interactive climate control devices into building components may contribute considerably to improving indoor climate (Fig. 12.1) and reduce energy consumption.

Considering that the aim for the Multimodal Apartment was to design a small apartment of 150 m^3 that has all the spatial qualities and functional performances of a standard 300 m^3 apartment, the initial assumption was that when a user is in the kitchen or living room, this user does not use the sleeping room at the same time implying that at one moment of the day large sections of the space could cater to only one to two functions. Basic recommendations for the design were inter al. use of scripting (implying that the design is generated and handled through scripting), NC fabrication, and dry assembly. The proof of concept required building 1:1 prototypes, which in case of the Pop-up Apartment it implied that spatial subdivision and furniture reconfiguration exploiting material and geometrical properties easily facilitate 24/7 change of use.

For reconfigurable buildings understanding 24/7 use by mapping activities in a 6 to 12–48 months period is of extreme importance as to understand individual and collective (in and outdoor) spatial use and respective requirements. Main consideration is that fast 24/7 changes such as spatial use, indoor climate, and energy management require real-time responses. Distributed, intelligent spatial, climate, and energy control devices embedded into building components aim to establish the required demand-driven use.

Such componential distributed systems operate as *self-organizing swarms* (Figs. 12.1, 12.2, 12.3, 12.4 and 12.5) consisting of simple (physical and virtual) agents that interact locally with one another and their environment based on simple rules leading to the emergence of complex, global behavior. Swarms are relevant in architecture and architectural design for many reasons but mainly because of their ability to embody both natural (human) and artificial (architecture related) aspects. Swarms are, basically, set up as parametric (virtual and physical) systems that can simulate and actuate behaviors in real-time.

Artificial agents are conceived similarly to natural agents as autonomous entities able to perceive through sensors and act upon an environment using actuators. Interactions between human or natural and artificial agents may follow principles as described in the Actor–Network Theory (ANT) implying that material–semiotic networks are acting as a whole whereas the clusters of actors or agents involved in creating meaning are both material and semiotic (Latour 2005). ANT, therefore, implies agency of both humans and non-humans, whereas agency is not located in one or the other, but in the heterogeneous associations between them.

In this context, human and non-human interaction may take place on virtual and physical level implying that spatial reconfiguration according to users' needs is implemented within the parametric design framework preliminarily defined by

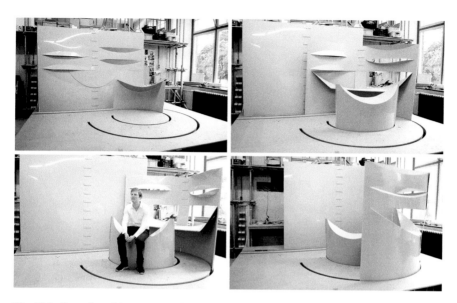

Fig. 12.3 Reconfigurable apartment developed by Hyperbody with MSc 2 students and industry partners at Hyperbody, TUD (Pop-up Apartment, 2013)

experts such as architects, engineers, etc. Such a framework is enabling users to choose preferred solutions from a set of possible solutions, while the amplitude of choice stays within the (scientifically sound and) valid solutions field, which is framed parametrically by experts (Bier and Ku 2013). This implies that users cannot generate arbitrarily (any kind of) solutions but rather contribute to and choose from a set of possible solutions. Parametric constraints for possible solutions are defined according to functional, formal, material, structural, environmental etc. requirements identified as such in architectural, engineering, and building sciences, thus excluding possibility of generating (scientifically) invalid solutions. For instance, spatial dimensioning may be numerically constrained in relation to min-max occupancy and use requirements; access opportunities may be defined in relation to shortest connecting path, indoor climate variations may be restricted to a range of recommended choices, etc.

This implies that non-human agency is conditioned to operate exclusively in interaction with human agency, and therefore, it procedurally facilitates human decision-making by compensating where human decision-making might be limited or overextended. For instance, same or similar (virtual and physical) agent systems produce multiple (and even endless) variations of architectural configurations under similar conditions due to the emergent properties of the system. While in design spatial and programmatic formations emerge from data-driven contextual (environmental, programmatic, etc.) interactions, robotic architecture employs real-time interaction in the actuation of architectural embodiments, which become dynamic, acting and re-acting in response to environmental and user-specific needs. Both employ swarm intelligence for generative and reconfiguration purposes,

Fig. 12.4 Protospace 4.0 is consisting of integrated, customizable, and specialized building components developed at Hyperbody, TUD (2010)

respectively, implying that not only design emerges from local interactions between human and non-human agents but also physically built space adapts and reconfigures locally according to human and environmental needs.

In this context, the interaction between artificial and natural agents requires further definition: Russell and Norvig (2003) classify artificial agents based on their degree of intelligence into simple and model-based reflex agents, goal- and utility-based agents, and learning agents. While, simple reflex agents ignore history and act only on current conditions based on if-condition-then-action rule, goal-based agents further expand on the capabilities of the model-based agents, by using goals. This allows agents to choose among multiple possibilities. They can, however, only distinguish between goal and non-goal states. By mapping performances that allow comparison between different (goal and non-goal) states utility agents make informed choices, while more advanced learning agents have the ability to even become competent in time.

Hyperbody employs populations of (natural and artificial) agents with different degrees of intelligence in order to achieve functional-, material- and energy-efficiency. The interaction between artificial and natural agents allows achieving required performance whereas control is performed by wirelessly networked components that are locally driven by users' preferences and indoor-outdoor environmental conditions. In such context, (1) spatial and (2) climate control components communicate not only with each other but also with all (other) building components,

Fig. 12.5 Protocology operating as a swarm of components interacting with each other and users by means of sound, light, proximity, and movement developed at Hyperbody, TUD (2009)

inhabitants and indoor-outdoor environment in order to provide conditions that may differ depending on local needs and individual demands from space-to-space or even place-to-place.

Spatial Reconfiguration

User-driven spatial reconfiguration involves users in the real-time transformation of physically built space. This requires development of building systems incorporating intelligent control, where reconfiguration is accomplished collectively by distributed building components that are operating in cooperation. Considering, for instance, that there is 6,9 million m² empty office space in Netherlands due to lack of spatial versatility, Hyperbody aims to address this problem by advancing multi- and trans-disciplinary knowledge in designing and engineering spatially reconfigurable and customizable building systems.

Reconfigurable architecture can be traced back to Archigram's vision in the 1960s of an architecture that could respond to open-ended and uncertain conditions, followed by Zuk and Clark's kinetic architecture in the 1970s presenting auditoriums and stadiums with movable seating and retractable roofs (Bier and Knight 2010), and Negroponte's responsive architecture (Negroponte 1970) resulting from the (ubiquitous) integration of computing power into built spaces and structures.

Today, advancements in robotic and networked systems change radically relevance, meaning, and use of physically built space. While both, the physical and the virtual facilitate the human interaction, the question of how does the built environment change when it incorporates robotics is of great relevance. Hyperbody projects attempt to answer this question by enabling real-time interaction between natural or artificial environments and users.

In this context, real-time interaction implies that physically built space responds in real-time to required changes by spatially and sensorially reconfiguring itself.

Fig. 12.6 Prototype built by means of robotic wire cutting in a wire cutting in a Hyperbody off-campus lab (2012)

This reconfiguration may imply slow to fast speed transformation depending on momentarily, daily, monthly, seasonally, or yearly changing needs. All employ human-robot interaction models that establish continuous feedback based on ubiquitous communication between natural (human) and artificial (robotic) agents. For RB, ubiquitous communication implies that robotic devices are embedded into objects (such as furniture, appliances, etc.) and spaces, communicate through high-speed (local or worldwide) networks, while required data and computational services are online accessible (Fig. 12.8).

The challenge is that robots and humans share the same physical space as well as share goals in terms of accomplishing tasks such as spatial or indoor climate reconfiguration. Also, environments located in private and public buildings have usually more complex interaction requirements than factories. The assumption is, however, that the factory of the future employs robots operating on-site, which requires as in private and public buildings that robotic devices need perceiving and understanding capacities allowing them to build dynamic models of their surroundings. They need, therefore, to categorize objects, recognize, and locate humans in space in order to address their needs.

Methods for perceiving humans in the built environment explored recently at Hyperbody are based on sensor information that is extracting, for instance, human kinematics (Kinect). These allow mapping dynamically bodily movement in relation to space, which reconfigures by employing a variety of distributed sensor-actuators. Depending on which sensor provides the most reliable data at the given time, the environment e.g. space is re-mapped and reconfigured semi- or completely autonomously.

Robotic devices ensuring spatial or indoor climate reconfiguration in response to human and environmental needs operate, therefore, semi- or completely autonomously transforming buildings into active participants in the dynamic and customizable use of physically built space.

Fig. 12.7 NC design to additive production of porous structures implemented at Hyperbody, TUD (2014)

Climate Control

Interactive climate control and environmental concerns are addressed at Hyperbody by developing new concepts for in building components embedded ventilation, heating, and lighting components that provide as much air, heat, and light, as needed at the specific time and location:

1. VENTILATION consisting of cooling, ventilation, and humidity control devices is distributed (in wall-, ceiling-, and skin-components) and intelligently controlled by sensor-actuators with the aim to passively and actively exploit potential of distributed control for efficient ventilation. For instance, in skin-integrated sensor-actuators (Fig. 12.2) allow for natural ventilation, whereas mechanical ventilation is implemented only if, when, and where needed.
2. HEATING employing heat convection, conduction or radiation is distributed (in furniture-, wall-, ceiling-, floor-, and skin-components) and intelligently controlled by sensor-actuator devices in order to ensure local comfort only if, when, and where needed.
3. LIGHT is distributed (in furniture-, wall-, ceiling-, floor-, and skin-components) and is intelligently controlled by sensor-actuators in order to reduce energy usage by providing natural and artificial light only when, where, and how much it is needed. Such Ambient Intelligence (AmI) may include occupancy control, daylight, heat, or air harvesting, and demand response (Aarts et al. 2001) by automatically diming or turning on and off lights, heating or ventilation. Such intelligent networked systems of devices may employ wireless (i.e. ZigBee) controls with respect to chronological (24 h) and astronomical time (sunrise and sunset), occupancy (using movement sensors), devices availability and use (combination of events by using if-then-else statements and logical operators) while adjustment of the system occurs both automatically or manually, at device locations and via software programs or other interfaces (Fig. 12.9).

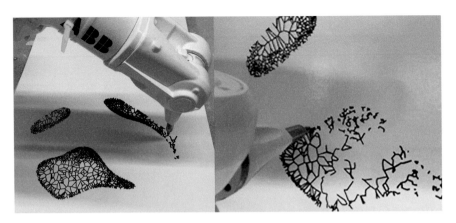

Fig. 12.8 Materialisation experiments showing material porosity with different (scalable) densities and gradient materials architectured for structurally- and energy-efficient building, first ideas and tests implemented at Hyperbody, TUD (2014)

The development of such systems requires advanced design to production processes. While knowledge in 3–4D modelling and simulation of indoor-outdoor climate conditions and NC designing and fabricating building components with integrated sensor-actuator devices is available to experts, there is no framework for an integrated approach that would indicate system requirements with respect to dimensions, complexity during installation, and degree of climate control that can be achieved, scalability and life-cycle, which Hyperbody aims to accomplish.

Scientific, fundamental challenges are, therefore, the development of efficient sensor-actuator mechanisms, intelligent control strategies, and effective NC and robotically driven design to production and operation processes. For instance, efficient sensor-actuator mechanisms imply use of sensors and performance indicators of indoor environment quality, while it is not always obvious what to use as indicator and most likely a combination of indicators needs to be employed (Bluyssen 2013) depending on the scenario studied (classroom, office, bedroom, kitchen, etc.). Furthermore, considering that state-of-the-art climate control is usually employing single (not multiple) sensor set-ups and is usually centralized, rendering demand-driven use inefficient and ineffective, the innovativeness of Hyperbody's research lies in the systemic integration of intelligent, distributed sensor-actuator mechanisms for controlling climate into building components.

Research results contribute to science at the level where (a) distributed, robotic or mechatronic systems incorporating intelligent control are integrated in architectural environments, and (b) climate control concepts and models are fundamentally innovated in order to address (individual) human needs and energy efficiency requirements at building scale.

In this context, intelligent control implies establishing an energy-climate-balance by means of computer-based continuous calculation of incoming-outgoing energy

Fig. 12.9 Hyperbody 2–3D materialisation experiments implemented at Hyperbody, TUD in order to identify correlation between material properties, deposition pattern and speed (2014)

and climate regulation needs. The scientific challenge is to conceptualize climate control as a distributed robotic system and embed it into architectural building components. Therefore, the main focus is on the development of reliable indoor climate performance indicators, robust control algorithms and fast deploying sensors-actuators, efficient communication protocols for distributed networks, and sustainable embedding procedures.

AmI and autonomous control for indoor climate control and energy management do not necessarily require Internet and are not part of Internet of Things (IoT). They employ a network of connected devices consisting of intelligent entities that act independently and collectively depending on situation and context. Climate control and energy management, for example, may be operated through a local network while IoT systems are in charge of collecting information with respect to natural ecosystems and buildings connected to the larger environmental sensing, energy management, and urban networks. AmI implies, in this context, that devices work together and support people in carrying out everyday life activities. Computation is embedded into objects or devices and spaces, while networked communication enables these to communicate with each other and users. This implies that computing is embedded everywhere and anywhere.

This new paradigm involves the IoT and employs distributed and networked systems and technologies that are embedded or integrated into the physically built environment and are context aware, customizable, and adaptive to changing context (inter al. Aarts et al. 2001) meaning that they can respond and to some extent even anticipate needs.

RB applies principles of AmI and IoT by embedding robotic devices into physically built environments. Distributed RB components accomplishing collectively either spatial reconfiguration or climate control and energy management require design to production processes that facilitate NC modeling, simulation, and robotically driven production. Such processes establish a direct link between not only design and production but also operation of robotic building components.

Numerically Controlled and Robotically Driven Building Processes

Physically built robotic environments rely on design to production and operation chains that may be (partially or completely) implemented by robotic means. In this context, the main consideration is that in architecture and building construction the factory of the future employs building materials and components that can be robotically processed and assembled. RB employs customised design to production processes that incorporate material properties in design, control all aspects of the design to production process numerically, and utilise parametric design principles that can be linked to the robotic production (Fig. 12.10).

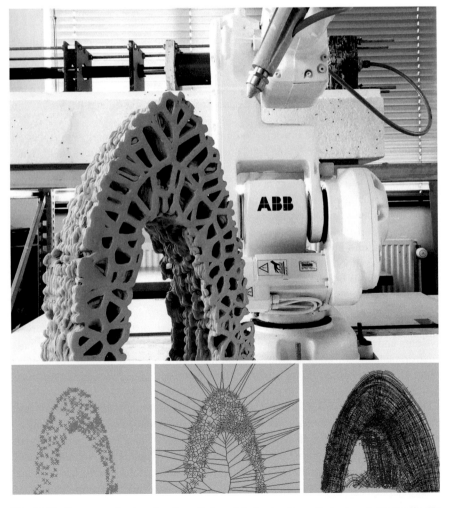

Fig. 12.10 Fragment of urban furniture (1:1 scale) structurally optimized and robotically 3D printed at Hyperbody, TUD (2015)

The design to production framework developed at Hyperbody for RB allows real-time connectivity between designers, engineers, manufacturers, and clients. It eliminates the current problem of missed optimization opportunities due to a fragmented and sequential process of architecture – engineering – manufacturing. With the design to production framework, it is easy to integrate a network of sensors and mechatronic components in the construction elements, and also integrate structural strength with high level of insulation into new types of materials and building components.

Material usage is also minimized, since design to production optimizes the use of materials quantitatively and performance-wise. In other words, novel materials (Fig. 12.7) and multi-material compounds, which allow the construction of building components with a. o. robotic additive (3D printing) technology, are developed. Together with structural optimizations during the design process, this technology may result in components with the minimal quantity and the right quality of materials to perform the integrated functions of the components.

Explorations in robotic building implying NC and robotically supported design to production and operation chains, have been implemented since 2012 at Hyperbody first with two large ABB robots, which were customized to perform tasks with specialized operating tools and programs (Oosterhuis and Bier 2013). A series of experiments were implemented with MSc 2 students in order to develop and test robotic fabrication methods by establishing a feedback loop between design and fabrication. The assumption was that by employing robotic fabrication, customized designs could be easily implemented so that end-users may be able to transform (extend, shrink, expand, etc.) physically built environments on demand. Such spatial reconfiguration has been understood as being slower as it takes place over longer periods of time (measured in not hours and days but months and years) corresponding to cycles of growing and shrinking family size and corresponding changing spatial requirements.

Initial experiments with robotic subtractive manufacturing (Fig. 12.6) where followed up by additive robotic production (Fig. 12.7), which implied linking design to materialisation by integrating all functionalities (from structural strength, to thermal insulation and climate control) in the design of building components. This was implemented by employing novel multi-performative design to production strategies: New materials were developed for the robotic production of multi-material building components and novel robotic production and assembly tools were deployed for testing the blueprint of future robotic building.

RB employs customised design to production processes that incorporate material properties in design, control all aspects of the design to production process numerically, and utilise parametric design principles that can be linked to the robotic production. This framework exploits expert and user involvement challenging the production-consumption gap by connecting parametric models with robotised production tools in order to achieve efficient production of custom-made parts e.g. building components for personalized use.

NC and robotic design to production processes enable production of free-formed, heterogeneous, optimized structures by additively and selectively depositing or manipulating materials in order to achieve specific porosity-density, flexibility-rigidity, etc. requirements in accordance to formal, functional, structural, climatic, environmental, and economic needs. This requires multi-robot production implying that several robots operate simultaneously or in short sequence in the process of production and assembly of multi-material building components. This is necessary in order to, for instance, deposit reinforcement fibres or granular insulation material, etc. in parallel to depositing cement-based materials, etc.

Such a robotic design to production system employs laser scanning to capture the current status of the building process. This allows for monitoring by establishing a feedback loop between the virtual and the physical environment. Furthermore, direct data streaming for interactive tool paths allows users not only to adjust robot tool-paths in real-time, but also receive immediate feedback regarding the robot position and possible interfacing with other devices. This is of relevance especially in production environments where robots and humans are involved simultaneously or in short sequence in the process of production.

Hyperbody's explorations with robotically supported design to production processes indicate that architectural production becomes procedural instead of object-oriented and architecture emerges from a process in which the interaction between all (human and non-human) parts of the system generates the result.

Human and non-human parts of the system may be involved as experts and users in the design to production and operation process. This implies that virtual and physical agents inform architecture at all stages of the process and the architect develops a meta-design establishing rules for user co-creation. Users customise designs employing web-based interfaces, and order resulting personalized products.

In this context, distributed design to production exploits the advantages of cloud computing by employing remote servers and software networks that allow data storage and online access to computer services and resources. This implies decentralized and geographically independent distributed design and production (inter al. Bopp 2010), which is of great relevance as it enables users to share infrastructure costs (of intangible and tangible resources) while taking advantage of the advanced capabilities of the NC and robotic production tools (inter al. Kostakis 2013).

As NC and robotic design to production processes become more accessible to users, the distinction between producer and user is increasingly blurred. While the industrial paradigm exploited the economies of global scale, NC production counters globalization, as users increasingly manufacture themselves products rather than engage in trade. This implies that production takes place in response to actual demand, not anticipated demand, and it becomes increasingly local and customized.

Conclusion

Physically built robotic environments and robotically supported building processes presented and discussed in this chapter are experimental. They rely on theories and applications of ANT, IoT, and distributed robotics where the role of the human is framed in terms of hybrid (human and non-human) agency. Their development towards real life applications and industrial production requires further development and testing aiming mid- and long-term at transferring knowledge to industry.

Research and experimental developments in interactive and robotic building implemented at Hyperbody and representatively presented in projects discussed in this chapter, are employing multiple and distributed sensor-actuators integrated into architectural components and architectural production tools. They confirm that distributed intelligent control is a viable option for addressing contemporary needs for reconfiguration and demand-driven production and use of physically built environments.

Hyperbody pushes developments in RB based on the understanding that the ongoing fusion of the physical and the virtual generates a physical-virtual continuum that is containing hybrid degrees of physical and virtual conditions and the distinction between physical and virtual is increasingly blurred.

In this context, RB exploits mainly two paradigm shifts implying (1) a move from mechanical, industrial production to NC and robotically driven mass-customization and (2) a transition from inanimate (inert, insentient) to animate (actuated, sentient) architectural environments. Hyperbody's research into concepts and applications related to these paradigm-shifts is relevant because of its impact on architecture with respect to energy-efficient building, demand-driven production and operation, and efficient use of resources. This implies that buildings are not demolished or remodeled to fit changing needs but are reconfigured and built space is efficiently used. Climate control and energy management responds not to average but real-time data ensuring customizable conform, while energy-loses through excessive or unnecessary illumination, ventilation, heating or cooling of little or even unoccupied spaces, etc. are reduced.

RB employs NC and robotically supported design to production and operation processes for the development of robotic building components and buildings. These processes rely on interactions between virtual and physical, non-human and human agents, while physically built space incorporating robotic agents (e.g. sensor-actuators embedded in building components) adapts and reconfigures (with respect to indoor climate and 24/7 use) in response to human agents' needs. This implies that architecture is not only produced (created or designed and fabricated) by NC and robotic means but is, actually, incorporating robotic mechanisms that enable them real-time operation e.g. interaction with environments and users. Data collected from e.g. outdoor environment informs on the one hand the design and on the other hand it informs the real-time operation of the interactive indoor climate control. Also, the data incorporated in design with respect to form, structure, and materialization informs the NC and robotic production. Data-driven design to production and operation implies, therefore, that data informs parametric models on which simulations are implemented. These, in turn, interface the real-time operation of physically built architectural systems implying that data-driven design establishes an unprecedented design to production and operation feedback loop (Bier and Knight 2014).

Robotic environments and robotically driven design to production and operation processes contribute to the reduction of economical inefficiency and environmental damage, since multiple use of built space in condensed timeframes renders an increase from 25 % to at least 75 % in operability, while design to production and operation processes establish a direct link between conceptualisation, design, engineering, fabrication and operation of buildings.

Users are involved in the design to production to operation process on many levels and have a great impact on the process and the result. While experts establish the parametric framework (as meta-design) that allows within certain constraints exploration of multiple designs by users, the architect becomes creator of meta-designs that the user is customizing participating as co-creator and even co-producer in the process. This implies that architects develop (virtual and physical) agents that produce hybrid architectural systems, and architectural production becomes the result of multiple, interacting natural (human) and artificial agents and systems. Such agent-based systems produce under similar conditions various architectural ecologies due to the emergent properties of the systems.

RB relies on the integration of robotic and cloud-computing technologies into architectural production and operation, which leads to new approaches (inter al. Wu, Rosen, and Schaefer 2014) that are exploiting technologies of the fourth industrial revolution. It implies the use of distributed robotic systems and the IoT in order to monitor physical processes by creating virtual representations of the physical world that support decentralized decisions making (Kagermann et al. 2013).

RB relies, therefore, on (1) interoperability, which is the ability of robotic systems, humans, and factories to connect and communicate via the IoT, (2) virtual-physical coupling by linking sensor-actuator data (from monitoring physical processes) with virtual models and simulations, (3) decentralization, which is exploiting the ability of robots to operate distributedly and autonomously, and (4) real-time operation implying that data is exchanged in real-time, which are the main Industry 4.0 characteristics (Hermann et al. 2015). RB employs all these concepts and extends them by including in the design to production loop the actual operation of buildings.

Acknowledgements This paper has profited from the input of Hyperbody researchers and students teams and is based on the Interactive-Robotic Building framework developed by the main author 2010–2013. Robotic Building (RB) has been supported 2014–2015 by 3TU, Delft Robotics Institute (DRI), 100 % Research, AE&T, KUKA, and ABB.

References

Aarts E, Harwig R, Schuurmans M (2001) Ambient intelligence, The invisible future: the seamless integration of technology into every-day life. McGraw-Hill, New York

Bier H (2013) Robotic building(s). In: Oosterhuis K (ed) 1st next generation building issue. Baltzer Science, Berlin

Bier H, Knight T (2010) Digitally-driven architecture. In: Bier H, Knight T (eds) 6th footprint issue. Stichting Footprint, Delft

Bier H, Knight T (2014) Dynamics of data-driven design. In: Bier H, Knight T (eds) 15th footprint issue. Stichting Footprint, Delft

Bier H, Ku Y (2013) Generative and participatory parametric frameworks for multi-player design games. In: Krivý M, Kaminer T (eds) 13th footprint issue. Stichting Footprint, Delft

Bluyssen P (2013) Indoor environment quality as a multi-level, multi-factor, multi-disciplinary and multi-stakeholder issue. HVAC J: REHVA 06/2003:40–43

Bopp F (2010) Rapid Manufacturing: Zukünftige Wertschöpfungsmodelle durch generative Fertigungsverfahren. Diplomica, Hamburg

Eastman C (1971) Adaptive-conditional architecture. In: Nigel C (ed) Design participation: proceedings of the design research society's conference Manchester. Academy Editions, London, pp 51–57

Gardiner V (2009) 24 rooms tucked into one. Retrieved 8 Aug 2015. http://www.nytimes.com/2009/01/15/garden/15hongkong.html?pagewanted=all&_r=0

Hermann M, Pentek T, Otto B (2015) Design principles for industry 4.0 scenarios. Retrieved 3 May 2015. http://www.snom.mb.tu-dortmund.de/cms/de/forschung/Arbeitsberichte/

Kagermann H, Wahlster W, Helbig J (2013) Recommendations for implementing the strategic initiative industry 4.0 – final report of the industry 4.0 working group. Acatech (http://www.acatech.de/de/publikationen/publikationssuche/detail/artikel/recommendations-for-implementing-the-strategic-initiative-industrie-40-final-report-of-the-industr.html)

Kohler M, Gramazio F, Willmann J (2014) The robotic touch – how robots change architecture. Park Books, Zurich

Kostakis V (2013) At the turning point of the current techno-economic paradigm: commons-based peer production, desktop manufacturing and the role of civil society in the Perezian framework. TripleC 11(1):173–190

Krieg OD, Menges A (2013) Potentials of robotic fabrication in wood construction: elastically bent timber sheets with robotically fabricated finger joints. ACADIA, Waterloo

Latour B (2005) Reassembling the social: an introduction to actor-network-theory. Oxford University Press, Oxford

Negroponte N (1970) The architecture machine: towards a more human environment. MIT Press, Cambridge

Oosterhuis K (2010) Towards a new kind of building. NAI Publishers, Rotterdam

Oosterhuis K, Bier H (2013) Robotics in architecture, IA #5. Jap Sam Books, Heijningen

Remoy HT, van der Voordt DJM (2014) Adaptive reuse of office buildings: opportunities and risks of conversion into housing in building in research & information. CIB, Delft, pp 381–390

Russell S, Norvig P (2003) Artificial intelligence – a modern approach. Upper Saddle River, Englewood Cliffs, pp 1–40

Walter W (1951) A machine that learns. Sci Am 185(2):60–63

Wiener N (1948) Cybernetics: or control and communication in the animal and the machine. Hermann & Cie, Paris

Wu D, Rosen DW, Schaefer D (2014) Cloud-based design and manufacturing: status and promise. In: Schaefer D (ed) Cloud-based design and manufacturing: a service-oriented product development paradigm for the 21st century. Springer, London, pp 1–2

Zuk W, Clark R (1970) Kinetic architecture. Van Nostrand Reinhold, New York

Part V
Sights and Manifestations

The site of an interactive space is an essential determinant of its context, whether this is its spatial, technical or social context. It is well understood that context needs to be considered when evaluating and when designing for interaction. Who frequents a particular location? For what reason are they there? Where are they heading? From internal spaces, such as those concerned with the health sector or learning environments, to urban space, where mobile computing and fixed interactive screens are employed, interaction is considered on a variety of scales. In this section, we consider the impact of site on interaction and the specific approaches that researchers have developed to address context.

Luusua et al. argued for what they call emplaced interaction design. They took and build upon the work of Paul Dourish, who suggests that one way to unify the wider field of interaction design is to use the notion of embodiment. This in many ways leads to the idea that what unifies computing and architecture is the notion of users/inhabitants interacting with each other and with the building or the machine. Dourish's vision of computing being unified through the notion of embodiment and to some extent phenomenology combines with a historical branch of architecture theory. Christian Norberg-Schlz, a Norwegian architect, educationalist and architectural theorist performed much the same role in Architecture as Dourish did 40 years later in computing. Bringing the philosophical aspects of phenomenology and embodiment to the subject. It makes sense then to explore the work beginning with the lens of phenomenology, ethnography, and place. Luusua approaches this from and architectural perspective and comes up with emplaced interaction as an extension of the Dourish work and embodied interaction. Here, place as well as the embodied mind become tools to conceptualize and communicate between disciplines. Indeed from this work the links are so strong we could envisage a unification of both subject areas at least on a theoretic basis.

Bedwell's chapter delivers research and extensive empirical experience to provide an excellent complement to *Luusua's* and *Deshpande's* work. *Bedwell's* chapter examines use of an interactive location-based experience, this entertainment and information experience fixes in practice some of the experiences of the other chapters in this section. It reminds us that tools for creators of urban experiences will be a vital part to the creation of these virtual places. This work echoes that of *Bolbroe* suggesting that before work can be crafted to fully take advantage of this new technology other prototypes and experience reflection or experience analytics will be needed to create compelling urban experiences.

Deshpande deepens the notion of space. It is well known in the field of urban social geography that there is a separation between space and place. While not wishing to engage in the deep philosophical debate behind these terms reaching as far back as Aristotle, it is interesting to reflect on their meaning in this work. Space can be seen as the container it is the shared physical experience. Place, on the other hand, is the emotional attachment one feels in a space. For example, the physical spatial side of the house can be easily defined as the number of square feet/meters of the floor area. The place can be one relationship to home. From this point of view one's home can be destroyed while the building can be easily rebuilt. This leads to the question how do we create 'place' where non exists before (Placemaking)? Deshpande explores the use of design of interactive architect artifacts to help create an emotional attachment to the location changing space into place. The idea of digital technology facilitating the place making process does speak strongly to the notion of the overlap between Urban Architecture and HCI.

Chapter 13
Northern Urban Lights: Emplaced Experiences of Urban Lighting as Digital Augmentation

Anna Luusua, Henrika Pihlajaniemi, and Johanna Ylipulli

Abstract The shift towards interactivity in the design of spaces and places has persuaded both architects and HCI practitioners to acknowledge that there is a need to work together. However, there is little knowledge of how we actually experience dynamic adaptation, informational services and interactivity in the built environment. As such, there is a pressing need to empirically study actual implementations of media architecture, urban interaction design and urban computing from an emic perspective. Consequently, this article examines participant experiences of an interactive urban lighting pilot, Urban Echoes (UE), which took place in a northern urban park. Collected as video and audio recorded material in walking interviews and semi-structured interviews, we examine the *emplaced* experiences of two differing participant groups, young adults (20–29 years old) and seniors (over 65 years old). Furthermore, we argue that the concept of emplacement, which highlights the importance of *place* and the *embodied mind*, can be a useful tool both as an analytical lens and as an effective way to conceptualize and communicate some essential aspects of architectural thinking in the interdisciplinary arena of media architecture and urban interaction design. Finally, building on the work of Paul Dourish on embodied interaction design, we argue for emplaced interaction design.

Introduction

Traversing through the contemporary urban environment, with smartphones in our pockets and passing by displays, sensors, and cameras on our way, we can see that digital technologies have arguably permeated the city in many ways. Urban displays and media façades, for example, have changed the visual cityscape as some of the basic material elements which form urban spaces have been integrated with dynamic and adaptive content (e.g. Fatah 2006). Mobiles and wireless networks, on the other hand, have affected the way we experience, behave in and use public urban places (e.g. Willis and Aurigi 2011; Coyne 2010). Importantly, digital technology has also

A. Luusua (✉) • H. Pihlajaniemi • J. Ylipulli
University of Oulu, Oulu, Finland
e-mail: Anna.Luusua@oulu.fi; Henrika.Pihlajaniemi@oulu.fi; Johanna.Ylipulli@oulu.fi

© Springer International Publishing Switzerland 2016
N.S. Dalton et al. (eds.), *Architecture and Interaction*,
Human–Computer Interaction Series, DOI 10.1007/978-3-319-30028-3_13

introduced the possibility to add a level of interactivity in urban places that has never been experienced before. Not only do we employ technologies to interact with each other in new ways in urban places, we now also possess the opportunity to be reacted to and genuinely interact with the urban environment itself through movement, speech or devices (McCullough 2005). This type of interaction – rapid and digital – marks a substantive change from the types of interaction we have had with our urban surroundings before. These have been, for instance, slow and gradual material changes: patina, wear and traces of use; or more intentional and rapid modifications of our surroundings, ranging from the introduction of personal belongings into work spaces to the temporary re-arranging or repurposing of an urban space. These are naturally still a central concern for architecture.

However, this *interactive shift*, as we might call it, in the design and experience of architectural spaces has also garnered the interest of the architectural research community, who have called for researchers and practitioners in the field to participate in the study and design of interactive technologies. The emerging field of *media architecture* (e.g. Brynskov et al. 2015) has formed around these phenomena, especially dealing with public and outdoor spaces so far. Indeed, the number of media architectural installations is growing rapidly. Within this emerging field we must take into account that digital interactivity might also raise interesting theoretical questions in regards to urban places. For instance, might it be possible for urban places to have a certain agency themselves? What will it mean for us to live in and with interactive urban places? What will happen when locational technologies interact with other locational technologies without human presence and interference?

Similarly, researchers and designers in the field of Human-Computer Interaction (HCI) have taken note of the new spatial and locational aspects of their field, giving rise to, e.g., *urban computing* (Kindberg et al. 2007) and *urban interaction design* (Brynskov et al. 2014). For almost two decades ago, Harrison and Dourish (1996) made the case for the importance of understanding *space* and *place* in HCI. Drawing heavily from other fields (Tuan 1977; Lakoff and Johnson 1980, 1999; Goffman 1959; Giddens 1984; Alexander 1977), Harrison and Dourish first provided their readers with "two accounts of spatiality – one geometric, mathematical or physical, the other social and cultural". The first descriptor was assigned to the concept of space, the latter to place. Ten years later, Dourish (2006) amended this discussion with the note that a possible dualistic 'layer-cake' model of these concepts – wherein 'places' are created on top of naturalistically existing 'spaces' – is not an adequate understanding of the concepts. Dourish drew attention to the well-established point of view that the spatial forms that we generate, and our experiences of them, are also socially constructed, thus meriting a more nuanced understanding of the concepts. Importantly, Dourish also discussed these issues in more detail in an influential book (Dourish 2004) which delved deeper into the subject of embodiment in HCI. Thus, some existing understandings from philosophy, the social sciences, and architecture were formally introduced into HCI.

To date, however, there is very little empirical knowledge of how we actually experience these digitally augmented places, as most of the research in HCI and related fields has focused on building more and more new applications of technologies (Kitchin 2014). Thus, we argue, they have not been properly studied as broadly experiential entities from a qualitative and empirical point of view – rather, they have been judged mostly through UX research methods, on the basis of their technological viability, and sometimes on their visual impact. Before urban technologies are implemented on larger scales, more knowledge is needed to understand their impact on the urban environment and our experience[1] of it. More specifically, we need to deepen our knowledge of how urban technologies are understood by different kinds of individuals and groups using public urban places (Williams and Dourish 2006; Ylipulli et al. 2014b; Luusua et al. in review). Arguably, a crucial goal for the practice of architecture and urban design is to support the creation of better places. As interactive technologies move into this territory (and indeed the very terms – media architecture, urban interaction design and urban computing – strongly suggest a desire to do so), they must also be employed in a responsible, inclusive and creative manner. This can only be done if we have a deep understanding of what public spaces and places are like as individual instances and as a larger phenomenon. For this purpose, we attest, both suitable theoretical concepts as well as empirical research of various kinds of groups' and individuals' experience are needed. We can identify not only a gap, but several gaps that occur between the traditional fields of engineering, architecture and social sciences, as experts from these fields struggle to understand the interactive shift in public places (e.g. Jurmu et al. 2015).

This, among others, was an aim of the Urban Echoes (UE) pilot study, an architecturally-led intervention into a real urban park in a northern city in wintertime, which employed adaptive urban lighting as a medium. UE was designed within the Adaptive Urban Lighting project at the Oulu School of Architecture, University of Oulu, Finland, and the resultant pilot was evaluated and studied in collaboration with the interdisciplinary UBI Metrics research project, using semi-structured and walking interviews as methods. One important aim of the study was to study participant experiences of an adaptive, informative and interactive urban lighting installation in a real urban place, in this case, a park. Thus, in this article, we examine the emplaced experiences of two differing participant groups, namely young adults between 20 and 29 years old, and seniors over 65 years old, through analysing the material gained in these interviews.

The aim of this article, then, is twofold. Firstly, we wish to provide our readers with a descriptive analysis of participant reflections and accounts of an actual deployment of an urban technology. Secondly, we consider *emplacement* as a useful concept for the field of study for architecture and HCI, arguing ultimately for the importance of *emplaced interaction design* for the making of environmentally integrated computing, such as media architecture.

---

[1]*Experience* is a nebulous concept which escapes easy definitions; thus, we approach it from a very broad perspective, through the theoretical lens explained in Chap. 3, where we explain the theoretical underpinnings of our work.

Research Setting

Our research site was the city of Oulu in Northern Finland, a Nordic country that is highly technologically developed: to illustrate, a broadband Internet access has been declared a citizen right in the country, and over half of all Finns have their own smartphone (OSF 2015). The city of Oulu especially has been known for its ICT industry and its smart city initiatives, such as the Open Ubiquitous Oulu (Ojala et al. 2010), which has deployed an extensive urban computing infrastructure in the city, with sensor networks and free public WiFi and public displays. Thus, our research was located in a high-tech city within a high-tech country.

The Otto Karhi Park, in which our pilot took place, is the size of one city block, approximately 90 by 90 m. At the time of our study, it was quartered by footpaths stretching from one end of the park to the other, as well as a small body of water, a narrow channel. The park was flanked on its southeastern side by a very busy two-lane street with heavy traffic; on its southwestern and northwestern side cars were allowed, but the amount of traffic was reduced; on its northeastern side, taxis gathered in a line to collect patrons. Many of the retail spaces surrounding the park were occupied by restaurants, bars and nightclubs; furthermore, the park was situated halfway between the pedestrian centre and the train station. Thus, the site was busy in the evening as well as during the day with passers-by. Notably, the site was, and continues to be, a northern urban park; thus, the winters are very cold and dark. The interviews were conducted in the middle of the winter, with only a few hours of sunlight every day – approximately 4–6 h in December and January, and 7–10 h in February (Finnish Meteorological Institute). The role of darkness and artificial lighting, then, arguably constitutes an important part of urban inhabitants' lives in this context.

This was the scene for which UE lighting was designed and implemented. It was determined to run on a path going alongside the water's edge. This path was used much less, as could be determined by the often untouched snow that had been trampled on other, busier pathways. One objective, then, for choosing this location was to see whether or not the new lighting design could attract more walkers on the path. In general, the park was illuminated with spherical luminaires dating from the 1980s along the footpaths, leaving much of the park and its vegetation in a fairly dimly lit condition.

Urban Echoes

UE was a temporary, adaptive park lighting installation, which provided urban information in the form of colourful lighting, and adapted to people's movements. Interaction was based on the use of mobile devices and motion detection through sensors. The installation of UE was implemented with LED luminaires. These luminaires were both suspended above a path that ran through the park, and positioned on the ground near trees and bushes. The selection of lights consisted of RGB spotlights with varying beam angles and 3,000 K LED luminaires with

Fig. 13.1 A light map
showing the locations of the
UE installation luminaires
and the test area in the
immediate urban context

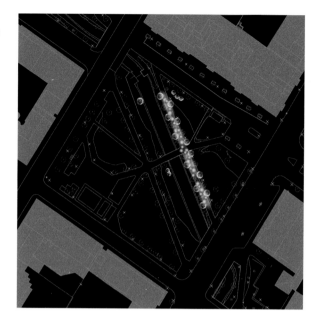

efficient street lighting optics. The park lighting was designed as a flexible system which was programmed to produce both even and uneven distributions of light creating light patches of various sizes on the surface of the path. The lighting reacted to park visitors' movements via a network of motion sensors installed on the trunks of the birch trees that flanked the path. The situation of the test area in the park and the locations of installation luminaires are seen in Fig. 13.1.

With their mobile devices, people could make inquiries about current events and the real-time activity levels of different districts in the city centre, and receive an answer visualised as light playing on the surfaces of the paths and the surrounding trees. The same information was readable as graphical and textual representations on their mobile devices. The service also provided real-time information on the current status of lighting in the park, and how much energy it was consuming. This information was displayed on the user's device. The UE mobile service web-sites were accessible from the park also through QR codes situated on the site (Pihlajaniemi 2013).

In the movement-adaptive scenarios, UE reacted with different lighting patterns to park-goers presence and movement. A protocol with several dynamically chang-ing lighting scenarios was designed for the interviews. In the scenarios, the level of expression gradually rose so that the first ones were very slow and calm with no colour, and the last ones were very intense with lots of colours and quick alterations. The variables changing in the scenarios were light levels, the distribution of light on the path, the use of tree lighting along the path, the colour of light (warm white light only, warm white light with effect colour, and coloured light only), the pace of dynamic changes, and the linearity or non-linearity of lighting behaviour (Pihlajaniemi et al. 2014).

Fig. 13.2 In the 'Events' service, the amount of ongoing events and the ones which are starting within 2 h were displayed in categories with theme colours on a mobile device. In the resulting lighting scheme, luminaires reproduced the amount of different events as spots of thematically coloured lights

Fig. 13.3 Scenario 2

The explicit user interaction with UE was based on the mobile services which provided the user with urban information displayed by park lights in real-time. The sensor-based adaptation to park-goers' presence and movements could be described more as reactive and implicitly interactive. This was due to the technical limitations of the motion sensors that were used. Altogether, each participant experienced 11–14 dynamic scenarios and two lighting schemes based on mobile services (Fig. 13.2). Two of these scenarios did not react to the park-users' movement; these were only programmed to be dynamically altering with changing colours. Examples of different scenarios are presented in Figs. 13.3, 13.4, 13.5, 13.6, and 13.7.

The research aims of the UE pilot were multifaceted. In addition to studying the park visitors' experiences, the design process of the scenarios was utilized in developing a new algorithmic design tool (VirtuAUL) and methodology for

Fig. 13.4 Scenario 4

Fig. 13.5 Scenario 7A

Fig. 13.6 Scenario 9B

Fig. 13.7 An informative and adaptive lighting scenario (Scenario 8A) where the accent colour represents *outdoor air temperature*. This was the default scenario which was on in the park whenever we were not conducting our interviews, or neither one of the 2 min long communicative lighting schemes was on

designing adaptive lighting, which was one of the targets of the Adaptive Urban Lighting project. The design process of the pilot and the development process of the design tool and method are discussed thoroughly in Pihlajaniemi et al. (2014) and Pihlajaniemi (2016), and the VirtuAUL design framework is described in Österlund and Pihlajaniemi (2015). In this article, we strive to gain perspectives into our *participants' emplaced experiences of UE as digital augmentation* through analyzing the research materials which were gathered in-situ in the urban park prior to and during the UE installation. Next, we will delve deeper into the concept of emplacement.

Emplaced Sense Experiences: Theoretical Underpinnings

While it is true that urban lighting can be arguably described as offering primarily visual experiences, we have to concede that even though light might seem ethereal, it is in itself a material phenomenon, and is necessarily cast on a material world. In the case of urban lighting, this is the city, which offers a wealth of sensory experiences. Bille and Sörensen (2007) note that acknowledging the fact that light "has a material dimension raises questions concerning the materiality and sociality of light," arguing further that "light is used to reveal people, places and things in culturally specific ways." Importantly, they go on to explain that they are interested in how light is used to orchestrate how we experience and use spaces and places. This point of view is naturally made more intriguing by the fact that designers' technical range of orchestrating light is increased as more and more 'intelligence' is programmed into luminaires and lighting systems, as is evident in UE; moreover, the line of separation between lighting and the projection of digital content is similarly obscured in urban places, as more and more projections have sprung up in urban centers. Thus, it is productive to understand these novel types of lighting systems as digital augmentation (Aurigi and De Cindio 2008) of spaces and places. Therefore we examine the UE pilot as a situated urban technology that employs intelligent lighting to orchestrate experiences of space and place.

For the examination of situated urban technologies and media architecture, we deem the concept of *emplacement* useful. This concept builds upon the well-established notion of *embodiment*, which was most famously developed by Merleau-Ponty (1945), building on the philosophies of Husserl and Heidegger. Embodiment as a concept is very broad. However, what is important to us here is that it rejects the notion of the duality of body and mind, a central problem in Western philosophy. Dreyfus (1996) has identified different meanings for 'embodiment' in Merleau-Ponty's own work; namely, the physical embodiment of human beings with material qualities and with accompanying *embodied capacities that have limitations*; embodiment as the set of *embodied skills and situational responses* that we develop in response to the natural environment; and the *cultural skills* that we similarly develop in response to the cultural environment. What is important about this notion is that it does not consider these aspects in juxtaposition, but holistically.

Since its conception, embodiment has been an issue of concern in many fields of study, including the social sciences from very early on; for example, Schutz (1967) developed the idea that embodiment is not in opposition with intersubjectivity, the notion that experiences can be shared, which naturally forms the basis of social and cultural studies. Embodiment, then, continues to be a widely used and productive concept in the social sciences. Interestingly, embodiment has become an important touchstone between philosophy and the natural sciences. The philosopher Daniel Dennett (1992) has explored the bodily basis of cognition and the phenomenological experience through examples from post-positivist experiments. From the point of view of linguistics, Lakoff and Johnson have argued at length for embodied cognition in their widely-read works (Lakoff and Johnson 1980, 1999). Furthermore, cognitive scientists Ward and Stapleton (2012), among others, argue for a *4e* model of cognition; the e's stand for enacted, embodied, embedded and extended (as well as affective). In the realm of applied sciences, issues around the theory of embodiment has been introduced into the field of human-computer interaction (HCI) by Winograd and Flores (1986), Lucy Suchman (1987) and Dourish (2004), as recounted by Marshall and Hornecker (2013). Thus, the concept of embodiment has garnered enormous interest in the wider research community not only across disciplinary boundaries, but also across differing ontological and epistemological notions.

Exploring embodiment from the point of view of the social sciences, it was David Howes who first called for a move beyond the notion of embodiment towards the paradigm of *emplacement*, which "suggests the sensuous interrelationship of body-mind-environment" (Howes 2005, p. 7). This Howes coupled with the feeling of being at home, juxtaposing it with the negative feeling of displacement. The notion of emplacement was soon championed further by Sarah Pink (2009, 2011). What is noteworthy about Pink's use of the concept is that she uses emplacement as a theoretical lens through which she conducts her analysis, rather than as a descriptor of a body of academic work or a positive feeling of situatedness, as Howes had done. However, while Pink (2011) maintains that the major contribution of *embodiment* to her own field, the social sciences and cultural anthropology in particular, is precisely the eradication of the distinction between the body and the mind, we have to acknowledge here that embodiment does not consider the embodied mind in isolation of *place* either; the notion of being-in-the-world, and thus, being in place, is absolutely central to the idea of embodiment.

In architectural theory, phenomenology has occurred in two waves according to Hale (2013). It was first brought centre-stage in the 1970s and 1980s, especially by Norberg-Schulz (1980), whose major interests lay in the study of places, which he described in the following manner:

A concrete term for environment is place. It is common usage to say that acts and occurrences take place. In fact it is meaningless to imagine any happening without reference to a locality. Place is evidently an integral part of existence.

What then, do we mean with the word 'place'? Obviously we mean something more than abstract location. We mean a totality made up of concrete things having material substance, shape, texture and colour. Together these things determine an 'environmental character'. (Norberg-Schulz 1980, p. 6)

In its second wave, Hale (2013, p. 22) identifies "a dramatic shift of interest from the macro to the micro scale" in architectural phenomenology. Issues of concern here deal with tectonics, materiality and the sensory connections between the built environment and experiencing subjects, with Frampton (1995) and Pallasmaa (2012) as important figures.

Against this background of scholarship, there is an obvious overlap in embodiment and emplacement, and they should not be seen in opposition. While emplacement is a later development, birthed out of the tradition of embodiment, emplacement should not be touted as a replacement to embodiment. Rather, owing to terminology, we consider these two terms to highlight different aspects of being-in-the-world; emplacement can be seen as bringing *place* to the fore. Since concepts are tremendously powerful, we wish to highlight the role of place as an important point of departure for understanding individual and cultural experiences. While embodiment recognizes that we are embodied subjects, experiencing our lifeworlds, we wish to underscore that we understand these lifeworlds as constituting of places with equally individual histories, having material properties, and existing themselves in a cultural and natural context. Thus emplacement as a concept also gives us an advantage in comparison to the concept of *embeddedness* of the 4e's (Ward and Stapleton 2012).

With its focus on the relationship between the sensuous body and its surroundings, emplacement seems a productive point of view for architectural research, in which place is a central concern. In fact, from an architectural perspective, Pink's (2009) summarizing comment that much of the current interdisciplinary scholarship urges us to "start thinking about bodies as parts of places" might even seem absurd to begin with; as it would seem inconceivable for architectural research and practice to consider anything as not being inherently situated in its real environment. After all, this is where the most foundational theory in the field departs from; this is where the first-year architectural studio project begins: the site, or place. On the other hand, many architects (Jacobs 1961; Gehl 2011 [1987]; Alexander et al. 1977) have already decades ago faulted their profession for having an insufficient understanding of different kinds of people and how they actually experience and use urban places. Through the concept of emplacement, then, we strive to approach lived reality with a firm understanding that not only do we need to understand places *and* bodies, but that they are inextricably intertwined.

Emplacement also highlights the role of the sensuous body through which we acquire knowledge about the material and socio-cultural world around us. Furthermore, we are cognizant that senses do not work in isolation; while sight might be the sense that is being predominantly served by lighting, we deem it important to take into account the intersensoriality (e.g. Howes 2005) of emplaced experience. Finally, we are aware of temporality and personal history as an important perspective of emplacement; we all have varying prior experiences and lifespans of varying lengths.

The fact that the notion of emplacement has arisen from the field of cultural anthropology is another factor that affects the application of the emplacement. As

Pink has done, emplacement is seen here as a theoretical lens through which we examine participants' experiences, attitudes, opinions and perceptions.

Methods and Materials

Due to the highly context-driven and dynamic nature of the study setting, we decided to employ walking interviews as the main method of gaining insight into our participants' experiences. These were complemented with semi-structured theme interviews conducted in the nearby café and in the park prior to the walks and before any adaptive lighting installations had been made. The purpose of these preliminary interviews was to collect background information about our participants and knowledge about their views concerning the site, and to gain a general sense of place that would inform our subsequent analysis of the UE walking interviews. However, it also gave our participants a chance to reflect on their personal relationship with the park, and their views and experiences of urban lighting, preparing them for the walking interviews.

As the name suggests, walking interviews refer to a set of qualitative research techniques used increasingly by, e.g., social scientists and geographers, where researchers walk with participants (Evans and Jones 2011). The strength of this particular approach lies in its assumed ability to provide an access to participants' attitudes, knowledge and perceptions regarding the surrounding environment. Thus, it can help the researcher to understand facets of local contexts, and for example, social architecture of settings (Carpiano 2009; Kusenbach 2003). According to the typology of walking interviews presented by Evans and Jones (2011), the method ranges from "natural go-alongs" to "guided walks"; the first type of walking interview refers to studies where researcher is walked through a route determined by the participant; the latter refers to an interview where the route is determined by the researcher. Naturally, these different approaches yield different types of research material; guided walks do not, for example, reveal anything about the ways people navigate in their surroundings.

Our choice was to employ "guided walks"; in practice, we walked back and forth along a predetermined route in the park with our participants. As explained earlier, the studied augmentation was installed along one pathway in the park which resulted in the relatively strict interview choreography. The other reason for orchestrating the walking interviews carefully beforehand was the large amount of studied scenarios and the designerly aim to present every one of them to each participant from the same perspective. Otherwise it would have been interesting to let people wander in the park and familiarize themselves with the lights more freely. Our method was somewhat characterized by restricted bodily movements, even though we told every participant that stopping, looking back, etc., is of course allowed. Some of them followed this advice but some just seemed to adjust their bodily movements to the movements of the researchers. The questions in the walking interviews were centered on the different scenarios. Immediately after the guided walks, participants were also interviewed about the overall experience. The interviews were recorded

Fig. 13.8 Walking interviews in the park with Urban Echoes

with an audio recorder and video camera. In total, four persons took part in each interview: one researcher was interviewing the participant, the designer was participating in the discussions and changed the scenarios with a smart phone, and a third person was operating the video camera.

Overall, the study setup was highly complex, with a live, real-world installation being used for the scenario-based interview. Thus, often the interviews were suddenly interrupted with one of the information based lightings by an unknown user. This provoked one of our participants to exclaim: "This gave me a shock!" The designer's presence was another major factor in the interviews. On the one hand, detailed information could be given to the participants about why or how the installation worked the way it did; on the other hand, shy interviewees might have been more lenient with their criticisms. However, we stressed the fact that we appreciated and valued all their opinions, and noted that during the interview many participants became very talkative and open about their opinions as they got used to the situation. Selecting the set of scenarios used in the interviews was rather challenging. Firstly, the amount of scenarios could not be very large in order to not exhaust the interviewees. In addition, the wintertime climate conditions were challenging as the temperature ranged between -17 and $+1$ °C, and sometimes it was snowing so much that the video camera had to be sheltered with a hat. Secondly, due to the complexity of the research setting and question, the various characteristics of the presented scenarios, as well as the order in which they were presented, could easily influence the answers.

During the process of 5 weeks of conducting the interviews, some more scenario variations were added to the protocol. This was due to the fact that we realised from the interview answers that the choice of colours in lighting schemes had a strong effect on the answers and attitudes. In some cases the dislike against chosen effect colour dominated the opinion substantially so that it overwhelmed the experience of other features of the scenario. Thus we showed another variation. Some of the interviewees' comments and wishes inspired further developments and refinements of some scenarios, and these were then presented in the following interviews. This enhanced the participatory and dialogic character of the research method.

To some extent, our study was inspired by ethnography; we understand it as a methodology based on joint knowledge production where researcher and study participant(s) create new understandings of phenomena together. The study especially resembles "short-term ethnography" which has been discussed by Pink and Morgan (2013) in their recent article. The authors claim their approach should not be understood as a "quick and dirty" path to doing qualitative research; rather, they argue it should be defined as a more deliberate and interventional way of conducting ethnography. According to Pink and Morgan, short-term ethnography is characterized by several forms of intensity that lead to deep ways of knowing. For instance, we have employed the probes methodology for similar purposes in our earlier studies (Luusua et al. 2015). For example, the use of the video represents a useful tool as it leaves rich traces of the short encounters with the study participants. Our study was an intervention meant to provoke new experiences in our participants, and intensity characterizes these encounters well. However, these encounters did not take place in everyday life situations of the study participants; rather, we enmeshed an everyday life locale with extraordinary, temporary elements.

We decided to recruit two groups of participants, one consisting of young adults (11 participants 20–29 years old; 6 females, 5 males) and seniors (5 participants over 65 years old; 3 females and 2 males). One of the young adults only participated in the preliminary interview. These groups were chosen initially because we wanted to question some essentialist everyday notions that are usually associated with these groups, where the youngsters are tech-savvy and the seniors technophobic. The in-depth manner in which these interviews were conducted in resulted in dozens of hours of intensely rich video material and audio transcripts. Due to the chosen method being highly work-intensive both on the field as well as in the analysis phase, this overall number of participants was deemed sensible.

We recruited our participants through various email lists – these included hobby groups, and student and professional organizations – and through visiting an activity center for elderly citizens. The volunteers represented a wealth of different educational, personal and employment backgrounds. They also had differing relationships to the park – some visited it often, some hardly ever. However, we must also acknowledge that there was a bias in recruiting participants, as those volunteering were probably more active personalities and may have had a prior interest in the subject at hand. Nevertheless, our participants came from diverse walks of life, from the arts and humanities to technical and medical fields, and from various educational backgrounds. These professional backgrounds played a part in their perceptions and attitudes. We consider these participant experiences as having prompted reflexive accounts, created in mutual knowledge-production with us as the researchers and interpreters of their stories. We did not strive to create totally naturalistic, observation-based results, as we were interested in participants' emic accounts.

Analysis

It is these theoretical underpinnings that inform our descriptive analysis of our walking interviews and semi-structured interviews. Thus, we read our research materials from the point of view of emplacement, with a special focus on the place in question: its identity, history, materiality, and future. Thus, we present our analysis in two parts: the first part consists of results pertaining to the park's sense of place. Secondly, we try to gain a knowledge about the informational, interactive and adaptive qualities of the UE pilot through our participant's experiences of the walking interviews. This analysis we conduct through an awareness of not only the park's sense of place, but also of our participants' embodied abilities as temporal, material and cultural beings.

Sense of Place

As stated, we conducted semi-structured theme interviews with our participants in-situ and in a nearby café before the installation was built. A major theme that emerged in the interviews was the dual nature of the park: It was perceived simultaneously as quite an attractive park, while being slightly shunned during the night. Most participants described the park in fairly positive terms, especially in the summer and autumn conditions. Several participants, especially senior ones, admired the work that had gone into the flower arrangements. The birch trees were often considered to convey a sense of Finnishness, and the small channel was equally a natural element that was viewed favourably. In the winter, when the interviews took place, participants mostly considered the park to be quite dull, except for one young adult male, who thought winter was the most attractive time of the year esthetically. This wintery dullness can be explained not only with the absence of vegetation, but with the then-prevailing lighting situation. This was deemed adequate by some, but mostly boring because of the spherical luminaires that flanked the paths. These provide all of the park's lighting besides the light that spilled from the surroundings, as our participants noted. One senior male saw the spherical luminaires as ugly and even wasteful, as they projected light indiscriminately in all directions. Other participants, regardless of age or gender, showed similar feelings.

Importantly, one our young adult female participants stated outright: "They warned us freshman year that all kinds of stuff has happened here, people call this the rape park", referring to the series of three rape incidents which had occurred 8 years prior (Kaleva 2006). Both young adults and seniors referenced these incidents during some point in their interview. The incidents shook the city to its core not only due to the fact that these incidents had occurred almost in plain sight (albeit in night-time), but also because Nordic countries have traditionally enjoyed a high level of security on the street-level. However, parks have garnered notoriety elsewhere as well, and as such, have been the subject of studies on the 'geographies of fear' (e.g. Madge 1997). At the time of the study, the park was also known to our participants for its late-night grill kiosk and its sometimes rowdy and intoxicated clientele. Many participants also mentioned that there were often intoxicated individuals in the park during the day as well. One elderly female said she never visited the park at all, as she had experienced something that gave her a feeling of not being safe. In a contradictory manner, a young adult male stated that although he did not feel unsafe, he had considered going around the park when he had seen a suspicious-looking crowd in there in the night.

Participants were unanimously of the opinion that functionally this was a "pass-through park", with many opting to use those particular words. The park's main path offers a "chance of a shortcut" in a city shaped in the form of a grid, encouraging a flow from the main pedestrian area towards residential areas and the train station. Stopping here to sit was not perceived of as an attractive option due to noise from the traffic and the intoxicated individuals that sometimes occupied the benches. Yet, for most of our participants this was a frequent route through which they either walked or bicycled.

We captured the sense of place in the park at a time of a definite sea-change in its long history. Some of our senior participants had long prior experiences of how the park had changed during their lifetime. One elderly female, who had lived in the city for 75 years, reminisced about the wooden pavilion that stood in place of the kiosk, and the small-two story wooden house next to the park. Yet she also reminisced about the fear that she had associated with the dark, badly lit night-time park 30 years ago. True enough, it was in the 1980s that the late-night grill kiosk was added, worsening the night-time situation. By the time of our interviews, the bus stop behind which the rapes took place had been moved elsewhere as public transit in the city has been rearranged to go on a designated 'public transport street'. The kiosk had been closed down, awaiting dismantling (after our research, it has been replaced by a high-end café), which many of the participants noted with pleasure. It was against this background that our participants experienced the UE pilot.

Bodily Rhythms, Control and Intelligent Adaptation

The walking interviews lasted for approximately 1–1,5 h due to the high number of lighting scenarios we explored which each participant, and thus, the walking interviews unfolded in a very iterative manner as we walked along the path back and forth. The mobile nature of the interviews inspired participants to envision different kinds of bodily rhythms and mobilities[2] that can take place in the park, and how this particular way of technological augmentation would suit them. For

---

[2]Here we are mainly interested with individuals' everyday mobilities. For a seminal text on the study of mobilities in general, see Urry (2000).

example, cycling is a highly popular way for students to get around the city and move between the campus and the city centre both in the summer and in the winter, and this was reflected in many of our young adult participants' views on mobility. However, it was also reflected in their personal experiences with the park, and this had an overall effect on their opinions, ideas and current experiences with the. Senior participants' mobilities, however, were much more heterogeneous. While one senior male participant described his everyday life as constant and deliberate movement by foot or by bicycle, going from place to place in a radius of several kilometres, another elderly female participant said she almost never visited the park, despite living only a couple of kilometers away in an adjoining part of the city. Very mobile participants seemed to underscore issues of adaptation rhythm, i.e., how quickly and in what manner UE was able to adapt to park-goers' movements. For one participant, one of our researchers even ran along the pathway to demonstrate that the lighting would be able to adapt to a fast pace. For another participant, however, the worry was rather about whether she would be left in the dark if she remained stationary and the sensors would not detect her. The overarching theme here was the concern of having their movements being controlled by the technology, rather than vice versa.

Yet overall, participants were clearly of the opinion that the fact that the light 'followed' them around as they moved on the path was a decisively positive aspect. All participants had different ways of justifying this explicitly. One participant stated that it made him feel like he personally mattered. Many felt that it enhanced safety. Some underscored the importance of economic or environmental aspects: not wasting lighting on places where it was not needed. Even when specifically questioned about issues of surveillance, participants were not worried about possible surveillance aspects. In the preliminary interviews, some participants had doubted whether or not it would be technologically and practically feasible to make urban lighting adapt to movement, but these participants did not react negatively when they experienced this themselves. Intelligent adaptation, at this level at least, garnered wide-ranging acceptance. Moreover, some participants noted that they themselves had motion-sensor lighting in their own driveways. Thus, we can hypothesize this type of a technology, although in a more crude form, had been somewhat domesticated as a consumer product by several of our participants, creating a continuum of prior experience (Ylipulli et al. 2014a) of using the technology at home to experiencing it in public places.

Digitally Augmented Sense of Place and Identity

Overall, the scenarios and mobile services clearly evoked change in the park's sense of place through adaptation, interactivity, and ambient and explicit informativity. For one young female participant, the scenario which included colourful spots of light on the pathway evoked the metaphor of "rag rug", a traditional rug which is made of recycled old clothing and thus is usually a mix of colours. This kind of a rug is normally only found in homes, and thus belongs in the sphere of very intimate spaces. This metaphor of domesticity was especially interesting since we were still in a highly public and busy place, with large amounts of people passing through. One young adult male participant said that one scenario would be perfect for a romantic walk with his girlfriend. While we did not ask, it would be dubious to suggest that this kind of an activity would have occurred to him in this ill-reputed park in its normal evening appearance. The most extreme scenario with rapidly changing colour lights, was unfailingly described as a "disco" by our participants. This was indeed meant as a horror scenario, indicative of the less desirable things that could be achieved with the technology, and true enough, most participants rejected it outright. However, participants also agreed that while the scenario was rather "epileptic", as stated by many, it would be suitable for an event, especially with music. The busy rhythm was very often coupled with the idea that music should play in the background. And true enough, we observed a group of young people dancing in the light, in the middle of the pathway while we were conducting an interview. During the interviews, we observed also other new ways of using the park, such as photography, staging a costume play, having a picnic, and sitting on the benches, all in below-freezing conditions. Thus, the scenarios were able to introduce novel ways of experiencing and using the space.

Appropriate Augmentation?

However, sense of place also strongly dictated what was considered appropriate for the augmentation. For example, one senior female participant exclaimed that shades of red and pink were definitely her favourite colours, but that they were not suitable for illuminating birch trees. She was utterly convinced that blue was the colour that suited better. Another senior female participant said that she did not like the red on the trees either, because it was reminiscent of a forest fire. The retired technician, a senior male, expressed indignation from a utilitarian point of view "Unnecessary, totally unnecessary for a park!" He associated the use of colour in the park as something exceedingly intimate ("These are bedroom colours"), and wasteful. Locational appropriateness pertaining to seasonal variation in the park was also reflected upon by many participants. The augmentation they felt, should adapt to the prevailing conditions, but there were two opposing tactics according to the time of the year: while some participants felt that the coldness should not be highlighted with cold colours, others felt that cool colours and hues were appropriate for winter. Warm colours were quite uniformly desired for autumn conditions. Similarly, it was commonly desired that lighting levels be higher in the autumn when there's no snow on the ground. A slow, softly, changing rhythm of change was generally regarded as suitable in the park. As discussed, the rhythm of change was a powerful way of orchestrating experience in UE. Overall, however, desirable esthetics were tied up with locational context. The interplay between the dynamic change in the materiality of place and the dynamic change induced by the technology produced a wealth of different experiences, reflected in our participants' commentary. One participant also explicitly stated that the pilot, if made permanent, might change the whole identity of the park, hypothesizing that this might become the 'purple park' if the scenario with the magenta-coloured scenario would be allowed to stay on. The influence of UE on the atmosphere of the park was, overall, very significant.

Ambient Information

Locational appropriateness factored in strongly with the informational aspects of the technology as well. The use of the pilot as an ambient display (Wisneski et al. 1998) was deemed a fascinating aspect by most of the participants, but individual opinions varied greatly in regards to the more sophisticated informational services it offered. For example, one young adult participant, who enjoyed going to events, was certain he would see what was available in the city through the ambient/mobile Events service, but many others were of the opinion that while the application was definitely "a fun idea", they might not use it personally. Similarly, the service that showed ambiently where people were in the city, by mapping Bluetooth sensors as a kind of a heatmap on top of the park, was considered interesting by many, especially if it ran constantly as the sole feature, as suggested by one young adult female participant. This would have made the feature more easily legible. Interestingly, one senior male participant felt that it would even encourage public fights, echoing the seniors' overarching preoccupation with safety. Similarly, the energy consumption service was considered very interesting by those participants who underscored either economic or environmental issues in general, but not by all. Prior interests and personal values, then, guided much of our participants' views, making both young adults' and seniors' groups quite heterogeneous when it came to what kind of ambient information they deemed interesting. Importantly, all participants noted that the legibility of the ambient information should be quite clear; many suggested the addition of some sort of physical placards to explain what services were being offered, and how to decode the meaning of ambient information.

Through the ambient informative services, anyone could change the colours and the general atmosphere in the park. This possibility was greeted with a generally positive attitude by our participants, and no one thought it a bad thing that someone else might do this as well. When asked whether they might want to use ambient lighting to communicate something else, a wealth of creative ideas emerged: some were related to awareness-raising or ideological purposes (staging a demonstration), some were related to personal and emotional expression, and some were related to advertising. Participants also expressed interest in producing their own content. Overall, then, these inherently participatory and interactive features of UE were greeted with interest and enthusiasm, which integrated the interactive properties with emplaced practices.

Meaningful Emplaced Experiences

However, the service that participants were most uniformly excited about was by far the simplest one: participants were told that the accent colour of the lights adapted dynamically according to the temperature: for example, they were told that since this day was a very cold day, the light was very blue, and when temperatures rose closer to 0° C (in the winter), the colour would become pinkish or reddish in hue. Participants were not aware that this feature had not actually been programmed into the system; rather, a suitably coloured ready-made scenario was summoned according to the temperature of the day. Thus, some participants saw blue hues and some more magenta-like colours. While some participants were of the opinion that they did not want the ambient colour to make them feel even colder (and thus, perhaps the colours should be reversed), our participants uniformly expressed great enthusiasm about this 'thermometer' feature as a fun and relevant ambient information service. While its simplicity as a technological application might be even frustrating from a designers' point of view, it is important to try to understand why this was the case with our participants.

In order to explain this phenomenon, we have to refer to our earlier work (Luusua et al. in press) as this was reminiscent of results we have gained in the study of a wholly other urban technology: public urban displays. Specifically, we have found that environmentally integrated computing applications (which constitutes most of what might be termed media architecture) that offer meaningful emplaced interactions are very popular. By this we mean, among other facets, that the service is connected to an aspect inherent to its immediate locational surroundings, the place; and that it relates to their whole bodies, and creates a continuum of usage with their prior experiences that renders the artefact understandable. In this case, this aspect was that of the temperature, a highly locational and ever-changing aspect of place that affects all embodied beings, and which also forms a continuum with their prior experiences with traditional thermometers. In the case of public displays, a meaningfully emplaced technology was the UBI Postcard application where users were able to take a picture of themselves and possibly their friends, with the cityscape visible behind them, and send this via email. In this case as well, we can observe that the application included the users as embodied beings with embodied cultural skills, all tied together in locational context.

Discussion: Towards Interdisciplinary and Emplaced Interaction Design

UE demonstrated a powerful way of affecting the experience of the park through digital augmentation. It was able to the change the atmosphere of the park within seconds, which was reflected in our walking interviews. The use of lighting as a medium enhanced the effectiveness of UE as digital augmentation, as light enmeshed itself effortlessly with the materiality of the place. Our participants' embodied skills and cultural abilities were of the essence in determining the manner, and to what extent, our participants were able to read and respond to this highly dynamic urban environment. Most participants regarded UE in an overall positive light due to esthetic, environmental, economic or safety reasons. However, many also noted its identity and image-building potential for the whole city, coupling it with the technology-identity of the city. Digital augmentation in this form as an urban competitiveness factor was unanimously seen as a beneficial aspect; no one considered it in a negative light. What emerged overall in the walking interviews, then, was the holistic nature of this technology. It is important to also point out that the context of the study played a crucial part in how UE actually came to life. Thus, it is necessary to study further various kinds of media architecture and urban computing installations through the lens of emplacement.

The digital augmentation of urban places, then, relates to all aspects of city-making and urban life. Thus, interdisciplinary work is necessary to understand this phenomenon; an issue that was evident in the UE pilot, which benefited from a close collaboration between architects and cultural anthropologists. The ambitious aim here was to not only inform design, a worthy goal in itself, but to also form a very broad understanding of UE as a phenomenon. Thus, a sensibility that merged both methodological and theoretical traditions and ideas in an interdisciplinary manner was useful. On the level of research practice, this meant the thoughtful re-conceptualisation and application of methods in the form of walking interviews in a real-world short-term pilot. Thus, our study also indicates that it can be highly useful to dismantle disciplinary boundaries within a design process.

Theoretical concepts, however, also hold tremendous power. It is important to be able to communicate what central ontological and epistemological convictions guide one's work, and what is valued in one's field. Embodiment is an important fundamental concept in the study of experiences, and through emplacement, a focus on place both highlights and effectively communicates what is held most dear by, for example, architectural researchers and practitioners. Communicating and conceptualising the fundamental aspects of one's own professional background is the basis of interdisciplinary work. Thus, the concept of emplacement proved itself to be an effective tool for both descriptive analysis and interdisciplinary communication.

An important overall realization achieved through the analysis of the gained materials was that even the more mundane-seeming, usability-oriented participant comments had deep roots in their embodied physical and cultural capabilities, their various urban movement patterns, prior experiences, expectations and personal value systems. These took specific form in the context of the park that also had its own sense of place, its own materiality, history and identity. Architectural places and spaces which have been infused by computing systems cannot be fully understood without taking place into account properly. Thus, while the larger tradition around the concept of embodiment, which has been brought over into HCI design and research, introduces a foundation on which we can begin to build interdisciplinary research and practice, we would like to highlight the necessity of what we might term 'emplaced interaction design', an interaction design practice that would acknowledge on a fundamental level the complexity of embodied interactions in *place*.

Acknowledgements We would like to thank our participants, the Academy of Finland for their support of the UBI Metrics and the Adaptive Urban Lighting projects, as well as the Nokia Foundation for their support. Special thanks to Dr. Tiina Suopajärvi, Dr. Aulikki Herneoja, Dr. Jonathan Hale, MSc. (Arch.) Toni Österlund, MSc. (Arch.) Anniina Valjus, MSc. (Arch) Tuulikki Tanska, and the students from the Multimedia Systems Course at the University of Oulu Department of Computer Science and Engineering. Figure 13.1 copyright Toni Österlund and Henrika Pihlajaniemi, Figs. 13.2, 13.3, 13.4, 13.5, 13.6, 13.7, and 13.8 copyright Henrika Pihlajaniemi.

References

Alexander C, Ishikawa S, Silverstein M (1977) A pattern language. Oxford University Press, New York

Aurigi A, De Cindio F (eds) (2008) Augmented urban spaces: articulating the physical and electronic city. Ashgate Publishing, Ltd, Aldershot

Bille M, Sørensen TF (2007) An anthropology of luminosity: the agency of light. J Mater Cult 12(3):263–284

Brynskov M, Bermudez J, Fernandez M, Korsgaard H, Mulder I, Piskorek K, Rekow L, de Waal M (2014) Urban interaction design: towards city making. Urban IxD Booksprint. [online] http://repository.tudelft.nl/view/ir/uuid:9b936bee-c846-4283-9dc9-1804018c8efe

Brynskov M, Dalsgaard P, Halskov K (2015) Media architecture: engaging urban experiences in public space. In: Loussau J, Stevens Q (eds) The uses of art in public space. Routledge, London

Carpiano RM (2009) Come take a walk with me: the "Go-Along" interview as a novel method for studying the implications of place for health and well-being. Health Place 15(1):263–272

Coyne R (2010) The tuning of place: sociable spaces and pervasive digital media. MIT Press, Cambridge, MA

Dennett D (1992) Consciousness explained. Penguin, London

Dourish P (2004) Where the action is: the foundations of embodied interaction. MIT Press, Cambridge, MA

Dourish P (2006) Re-space-ing place: "place" and "space" ten years on. In: Proceedings of the 2006 20th anniversary conference on Computer supported cooperative work (CSCW '06). ACM, New York, pp 299–308. Doi:10.1145/1180875.1180921

Dreyfus HL (1996) The current relevance of Merleau-Ponty's phenomenology of embodiment. Electron J Anal Philos 4:1–16

Evans J, Jones P (2011) The walking interview: methodology, mobility and place. Appl Geogr 31(2):849–858

Fatah gen Schieck A (2006) Towards an integrated architectural media space. First Monday, Special Issue, (4). [online]

Finnish Meteorological Institute. Oulun paikallissää. Referred 14.08.2015. http://ilmatieteenlaitos.fi/saa/oulu

Frampton K (1995) In: Cava J (ed) Studies in tectonic culture: the poetics of construction in nineteenth and twentieth century architecture. MIT Press, Cambridge, MA

Gehl J (2011) [1987] Life between buildings: using public space. The Danish Architectural Press, Copenhagen

Giddens A (1984) The constitution of society. Polity Press, Cambridge

Goffman E (1959) The presentation of self in everyday life. Penguin, New York

Hale J (2013) Critical phenomenology: architecture and embodiment. Archit Ideas XII:18–37
Harrison S, Dourish P (1996) Re-place-ing space: the roles of place and space in collaborative systems. In Ackerman MS (ed) Proceedings of the 1996 ACM conference on Computer supported cooperative work (CSCW '96). ACM, New York, pp 67–76. 10.1145/240080.240193
Howes D (2005) Empire of the senses. Berg Publishers, Oxford
Jacobs J (1961) The death and life of great American cities. The Modern Library, New York
Jurmu M, Ylipulli J, Luusua A (2015) I've had it: group therapy for interdisciplinary researchers. In: Proceedings of the 5th decennial Aarhus conference: critical alternatives, vol 2. pp 27–29. Computer Science, Aarhus University, Denmark
Kaleva (2006) Joukkoraiskaus keskellä Oulua. Retreived 16 Aug 2015. http://www.kaleva.fi/uutiset/oulu/joukkoraiskaus-keskella-oulua/121073/
Kindberg T, Chalmers M, Paulos E (2007) Guest editors' introduction: urban computing. IEEE Pervasive Comput 6(3):18–20
Kitchin R (2014) Making sense of smart cities: addressing present shortcomings. Camb J Reg Econ Soci. First published online 21 Oct. http://cjres.oxfordjournals.org/content/early/2014/10/20/cjres.rsu027
Kusenbach M (2003) Street phenomenology: the go-along as ethnographic research tool. Ethnography 4(3):455–485
Lakoff G, Johnson M (1980) Metaphors we live by. University of Chicago Press, Chicago
Lakoff G, Johnson M (1999) Philosophy in the flesh: the embodied mind and its challenge to western thought. Basic Books, New York
Luusua A, Ylipulli J, Kukka H, Ojala T (in press) Experiencing the Hybrid City: The role of digital technology in public urban places. In: Hannigan J, Richards G (eds) The SAGE handbook of urban studies. SAGE, London
Luusua A, Ylipulli J, Jurmu M, Pihlajaniemi H, Markkanen P, Ojala T (2015) Evaluation probes. In: Proceedings of the SIGCHI conference on human factors in computing systems. ACM, New York, pp 85–94.
Madge C (1997) Public parks and the geography of fear. Tijdschr Econ Soc Geogr 88:237–250
McCullough M (2005) Digital ground: architecture, pervasive computing, and environmental knowing. MIT Press, Cambridge MA
Merleau-Ponty M ([1945] 2013) Phenomenology of perception. Routledge, London
Norberg-Schulz C (1980) Genius loci: towards a phenomenology of architecture. Rizzoli, New York
Official Statistics of Finland (OSF) (2015) Use of information and communications technology by individuals [e-publication]. ISSN=2341-8710. 2013. Statistics Finland, Helsinki. Referred: 14.8.2015.
Ojala T, Kukka H, Lindén T, Heikkinen T, Jurmu M, Hosio S, Kruger F (2010) UBI-hotspot 1.0: large-scale long-term deployment of interactive public displays in a city center. In: Internet and web applications and services (ICIW), 2010 fifth international conference on, IEEE Washington, DC, pp 285–294.
Österlund T, Pihlajaniemi H (2015) VirtuAUL – a design framework for adaptive lighting. Proceedings of eCAADe 2015 – 33rd annual conference 16th-18th September 2015. Wien
Pallasmaa J (2012) The eyes of the skin: architecture and the senses. Wiley, Hoboken NJ
Pihlajaniemi H (2013) Stories and echoes – communicating through adaptive urban lighting. In: Proceedings of PLDC 4th global lighting design convention 30.10.-2.11.2013 in Copenhagen/Denmark. VIA-Verlag, Gütersloh, Germany. ISBN 978-3-9811940-2-9
Pihlajaniemi H (2016) Designing and experiencing adaptive lighting. Case studies with adaptation, interaction and participation. Doctoral dissertation. University of Oulu Graduate School; University of Oulu, Oulu School of Architecture, Acta Universitatis Ouluensis H 3
Pihlajaniemi H, Österlund T, Herneoja A (2014) Urban echoes: adaptive and communicative urban lighting in the virtual and the real. In: Proceedings of the 2nd media architecture biennale conference: world cities. ACM, New York, pp 48–57.
Pink S (2009) Doing sensory ethnography. Sage Publications, London

Pink S (2011) From embodiment to emplacement: re-thinking competing bodies, senses and spatialities. Sport Educ Soc 16(3):343–355

Pink S, Morgan J (2013) Short-term ethnography: intense routes to knowing. Symb Interact 36(3):351–361. Taylor & Francis, Abingdon

Schutz A (1967) The phenomenology of the social world. Northwestern University Press, Evanston

Tuan YF (1977) Space and place: the perspective of experience. University of Minnesota Press, Minneapolis

Urry J (2000) Sociology beyond societies: mobilities for the twenty-first century. Routledge, London

Ward D, Stapleton M (2012) Es are good. Cognition as enacted, embodied, embedded, affective and extended. In: Paglieri F (ed) Consciousness in interaction: the role of the natural and social context in shaping consciousness. John Benjamins Publishing, Amsterdam

Winograd T, Flores F (1986) Understanding computers and cognition: a new foundation for design. Intellect Books

Williams A, Dourish P (2006) Imagining the city: the cultural dimensions of urban computing. Computer 39(9):38–43

Willis KS, Aurigi A (2011) Hybrid spaces: presence, rhythms and performativity. In: Intelligent Environments (IE), 2011 7th international conference on, IEEE, New York, pp 100–106

Wisneski C, Ishii H, Dahley A (1998) Ambient displays: turning architectural space into an interface between people and digital information. Cooperative buildings: integrating information, organization, and architecture. pp 22–32

Ylipulli J, Luusua A, Kukka H, Ojala T (2014a) Winter is coming: introducing climate sensitive urban computing. In: Proceedings of the 2014 conference on designing interactive systems. ACM, New York, pp 647–656

Ylipulli J, Suopajärvi T, Ojala T, Kostakos V, Kukka H (2014b) Municipal WiFi and interactive displays: appropriation of new technologies in public urban spaces. Technol Forecast Soc Chang 89:145–160

Chapter 14
Reading and Responding to the Digital Footprints of Mobile Visitors

Ben Bedwell

Abstract Improvements in wireless infrastructures and personal mobile devices now make it possible for visitor sites to offer locative media experiences as an option for outdoor visitor experiences. However, while developing a design for such experiences is relatively easy, understanding how that design will play out in the real world is not. This chapter presents findings from three research engagements in which partners from the cultural heritage sector used a web-based tool to design and deploy locative media experiences. From thematic analysis of the findings, we show how our partners appropriated visualisations of digital footprints – geolocation data reported by visitors' mobile devices – to understand visitor behaviour and the interaction between the experience designs, wireless infrastructures and physical environment. We demonstrate how data interrogation "at the desk" and observation "in the field" can be combined in an effective cycle of iterative refinement, in an approach to location-based experience design that fitted around our partners' day-to-day work to manage outdoor visitor attractions.

Introduction

Location-based experiences and "locative media[1]" can be attributed an extensive history of investigation by Human Computer Interaction (HCI) researchers, initiated by seminal work such as ParcTab (Schilit et al. 1994) and Cyberguide (Long et al. 1996). Drawing on a technology-mediated convergence (or "spatial turn" (Thielmann 2010) of numerous other disciplines, including architecture, media and the social sciences (Hemment 2006) and supported by the ubiquity of location-aware mobile devices, physical space is used to add context to digital media (and vice versa) (Galloway and Ward 2006). This has resulted in applications that create a

---

[1]Digital media tied to particular locations, coined at http://locative.x-i.net

B. Bedwell (✉)
Horizon Digital Economy Research Institute, The University of Nottingham, Jubilee Campus, Triumph Road, Nottingham, NG72TU, UK
e-mail: benjamin.bedwell@nottingham.ac.uk

© Springer International Publishing Switzerland 2016
N.S. Dalton et al. (eds.), *Architecture and Interaction*,
Human–Computer Interaction Series, DOI 10.1007/978-3-319-30028-3_14

spectrum of augmented reality and 'hybrid spaces' (de Souza e Silva 2006) where a person's location and movement (as reported by their mobile device) determine what digital content is delivered by their mobile.

A rich array of location-based experiences (LBEs) have emerged, including pervasive games (Benford et al. 2004), art (Tuters and Varnelis 2006), performance (Bedwell et al. 2009), culture and heritage (Rennick-Egglestone et al. 2013), and tourism (Durrant et al. 2012; Hawking et al. 2005). In this chapter we reflect on our research into the process of *designing* LBEs, specifically those created around locative media. Interest in supporting the design process is not new: previous HCI research has contributed software that enables authors to easily translate an experience concept into an end-product for users to access on-location through their mobile device, e.g. Hull et al. (2004) and Wetzel et al. (2012). However, predicting the ways in which users will act in the real world is not trivial, and research has shown that designs of location-based experiences rarely play out as expected (Weal et al. 2006). LBEs can provoke surprising behaviour from participants who encounter a complex blend of distractions and cues from their mobiles and the world around them (Norman 2008).

Using traditional qualitative evaluation methods – observation, contextual inquiry and interview – researchers have studied the behaviour of participants to unpack the reality of LBEs (Chamberlain et al. 2011), demonstrating the tendency for mobiles to distract attention from surroundings (Pielot et al. 2011), the contradictory nature of imperfect GPS service (Hull et al. 2004), the effects of lighting and ambient noise on the experience of mobile media (Barnard et al. 2007), and the ways in which mobile technologies can de-socialise public spaces (Landry and Wood 2012).

Despite providing valuable insights, the HCI fieldwork methods that typically provide our insights into user behaviour are also expensive, and consider only "snapshots of use" (Kjeldskov and Skov 2014). In contrast, research on the impact of changeable and heterogeneous wireless infrastructures has used geolocation data from mobiles to evidence the effects on mobile user experience (Chalmers and Galani 2004), describing the edges of infrastructures (e.g. the limits of wifi hotspots, or GPS shadows) as "seams". By studying data generated by players' mobiles in location-based games, Barkhuus et al. saw strategies of game players for coping with seams emerge (Barkhuus et al. 2005). This data-driven approach was adopted in the design and refinement of *Feeding Yoshi* (Bell et al. 2006). Based on the process of authoring several experiences, Oppermann et al. suggest value in software that reveals wireless hotspots, signal strength and positioning accuracy (Oppermann et al. 2006). Recounting the experience of co-developing a location-based mobile experience, researchers highlight the degree of "guesswork" that experience designers use in the absence of this information (Chamberlain et al. 2011). Work to evaluate mobile guides has also suggested that statistical analysis of geolocation data, giving measures such as walking speed and bearing, might reveal issues with the design of an LBE (Goodman et al. 2004).

As a response to these issues, our recent research has considered how data generated by visitors participating in an LBE might be tapped for insights into their

Fig. 14.1 Photograph showing a desire line trodden by visitors diverging left from the *intended* path

behaviour in response to the LBE and their surroundings. One particularly useful analogy is that of *desire lines* – the paths that emerge through erosion as many people tread the same desirable path to a destination (e.g. see Fig. 14.1). Desire lines are a tangible response to affordances and signifiers in the surroundings, as well as to cues from technologies (Myhill 2004). In urban planning, desire lines hint at the optimal place (from the walker's perspective) to lay a brand new path or where existing paths should be relocated to (see Rogers and Berendt 1987).

Drawing on the analogy of desire lines, we suggest that stepping back and reflecting on the *digital* footprints of mobile users may tell us more about how place and space affect the use of mobile LBEs. To explore the utility of visitors' digital footprints we provided our research partners with a novel tool: *Wander Anywhere*. During the design of three location-specific mobile experiences, authors of the LBEs appropriated visual representations of geolocation traces of visitors – provided by *Wander Anywhere* – to adapt their designs. The tool became a valuable element of the refinement process: by analysing their use of the visualisations we illustrate four particular strategies adopted by our partners, made possible by their newfound ability to interrogate visitor data.

Wander Anywhere

To explore the utility of geolocation data – digital desire lines – in the design and refinement of location-based experiences we developed the website *Wander Anywhere*.[2]

---

[2]See http://wanderanywhere.com/

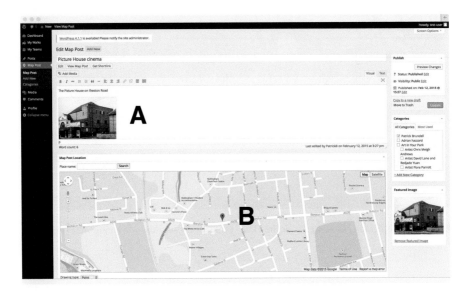

Fig. 14.2 Screenshot of the authoring interface, showing *content* in the upper pane (labelled "A") and the content's *trigger location* in the lower pane (labelled "B")

Authoring: Authors visit the *Wander Anywhere* website in a standard desktop web browser. This desktop website is based on the open source *WordPress* content-management system[3] that allows users to create blog posts using a WYSIWYG editor. Users can upload multimedia and combine this with text to create rich web pages. *Wander Anywhere* extends the core blogging interface (see Fig. 14.2) to allow users to "geo-tag" their content, locking it to a specific geographical location, creating *locative media*.

Like other locative media authoring tools such as Hull et al. (2004) the author geo-tags their content using a cartographic interface: an author drops a pin on a map to indicate a precise trigger location, or draws the vertices of a polygon to dedicate a larger trigger area.

Experiencing: By pointing a GPS-enabled mobile device at the same website, users can access a mobile-friendly HTML5 version of the site. This web client allows mobile users first to choose one of the collections of locative media created by *Wander Anywhere* authors, then helps them to find the location of the nearest piece of content in that collection. Mobile users can choose a desirable method of navigation from a selection of a map, compass bearings or a "solar compass" (see Fig. 14.3). On location, the mobile user is then permitted to unlock and view the blog post, then move on to the next nearest.

Reflecting: Whenever mobile users access the *Wander Anywhere* website to search for locative media they leave a digital footprint. Specifically, *Wander Anywhere* keeps anonymous logs of the geographical trajectories of participants,

---

[3] See http://www.wordpress.org/

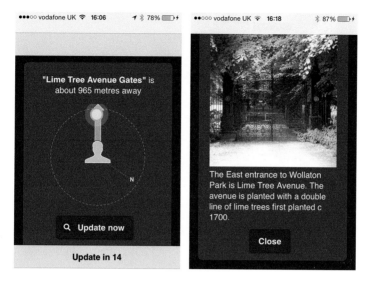

Fig. 14.3 Screenshots of the mobile website during an experience, showing guidance to the nearest piece of locative media (*left*) – in this case telling the user to walk towards the sun – and the unlocked piece of media being viewed on location (*right*)

in the form of the *latitude and longitude* reported by their mobile device approximately every 5 s. As a result, participants generate detailed traces with data points frequent enough to reveal short-term changes in direction and pace. In addition to reporting a latitude and longitude, mobile devices also report a measure of the *accuracy* of the coordinate. Most mobile devices draw on a range of technologies to calculate their position, including GPS, wifi (by triangulating the confirmed geographical positions of nearby hotspots), and phone networks (by triangulating the geographical positions of nearby cells). Each of these infrastructures provides different degrees of accuracy, and are affected to differing extents by the weather, nearby architecture and geographical features. A mobile assesses the capability and quality of the infrastructures that it leverages with each reading, and provides a 95 % confidence interval, indicating the ambiguity – in terms of metres – in each lat-long coordinate.

Authors can return to the desktop website to view traces of users who have experienced their collections (e.g. Fig. 14.4), interrogate individual steps (to see the exact time, latitude, longitude and accuracy), and compare traces left on different days.

Research Method

Our research shares aspects of *technology probe* approaches. In the current case *Wander Anywhere* is a technology probe: a novel technological artefact, at least in the situations into which it was deployed. Technology probes are not prototypes in

Fig. 14.4 The digital footprints (*blue points*) of a several visitors visualised by *Wander Anywhere*, forming trajectories between the locations of locative media (*red pins*)

the accepted sense of the word: rather they are technologies that may fail, but more importantly may cause unexpected disruptions to practices in order to reveal future design opportunities (Hutchinson et al. 2003). By handing over technology probes to real end-users we hope for *appropriation*, and learn from the practices that emerge around the probes (Taylor et al. 2007).

Our research was conducted with the cultural heritage sector: organisations and individuals who work to preserve monuments, natural environments, historical records, art and cultural practices. This sector has begun to engage with location-based technologies to enhance visiting experiences. Experimentation with products including *7scenes*[4] and *AppFurnace*,[5] has lead to mobile LBEs such as "Soho Stories[6]" that visitors can access through their own mobiles. However, broadly speaking penetration of mobile visitor offerings is low.

Over several years (mid 2012 to early 2015) we promoted *Wander Anywhere* within the cultural heritage sector in the UK, engaging with a number of smaller organisations from the sector to carry out collaborative research on the authoring, end-user experience and refinement of LBEs for cultural heritage visiting.[7] None

---

[4] See http://7scenes.com/

[5] See http://appfurnace.com/

[6] See http://www.nationaltrust.org.uk/article-1356398419972/

[7] See http://wanderanywhere.com/portfolio/ for short case studies.

Table 14.1 LBE research engagements

#	Name	Location	End-users
1	Wander Thoresby (2012)	Rural parkland and country estate	29 visitors during 2 public test sessions; 98 visitors during 6-week public release
2	Art in Your Park (2013)	Urban parkland	33 visitors during 4 public test sessions; 57 visitors during 1-month public release
3	Collections in the Landscape (2014)	Urban centre and parkland	51 visitors during 3 public test sessions

of our partners had previously offered mobile visitor experiences or had experience designing locative media, but they do offer traditional outdoor activities to encourage visitors to explore the sites that they manage.

The insights that are presented in this chapter are drawn from three specific research engagements, outlined in Table 14.1. During these engagements, researchers and the partner organisations co-developed location-based experiences for outdoor cultural heritage visitor sites using *Wander Anywhere*. The LBEs were subsequently tested with volunteers in part-facilitated sessions, then released to real visitors as an open attraction (in the cases of engagements 1 & 2).

During test sessions and public releases, site partners spent time reviewing the digital footprints left by volunteers and visitors and revising the design of the mobile experiences. This chapter focuses on this iterative aspect of the design process.

Iteration and Refinement

Wander Anywhere supports rapid iteration of LBE design: authors can return to the website at any point and edit both the web content and the location of the web content, with any changes going live immediately. As a result of editing the mobile experiences via *Wander Anywhere*, each of the LBEs passed through several evolutions. Working with members of site staff on "Wander Thoresby", an initial collection – 8 pieces of locative media spread across an area of approximately 0.5 km² – *grew* through several design iterations to include 24 pieces at the time of release, covering a larger area of approx. 2 km². During "Art in Your Park" an initial collection of 10 pieces was not added to, but all pieces were *moved*. The set of content in "Collection in the Landscape" stayed in the same locations, but the *shapes* of the trigger regions were refined.

Researchers observed the data reflection process where possible, keeping field logs of the process, collecting the thoughts of partner staff through *contextual inquiry*. Snapshots of the visitor traces – as referred to by the partners at decision points during the process of refinement – were also collected: these snapshots provided prompts for *semi-structured interviews* with the partners after the final releases of the LBEs exploring the decisions made during the refinement process. Interview notes were then *thematically analysed* into sets of common insights and responses – four *themes*, presented in section "Themes: Data, Insights and Responses" – that reveal a generalised picture of how the authors appropriated the visualisations of visitors' digital footprints in the refinement process.

Themes: Data, Insights and Responses

Each of the four themes represents *distinct reactions* that authors had to *particular visualisations*. In the following descriptions of the themes, we describe for each: the characteristics of the **data visualisations** that caught the attention of the authors, the **insights** that authors were led to by investigating those visualisations, and the **design responses** made by authors based on those insights. Quotes coded within the themes are used as illustrations and are attributed to site partners in the particular research engagement/LBE that they worked on.

Staging: Expected and Unexpected Entrances

The first common theme to emerge from the research engagements relates to the way that locative media experiences are **staged**, bringing together observations by authors that digital footprints revealed *unexpected entrances* to their LBEs, insights into why visitors made their entrances in this way, and their responses to shape this entrance.

The designs emerging from our three engagements can be considered *linear* experiences. Our partners naturally tended toward this structure:

> We deal in linear routes – set stories – it helps us manage visitors and keep surprises to a minimum. (Partner *Collections in the Landscape*)

In the case of Wander Thoresby, the locative media contained parts of a rhetorical dialogue with the visitor: later content referred back to previous parts of the dialogue. In Art in Your Park, content was a sequence of images cut from a video. In Collections in the Landscape, content pieces were not explicitly interdependant, but did represent a historical sequence if visited in a particular order. In these cases, the experiences had expected *entry points*, from which the designed narrative began. Reflecting on the progress of the public release of Wander Thoresby, this member of staff explains the author expectations:

> When you're here every day you don't even think about it: everyone comes to the courtyard first to get their bearings, right? So this is the logical place to start. It's the center of all activity here – you don't even need to stick up signs to tell people to come in. (Partner *Wander Thoresby*)

This strategy of aligning a physical staging area – e.g. a central courtyard in Wander Thoresby (see Fig. 14.5), a café in Art in Your Park, a museum in

Fig. 14.5 Wander Thoresby's *portal* in the focal courtyard: a QR code outside the gallery and URL inside both provide access to the LBE that starts nearby

Collections in the Landscape – with the digital entry point to create a "portal" for an LBE provides a clear, symbolic threshold for the experience.

Portals were deemed by our partners to be "focal points" and an important part of the experience where visitors to find out about and start the LBEs, i.e. where their expectations are set. Drawing out commonalities from the comments, these locations were typically perceived as points where visitors were already known to *converge and dwell*:

> The café sticks out: it's where people come for a hot drink and a sit down before or after they walk around the lake. It's the only single place visitors really spend a significant amount of time. (Partner *Art in Your Park*)

> Locals know the museum. I suppose there are plenty of meeting points around here – we're in a town centre after all – but this is the cultural hotspot. (Partner *Collections in the Landscape*)

Following observation of the public releases of the LBEs, unexpected patterns in the digital footprints of visitors emerged, challenging the authors' assumptions. Figure 14.6 shows a view of visitors' digital footprints discussed part-way through the Wander Thoresby public release: this view plots the *first position* reported by the mobile of each visitor engaging with the LBE. In the figure, the intended entry point – the courtyard – is labelled "A", surrounded by an expected cluster of first steps.

Despite this cluster, first steps were spread widely: the furthest entrance to the experience (labelled "B" in Fig. 14.6) was over a kilometre from the intended start point, provoking confusion:

> Who knew that we had so many "unofficial" visitors? The edge of the estate is more leaky than we expected. I don't get how they're *finding* the experience, let alone if what they find will make sense . . . (Partner *Wander Thoresby*)

Similar findings emerged from the two other engagements, revealing multiple unexpected entrance points to the experiences. Authors questioned the cause

Fig. 14.6 First footsteps in Wander Thoresby experiences plotted alongside content locations. For convenience of illustrating the data points, the map is shown in greyscale and labels have been removed

of these unexpected entrances. Inspecting the data visualisations, authors noted correlations between the locations of content and entrance points:

> It looks like people are joining in at trigger points further around the walk. Something about those spots is advertising the walk – there's some kind of guerrilla marketing going on. [This effect] isn't very helpful – they'll have missed the setup at the start. (Partner *Art in Your Park*)

These observations led authors to question the visitors, and to discover the attractive effect of public interaction. Discussion with some visitors revealed that they were curious to see others using their mobile phones to view content, "snooped", then followed their lead. As visitors converge on trigger locations occasional groups of visitors occurred, which magnified the effect on bystanders:

> We didn't think much about this beforehand: we're creating behaviour that *really sticks out*. You can see several people sort of wandering in circles together trying to hunt down this trigger, then looking smug when they do. The guy I spoke to said he saw someone else do it, then wanted in on the action. (Partner *Art in Your Park*)

Our partners remained unsure about how to respond to this effect, or indeed whether the impact was negative or positive. On one hand, authors suggested that the effect may draw in more visitors than attempting to restrict access to one dedicated portal location. On the other, concerns remained that the experiences would not be correctly framed if begun in such an ad-hoc manner:

> It's great that we've got visitors advertising for us, but I'm worried that they start and then have no idea what's going on. That could reflect badly on us. (Partner *Wander Thoresby*)

Orphaned Content and Desire Lines

The second theme encompasses concerns of the authors that none of the content they created be missed by visitors. During the design processes, viewing the digital footprint visualisations led authors to the realisation that various pieces of content had become **orphaned**, i.e. to be ignored by visitors. We illustrate here what insights they gained from exploring this phenomenon, and their responses.

Early reviews of visitor traces in each engagement revealed that visitors did not take time to find every piece of content; instead, authors noted a disparity between pieces that seemed to attract many visitors, and pieces that were rarely (or never) visited. Figure 14.7 is part of a view of digital footprints from an iteration of the Wander Thoresby LBE. This visualisation was viewed by authors after the addition of a new piece of content (its trigger area is circled) to review its impact on the flow of visitors: it shows the paths of multiple visitors after the introduction of the piece, forming a *desire line* ignoring it.

Orphaned content appeared regularly enough to be a distinct source of frustration for authors, and a topic of discussion around the impact of environmental signifiers:

> They [visitors] follow paths like ants. If there's a paved path they clearly follow it, regardless of whatever the phone tells them. (Partner *Wander Thoresby*)

Authors became wary of anticipating the "push and pull" of distractions in the environment, citing a tension between instructions presented by the mobile website and cues from the surroundings. In response to Fig. 14.7, authors noted that:

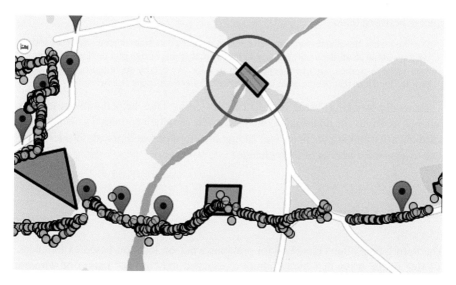

Fig. 14.7   An orphaned piece of content in Wander Thoresby, 200 m from a desire line

It's like trying to change a river, isn't it? Maybe visitors do see the mobile telling them to head north, but the only way to get out of the field is the stile on the east side. Once they get there, the phone switches to pointing to the content to the east, so they probably think it was a glitch before. We'll have to rethink the content on the bridge ... (Partner *Wander Thoresby*)

Persisting in attempts to divert visitors, some authors laid down pieces of closely spaced content as "breadcrumbs" to isolated locations, and included encouraging or persuasive messages in other content to entice visitors:

This location is important. I think [the visitors] are scared: there's something making them all take that other path, [so] we need to let them know they can walk here. We need more content closer together so they can't miss it, and we need the Countess [the narrative's protagonist] to tell them what they should be walking towards. (Partner *Wander Thoresby*)

This strategy was employed most often in Wander Thoresby, leading to a significant increase in the number of pieces of content in the experience.

In the other engagements, design teams sought to *leverage* desire lines rather than change them. In Art in Your Park, triggers were initially placed in secluded areas off thoroughfares: the design team noted that several of these were missed as visitors followed the established paths:

It's as if they're on a roller-coaster; they don't seem to break out much. (Partner *Art in Your Park*)

In response, the trigger locations were moved *on to* the desire lines (considering the flow immovable), and a prompt was added to each piece of locative media to encourage the visitors to walk off the paths before viewing the media.

The authors of Collections in the Landscape adopted a *preemptive approach*, placing four location-specific pieces of content explicitly to allow desire lines to emerge between them:

Based on what you [the researchers] have shown us in the data from other experiences and what we know about deploying signage in the town, it seems best to plot the locations that *have to be there* then see where people want to walk. We can be opportunistic, and then pick the locations that people want to go. (Partner *Collections in the Landscape*)

Generally speaking, being able to identify desire lines helped authors identify suitable locations for additional content, as well as which content was isolated. In addition, after making changes, e.g. adding breadcrumbs, authors could refer to the data to assess the impact of their changes.

Identifying Seams

The third theme aligns closely with previous work on location-based experiences, relating to the ways in which authors recognised the "messy" nature of wireless infrastructures, e.g. as **seams** in the data, and insights into the impact on the user experience.

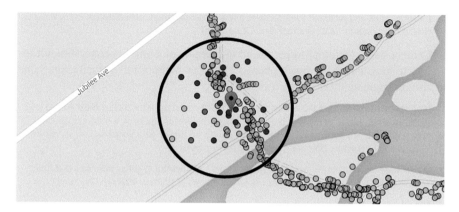

Fig. 14.8 A region (*circled*) within the Art in Your Park deployment area, highlighted by the author as problematic

As described in section "Orphaned Content and Desire Lines", being able to visually recognise desire lines was useful within the design process. However, as public deployments progressed, authors noted factors that appeared to affect the clarity of the data. Sometimes these factors were abstract:

> When it's really hot and humid – when we get the most visitors walking out into the park – the phones seem to play up more than usual and produce weird trails. Oddly, fresher days seem to give more reliability. I'm probably reading into it too much ... (Partner *Wander Thoresby*)

In other cases, authors noted specific locations in the deployment sites where desire lines appeared to break apart. Figure 14.8 captured during the design process illustrates one such area. In the visualisation, varying levels of accuracy are represented by the colour of the data points (where green is high, blue is low, i.e. ±50 m, and red is very low, i.e. ±200 m).

In some cases network connectivity reduced to zero and so no data points were logged, giving the impression of visitors disappearing only to reappear some distance later. Authors developed an understanding of the realities of GPS and mobile networks in their own tests, attributing blame to architecture and vegetation:

> Walking with *Wander Anywhere* is much more "visceral" than using a sat-nav: you really get a sense that [being near] buildings make the navigation aspect stutter and slow down. You can also tell when you're wandering into a situation where its about to give up (Partner *Collections in the Landscape*)

> We had some complaints about some particular pieces – it's only after we had a few traces on here that it becomes really obvious that the trees are causing an issue. Who knew? (Partner *Art in Your Park*)

Authors found it difficult to predict the effect of these seams on the visitor experience, preferring to design around them. Referring to the area highlighted in Fig. 14.8, the site partners said:

I've gone back and [walked] through there a few times: my phone acts different every time! How do you plan for that? (Partner *Art in Your Park*)

Content that was found to be placed in a seam sometimes became difficult for visitors to find, and so became orphaned. However, authors did appreciate the value in visitors mapping these seams for them:

It's impossible to find all these dips in connectivity ourselves with such a short period to spend creating. It also seems like they're in different places if you're on a different [mobile] network. Once you know what you're looking for here [in the data visualisation] its easier to see the gaps emerge. (Partner *Collections in the Landscape*)

We should encourage brave people to be "pioneers": it's helpful to get a consensus that [that area] is really a problem, and not just my phone glitching. (Partner *Wander Thoresby*)

Finally, authors noted that the seams in the wireless infrastructures were likely to change over time. This *fluidity* is not discussed in previous research, arguably because that research has considered short-lived LBEs; however it was a concern for our partners:

We wouldn't build an experience for a weekend – it would need to last to be cost-effective. So ... even if we could go out and map connectivity ourselves now – which we don't have the time to do, by the way – isn't it all going to be immediately out-of-date? If the [mobile network providers] are always chopping and changing, and buildings are going up and down, we need to be re-mapping the place constantly. (Partner *Collections in the Landscape*)

Realigning Signifiers

The final theme brings together findings relating to the relationship between digital trigger locations and environmental signifiers, specifically **alignment** of these. The impact of this relationship on visitor behaviour became visible through motifs in the digital footprints; authors also took action to correct misalignment.

In contrast to loose distributions of data points like Fig. 14.8 caused by inaccuracy in the geolocation process, authors also noted *tight* clusters of accurate data points:

We look hard at the clusters to see what's going on. If we expect participants to stop for some reason, fine. If there's *not* content there then something might need addressing ... (Partner *Collections in the Landscape*)

Figure 14.9 shows two examples of tight clusters, captured during reviews of Wander Thoresby. Tight clusters are caused by visitors' mobiles reporting their location at a constant rate, while visitors *slow their pace*.

The lefthand example in Fig. 14.9 was expected by authors: convergence on a trigger location was diagnosed as the visitors pausing to experience the locative media, before moving on:

It's great to see these big blobs of dots on the pins: you can just tell that the website is working – that someone has been caught up in the moment. (Partner *Art in Your Park*)

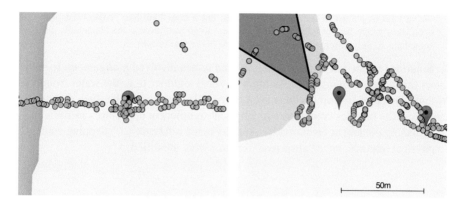

Fig. 14.9 Clusters representing slow moving visitors converging on a trigger location (*left*) and struggling to find a trigger location (*right*)

When asked to describe their most effective choices of trigger location, authors said that good locations should be *obvious* to visitors:

> I'd say we follow the same intuition that we do when we put up interpretation boards or signage: pick "vantage points". (Partner *Collections in the Landscape*)

On the other hand, authors noted pieces that visitors appeared keen to find but struggled to do so, often walking in circles or zig-zags to find the trigger location. Authors could visually identify this "searching" behaviour in the traces as distinct from the usually direct paths of visitors. The righthand plot in Fig. 14.9 was highlighted as one such example:

> Look: this part has caused real problems, and its not a problem with the technology. Accuracy is good. Probably the trigger location is too small, but there's also not really anything visible to lock onto: the content describes old railway sleepers that are hidden in the grass. You can't see them until you're standing on them. People literally walk in circles trying to follow compass bearings on their phone! (Partner *Wander Thoresby*)

The authors revisited the troublesome trigger locations for insights into searching issues. To their surprise, authors found that physical features of some trigger locations had changed since they originally geotagged the locative media, leaving no *signifier* to indicate where a visitor might search:

> There was a big old water trough right where I put the piece: it was really obvious that this is where the trail headed to. Now it's been moved to another field and there's nothing [at the location]. Not surprised people don't know what the hell they're aiming for! (Partner *Wander Thoresby*)

Elsewhere authors found that visitors were distracted by other features, mistaking them for the logical place where content would be found. In Art in Your Park – as described in section "Orphaned Content and Desire Lines" – it seemed that visitors expected content to be placed on paved paths; in Collections in the Landscape, authors noted that visitors headed towards cross-roads and junctions:

We've kind of played to the metaphor anyway, but it does look like people head to the open spots where they're used to choosing where to go next, even if the phone tells them something slightly different. (Partner *Collections in the Landscape*)

Solutions to each of these signifier-related issues involved *realignment*. In some cases this meant moving or replacing a physical signifier (e.g. the water trough in Wander Thoresby); in others this meant moving the locative media, such that digital cues from the mobiles coincided with physical signifiers in the visitors surroundings (e.g. placing content at cross-roads). Authors made reference to "snapping content" to physical features, once "attractive" features were identified.

Discussion

Our analysis highlights several *appropriations* of data visualisations emerging from work by the design team in each of the three LBEs that we studied. The ability to reflect on visitors' trajectories became embedded in the design process: initially the "reflection view" of *Wander Anywhere* was simply an object of interest, but later became a tool for interrogation and diagnosis. In particular, our analysis demonstrates the utility in enabling certain types of data interrogation:

- Being able to pinpoint the *first steps* of visitors allowed authors to assess their choice of portals (the expected entry points to their LBEs), to become aware of alternative routes into the experience, prompting them to consider how to cater for this "ad-hoc" audience
- Being able to *compare desire lines to trigger locations*, authors could identify orphaned content and attempt to shift the visitor flow or revise their choice of trigger locations
- By revealing *erratic or errant segments of trajectories*, authors could identify seams in wireless connectivity and adjust their designs to avoid the unpredictability of these locations
- By visualising *clusters of steps*, authors could judge whether locative media was difficult to find, subsequently revealing confounding effects of digital and physical signifiers

To enable our ongoing research, we are building support for these strategies into *Wander Anywhere* as features. We believe that it is important to retain the *simplicity and playfulness* of the reflection view in order to make it accessible to our partners, who had no technical staff to devote to experience design. We saw that appropriation of the tool happened little and often to *fit around our partners' existing practices*, and that it encouraged *iterative refinement* that involved investigation of data "at the desk" and corroboration "in the field". Further studies will consider how widely useful the strategies are: are they still applicable with greater numbers of visitors? Other researchers suggest that sets of geolocation data can rapidly become overwhelmingly complex (Oppermann et al. 2008). Do the strategies become more or less applicable over longer deployments? New strategies may emerge as authors' refinements become more subtle, or their capability at handling data increases.

We are also looking outwards towards spatial practices – architecture and environmental/urban planning – for concepts that predict and explain the insights that have emerged. Studies have shown that visitors' movement through space correlates with measures of *visibility* in those spaces, linking visibility to fundamental behavioural responses such as "prospect and refuge" (Wiener and Franz 2005). The *Space Syntax*[8] approach extends both visibility analysis and measures of spatial connectivity (Turner et al. 2001) to predict visitor flow and has been used to inform the design of outdoor spaces. Accepting that the physical environment exerts a degree of control over the participant in an LBE is a necessary concession; being able to explain and predict that effect is valuable, yet reference to this knowledge or toolbase is minimal in HCI. Our partners on Collections in the Landscape were familiar with Space Syntax, and suggested that their "intuitive" choices of locations for content aligned with the best practice suggested by the approach; they noted that the signifiers in many cases are not physical "things" but the characteristics that make up vantage points, i.e. visibility and connectivity.

More well-known within the HCI community is the concept of *proxemics* (Greenberg et al. 2011). Proxemics describes spatial mediation of *interpersonal relations*; the HCI community has extended this concept to include human-computer relations (see Hurtienne et al. 2014). Proxemics suggests that co-presence of people and technology can disrupt the *local behaviour* of an individual in space. For example, interaction with technology can create a *spectacle* (Reeves et al. 2005), which in turn can cause a "honey-pot" effect – as noted by our partners in Wander Thoresby – drawing in passers-by to become bystanders, or even participate (Brignull and Rogers 2003). If insights continue to emerge from our real-world studies that mirror effects predicted by spatial theories of proxemics and Space Syntax, we will look to more explicitly design this predictive power into *Wander Anywhere*.

Other Opportunities and Concerns

Despite focusing on four key themes relating to strategies for design refinement, other themes did emerge. As engagements progressed, our partners saw opportunities to exploit visitors' digital footprints for *other purposes*. Each partner referred to ways in which the data might aid general management of their outdoor sites, particularly when planning to redeploy resources.

> A big part of our remit is to make sure that visitors use *all* of the grounds – to make management cost effective. Currently we judge flow by eye … but the traces give us much more detail that we could even use to back up funding applications – for example for new bins or washrooms – and conservation strategy. (Partner *Wander Thoresby*)

---

[8] See http://www.spacesyntax.net/

Each of the partners compared the process of collecting digital footprints to *crowd-sourcing* or *volunteering*, hinting at an effect that collecting data might have on their relationship with visitors. In the cultural heritage sector, volunteers play a major role in the running of visitor sites. Our partners suggested that LBEs might allow volunteering on a much greater scale than is currently possible, involving visitors who might not normally contribute:

> Right now we run on volunteers and we try to make it possible for *everyone* to volunteer. Now everyone who uses their phone can be providing us with useful evidence – I think this would be a real pay-off for lots of visitors. (Partner *Collections in the Landscape*)

There were some concerns over *privacy*. Authors spoke of feeling like "voyeurs" or "spies":

> If you rationalise it – we know that everyone tracks us – but when you see it [the data] it really hits home about what you can infer. I'd feel uncomfortable spying like this without telling them. (Partner *Art in Your Park*)

In each engagement, visitors were clearly told that data would be collected. However, in Wander Thoresby the data was revealed to visitors in the form of a gallery installation (see Fig. 14.10). As well as believing that this provided transparency, it also made an effective *spectacle*, encouraging bystanders to participate:

> The projection gets a lot of attention and made a few more people take that leap – it shows that others had gone first and that it [the mobile experience] was *doable*, not just techy. I think it also made visitors realise that its OK to walk out [further] into the park. (Partner *Wander Thoresby*)

The authors suggested that there was untapped potential to *feed back* trajectories to their owners and that reflecting on their traces might enhance a visitor's understanding of a site. In particular, the authors were keen that visitors might see which locations they hadn't visited.

Our partner also used the installation as a means of sourcing more help from their visitors. Blank cards, pens and adhesive were available for visitors to annotate the installation (see Fig. 14.10 (right)) with information about the locations:

> The contributions are surprisingly helpful. We've got cards that describe what used to be built here, who lived there, [...] what wildlife visitors spotted, [...] corrections to the content, telling us that the text was in the wrong place. A note explaining why a visitor's trace went one way rather than another. And it always seems to be users of the mobile site that come back and add the notes. (Partner *Wander Thoresby*)

Finally, our partners did express concerns about how *representative* the data was. Some authors were critical about wider utility of the visitor data, warning that managers might be led to conclusions about visitors in general, based on the trajectories of LBE participants:

> Of course we've sculpted an experience: this isn't how normal people – you know, other walkers – act. You wouldn't want to redesign the park based [only] on what our participants do. (Partner *Art in Your Park*)

Fig. 14.10 Installation at Wander Thoresby portal. Live visitor traces were projected over a large printed map (*left*) and visitors were allowed to add annotations (*right*)

Conclusion

Previous research on location-based experiences has shown that authoring can be difficult. LBEs can provoke surprising behaviour from participants who encounter a unique blend of cues from their mobiles and the world around them: observation – the mainstay of HCI research – can reveal insights into the visitor experience, but is an expensive approach. Our research into the design and experience of LBEs "in the wild" has demonstrated that visualisations of participants' digital footprints – data captured during mobile geolocation – has utility during the design process.

We positioned *Wander Anywhere* as a technology probe. By making available a website that allows authors to create mobile experiences and also view the raw geolocation data generated by mobile users, various strategies emerged for appropriating the visualisations to refine the designs of the LBEs. Four themes reflect four different ways in which the visualisations were used by authors to gain insights about their sites, the way the physical environment interacts with wireless infrastructures, the way visitors behave when participating in LBEs, and the way that bystanders might be implicated in the experience. In contrast to experiences of designing other outdoor activities, our partners described how *Wander Anywhere* encouraged iteration – systematic cycles of trial and evaluation – to learn about visitors and the site, to design "better" experiences.

Moving forward, the emergent themes hint at opportunities to "design in" insights into LBE authoring tools. Characteristic motifs – clustering of data points, regional spread of inaccurate data points, isolated trigger locations and the locations of "first steps" – could all be *explicitly highlighted* to authors to accelerate the refinement of LBE designs. Unlike observational field techniques, which must focus on "snapshots" of use, the motifs we highlight will become clearer as numbers of participants increase, just as desire lines become clearer as footfall increases.

It is important to emphasise the complimentary relationship between observation in the field and the data reflection activities: each of our themes involved authors following up data reflection with observation or vice versa. Data interrogation might also highlight particular participants to target with qualitative techniques.

In our ongoing research and development, we continue to explore the potential for novel tools to support the design of LBEs. In part, this includes designing support for the four strategies emerging from our studies into *Wander Anywhere*; it also involves widening our collaboration to draw on the expertise of other academic disciplines and practitioners who work at the intersection of location-based services, architecture, planning and human behaviour, to identify convergence and inform the technologies that we build.

Acknowledgements This work was supported by Research Council UK's Horizon Digital Economy Research Hub grant (EP/G065802/1), and The University of Nottingham's Creative Knowledge Exchange Programme, funded by the Arts & Humanities Research Council.

References

Barkhuus L, Chalmers M, Tennent P, Hall M, Bell M, Sherwood S, Brown B (2005) Picking pockets on the lawn: the development of tactics and strategies in a mobile game. In: Proceedings of Ubicomp, Tokyo, pp 358–374

Barnard L, Yi JS, Jacko JA, Sears A (2007) Capturing the effects of context on human performance in mobile computing systems. Pers Ubiq Comput 11(2):81–96

Bedwell B, Schnädelbach H, Benford S, Rodden T, Koleva B (2009) In support of city exploration. In: Proceedings of CHI, Boston, pp 1171–1180

Bell M, Chalmers M, Barkhuus L, Hall M, Sherwood S, Tennent P, Brown B, Rowland D, Benford S, Capra M, Hampshire A (2006) Interweaving mobile games with everyday life. In: Proceedings of CHI, Montréal

Benford S, Flintham M, Drozd A, Anastasi R, Rowland D, Tandavanitj N, Adams M, Row-Farr J, Oldroyd A, Sutton J (2004) Uncle Roy all around you: implicating the city in a location-based performance. In: Proceedings of ACE, Singapore

Brignull H, Rogers Y (2003) Enticing people to interact with large public displays in public spaces. In: Proceedings of INTERACT, Zurich, vol 3, pp 17–24

Chalmers M, Galani A (2004) Seamful interweaving: heterogeneity in the theory and design of interactive systems. In: Proceedings of DIS, Cambridge, pp 243–252

Chamberlain A, Oppermann L, Flintham M, Benford S, Tolmie P, Adams M, Farr JR, Tandavanitj N, Marshall J, Rodden T (2011) Locating experience: touring a pervasive performance. Pers Ubiq Comput 15(7):717–730

de Souza e Silva A (2006) From cyber to hybrid mobile technologies as interfaces of hybrid spaces. Space Cult 9(3):261–278

Durrant A, Kirk DS, Benford S, Rodden T (2012) Pursuing leisure: reflections on theme park visiting. Comput Support Coop Work 21(1):43–79

Galloway A, Ward M (2006) Locative media as socialising and spatialising practices: learning from archaeology. Leon Electron Alm 14(3)

Goodman J, Brewster S, Gray P (2004) Using field experiments to evaluate mobile guides. In: HCI in mobile guides workshop at MobileHCI, Glasgow

Greenberg S, Marquardt N, Ballendat T, Diaz-Marino R, Wang M (2011) Proxemic interactions: the new ubicomp? Interactions 18(1):42–50

Hawking P, Stein A, Zeleznikow J, Sharma P, Nugent D, Dawson L, Foster S (2005) Emerging issues in location based tourism systems. In: Proceedings of ICMB, Sydney, pp 75–81

Hemment D (2006) Locative arts. Leonardo 39(4):348–355

Hull R, Clayton B, Melamed T (2004) Rapid authoring of mediascapes. In: Davies N, Mynatt E, Siio I (eds) UbiComp 2004: ubiquitous computing. Lecture notes in computer science, vol 3205. Springer, Berlin/Heidelberg, pp 125–142

Hurtienne J, Jetter HC, Marquardt N, Pederson T (2014) Ubicomp beyond devices: people, objects, space and meaning. In: Proceedings of NordiCHI. ACM, New York, pp 837–840

Hutchinson H, Mackay W, Westerlund B, Bederson BB, Druin A, Plaisant C, Beaudouin-Lafon M, Conversy S, Evans H, Hansen H, Roussel N, Eiderbäck B (2003) Technology probes: inspiring design for and with families. In: Proceedings of CHI, New York, pp 17–24

Kjeldskov J, Skov MB (2014) Was it worth the hassle? Ten years of mobile hci research discussions on lab and field evaluations. In: Proceedings of MobileHCI. ACM, New York, pp 43–52

Landry C, Wood P (2012) The intercultural city: planning for diversity advantage. Taylor & Francis, Hoboken

Long S, Kooper R, Abowd GD, Atkeson CG (1996) Rapid prototyping of mobile context-aware applications: the cyberguide case study. In: Proceedings of MobiCom, New York, pp 97–107

Myhill C (2004) Commercial success by looking for desire lines. In: Proceedings of APCHI, Rotorua

Norman DA (2008) The way i see it: signifiers, not affordances. Interactions 15(6):18–19

Oppermann L, Broll G, Capra M, Benford S (2006) Extending authoring tools for location-aware applications with an infrastructure visualization layer. In: Proceedings of Ubicomp, Orange County, pp 52–68

Oppermann L, Koleva B, Benford S, Watkins M, Jacobs R (2008) Fighting with jelly: user-centered development of wireless infrastructure visualization tools for authoring location-based experiences. In: Proceedings of ACE, Yokohama, pp 322–329

Pielot M, Poppinga B, Heuten W, Boll S (2011) A tactile compass for eyes-free pedestrian navigation. In: Human-Computer Interaction–INTERACT 2011, Lisbon, pp 640–656

Reeves S, Benford S, O'Malley C, Fraser M (2005) Designing the spectator experience. In: Proceedings of CHI. ACM, New York, pp 741–750

Rennick-Egglestone S, Roussou M, Brundell P, Chaffardon C, Kourtis V, Koleva B, Benford S (2013) Indoors and outdoors: designing mobile experiences for cité de l'espace. In: Proceedings of NODEM, Stockholm, pp 89–97

Rogers EB, Berendt J, Department of Parks and Recreation (New York), Central Park Conservancy (New York) (1987) Rebuilding Central Park: a management and restoration plan. MIT, Cambridge

Schilit B, Adams N, Want R (1994) Context-aware computing applications. In: WMCSA workshop. IEEE, Santa Cruz, pp 85–90

Taylor N, Cheverst K, Fitton D, Race NJP, Rouncefield M, Graham C (2007) Probing communities: study of a village photo display. In: Proceedings of OZCHI, New York, pp 17–24

Thielmann T (2010) Locative media and mediated localities: an introduction to media geography. Aether 5a

Turner A, Doxa M, O'Sullivan D, Penn A (2001) From isovists to visibility graphs: a methodology for the analysis of architectural space. Environ Plan B Plan Des 28(1):103–121

Tuters M, Varnelis K (2006) Beyond locative media: giving shape to the internet of things. Leonardo 39(4):357–363

Weal MJ, Hornecker E, Cruickshank DG, Michaelides DT, Millard DE, Halloran J, De Roure DC, Fitzpatrick G (2006) Requirements for in-situ authoring of location based experiences. In: Proceedings of MobileHCI, New York, pp 121–128

Wetzel R, Blum L, Oppermann L (2012) Tidy city: a location-based game supported by in-situ and web-based authoring tools to enable user-created content. In: Proceedings of FDG, New York, pp 238–241

Wiener J, Franz G (2005) Isovists as a means to predict spatial experience and behavior. In: Freksa C, Knauff M, Krieg-Brückner B, Nebel B, Barkowsky T (eds) Spatial cognition IV. Reasoning, action, interaction. Lecture notes in computer science, vol 3343. Springer, Berlin/Heidelberg, pp 42–57

Chapter 15
On Potential Application of Interaction Design for Placemaking

Parag Deshpande

It is difficult to design a space that will not attract people. What is remarkable is how often this has been accomplished.

William H. Whyte

Abstract While the notion of place has been discussed exhaustively within the field of interaction design, the idea of Placemaking or creation of places is yet to receive attention. Placemaking is an established approach used by disciplines, such as, Urban Planning, Urban Design, Landscape architecture and Architecture, to create public places that people want to live and work in. So far, various approaches to Placemaking have been largely limited to the above-mentioned fields. Drawing on evaluation of four interaction design projects (carried out by the author and by his students under his tutelage) and on author's extensive experience of designing novel interactive artefacts for public places, it is pointed out that interactive artefacts, due to their novel nature, may have the potential to contribute to the process of Placemaking. The chapter concludes by arguing for deeper examination of the field of interaction design for its potential to contribute to the process of Placemaking.

Placemaking

While we are surrounded by a number of man-made and nature entities, such as buildings, trees, street furniture etc., our built environment cannot be seen just as an agglomeration of physical and natural entities. A better way of thinking about our built environment is to think of it in terms of a network of places – both public and private. Places are constituted of two elements, one, a Euclidian space and people's experience resulting from their interaction with and within this Euclidian space (e.g. Harrison and Dourish 1996; Tuan 1996 etc.). A place therefore is not just constituted of physical structures but also of imagined worlds (Anderson 1983).

P. Deshpande (✉)
HiQ Stockholm AB, Stockholm, Sweden
e-mail: parag.deshpande@hiq.se

© Springer International Publishing Switzerland 2016
N.S. Dalton et al. (eds.), *Architecture and Interaction*,
Human–Computer Interaction Series, DOI 10.1007/978-3-319-30028-3_15

And it is continuously shaped by a patchwork of actions and everyday practices that, over time, contribute to patterns of familiarity (e.g. De Certeau 1984; Jacobs 1961; Massey 1995; Cresswell 2005 etc.).

Over the years, the character of our built environment, especially our cities, has changed considerably (e.g. Low 2006 etc.). Growth of population (which is exponential in some cases), has imposed impossible demands on our cities infrastructure resulting in many problems such as traffic jams and disappearing greens spaces, within our midst. Most notable amongst such changes is the deterioration of our everyday places – especially public places – that constitute our built environment (Low 2006). In many cases, such places have seen significant change in the land/building use, encroachment and most significantly, deterioration of social activities for people to engage with. The loss of the character of public places that constitute our built environment is a matter of serious concern because of many reasons (Low 2006). For example –

1. Deteriorated places discourage social activities. Cities, as Cullen notes, are locations where a number of families come together and this has many advantages (Cullen 1971). They can gather around and have a party, they can go and see a play, they can have a discussion on issues of social and cultural importance and so on. The public places have been the traditional hubs of such social activities and therefore deterioration of such places discourages such social activities.
2. The deterioration of public places encourages anti-social activities and this further discourages people from using such places.
3. The drop in inflow of people to a public place impacts its economic activities. This, for example, forces the street vendor and people's activities associated with them, out of such places and thereby making such places lifeless.
4. Many such public places provide identity to the cities. For example, the St Mark's plaza provides identity to the city of Venice. Loss of such places therefore impinges on the identity of the city itself.
5. Finally, deterioration of places often leads to their turning into traffic islands and therefore eyesores that the populace of the city tends to avoid.

Over the years, the issue of deterioration of public places has received significant attention within the disciplines dealing with design and use of public places (such as architecture, urban design, urban planning, landscape architecture etc.) and a number of studies to understand the reasons for degradation of public places have been carried out (e.g. Low 2006; Carmona et al. 2003 etc.). Such studies have followed the early and seminal work of William Whyte and Jane Jacobs carried out in the 1960s that argued against the design of cities that catered to cars instead of people. To sustain the people centred nature of public places and to rejuvenate the deteriorating ones, Whyte and Jacobs argued for infusion of social life into such places (Jacobs 1961; Whyte 1980). Many such early ideas proposed by Whyte and Jacobs led to evolution of an approach called Placemaking that deals with planning, design and management of public places.

The Placemaking approach has evolved significantly since then with contributions from several influential researchers. For example, Fred Kent, a disciple of Whyte formed the Project for Public Places to pursue the idea of Placemaking (http://www.pps.org/). Christopher Alexander in the *Pattern Language* argued in favour of learning from patterns of people space interaction and reject top down approach adopted by Architects and Urban designers at that time (Alexander et al. 1977). Other noted researchers such as philosopher Henri Lefebvre (Lefebvre and Nicholson-Smith 1991), Ray Oldenburg (2002), urban sociologist Richard Sennett (Sennett 1992) and more recently Robert Putnam (2001) have also contributed to the development of Placemaking approach.

Today, Placemaking is concerned with how people experience their public spaces and how they develop a sense of place. The aim of Placemaking then is to create positive experience and to create public places that that people want to live, and work in. This approach now also incorporates a number of people centric aspects such as concern for healthy living, economic revitalization, community capacity building etc. (Silberberg 2013).

What Is Involved in Placemaking?

Let's first examine what is involved in creation of a place. A place is constituted of its following two elements:

1. A Euclidian space that acts as a 'container' for human activities, and
2. A judicious mix of human activities that occupies the 'container'

The existence of the above two elements is necessary for people to engage, dialogically, with their Euclidian spaces and develop a sense of place. Creation of a Place, therefore, involves following two activities –

- Architectural design of a Euclidian space that acts as a 'container' for human activities

Cullen, in Townscape, discusses how architectural design of everyday spaces contributes to people's experience (Cullen 1971). And a number of strategies concerning physical form of such spaces (e.g., human scale of the space, degree of enclosure of the space, rendering of the surfaces etc.) are employed by architects, urban designers and landscape architects when designing such spaces.

- Infusion of human activities within such Euclidian spaces.

Gehl notes that active and popular places, especially public places, have a judicious mix of three different types of human activities, namely, *necessary activities*, *optional activities* and *social activities* (Gehl 1987).

The process of Placemaking, ideally, involves both above-mentioned elements of a place. However, in this age of scarcity – of both the finances and the land – creation of new places is a very difficult, if not impossible, task. The prevalent process of Placemaking, therefore, is often concerned with an existing place/public place with little or no scope of intervening into the architectural design of its 'container'. Consequently, the focus of Placemaking process remains primarily on the infusion of human activities into the 'container' of a given public place with minor and often temporary modifications to the 'container' (Silberberg 2013).

It can be noted that when intervening in an existing public place, the process of Placemaking attempts to bring in various types of activities that are optional and social in nature (using Gehl's terminology). For example, introduction of activities such as weekly public events (such as talks by artists and others), introduction of book boxes, chair bombing, organization of walks have been considered by Placemaking projects (Silberberg 2013). In addition to this, deployment of artistic installations and street furniture have also been part of Placemaking projects (Silberberg 2013). The objective of such interventions is –

- to offer variety of activities within the place and,
- to provide opportunities for triangulation for people using the place (Whyte 1980)

and thus fulfil the two central principles of Placemaking from design perspective (www.pps.org).

Disciplines Involved in Placemaking

Currently, Placemaking approach continues to be practiced, largely by the disciplines of Urban Planning, Environmental Planning, Transportation Planning, Urban design, Landscape Architecture, and Architecture. However, such disciplines do not limit their contribution to the process of Placemaking to their disciplinary boundaries and often take help of other professionals, such as artists, performers etc., when engaged in the process of Placemaking. Given this, could the discipline of interaction design be seen as a potential contributor to the process of Placemaking?

Interaction Design as a Potential Contributor to Placemaking

The discipline of interaction design is concerned with design and deployment of interactive artefacts in a variety of human activity settings. Such artefacts can vary is scale and appearance. Such artefacts can also vary in terms of how they are deployed within human activity settings. That is, such artefacts could be deployed on Desktop computers, on mobile devices, within a space as a stand-alone artefact and could be embedded within the 'container' of the space. Furthermore, such artefact could vary in terms how people interact with them, e.g. by using keyboard and mouse, by using a touch screen, by using sensors such as movement sensor etc.. Regardless of their scale, appearance, manner of deployment and modality of interaction, supporting human activities associated with a given setting is at the heart of their design.

Over the years, the design boundaries of the disciplines of Interaction Design vis a vis human activity settings have expanded from the workspaces to private spaces to third spaces and also to quasi public and public spaces. Researchers have argued that for design and deployment of interactive aftetacts, there maybe advantages in thinking about such settings as places, instead of mere physical spaces as containers for human activities (e.g. Harrison and Dourish 1996).

Harrison and Dourish, drawing on architectural way of thinking about spaces and places, considered places as spaces that are invested with meaning. Their notion of place was later expanded by Dourish (2006) by recognising both spaces and places as complex and subjective constructs. Dourish's notion of place drew on research carried out in cultural geography (e.g. De Certeau 1984 etc.) and distinguished between strategic practices of space (concerned with design) and tactical practices of space (concerned with use of the space). He, thus, pointed out the difference between the formation of space (by design) and the formation of place as a result of people's interaction with and within the space. Many other perspectives on place from phenomenology (Turner and Turner 2003), architectural theory (Munro et al. 1999), sociology (Crabtree 2000), geography (Brown and Perry 2001) etc. have been discussed within the interaction design research.

The notion of place, thus, has received significant attention within the interaction design research. However, the research within interaction design is yet to examine the process of creation or activation of places (which is the primary objective of the process of Placemaking) and the potential role that the discipline of interaction design could play in the process of Placemaking. That said, the overall objective of the discipline of interaction design and that of Placemaking appears to be similar – that is to contribute to the (positive) human experience associated with variety of human activity setting. Given that public space have emerged as a design setting for interaction design, could the discipline of interaction design contribute to the process of Placemaking?

This question was at the back of author's mind when working as an interaction designer and a tutor (from 2004 to 2012) he got involved in a number of Interaction Design projects, with public places as their design setting. Such public places varied from farmer's market, to city streets, to city squares, to public places situated within University campuses and to airports. Such projects were part of two different activities

1. A research project titled **Shared Worlds** carried out from 2003 to 2007 at the University of Limerick, Ireland. The aim of this project was to examine conceptual and methodological issues associated with design, deployment and use of novel interactive artefacts in public spaces.
2. An elective course titled 'Interactive media in public spaces' offered as a part of postgraduate program in Interactive Media at the University of Limerick, Ireland.

Limitations of the Projects

Such projects were designed to explore public space as a design space from interaction design perspective. The scope of such projects, therefore was limited and none of these interaction design projects were carried out to contribute to the process of Placemaking and activation or rejuvenation of the spaces or settings of their deployment. Nevertheless, evaluation of such projects highlighted aspects that could potentially contribute to the process of Placemaking.

The objective of this chapter is to share author's thoughts with the community on such interaction design projects vis a vis the process of Placemaking. In what follows, readers are invited to a brief journey through the interaction design projects carried out. The next section discusses the interaction design projects carried out as part of the research project Shared Worlds. And the subsequent section discusses some of the projects carried out by the students. The following section reflects on the findings of the evaluation of such interaction design projects and on the usefulness of interaction design projects for the Placemaking process.

Interaction Design in Public Spaces: Shared Worlds Research Project

The Shared Worlds research project was a four year research project (2003–2007), funded by the Science Foundation of Ireland. It was carried out at The Interaction Design Centre, University of Limerick, Ireland under the leadership of Prof. Liam Bannon. The project investigated the development and use of novel interactive artefacts and environments within public shared spaces. To achieve its research objectives the Shared Worlds project focused on public spaces, such as, museums, airports, libraries, shopping malls etc. as a setting for design of interactive artefacts. The reasons for identifying shared public spaces as design settings were two-fold. One, the Shared Worlds research team wanted to build on its existing expertise in the area of interaction design for public spaces such as Museums (Ciolfi and Bannon 2003). Two, the Shared Worlds research team wished to examine the nature of public spaces as a setting for design, as they are complex in nature with heterogeneous mixes of people and activities.

At the outset of the project the research team carried out an extensive survey of several public spaces, in and around the city of Limerick, keeping in mind the research objectives vis a vis the expertise of the Shared Worlds research team and other practical constraints (such as the transient nature of deployment of the interactive artefact etc.). This resulted in the research team identifying two public spaces for more detailed examination – Shannon Airport, situated in County Clare and the Milk Market, situated in the heart of the Limerick city. There public space were distinct in character. i.e. while the Milk Market was an open to sky urban public space, the Shannon airport was an internal semi-public space.

The author was part of the two multidisciplinary design teams of the Shared Worlds project that carried out the design activities at both these public spaces. While the author led the design activities carried out at the Milk Market, he worked as a member of the multidisciplinary team and participated in the design activities carried out at the Shannon Airport. The Shared Worlds design team developed two different interactive artefacts for the two identified public spaces, namely, the Recipe Station (Deshpande 2009) and the Shannon Portal (Ciolfi et al. 2007).

The Recipe Station: The Milk Market Project

The Setting

The Milk Market is a farmer's market situated at the heart of the city of Limerick, Ireland. It comes into being in large courtyard of a purpose built 150-year-old market building that at the time when the project was carried out was open to sky and therefore to the elements. This open to sky courtyard used to work as a parking space during the weekdays. But on Saturdays, it was occupied by temporary vending stalls set up by vendors from nearby towns from 6 am to 2 pm. Such vending stalls sold a variety of food items, garden plants and other items of interest (such as handicraft etc.). In addition to this, the market building also housed two cafes with small sitting space for patrons to rest and enjoy the market environment. The friendly setting for socialization offered by the Market made it a popular public place and brought in people from various walks of life.

The Recipe Station

The Recipe Station (Fig. 15.1) was an interactive artefact designed to augment social activities of the market by facilitating users to search and exchange everyday and gourmet recipes. It was envisaged that, when deployed in the Milk Market, it would create an activity node (Lynch 1960) that was similar in nature to the other numerous activity nodes (such as vendor stalls) constituting the Milk Market. And for this reason, the Recipe station was designed as a temporary vending stall that was physically anchored to a location within the Market space, similar to the other vending stalls of the Market. The Recipe Station's temporary vending stall was constituted of three pieces of 'vending furniture', the Recipe Station artefact, the display table and the wall mounted display area.

Keeping in mind the temporary nature of the Market and therefore the need to deploy the vending stall on each Market day, the Recipe Station artifact was made out of three wooden boxes/sections that could be assembled in quick time. When assembled, the square wooden structure of the Recipe Station stood approximately 4 ft tall. It incorporated two touch screen displays, two RFID readers, two computers and a thermal printer.

Fig. 15.1 Recipe station in use, Milk Market, Limerick, Ireland

The display table exhibited 'ingredient' cards used to initiate interaction with the Recipe Station. The purpose of this display was to allow people to come and examine such cards and use them to interact with the recipe station. The display board inside exhibited a sketch of the recipe station along with a few sample recipes that could be obtained from the recipe station.

All such artefacts were constructed in wood and were rendered with white and red colours and with hand drawn sketches of food items available in the Milk Market. This rendering scheme used for the external surface of the wooden box was in harmony with the visual characteristics of the items and furniture used by Milk Market vendors and this allowed the Recipe Station to blend into the market environment.

A blue foldable marquee ($10' \times 10'$) made from water resistant fabric sheltered our stall. The marquee had foldable walls on all four sides, which allowed for extra protection from rain. At the same time, such walls could be opened during better weather conditions which allowed us to improve visibility of the stall and the activities taking place inside it.

'Ingredient' cards used to initiate interaction with the Recipe Station were, essentially, business cards for the market vendors with their business address on one side and a photograph of the food item(s) sold by them on the other side. Such 'ingredient' cards were embedded with RFID chips that stored information about the food item, the photograph of which was printed on them. A user could collect such 'ingredient' cards from the Market vendors as well as from the display space at the Recipe Station vending stall and drop one or more such cards inside the Recipe

Station to initiate interaction with it. The Recipe Station read the information stored on such cards and the same was displayed on the touch screens located at the top of the Recipe Station structure. The touch screen allowed users to search recipes that could be made by the 'ingredients' dropped in by them and then print such recipes to take home.

The interaction with the Recipe Station, however, was not limited to the users interacting with its touch screen displays. The shape of the Recipe Station structure allowed people to move and gather around it and engage with it from all sides. Its transparent middle section allowed users to see the ingredient cards dropped by users from a distance as well as when interacting with the Recipe Station. Two touch screen displays allowed more than one user to interact with it at the same time. And one printer, connected to both these touch screen displays, created opportunities for initiating conversation amongst people.

Designing the Recipe Station

Following the Human Centered Design process (Bannon 2005), an in-depth study of the Milk Market was carried out in the first stage of the design process. The objective of the study was to understand aspects (of the Market space) that contribute to people's experience of the space. For this purpose, a two-pronged study was carried that which involved, one, analysis of the space using Cullen's notion of Serial Vision (Cullen 1971) and two, semi-structured interviews with the market visitors as well as the market vendors. The study allowed us to gain insight into,

- one, the morphology of the Market space consisting of various types activity nodes and linkages (Lynch 1960),
- two, the manner of engagement of people with the Market space, i.e. active or passive engagement (Carr et al. 1992),
- three, the motivation and outcome of such engagement, i.e. curiosity, discovery, surprise, and
- four, qualities that characterised the Market space, i.e. novelty, variety and richness.

Such insights allowed the design team to get a good grip on not just what people do and how they experience the space, but also on how the organization of the space and people's interaction with the space supports people's experience. Based on such insights, in the second stage of the design process, a number of design concepts were developed. Given that the Milk Market was already a space that was deeply rooted in people's collective consciousness, the overall aim guiding such design concepts was to conserve how people experienced the space.

The design team then developed over 20 design solutions of diverse nature. Each such solution developed was then critiqued for its strength and weakness vis a vis insights illuminated by the study of the Market carried out in the first stage. The critique allowed us to short-list four design solutions, which were then further detailed out using 5Ws and H approach (Apte et al. 2001). This process allowed us to identify the Recipe Station as the best solution (amongst the design solution developed) that addressed majority of the aspects illuminated by the study.

In the third stage of the deign process, the design concept Recipe Station was detailed out and a rough prototype was built to evaluate the user interface. An in-lab evaluation of this prototype was then carried out by users. This allowed the design team to identify some flaws in the user interface. Following this, another prototype of the Recipe Station was built to evaluate the ergonomic aspects of the recipe station. Once again, an in-lab evaluation of the prototype was carried out and feedback from the users was noted. This was followed by another prototype – this time an elaborate one after rectification of the flaws identified by the evaluation of the early two prototypes. This prototype was built for a dry-run in the Milk Market for its evaluation with the Market visitors. This involved setting up the stall and running the Recipe Station during the Market hours. The prototype was used by a number of Market visitors who gave valuable feedback to the design team. Finally, the Recipe Station solution was implemented with detailed out form and aesthetics and deployed in the Milk Market.

In the fourth stage of the design process, an in-situ evaluation of the Recipe Station was carried out. The objective of this evaluation was to ascertain if we were able create an activity node by deploying the installation in the Milk Market which was the objective of the design of the Recipe Station. For this purpose we studied how people interacted with the space of deployment of the installation as well as the installation itself.

Evaluating the Recipe Station in Use

We used a two-pronged approach to study people's interaction with the space of deployment of the installation as well as with the installation itself. Firstly, we made notes and took photographs and videos to document people's behaviour in and around the space of installation. Secondly, we conducted semi-structured interviews with the people to gain insight into their experience of interaction with the space of the installation as well as the installation itself.

The evaluation of the Recipe Station was carried out for five market days and during this time it was used by over 1500 users. The analysis of the data collected from our observational studies highlighted the following:

- It was observed that the Recipe Station, immediately after its deployment in the Milk Market, emerged as an *activity node* (using Lynch's terminology) within the Market. This was evident from the fact that it was used consistently everyday by over 300 users out of approximately 1000 users who visited the Market. There was interest (and repeated interest in many cases) amongst users in interacting with the artifact, search for recipes and take one or more recipes home.
- A 'layered' form of interaction (Brignull and Rogers 2003) with the Recipe Station, designed to use 'peripheral participation' as means to 'entice' users to move towards hands-on interaction with the artifact worked well. This was the

form of user interaction associated with the vendor stalls in the Market that user were familiar with. The replication of the 'layered' form of interaction helped in bringing in the element of surprise and curiosity.

- The nature of the Recipe Station and what it offered to the users in the Market (i.e. searching for recipes using a wooden box) was in stark contract with the items sold by vendors in the Milk Market. And this made users *curious* about the Recipe Station and encouraged them to *discover* what it does.
- The novel nature of the Recipe Station was highlighted by the use of RFID embedded 'ingredient' card used to initiate interaction with it and the magical appearance of the printed recipe.
- Finally, It was observed that the presence of the Recipe Station as well as its use led to interesting conversations amongst users. This was evident by the fact that people often used the Recipe Station in groups of two or three and had interesting discussions about food and recipes amongst them. The presence of two touch screen displays and one printer also triggered many conversations as expected.

While the Recipe Station project successfully contributed to the objectives of the Shared Worlds project, it also allowed design team to examine design methodologies from architecture (e.g. Cullen's Serial vision approach etc.). Additionally, it also allowed the design team to understand and address the practical issues associated with design and deployment of interactive artefacts in public places.

The Shannon Portal: The Shannon Airport Project

The Setting

The Shannon airport, situated in County Clare, West of Ireland, is one of Ireland's three key airports. This airport links Ireland to USA and Canada as well as to the UK and mainland Europe and therefore it remains busy all year. This airport is historically significant. Its origins go back to the 1930s when it started functioning as a terminal for the flying boats that dominated transatlantic air traffic at that time. Since then, it has remained a major air traffic hub linking European continent to the American continent.

Shannon airport is a busy public place. The arrival lounge, the departure lounge and the waiting areas of the Shannon airport remain busy all day. The airport also has restaurants, bars and shops that cater to the airport visitors all day. However, from user's perspective, this public place is somewhat different than the public places that constitute our built environment. Unlike other public places, its users do not see it as their destination. Users come here to wait – temporarily – before continuing their journey to their destination. And therefore, the lived experience of such places is constructed by its users on the fly as they arrive, wait and leave such places.

Fig. 15.2 Shannon Portal in use, Shannon Airport, County Clare, Ireland

The Shannon Portal

The Shannon Portal (Fig. 15.2) was an assemblage of interactive artefacts that was designed to be deployed in the area used by passengers waiting to board their flight. The Shannon Portal assemblage was constituted of three artefacts:

1. Interactive Dolmen

A Dolmen, also known as *cromlech* or *portal tomb* is a type of tomb constructed during the Neolithic period (4000–3000 BC). Although there are many variants, it is usually constructed of two upright stones covered with a flat horizontal capstone. Such tombs were seen as portals – between earth and heaven – and in this sense, a temporary resting place for the departed souls.

Such Dolmens can be found in large numbers in county Clare, the county where the Shannon airport is situated. Given that airports can be seen as portals – that link one geographical region to another and that are temporary 'resting' or waiting spaces for the passengers, a strong link existed between the past culture of this geographical region and the airport in this case. To strengthen this link further, a modern-day technologically enhanced dolmen was proposed to be a part of the Shannon portal. This interactive dolmen allowed travellers/users to upload their photographs, annotate them with personal messages and mail them to their friends and families.

2. The image wall

The Image Wall allowed users to browse images uploaded by users using the Interactive Dolmen. At any given time, the Image Wall displayed a collage of a small number of recently uploaded of images and a virtual magnifying glass floating around the display. Users, by their bodily movements, could control the virtual magnifying glass (to make it go up or down with their hands gestures, and to make it go left and right by moving left or right in front of the Image Wall) and thus browse the entire database of the uploaded images. User's experience of manipulating the virtual magnifying glass was further enhanced by adding an auditory display dimension, in form of an inharmonic Shepard tone illusion (Shepard 1964), to the Image Wall. This inharmonic series was carefully chosen to fit the general noise spectrum of the waiting area while still being easy to segregate.

3. Web Image Wall

The third artifact constituting the Shannon Portal assemblage was the Web Image Wall. The Web Image Wall was a website that displayed the images uploaded by the users using the Interactive Dolmen. This allowed users to access the uploaded images both at the Shannon airport and from any geographical location in the world.

Designing the Shannon Portal

Once again, the design team followed the Human Centred Design process (Bannon 2005) to design the Shannon Portal.

The first stage of the design process focused on how Shannon Airport as a public place is experienced by people. The design team used a combination of qualitative methods such as observation of people's activites, video and photo documentation of people's activities, semi-structured interviews and conversations with passengers, visitors, and staff. The study illuminated, amongst other things, people's personal stories associated with Shannon airport, their experience of using airports as air travellers and their use of technology within the place. The findings of the study allowed us to gain insight into issues such as:

- Absence of a cultural rootedness for Shannon Airport – Shannon airport is situated in a historically and culturally rich area that brings large number of travellers to Ireland every year. Several interviewees commented on the lack of a strong link between the airport and its larger cultural historical setting.
- Activities carried out by people while they wait in the waiting space, such as reading, playing games on their phones and tablets, etc.
- Lack of engaging activities within the waiting area – the area had a bar and duty free shopping but the need for having something that is more engaging, such as a novel form of entertainment that was not too intrusive, demanding or distracting, was expressed by people.

Based on such insights, in the second stage, the design team developed a number of design concepts. The development of design concepts was spread over several design sessions. Initial design session focused on design concepts based on the themes of flow and people's trajectory (in and around the airport), baggage (that accompanies everyone coming to and going from the airport), plane watching and postcard (that people often buy when travelling). In the subsequent design session, the design team selected an initial idea based on the post card theme that would let passengers and visitors share their experience of their trip with others. This idea was further detailed out based on discussions with the airport management staff and it evolved into an artefact that would enable users to create e-cards of their own photos and annotate them, thus allowing users to make for individual contributions to the artefact.

In the subsequent design session, the design team developed the following set of design criteria to detail out the artefact:

- Developing an artifact that is anchored to a location in the waiting space, instead of a pervasive or mobile artifact to keep it avoid intruding into people's activities
- Freedom to engage with the artifact at different levels – from onlooking to active participation
- Ensuring anonymity of passengers and respecting airport security policies
- Introduction of an element of entertainment in waiting space of the airport
- Creating a link between the airport and its cultural historical context

The initial form of the artifact followed an old-fashioned post office counter, the post office being a traditional meeting and connection point in Irish society. The idea of establishing a strong link between the airport and its cultural historical setting pushed the design team to come up with a novel design concept based with strong cultural, historical, and geographical connections. Dolmen, the portal tombs that the region is associated with, became the inspiration for the artifact and it was developed into a modern-day, technologically enhanced dolmen.

Following this, the design concept Shannon Portal (interactive dolmen) was further detailed out. It was developed along the lines of 'make your own print' machines that allow users to upload their photos and print them. However, instead of printing photos, the Dolmen was designed to allow users to, one, draw and annotate their photos with an electronic stylus and two, e-mail their photos to their friends. Keeping this in mind, a touch screen tablet was introduced to the inclined top panel of the Dolmen and it was raised to the height of 1.2 m. Additionally, the interactive Dolmen was finished with stone like rendering to make it look similar to the Dolmens found in the region surrounding the airport.

The functionality of the Interactive Dolmen was extended further by addition of two more artefacts – a physical one, the image wall and a virtual one, the portal web site. The Image Wall was developed to display images uploaded by the users and allow them to browse such images. The Web site was developed to mimic the Image wall on an online platform and to allow users to browse uploaded photos at the airport as well as at other geographical locations.

In order to facilitate photo browsing by users, the Image Wall was envisaged as a stand-alone object, detached from the Interactive Dolmen. Furthermore, it was envisaged that the users would browse photos displayed by physically moving in front of the Image Wall. Given this, the height of the Image Wall was fixed at 3 m with a projection screen that display photos. The link between the Interactive Dolmen and the Image Wall was articulated by an animated image that smoothly leave the dolmen's screen interface to reappear on the Image Wall, sliding into place.

In the third stage, all three elements constituting the Shannon Portal were then iterated upon and evaluated in the lab. This allowed design team to iron out flaws associated with the user interface of the Interactive Dolmen. It also allowed the design team to fine-tune the graphical display of the Image Wall.

Following this, the fourth stage involved deployment and evaluation of the Shannon Portal at the Shannon Airport. For this purpose, a location within the airport waiting area was identified and a layout for deployment of the Shannon Portal was prepared. The deployment of the Shannon Portal began with the preparation of the floor and artificial grass was used for this purpose. Following this, both the Interactive Dolmen as well as the Image was assembled in-situ. Once complete the Shannon Portal was then opened for public use. The Shannon Portal remained open to the public for 3 weeks. During that time, approximately 1,500 people interacted with it in some form: Specifically, 432 photographs were uploaded to the image wall and a total of 535 e-mails were sent.

During its deployment, the Shannon Portal was evaluated extensively in-situ. This involved conversations and informal interviews with passengers and airport staff as well as observations supported by audio and video documentation of people's interaction with the Shannon Portal. The evaluation highlighted the following:

1. The Shannon Portal emerged as an *activity node* (following Lynch's terminology) after its deployment in the waiting lounge of the airport. The Portal observed constant presence of visitors in small groups of three to four and sometimes larger groups of eight to ten people. It supported collaborative annotation and drawing, joint exploration of the image wall, and exploration of the piece by two or more users who gave directions to each other.
2. A 'layered' form of interaction was clearly visible. The Portal supported multiple levels of engagement, facilitating a variety of behaviours ranging from on-looking to active participation and interaction with the Interactive Dolmen and/or the Image Wall.
3. The novel nature of Image Wall attracted many users of all ages. The audio dimension associated with it also invoked a lot of interest.
4. Finally, it was observed the presence of the Shannon Portal within the waiting area led to conversations between people – both while they interacted with it and while they watched others interact with it. The two physical components of the Portal, the Interactive Dolmen and the Image Wall, attracted attention of users and it was a common sight to see users in groups of two/three interacting with these components.

The Shannon Portal thus contributed to the overall objectives of the Shared Worlds project and allowed design team to get better grip on design and deployment of interactive artefacts in public spaces that are liminal in nature.

Interaction Design in Public Spaces: Student Projects

The postgraduate program in Interactive Media, offered by the University of Limerick, Ireland is one of the oldest interaction design programs in the country. In past, this program offered an elective course titled 'Interactive Media in Public Spaces', the objective of which was to explore public spaces as a design space for design and use of interactive media. The author was involved in running this elective course from 2005 to 2010 and his responsibilities included planning and tutoring this course.

This 14-week duration course was kicked off by formulation of an open-ended design brief, which focused on design of novel interactive artefacts to be deployed in public spaces. The open-ended nature of the design brief was crucial for the success of the course as it gave students the creative freedom and did not constrain them in any way. This was followed by identification of a number of public spaces as required by the design brief. Such public spaces ranged from internal public spaces (such as railway station, museums, university plazas etc.) as well as external public spaces such as farmer's market, commercial streets of the city as well as various courtyards situation within the University campus. Students attending this course were then divided into groups (of three to four students each) and each group was then assigned one public space for its exploration as a design space.

The student groups then followed the Human Centred Design process (Bannon 2005) to design interactive artefacts, as required by the design brief, to be deployed in the given public spaces. In the first stage, the student groups carried out in-depth study of the assigned public spaces to initiate the design process. Following this, they developed a number of design concepts that were expressed by sketches and storyboards. The student design team(s) were then asked to present their design concepts to the entire class and sometimes, also the actual users of the identified design spaces. In addition to this, student groups also evaluated their design concepts with other student groups as well as university staff who were actual users of the design spaces. Such presentations as well as one-on-one evaluation allowed students to get feedback on their design process as well as the design concepts developed.

Such presentations and evaluations were carried out on a periodic basis, which allowed students to iterate their design solutions. Towards the end of the course, students presented their design concepts, in form of mid fi or high fi prototypes. In addition to this, students were also asked to write a report to discuss their design process and to reflect on the activity of design carried out.

Here are two examples of the design projects carried out by students attending the course –

Fig. 15.3 Interactive portholes designed for the Stables Courtyard, University of Limerick, Ireland

Design project – Interactive Portholes (by Deirdre Coleman, Manuela Feist, Jimmy Fitzgerald, Shelagh Honan and Sharon Le Gear, iMedia, University of Limerick, Ireland, 2008–2009).

The design concept Interactive Portholes (Fig. 15.3) was proposed for a courtyard – called 'Stables' – situated within the campus of the University of Limerick. The Stables courtyard is a prominent public space of the University. The courtyard is surrounded by a small number of shops and is frequented by students and staff all days of the week. However, the courtyard remains underused because of a number of reasons, such as, limited number of activity nodes, amongst others.

The aim of the design concept Interactive Portholes was to invite users to use this courtyard more frequently. It involved a number of portholes – resembling ice holes created in snow – constructed in the floor of the courtyard. Such portholes were rimmed with a metal ring and covered with glass. Inside the porthole was a video screen that could be seen through the glass covering the portholes. Sensing the user around the porthole, the screen displayed a virtual fish, swimming around in the pothole, as if it is trapped within it.

Interaction with a porthole was initiated with a user tapped on the rim of a porthole. This caused the virtual fish to react and users then could see the virtual fish swimming away from the porthole to another one. This made the user wonder about the virtual fish, in terms of where it went, and made him/her look into other portholes in order to find it. Once the user found the virtual fish, the routine was then repeated again. The design concept, thus, supported interaction at multiple levels with the user was not just interacting with one porthole, but with many of them in a random manner. User's movements when interacting with the portholes attracted attention of the onlookers and involved them in the activity by making them curious. Additionally, participation of more than one user at a time opened up possibilities of collaboration between them (to find the fish) and made the interaction engaging for both the users as well as the onlookers.

Fig. 15.4 Illumasol: Interactive canopy designed for the Bedford Row, Limerick City Centre, Limerick, Ireland

The student group made a video prototype of the solution, which captured the interaction discussed above. This prototype was then used to evaluate the design concept with regular users of the Stables courtyard. The evaluation clearly showed that the following:

- that the design concept would help in encouraging conversations between the users of the courtyard since it made them wonder about the location of the fish
- that the design concept would enhance the space because of it novel nature since it allowed users to interact with a virtual fish and follow its movement

In addition to this, the design team was encouraged by the user of the courtyard to continue working on the design concept and develop it further.

Design project – Illumasol (by Fiona Kiely, Chris Hackett Li Hao Sun, Fernando Gomez Marin, iMedia, University of Limerick, Ireland, 2006–2007).

Illumasol (Illuminated Parasol) was a design solution proposed for the Bedford Row, a commercial street situated in the heart of the Limerick city (Fig. 15.4). Bedford Row is one of the pedestrianized streets of the city and is used by shoppers throughout the year. There are a number of shops along this street, which, at the time of the project, were under construction. In past, the street served a well-known theatre of the Limerick city, which at that time, functioned as one of the major activity nodes.

The aim of the Illumasol concept was to provide identity to the Bedford Row. The design concept proposed installation of three freestanding parasols as part of the street furniture of the Bedford Row. As the Bedford Row is open to sky and it rains frequently in Limerick, the parasols were meant for people to take shelter as and when required. At the same time, people could interact with such parasols with their bodily movements to create music and video projections.

The group made a physical model of the proposal and a qualitative evaluation of the proposal was carried out. The evaluation showed that

- The parasols provided opportunities for people to come together – because of practical reasons as well as because of the inclusion of interactive elements – which made it possible for such parasols to emerge as temporary activity nodes
- The novel nature of the parasols added to the character of the space

The feedback from the evaluation was encouraging for the group. Based on the feedback, the design concept was evolved further and presented during the Siena Design Project, 2007 at Siena, Italy.

Interaction Design in Public Places: Potential for Placemaking

As discussed earlier, the above mentioned interaction design projects were not designed and deployed to contribute to the process of Placemaking. The objective such project was limited to explore public space as a design space for interaction design. Nevertheless, the evaluation of such projects highlight following aspects considered central to the process of Placemaking. For example

1. Interactive artefacts can successfully create *activity nodes* (using Lynch's terminology) in public spaces

This was clearly observed in case of the Recipe Station as well as the Shannon Portal as when deployed in public spaces, both artefacts attracted people's attention and emerged as *activity nodes*. While the student projects, the Interactive Portholes and the Illumasol, were not physically deployed in their respective public spaces, the evaluation showed that they offered strong potential to support formation of *activity nodes*.

Activity nodes (or hubs or human activity) are essential constituent elements of a place. The fact that the design and deployment of interactive artefacts could generate an activity node indicates that such projects could potentially contribute to the process of Placemaking.

2. Interactive artefacts supporting social as well as optional activities help in forming activity nodes

The above discussed interaction design solutions were designed to support optional and social activities of the given public spaces. And the evaluation showed that the nature of such activities, especially social activities, helped in formation of activity nodes. For example, while both the Recipe Station as well as the Shannon Portal supported optional activities of searching recipes and sending annotated photos, it was the social dimension offered by such artefacts that offered the 'glue' to bring people together.

An examination of interaction design projects carried out in recent years also shows that the central design objective of such projects has been to support optional and social activities of the public setting (Deshpande 2009). Such projects have refrained from replacing one or more existing activities of that space. Instead, the objective of design has been to add to the existing set of activities offered by the space to its users. Several design objectives have been pursued to achieve this fundamental design objective. For example

- To introduce activities to address issues associated with use of public spaces as identified by research in the fields associated with design (such as architecture and urban design etc.) as well as human behaviour in public spaces (e.g. O'Hara et al. 2004; Memarovic et al. 2012; Ludvigsen 2005).
- To introduce activities to probe issues, such as, proxemics, location, form, modality of interaction etc., related with deployment and the use of an interactive artefact in a public space (e.g. Mazé and Jacobs 2003; Jacobs and Gaye 2003).
- To introduce a novel interactive object to create ambience or simply to add an aesthetic element in a public space to enhance the overall user experience associated with activities of a public space (e.g. *Duality*, ART+COM 2007).

It thus appears that interaction design artefacts in public places have mainly contributed to the introduction of optional activities and social (Gehl 1987) in a public space. Given that the Placemaking approach employs a variety of activity generators that lead to the generation of activities of optional in nature, such interactive artefacts, could potentially contribute to the Placemaking process.

3. Interactive artefacts could support *triangulation* and support sociality

Whyte argued that the process of triangulation could help in the process of placemaking. He defined triangulation as a phenomenon in which an external stimulus provides a social bond between people and prompts strangers to talk to each other (Whyte 1980). Such stimulus could be present in form of a physical object or sight such as fountain, sculpture etc.

The evaluation of the interaction design projects showed that their use by people indeed worked as a stimulus and encouraged people to talk to each other – both amongst people they knew as well as strangers. The novelty of the artefacts deployed in public spaces could be seen as one of contributing attributes that made such artefacts stimulate discussions amongst people and therefore triangulation.

4. Interactive artefacts, due to their novel nature, could contribute to the identity of place

In case of Recipe Station and Shannon Portal, it was also observed that an interactive artefact, due to its novel nature could encourage inflow of people into the public space. At the same time, it was apparent that if designed appropriately (in terms of its scale and functionality), an interactive artefact could also provide identity to a public place and thus contribute to the activity of Placemaking.

5. Interactive artefacts could engage users/people at various levels

People come to public spaces for various reasons and interact with it at different levels – some remain onlookers and some prefer active participation in what the space has to offer (Carr et al. 1992). The artefacts discussed earlier shows that such artefacts could be designed to support people's interaction at various levels and thus contribute to the formation of activity nodes and therefore could potentially contribute to the process of Placemaking.

Based on such insights gained from evaluations of interaction design projects designed to be deployed in public spaces it can be said that novel interactive artefacts could positively influence the qualitative characters of public spaces and thus contribute to the process of Placemaking. As discussed earlier, the objective of the interaction design projects discussed in the chapter was not to contribute to the process of Placemaking. However, it can be seen that the design and deployment of such artefacts brought in variety of above-mentioned attributes that are considered crucial from the perspective of Placemaking. Such attributed could be further amplified when such design projects are carried out with the sole objective of Placemaking. And in such cases, such artefacts could vary in size and their functionality. Additionally, the material used to build such artefacts could also add to their quality and improve their impact on the Placemaking process.

Concluding Remarks

Various studies carried out on our urban environment have noted that it could benefit from existence of places that people enjoy living and working in. And given this, the importance of the process of Placemaking cannot be underestimated. The process of Placemaking, at the moment, is limited to a handful of disciplines, such as Urban Design, Architecture etc. that primarily deal with design of spaces for human habitation. It can be noted however, that such disciplines draw from other disciplines such as, arts and crafts when engaged with the Placemaking process. Given that the discipline of interaction design aims to design for human experience associated with everyday human activity settings, including public places, the chapter questions if the discipline of interaction design could contribute to the process of Placemaking. Based on the discussions of four interaction design projects, the chapter points out that novel interactive artefacts with their activity and interaction attributes may indeed have potential to positively contribute to the process of Placemaking. It is therefore suggested that it might be worthwhile to examine the application of interaction design for Placemaking by designing and deploying specifically designed interactive artefacts in public spaces followed by evaluation of their impact on the process of Placemaking.

Acknowledgments The author would like to thank colleagues at the University of Limerick, Ireland who worked with him on the Shared Worlds project and former students of Interactive Media course, University of Limerick, Ireland who enthusiastically opted for the Interactive media in public spaces elective and developed the design concepts included in this paper.

References

Alexander C, Ishikawa S, Silverstein M, Jacobson MA (1977) Pattern language: towns, buildings, construction. Oxford University Press, New York

Anderson B (1983) Imagined communities. Verso, London

Apte PA, Mann DL, Shah H (2001) 5Ws and an H of Innovation: TRIZ. TRIZ J. www.triz-journal.com

ART+COM (2007) Duality [online] available: http://www.artcom.de/index.php?lang=en&option=com_acprojects&id=56&Itemid=144&page=6. Accessed 17 Oct 09.

Bannon L (2005) A human-centred perspective on interaction design. In: Pirhonen A, Isomäki H, Roast C, Saariluoma P (eds) Future interaction design. Springer, Berlin, pp 9–30

Brignull H, Rogers Y (2003) Enticing people to interact with large public displays in public Spaces'. In: Proc. INTERACT

Brown B, Perry M (2001) Of maps and guidebooks: designing geographical technologies. In: Proceedings of the conference on Designing interactive systems: processes, practices, methods, and techniques. ACM, New York

Carmona M, Heath T, Tiesdell S (2003) Public spaces urban places: the dimensions of urban design. The Architectural Press, London

Carr S, Francis M, Rivlin LG, Stone AM (1992) Public space. Cambridge University Press, Cambridge

Ciolfi L, Bannon L (2003) Learning from museum visits: shaping design sensitivities. In: Jacko, J, Stephanidis C (eds) Proceedings of HCI international 2003- vol. 1, Lawrence Erlbaum Associates, Inc., Crete, Greece

Ciolfi L, Fernström M, Bannon LJ, Deshpande P, Gallagher P, McGettrick C, Quinn N, Shirley S (2007) The Shannon portal installation: an example of interaction design for public places. IEEE Comput 2007:65–72

Crabtree A (2000) Remarks on the social organization of space and place. J Mundane Behav. 1(1):25–44

Cresswell T (2005) Place: a short introduction. Blackwell Publishing, Oxford. ISBN 1-4051-0672-7

Cullen G (1971) The concise townscape. The Architectural Press, London

De Certeau M (1984) The practice of everyday life. University of California Press, Berkeley

Deshpande P (2009) Bringing an interactive artefact into being: examining the use of an architectural design model in interaction design. Unpublished PhD thesis, Department of CSIS, University of Limerick, Ireland

Dourish P (2006) Re-space-ing place: "place" and "space" ten years on. Proc. CSCW'06

Gehl J (1987) Life between buildings: using public space, (trans by J. Koch) Van Nostrand Reinhold, New York

Harrison S, Dourish P (1996) Re-place-ing space: the roles of place and space in collaborative systems. In: Proceedings of CSCW 1996. ACM, New York

Jacobs J (1961) The death and life of great American cities. The Modern Library, New York

Jacobs M, Gaye L (2003) Tejp: ubiquitous computing as a expressive means of personalising public space. In: Adjunct proceedings of Ubicomp'03, Seattle

Lefebvre H, Nicholson-Smith D (1991) The production of space, vol 30. Blackwell, Oxford

Low S (2006) The erosion of public space and the public realm: paranoia, surveillance and privatization in New York City. City Soc 18(1):43–49

Ludvigsen M (2005) Designing for social use in public places. In: Proceeding of designing pleasurable products interfaces (Eindhoven, The Netherlands, October 24–27, 2005). DPPI 2005. Springer, Berlin, pp 389–408

Lynch K (1960) Images of a city. MIT Press, Cambridge, MA

Massey D (1995) The conceptualization of place. In: Massey D, Jess P (eds) A place in the world? Oxford University Press, Oxford

Mazé R, Jacobs M (2003) Underdogs & superheroes: designing for new

Memarovic N, Langheinrich M, Alt F, Elhart I, Hosio S, Rubegni E (2012) Using public displays to stimulate passive engagement, active engagement, and discovery in public spaces. In: Proceedings of the 4th media architecture biennale conference: participation (MAB '12). ACM, New York, pp 55–64

Munro AJ, Höök K, Benyon D (eds) (1999) Social navigation of information space. Springer, Heidelberg

O'Hara K, Lipson M, Jansen M, Unger A, Jeffries H, Macer P (2004) Jukola: democratic music choice in a public space. In: Proceedings of the 5th conference on designing interactive systems: processes, practices, methods, and techniques, DIS '04, ACM, New York, pp 145–154

Oldenburg R (ed) (2002) Celebrating the third place: inspiring stories about the "great good places" at the heart of our communities. Da Capo Press, Cambridge, MA

Putnam R (2001) Bowling alone. Simon & Schuster, New York

Sennett R (1992) The fall of public man. W.W. Norton & Company, New York

Shepard RN (1964) Circularity in judgments of relative pitch. J Acoust Soc Am 36:2346–2353

Silberberg S (2013) Place in the making: how place making builds places and communities. White Paper. http://dusp.mit.edu/cdd/project/placemaking

Tuan Y-F (1996) Cosmos and hearth: a Cosmopolite's viewpoint. University of Minnesota Press, Minneapolis

Turner P, Turner S (2003) Two phenomenological studies of place. In: O'Neill E, Palanque P, Johnson P (eds) InPeople and computers XVII- designing for society. Springer, London

Whyte W (1980) The social life of small urban spaces. The Conservation Foundation, Washington, DC

Printed in the United States
By Bookmasters